THE ECONOMICS OF SCIENCE

Science is difficult and costly to do well. This study systematically creates an economics of science. Many aspects of science are explored from an economic point of view. The scientist is treated as an economically rational individual. The book begins with economic models of misconduct in science and the legitimate, normal practices of science, moving on to market failure, the marketplace of ideas, self-correctiveness, and the organizational and institutional structures of science. An exploration of broader methodological themes raised by an economics of science ends the book.

Overall, the economics of science portrays science as a process which can be explained only partially in economic terms. In the short run, the allocation of resources within science has significant flaws. However, flaws such as fraud, replication failure, and market failure do not lead to systemic science failure. In the long run, science seems to be mostly self-corrective. From an economic point of view, science seems to move forward most rapidly when structured as small-numbers pluralism. Progress in science, to the extent that it occurs, is a consequence of focusing scarce scientific resources and the best scientific minds on the very best theories and their next best alternatives.

James R. Wible has been a member of the economics faculty at the Whittemore School of Business and Economics, University of New Hampshire in Durham for more than a decade. His main research interests are economic methodology and the economics of science, the economics and philosophy of Charles Sanders Peirce, and macroeconomics and monetary theory. His published articles on the economics of science have appeared in the *Journal of Economic Methodology*, *Philosophy of the Social Sciences*, *Review of Political Economy*, *Review of Social Economy* and the *Southern Economic Journal*.

ROUTLEDGE FRONTIERS OF POLITICAL ECONOMY

1 EQUILIBRIUM VERSUS UNDERSTANDING
Towards the rehumanization of economics within social theory
Mark Addleson

2 EVOLUTION, ORDER AND COMPLEXITY
Edited by Elias L. Khalil and Kenneth E. Boulding

3 INTERACTIONS IN POLITICAL ECONOMY
Malvern after ten years
Edited by Steven Pressman

4 THE END OF ECONOMICS
Michael Perelman

5 PROBABILITY IN ECONOMICS
Omar F. Hamouda and Robin Rowley

6 CAPITAL CONTROVERSY, POST KEYNESIAN ECONOMICS AND THE HISTORY
OF ECONOMIC THEORY
Essays in honour of Geoff Harcourt, Volume One
Edited by Philip Arestis, Gabriel Palma and Malcolm Sawyer

7 MARKETS, UNEMPLOYMENT AND ECONOMIC POLICY
Essays in honour of Geoff Harcourt, Volume Two
Edited by Philip Arestis, Gabriel Palma and Malcolm Sawyer

8 SOCIAL ECONOMY
The logic of capitalist development
Clark Everling

9 NEW KEYNESIAN ECONOMICS/POST-KEYNESIAN ALTERNATIVES
Edited by Roy J. Rotheim

10 THE REPRESENTATIVE AGENT IN MACROECONOMICS
James E. Hartley

11 BORDERLANDS OF ECONOMICS
Essays in honour of Daniel R. Fusfeld
Edited by Nahid Aslanbeigui and Young Back Choi

12 VALUE DISTRIBUTION AND CAPITAL
Edited by Gary Mongiovi and Fabio Petri

13 THE ECONOMICS OF SCIENCE
James R. Wible

THE ECONOMICS OF SCIENCE

Methodology and epistemology as if economics
really mattered

James R. Wible

London and New York

First published 1998
by Routledge
11 New Fetter Lane, London EC4P 4EE

Simultaneously published in the USA and Canada
by Routledge
29 West 35th Street, New York, NY 10001

Typeset in Garamond by Keystroke, Jacaranda Lodge, Wolverhampton
Printed and bound in Great Britain by Creative Print and Design (Wales), Ebbw Vale

British Library Cataloguing in Publication Data
A catalogue record for this book is available from the British Library

Library of Congress Cataloging in Publication Data
Wible, James R., 1951–
The economics of science: methodology and epistemology as if
economics really mattered / James R. Wible.
p.   cm.
Includes bibliographical references and index.
1. Science–Social aspects. 2. Fraud in science. I. Title.
Q175.5.W52 1998
303.48'3–dc21   97–15191
CIP

ISBN 0–415–17257–8

To my Mother and the memory of my late Father

CONTENTS

List of figures		xi
List of tables		xii
Preface		xiii
Acknowledgements		xvii

1 WHY AN ECONOMICS OF SCIENCE? 1
Science as an economically rational activity 1
Misconduct, market failure, and the marketplace of ideas 2
The substitutes argumentative structure of mainstream economics and an economics of science 5
Mechanism versus evolution 8
Positive economic science and the sociology of science 10
The problem of self-reference 13
Why an economics of science? 14
The structure of this book 18
Caveats and internal criticism 19

2 AN ECONOMIC THEORY OF REPLICATION FAILURE 23
Misconduct as a point of departure 23
Replication failure as an economic phenomenon 24
Concepts of replication in science 27
An economic model of replication failure 31
Some extensions and applications of the model 37
Conclusions 42

3 AN ECONOMIC THEORY OF FRAUD IN SCIENCE 43
Fraud as an economic phenomenon 43
Recent episodes of fraud in science 44
An economic approach to fraud in science 50
Conclusions 56
Mathematical appendix: the Ehrlich model of choice under uncertainty 57

4 PEIRCE'S ECONOMICS OF RESEARCH PROJECT
   SELECTION   61
   Research project selection as an economic problem   61
   The role of economics in Peirce's thought   63
   Peirce's economic model of research project selection   67
   The notion of probable error and the earliest correct usage of the logic
   of statistical inference   71
   Peirce's note as the first scientific piece in economics   73
   Nicholas Rescher on Peirce's economy of research   76
   Rescher's Peircean interpretation of Karl Popper   78
   Conclusions   81

5 A COST-BENEFIT APPROACH TO RESEARCH PROJECT
   SELECTION, POPPER'S METHODOLOGY, AND SCIENTIFIC
   PROGRESS   83
   A cost-benefit logic of science   83
   Radnitzky's cost-benefit interpretation of Popper   84
   A cost-benefit model of research project selection   86
   A cost-benefit approach to the selection of facts, theories, and research
   programs   90
   An appraisal of Radnitzky's cost-benefit interpretation of Popper 93
   Conclusions   95

6 MARKET FAILURE IN THE MARKETPLACE OF IDEAS: THE
   CASES OF KARL POPPER AND THE ECONOMICS
   PROFESSION   96
   Market failure in science and philosophy   96
   Bartley's economic critique of science and universities   98
   Market failure in the marketplace of ideas and philosophy of science:
   the case of Karl Popper   102
   A critique of Bartley's defense of Popper   105
   Market failure and the economics profession: the case of free market
   economics   110
   Conclusions   113

7 MARKET FAILURE IN THE MARKETPLACE OF IDEAS: THE
   CASE OF FRIEDMAN'S ESSAY   115
   Market failure in economic methodology   115
   Friedman's essay   116
   Innovation in philosophy of science and Friedman's essay   119
   Boland's defense of Friedman's essay   123
   Friedman's essay: a case for market failure in the marketplace of ideas 125
   Friedman's somewhat unwarranted dominance of two similar
   methodological rivals: Dewey and Samuelson   128
   Conclusions   132

8 SELF-CORRECTIVE SCIENCE IN THE CONTEXT OF
   MARKET FAILURE: THE MARKETPLACE OF IDEAS IS
   NOT REALLY A MARKET   133
   Markets, self-correctiveness, and science   133
   Noneconomic conceptions of the self-correctiveness of science   135
   The noneconomic origin of the marketplace of ideas   137
   Polanyi's nonmarket, self-corrective republic of science   141
   Hayek's theory of science as a noncommercial, rule-governed order   144
   Rescher's logarithmic retardation theory and scientific progress   150
   Partially endogenizing science as an economic process   153
   Conclusions   156

9 ON THE ECONOMIC ORGANIZATION OF SCIENCE, THE
   FIRM, AND THE MARKETPLACE   158
   *From cost-benefit theory and market failure to the economic organization
   of science*   158
   *Science as an anomaly to the substitutes theory of institutions in
   mainstream economics*   159
   Why do firms exist? The substitutes view   164
   Why does science exist? The substitutes view   170
   Why do markets exist? The complements view   172
   Why does science exist? The complements view   175
   A dual economy in the philosophy of science literature   180
   Transactions costs and the economic organization of science   186
   Conclusions   187

10 TOWARDS AN EVOLUTIONARY CONCEPTION OF
   RATIONALITY IN SCIENCE AND ECONOMICS   190
   Towards an evolutionary, processive conception of rationality   190
   Scientific rationality and the problem of induction   192
   An evolutionary conception of rationality in science   193
   An evolutionary conception of economic rationality   198
   Towards an economic conception of scientific rationality   200
   Conclusions   202

11 INTERNAL CRITICISM AND THE PROBLEM OF
   SELF-REFERENCE   203
   An economics of science and self-reference   203
   William Bartley on self-reference and the tu quoque *dilemma*   204
   The problem of induction in science again   205
   Self-reference in mathematics and Gödel's theorems   208
   Falsification and the problem of self-reference   211
   An economic response to the problems generated by self-reference   213
   Conclusions   216

CONTENTS

12 AN ECONOMIC CRITIQUE OF THE ARCHITECTURE OF
ECONOMIC THEORY AND METHOD   218
   The economics of science and the problem of self-reference   218
   Regressive conceptions of economic competition   219
   Methodological competition in the scientific marketplace of ideas 222
   The architecture of economic theory and method   225
   An economics of science critique of the architecture of economic
   science   227
   Conclusions   229

Notes   231
Bibliography   248
Index   261

FIGURES

2.1 The optimization problem of the time-constrained positive
    economist   36
2.2 Lexicographic preferences of a methodologically pure economist   38
2.3 A methodologically preferred change in article output   39
2.4 The negative methodological impact of a publication rate
    requirement on the economically rational positive economist   40
2.5 The optimization problem of the time-constrained pure theorist   41
3.1 The optimization problem confronting the fraudulent scientist
    under uncertainty   54
3.2 A scientist who is induced to commit fraud because of a rise in the
    return to fraudulent activities   56
4.1 Peirce's graphical portrayal of the economy of research   70
8.1 Three conceptual distinctions concerning science and the economy   155
9.1 The substitutes theory of economic organization   163
9.2 The complements theory of economic organization   174
9.3 A dual economy of science from the complements theory of
    economic organization   178
9.4 The dual economy of the literature: an individualized marketplace
    of ideas   182
9.5 The dual economy of the literature: institutionally organized
    science   183
11.1 A schematic representation of Gödel's incompleteness
    demonstration   209
12.1 The Gödel-like architecture of economic theory and method   225

TABLES

3.1 Some recent cases of known or suspected fraud in science   47

6.1 Citation space devoted to well-known figures in the history of
Western thought for the years 1979, 1984, 1989, and 1994   108

7.1 The justificationist metatheory and philosophies of science as
they relate to interpretations of Friedmanian positive economics   121

7.2 The nonjustificationist metatheory and philosophies of science as
they relate to interpretations of Friedmanian positive economics   122

8.1 The major sectors or markets of the economy including science as a
partially endogenized economic process   156

9.1 The substitutes argumentative structure of most mainstream
economics texts: sequence of argument   160

10.1 Weimer's synthesis of Popper, Kuhn, and Lakatos   196

10.2 Nonjustificational modes of criticism delineating aspects of a
multidimensional, nonjustificational conception of scientific
rationality   198

10.3 A nonjustificational conception of economic rationality with
maximization as a special case   199

11.1 An infinite regress of conceptions of falsification in recent
philosophy of science   214

the markets for scientific and technological personnel. There are sociological studies which use economic metaphors and discuss the role of various nonprice incentives motivating the actions and conduct of scientists. There are narratives of various episodes in the history and philosophy of science. There are ranking studies of graduate programs, particularly in economics. There is a literature on the role of research and development in the processes of long-run economic growth, and quite recently, mostly since this book has been in the process of writing, there are some systematic attempts at an economics of science by a few economists and philosophers.

The economics of science in this book is not a survey or synthesis of most of the preceding literature now retrospectively identified as contributing to the economics of science. Instead, this book focuses on two things: (1) creating a systematic economics of science and (2) the methodological and philosophical issues which result from an economics of science. Much of the existing literature on the economics of science is *ad hoc*. It does not take economic theory or economic analysis seriously. In order to create an authentic economics of science, one must assume that the scientist is a rational economic agent and that scarcity pervades and constrains what scientists do. To put it another way more familiar to economists, economic methodology, philosophy of science, and much of the literature on the economics of science is like the field of macroeconomics before the rational expectations revolution. Almost all of the literature on the economics of science does not assume enough economic rationality. This book attempts to rectify this problem. It initially assumes that the scientist is economically rational and then deals with the methodological and philosophical problems which follow from this assumption. These problems must be considered for a more complete vision of an economics of science. At a subsequent stage of the argument, we will find that the assumption of rationality needs to be broadened and significantly reinterpreted, that some sense needs to be made of the "marketplace of ideas," that whatever nonmarket organizational structures there are in science need to be identified and considered from an economic point of view, that the self-correctiveness of science in the context of misconduct and pervasive market failure needs to be scrutinized, and that the reflexive problem of creating an economics of economics needs to be explored.

While theoretical and philosophical problems have guided the organization of the chapters in the book, the process of discovery was quite different. The material on self-reference or reflexivity in Chapters 11 and 12 was drafted more than a decade ago. I first became aware of reflexivity while on the faculty at the University of Maine. There a good colleague and friend, Mark Lutz, encouraged me to accompany him in attending a semester-long seminar on mathematical logic and Gödel's theorems. Mark and I talked at length about mathematics and philosophy of science, and offered an undergraduate seminar together. My very first publication reflected this interest in self-reference. Another very crude paper followed, but no one could imagine what an economic theory of economics would look like. At that point in time, there were very few explicit applications of economic analysis to science. So the next task was to create some economic models of science. This work became Chapters 2 through 5 covering replication failure, fraud, Peirce's economic model of research project selection, and a cost-benefit model of science. The third phase of the project was to write Chapters 6 through 9 on the institutional structure of science, the problems of market failure in science, and the marketplace of ideas. The last phase was to rewrite another of my early articles on evolutionary conceptions of rationality in science and economics as Chapter 10. The implication is that a narrow conception of the economic rationality of science is quite inadequate and alternatively science must be considered as a multidimensional and multileveled evolutionary process of social and individual choice.

The argumentative strategy for the book was one of internal dissent. I consider myself a mainstream economist and methodologist who recognizes that there are considerable theoretical, philosophical, methodological, conceptual, and empirical problems with mainstream economics. Furthermore, alternative approaches to economics on the radical right or left suffer from a similar array of problems to an even greater degree. Thus they are even less attractive points of view to me than mainstream economics. Rather than adopting an alternative view of economics and criticizing the mainstream from without, the opposite tack was taken. An attempt has been made to show how microeconomics can be used to say some interesting and perhaps important things about the nature and conduct of science using conventional microeconomics. Economists have routinely used their analytical tools to criticize other professions such as medicine, law, business, and government. There is no reason why such tools cannot be used to criticize both science and economics. Once such models are created, they provide the subject matter for philosophical and methodological investigation. My guess is that the application of microeconomics to science has only just begun. However, the more economics gets applied to science, the more self-critical economists could become of their own discipline and the more clearly the limits of economics could be encountered explicitly rather than just imagined. In the end, what I hope will emerge is an analytical, evolutionary economics of science with important applications for both science in general and the economics profession in particular. Such an economics of science would contain significant economic content and would also exemplify its own incompleteness.

Now a word with regard to graduate education. Every two or three years, I have been privileged to offer a graduate seminar on economic methodology and philosophy of science in the masters and doctoral programs in economics at New Hampshire. This is a program which also routinely requires PhD students to take a course in the history of economic thought. This is a privilege because few graduate programs in economics offer such instruction and most economists who are interested in the history of economic thought and methodology do not have the opportunity to teach these fields especially at the graduate level. It is also a well-known fact that graduate students at our best universities are disenchanted and have become disillusioned with the technique-oriented graduate programs which have come to dominate graduate economics training in the United States. Arjo Klamer and David Colander have documented this in their book, *The Making of An Economist*. What I have found in my graduate seminar is that advanced graduate students are more than ready to begin a self-critical inquiry about the nature of economic science and the economics profession. They will readily read more traditional materials about the methodology, philosophy, sociology, and history of science if they are complemented with an economics of science literature which uses the analytical tools of their graduate training. Graduate students have a hunger for intellectual context. Traditional economics graduate programs do not meet this need. An economics of science broadly interpreted to include contributions from the other disciplinary approaches to science and coupled with the history of economic thought goes along way to meeting this need. Carried out on a broader scale in many institutions of higher learning, such instruction could intellectually transform graduate education in economics. It is my hope that this book might contribute to an intellectual reawakening in graduate economics education particularly in the United States.

January 28, 1997

ACKNOWLEDGEMENTS

Words of appreciation need to be expressed for support and encouragement in writing this book. Over a period of several years, Wade Hands has read much of what I have written and encouraged its development into a book-length manuscript. Wade and David Hull have read the whole manuscript and made important suggestions. I am grateful for their help. Several research grants have helped to make the book possible. A sabbatical, a Faculty Scholar's grant from the Provost for Academic Affairs at New Hampshire, and several summer research grants from the Whittemore School of Business and Economics have supported this project. Both of my recent department chairs, Richard England and Allen Thompson, and a colleague, Robert Puth, have been particularly supportive. There are a number of individuals who have commented on specific chapters. Paul Wendt, David Warsh, Bill Butos, Mark Lutz, Robert Dorfman, Jeff Sohl, and Avi Cohen have made important suggestions for revisions. The entire manuscript has been presented to the Kress Society in Boston and to the Austrian Economics Seminar at New York University. Also, I want to thank the graduate students in the economics department at New Hampshire. Their day-to-day responses and criticisms of the book when used in my seminar have been invaluable. At a personal level, my wife Susan has encouraged me at every stage of the project.

Several of the chapters of this book appeared first as journal articles or part of a review article. I would like to thank the editors and publishers of the following journals for their permission to make use of previously published material: *Review of Political Economy*, *The Journal of Economic Methodology*, *Southern Economic Journal*, *Review of Social Economics*, and *Philosophy of the Social Sciences*.

"Maximization, Replication, and the Economic Rationality of Positive Economic Science," *Review of Political Economy*, vol. 3, 1984, pp. 164–86. Carfax Publishing Company, PO Box 25, Abingdon, Oxfordshire OX14 3UE, United Kingdom.

"Fraud in Science: An Economic Approach," *Philosophy of the Social Sciences*," vol. 22, no. 1, 1992, pp. 5–27, and "The Economic Organization of Science, the Firm, and the Marketplace," *Philosophy of the Social Sciences*, vol. 25, no. 1, March 1995, pp. 35–68, copyright © by Sage Publications. Reprinted by Permission of Sage Publications, Inc.

"Charles Sanders Peirce's Economy of Research," *Journal of Economic Methodology*, vol. 1, no. 1, 1994, pp. 135–60 and "Rescher's Economic Philosophy of Science," *Journal of Economic Methodology*, vol. 1, no. 2, pp. 314–29. Routledge, London, UK.

"Towards a Process Conception of Rationality in Economics and Science," *Review of Social Economy*, October, pp. 89–104. Routledge, London, UK.

"Friedman's Positive Economics and Philosophy of Science," *Southern Economic Journal*, vol. 49, no. 2, pp. 350–60. Permission from the Southern Economics Association.

1

WHY AN ECONOMICS OF SCIENCE?

If in a limited lifetime, I would wish to be both a philosopher and a mathematician, but my rate of acquisition of knowledge is such that I cannot do both completely, then some part of my wish for philosophical or mathematical competence must be relinquished.

(Robbins 1935: 14)

No human activity comes free of charge; everything we do has costs in terms of time, energy, effort, physical goods, or the like. Throughout the entire range of our endeavors in this world, we are involved in the expenditure of limited resources. And knowledge is no exception to this rule. . . . The problems of knowledge acquisition are certainly not without their economic ramifications.

(Rescher 1989: 9)

SCIENCE AS AN ECONOMICALLY RATIONAL ACTIVITY

Science is difficult and costly to do well. The remarkable benefits of scientific research require the efforts, time, and talents of some the very best minds and research teams in the world and the expenditure of significant sums of material and financial resources. Consequently, science is an economic phenomenon. This book systematically creates an economics of science. Many aspects of science are explored from an economic point of view. Throughout the work, the scientist is assumed to be a rational economic agent. Without the assumption of rationality, the resulting theory would have little claim to being economic. Broadly speaking, this economics of science begins with rational economic models of individual scientific activity. The models present an economic approach to both misconduct in science and to the legitimate, normal practices of professional scientists.[1] From these issues, this economics of sciences moves to aggregate economic analysis. Here the focus is on market failure, the marketplace of ideas, self-correctiveness, and the organizational and institutional structures of science. Finally, this inquiry ends with an exploration of broader philosophical and methodological themes which result from a systematic economics of science.

1

Themes such as evolutionary conceptions of economic and scientific rationality, incompleteness versus the inconsistency of theoretical frameworks, the problem of induction, and the problem of self-reference are all raised by an economics of science.

Overall this economics of science portrays science as a partially endogenized economic process. In the short run, the allocation of resources to specific lines of research and to individual scientists has significant flaws. However, the flaws do not suggest systemic science failure. There is no reason to expect that misconduct and market failure are worse than in other noncommercial economic processes with imperfect human decision makers. In the long run, science seems to be mostly self-corrective in spite of the problems of misconduct and market failure. From an economic point of view, science seems to move forward most rapidly when structured as small-numbers pluralism. Progress in science, to the extent that it occurs, is a consequence of focusing scarce scientific resources and the best scientific minds on the very best theories and their next best alternatives. This is the basic economic idea of opportunity cost operating in the domain of knowledge creation. Such economic concerns imply that both scientific monism and anarchy are inefficient and wasteful. When science is dominated by a single paradigm, one would expect an underproduction of rival theories and hypotheses in science. When there is an anarchy and a proliferation of too many competing alternatives, then science becomes highly fragmented overproducing theoretical constructs and providing too little evidence for adequate evaluation and comparative ranking. Such circumstances would seem to retard the growth of science.

MISCONDUCT, MARKET FAILURE, AND THE MARKETPLACE OF IDEAS

This economics of science initially considers the special problem of misconduct in science. In the past decade or so there have been significant episodes of documentable misconduct which have greatly and perhaps gravely damaged the reputation of science. The broader scientific community has been appalled and has condemned these well-known instances of misconduct. Misconduct concerns falsification of data, fabrication of experimental results, sloppy research habits resulting in replication failure, and plagiarism. One area which has been hit hard with the problem of misconduct is the biomedical area. There are instances where treatments and therapies have been reported as effective when in fact they have not even been tested or the data has been significantly altered. The moral issues are trust and subsidy. Can science as an institutional process be trusted to provide solutions for human difficulties and illness that do not unduly worsen rather than reduce human suffering? Is science as an institutional process deserving of the tax subsidies that it now receives through government funding and the research support dollars provided to universities and research institutes? Misconduct at whatever level undermines confidence in science, diminishes its reputation and support, and thereby impedes scientific progress.

2

An economic approach to misconduct in science can provide a theoretical framework for analyzing the issues. Neither scientists (including editors of scientific journals) nor journalists who cover science have a conceptual framework capable of characterizing alternative forms of misconduct in science. Professional scientists tend to dismiss the significance of the problem while journalists tend to see it as pervasive. An economic approach raises the possibility of categorizing some forms of misconduct as pervasive almost routine in nature and others as being exceptional perhaps "criminal" in nature. Misconduct from fraud, to replication failure, to plagiarism seems to be an aspect of the behavior of scientists that would be particularly amenable to economic analysis. Relatively simple and straightforward extensions of conventional microeconomics can be applied to the problem of scientific misconduct.

An economic understanding of the most important aspects of scientific inquiry is another matter entirely. It would be quite an intellectual and theoretical challenge to explain the very core of scientific activity as an economic process. This economics of science also extends to the normal, nonaberrational behavior of the scientist. There is an economic dimension to almost every aspect of science. The theoretical core is a cost-benefit logic of the choices facing the scientist. A cost-benefit theory of science is not without precedent. Contemporary philosophers Nicholas Rescher and Gerard Radnitzky have explored the cost-benefit approach to science, and Charles Sanders Peirce created an economic model of research project selection more than a century ago. Rescher's cost-benefit approach stems in part from Peirce's economy of research project selection while Radnitzky presents a cost-benefit interpretation of Popper's methodology of science. With a cost-benefit approach, an economics of science can be extended beyond misconduct to explain key aspects of science such as the selection of particular research projects, the choice of data taken as facts, and the adoption of one among several competing theoretical frameworks or research traditions. It is even conceivable that scientific revolutions might be amenable to economic analysis.

Having created a cost-benefit logic of individual choice, an economics of science raises the issue of intellectual and economic concentration in science. Economic concentration is one venue for market failure. One of the virtues of cost-benefit theory is a clear recognition of the problem of market failure. If commercial economic processes efficiently organized most domains of human behavior, then cost-benefit analysis would not have been created. Thus the mere use of cost-benefit analysis is a strong indication that market failure problems exist. In science, one form of market failure is the domination of a discipline by one or a small number of points of view. A dominating point of view in science also seems to control the flow of resources. William Bartley has raised this issue in the discipline of philosophy. Bartley has maintained that Karl Popper's ideas and those of his students have been excluded from professional philosophy. This exclusion is not because of the inherent intellectual merit of Popperian ideas. Instead those who dislike Popper's philosophy apparently have the market

3

power to carry out anticompetitive biases. Similar questions also are raised for the discipline of economics and economic methodology. In the absence of the competitive forces of commercial markets in the economics profession, is economics dominated by anticompetitive biases? For example, can the success of free market economics or Friedman's essay on positive economics be attributed to intellectual merit? Or is the success of free market economics and Friedman's essay a consequence of a certain point of view whose dominance can be attributed to market failure in the domain of professional economic science? If the dominance of Friedman's essay can be attributed to market failure in the marketplace of ideas, then the success of the essay is more an economic than an intellectual phenomenon. It may be difficult to come to a definitive conclusion, but this is the sort of question that can be raised with an economic approach to science.

If there is market failure in science, then an economics of science needs to reconsider a well-known metaphor for thinking about science. This notion is that science is a self-corrective marketplace of ideas. Science, like the commercial marketplace, is often viewed as having a superior self-corrective dimension. An economics of science requires making real economic sense of two things: (1) whether the metaphor of science as a marketplace of ideas has any economic content and (2) whether there is an economic dimension to the self-correctiveness of science if it does not function like a market. If science is mostly a nonmarket process, then another approach to science might make sense. Perhaps the recent economic research on nonmarket processes and internal structures of organizations is more relevant to science than economic theories relating to competitive market processes. Science has many unique organizational and institutional structures. It could be that they exist to solve some of the economic problems that would otherwise inhibit the success of science as an economic process. Perhaps it is the nonmarket processes of science which are responsible for the self-correctiveness of science.

Ultimately, an economic approach to science may change the way we conceive of economics. Although a narrow interpretation is assumed initially, rational economic behavior requires a much broader interpretation than is found in most economics texts and literature. Economists mostly are taught a rigid, logical interpretation of economic rationality in their formal training. But in their scientific applications, they are taught creative ways of liberalizing an otherwise sterile approach to understanding human behavior. This economics of science, begins with a rather rigid interpretation of economic rationality which is then liberalized in a self-conscious way. Most mainstream economists, despite their formal training have been taught tacitly and intuitively to liberalize economic rationality in this manner. An economics of science is not unique in the way that economic theories are actually applied.

THE SUBSTITUTES ARGUMENTATIVE STRUCTURE OF MAINSTREAM ECONOMICS AND AN ECONOMICS OF SCIENCE

Mainstream economics has strengths and weaknesses. Its virtues and flaws are a consequence of an argumentative structure shared by those in the mainstream. This argumentative structure can be reevaluated in light of an economics of science. This argumentative structure has both stimulated and inhibited scientific progress in economics. It is present in most texts and professional journals, and largely has gone unobserved. In professional journals, complex technical expression and the fulfillment of complicated demands of scientific inference require formal modes of expression. These technical, formal modes of professional discourse obscure the broad, overarching arguments that the mainstream of the discipline sets forth. The argumentative structure of mainstream economics is more readily apparent in texts, although none of the texts explicitly present it. To my knowledge no one else has written about it. Because all of the models are presented in a qualitative way with descriptive rather than inferential evidential support, textbook economics is really prescientific, except at the graduate level. Furthermore, the argumentative structure of economics unfolds as an ahistorical, analytical story regarding the efficacy of competition and free markets. The role of knowledge and information in such a process is usually totally ignored because transactors are often assumed to have almost perfect information.

The argumentative structure of mainstream economics that can be found in virtually every mainstream economics text takes the form of a sequence of arguments. This sequence can be called the substitutes argumentative structure because it begins with the primacy of competitive markets and theorizes that all other forms of organized economic activity are deviations from and substitutes for competitive markets. In broad outline, the substitutes argumentative structure takes the following form:

1 Market efficiency
2 Market failure
3 Government intervention
4 Government failure
5 Institutional change.

The substitutes argumentative structure unfolds with the presumption that competitive markets are the most efficient organizers of economic activity. If there are imperfections in the marketplace, then the story of competition is modified to allow for market failures such as incomplete information, externalities such as pollution, free rider behavior, moral hazard, and adverse selection. Since market failure is a real possibility, the issue of correcting such failures arises. In theory, if the sources of market failure are known, then a case can be made for some form of intervention so that the worst aspects of market failure can be surmounted. Micro and macro policies of the past few decades appear to be justified with the view that market failure can and should be corrected by government.

While the favorable effects of government intervention in the economy are theoretically possible because of market failure, it is also possible that government may fail. Government may fail to implement adequately those worthy policies which ameliorate the worst effects of unfettered capitalism. Government failure may be just as much a possibility in the economy as market failure. On the contemporary landscape of political economy, newer versions of liberalism and conservatism have emerged. Contemporary conservatives, while recognizing that government intervention is a theoretical possibility, now take the position that government failure is worse than market failure. Liberals have become more pragmatic and hold to the view that market failure is often worse than government failure. Thus while the case for a large role of government in the economy is not as strong as it once was, liberals are still optimistic regarding the achievements of government in addressing the worst problems of capitalism.

The last stage in the substitutes argumentative structure calls for institutional change. If the problems of government failure and market failure are particularly severe, then the basic rules of the game may need to be changed. Proposals for a balanced budget amendment or an incomes tax policy are tantamount to a constitutional-level restructuring of the relationship between government and the economy. Similarly the notion of a return to a gold standard to contain inflation or the idea of a line item veto for the chief executive are attempts to change the fundamental rules relating government and the private sector.

An economics of science can play an important role in reappraising the substitutes argumentative structure of mainstream economics. Science is an anomaly for the substitutes argumentative structure of mainstream economics. The arguments of mainstream economics have not been extended to science. This is a glaring oversight that must be accounted for and understood in some way. Perhaps some aspects of science can be understood from the perspective of the substitutes approach. Perhaps science can be understood in some of its dimensions as a substitute for the market. However, a more complete understanding of science may require a significantly modified mainstream argumentative structure. Indeed, the possibility exists that a substitutes economic explanation of science would be fundamentally incomplete. Mainstream economics needs an economics of science to be a mature discipline. Otherwise, economic science and all of science will continue to be seen as a noneconomic endeavor. While those in other disciplines and professions may want to keep economics external to an understanding of science, I think it is unacceptable and inconsistent for economists to adopt such a position. An economics of science could teach us much about private, nonmarket processes of economic organization and the limits of economics as a science. What all of this means is that the argumentative structure of mainstream economics needs to be modified and reconceived with science as the paradigm of nonmarket economic activity. In

6

the same way that an auction market serves as a model for a well-functioning and efficient market, perhaps science can be seen as a model for understanding non-market processes and organizations in the private sector.

Interpreting science to be the economic opposite of an auction market, has significant implications for macroeconomics. A macro theoretical example may shed further light on the economic significance of an economics of science. In macroeconomics and monetary theory, there are at least four major categories of markets that are considered in most models of aggregate economic activity: goods, money, bonds (financial), and labor. Sometimes capital goods are analyzed separately, if they are not included as a subcomponent of the goods market. The conservative New Classical economists basically have presupposed the relevance of the financial auction market conception to all of these markets or sectors of the economy. This is one way of implementing the belief in the competitive efficacy of the marketplace and a minimal role for government in the economy. The universal relevance of auction markets has been questioned in different ways by Keynesians, Monetarists, and Institutionalists and more recently by New Keynesians and New Institutionalists. These schools perceive differences in the speed of adjustment in these markets. If such differences are recognized, a step has been taken toward recognizing the limits of the auction market paradigm as the only understanding of economic processes. The bond or financial markets in New York, Chicago, and elsewhere are recognized almost universally by economists as closely approximating the auction market paradigm. The goods market and the market for financial services from banking institutions are seen to be much less auction market in nature. In this theoretical scheme, labor comes closest to being the economic opposite of an auction market process, unless capital goods are explicitly recognized as well. Both labor and the planning and implementation of capital goods are recognized as being some of the longest term processes in the economy. This contrasts with financial and commodity markets where transactions are conducted almost instantaneously.

Science could take its place among the other major categories of economic processes in economic theory. Science could be interpreted to be the economic opposite of auction markets. Science has a longer time horizon than the labor and capital goods sectors of the economy. Goods, money, bonds, labor, *and* science would be the major categories of economic theory needed to understand the modern, informationally based economy. Ranked according to speed of adjustment from fastest to slowest in terms of adjustment processes, we have:

1 Bonds (financial markets)
2 Money
3 Goods and services
4 Labor and capital goods
5 Science.

Thorough analysis of the economy requires not only an understanding of auction markets and the social processes to which the auction market paradigm might suitably be extended, but also an understanding of nonmarket processes. Rather than taking labor or capital goods, science will be taken as an example of the most extreme departure from auction markets. Science will be taken as the paradigm of nonmarket processes which are vital to the growth and efficiency of the economy. Science is the economic opposite of auction markets. An economic understanding of science not only will help us better understand science, it will also help us better understand the nonmarket aspects of the economy.

MECHANISM VERSUS EVOLUTION

Although this economics of science begins with a conventional premise of economic rationality being applied to scientific misconduct, it will not end there. An economics of science may provide the occasion to transform and broaden the conception of economic rationality. A mechanistic interpretation will gradually give way to an evolutionary view of rational economic behavior. An evolutionary view is one way of expressing the limitations of mechanism. There are important domains of human activity that can be characterized as being mechanical within a broader context of evolutionary change and adaptation. Important aspects of our lives are mechanical, and other significant dimensions of our existence are evolutionary. Using terminology from economics, mechanism and evolution need to be viewed as complements not substitutes. Or to state it differently, machines exist even in an evolutionary world. Economic behavior may be viewed as being highly patterned and ordered, locally and individually, but there are limitations on such order that can only be considered from an evolutionary point of view.

Mechanism as a thesis regarding human conduct invites further comment. In the history of science, I contend that one of the most successful hypotheses that ever has existed is mechanism. The hypothesis that "X is a machine," where X is some newly observed phenomenon, has been one of the most fruitful scientific hypotheses ever advanced by human kind. It has taken many forms: Descartes idea of man as an automaton, Newton's laws of motion, LeMettrie's physiology, Harvey's view of the circulation of the blood, Freud's conception of the mind and the unconscious, Skinner's behaviorism, Samuelson's operational revealed preference theory, and recent notions of artificial intelligence and the attempt to make thinking machines that emulate, if not mimic, human thought. Similarly, the hypothesis that an individual is economically rational clearly implies aspects of mechanism – that humans in their economic behavior act mechanically. If, as I believe, mechanism has been an extremely fruitful hypothesis, its adoption by economists should come as no surprise. It would be wasteful of economists not to adopt this viewpoint. Thus I suspect that the hypothesis of mechanism will continue to be highly productive. There will be more innovative discoveries in science and economics based on the guess that "X is a machine."

Doctrinal disputes in economics concerning mechanism and evolution have been exceptionally rigid.[2] Conventional microeconomics is rarely placed in an evolutionary context particularly in graduate instruction. Most traces of an evolutionary interpretation of mainstream microeconomics are either banished or lost when the advanced theory course peaks with an emphasis on general equilibrium theory. General equilibrium theory analyzes the entire economy as one grand, multimarket machine with individuals as cogs in this grand machine. Furthermore, nonmainstream evolutionary views of the economy are dismissed as *ad hoc*, qualitative, and lacking the rigor required of scientific inquiry. One of the major evolutionary alternatives to conventional microeconomics is just as rigid in its views. Among the most persistent critics of neoclassical microeconomics are the American Institutionalists. Their evolutionary perspective descends from American pragmatism in philosophy. Institutionalists have mostly rejected mainstream microeconomics because of its rigidly mechanistic, anti-evolutionary view. Mathematical models of a neoclassical variety have been banished from the professional publications of the Institutionalist school.

What is new in my position is the explicit limited adoption of analytical, neoclassical microeconomics within the broader context of an evolutionary view of systemic social change.[3] Mechanism is the special case, evolution is the general theory. Conventional microeconomics is just one way of analyzing the most ordered aspects of individual economic behavior. But it is not the only way. In this regard, two extremes must be avoided. Neoclassical microeconomics is not the only way to analyze the high levels of order and pattern apparent in individual behavior. Nor should it be rejected out of hand for its failure to be relevant to evolutionary economic phenomena it could not possibly explain. Two evolutionary thinkers who have influenced this economics of science greatly are Charles Sanders Peirce and Karl Popper.[4] Peirce was probably the first evolutionary indeterminist and he also had some influence on Popper. The proposed path of placing neoclassical microeconomics in a broader evolutionary context was blazed by Peirce. Peirce made a path-breaking contribution to mathematical economics. Peirce used mathematical microeconomics of the neoclassical variety to advocate an economics of research project selection. But he never abandoned his evolutionism. The use of conventional microeconomics in this economics of science follows Peirce's lead. Mechanical rigidity exists but ultimately breaks down requiring an indeterministic, evolutionary view of the world.

The vision of science implied by the preceding remarks is multifaceted. Science is a multileveled, individual, social and economic process for appraising and creating theoretical abstractions called scientific theories.[5] Science is a partly ordered process. The most ordered aspects of science can be modeled with mechanical models of human behavior like those found in conventional microeconomics. Less ordered aspects of science press the limits of mechanically interpreted, rational economic behavior and require a less restrictive view. An evolutionary interpretation of rational scientific conduct emerges. The more

9

mechanical aspects of scientific behavior are nested within less rigid, evolutionary processes and practices of scientific conduct. Paraphrasing Karl Popper's (1972b: 215) discussion of human evolution, each individual person can be regarded as a hierarchical system of control over subsystems. The subsystems of the individual are partly controlled by and partly control the individual. Controlled subsystems of the individual make trial and error corrections which are partly suppressed and partly restrained by the individual.

Extending Popper's insight to science, science can also be viewed as a system of hierarchical controls and subsystems. The subsystems of science are partly controlled and partly controlling. Similarly, economic constraints partly control and are controlled by the individual scientist. Trial and error corrections are made by individuals within the system and the subsystems. Individuals are part of the systems and subsystems of science. They partly control and are partly controlled by science, by its subsystems, and by its economic constraints. Scientists create the structure of rules for science within which they may operate in a highly rigid and patterned fashion for quite sometime. The rules of science thus direct and restrain individual behavior. But eventually, scientists change the rules. In the long run science is a slowly evolving, hierarchical system of created constraints, but in the short run the rule-governed constraints are so rigid possibly to the point of assuming the characteristics of absolutes. Scientists can function for decades, perhaps even their whole careers, within the context of these scientific "absolutes." An economics of science can help us understand behavior within the context of the rules of science and also the evolutionary adaptation of the rules of science.

Some aspects of the behavior of scientists will be explainable with a conventional interpretation of individual activity as mechanical, optimizing behavior. Other aspects will not. Conventional microeconomics rarely has been applied to science. It is time to begin such applications. Other aspects of science require a broader, evolutionary interpretation of economically rational behavior in science. There are many nonmarket economic aspects of science and they require an economic interpretation as well. Science may be an excellent domain for exploring the applicability of a broader conception of economic rationality. Scientists may embody rational economic behavior in ways that have yet to be recognized. One of the aims of an economics of science is to show both the surprising fertility *and* the unexpected limitations of an economic view of science.

POSITIVE ECONOMIC SCIENCE AND THE SOCIOLOGY OF SCIENCE

Economists do not have an economics of science.[6] However, they do have a methodology of science. For the noneconomist who may have an interest in an economics of science, the traditional methodology of economic science is known as "positive economics." The most widely read version is Milton Friedman's

(1953) essay, "Methodology of Positive Economics." This essay has proven to be quite controversial. And it has been quite difficult to locate philosophically. Friedman's essay contains terminology from differing philosophies of science. Apparently Friedman did not write his positive economics essay with any particular philosophy of science in mind. While it is interesting and perhaps useful to ask which philosophy of science may be implicit in Friedman's essay, Friedman is not a philosopher and his essay does not embody a philosopher's sensitivity and standards of consistency and coherence. Before Friedman, positive economics as a scientific tradition reached back into the nineteenth century. Mark Blaug (1980) has traced the historical development of the fundamental ideas of positive economics to John Neville Keynes, John Stuart Mill, and others.

What is interesting about positive economic methodology is its apparent disregard of economic ideas. Like philosophers, economists have theorized as though science and economic science can be done without paying attention to scarcity and resource costs. Furthermore, another economic idea, an economic metaphor – the competitive marketplace of ideas – plays no role in positive economic methodology. Positive economics as typically conceived is a noneconomic methodology of economic science. One can peruse Friedman's essay and the many articles and books interpreting the essay and little, if any, economics is mentioned. In the essay, Friedman did not think that economic issues were relevant to progress in economic science:

> Progress in positive economics will require not only the testing and elaboration of existing hypotheses but also the construction of new hypotheses. On this problem there is little to say on a formal level. The construction of hypotheses is a creative act of inspiration, intuition, invention; its essence is the vision of something new in familiar material. The process must be discussed in psychological, not logical categories; studied in autobiographies and biographies, not treatises on scientific method; and promoted by maxim and example, not syllogism or theorem.
>
> (Friedman 1953: 42–3)

It may be that Friedman is merely restating the familiar positivist distinction between the context of justification and the context of discovery and that he has no intention of excluding economics as an approach to understanding science. While it has been argued that Friedman is not a positivist (Boland 1979, Hirsch and de Marchi 1990), a tacit, limited acceptance of such a positivist distinction is merely one way of excluding economic aspects of science. If economic analysis is associated with Friedman's "logical categories," then it is quite clear that a view such as Friedman's would tend to retard the exploration of science from an economic point of view. Most other economic methodologists have followed the same path as Friedman and ignored the economic dimensions of science and economic science.

11

In contrast to Friedman, there is another well-known Chicago economist, George Stigler, who has advocated an economics of science. Most of the economics profession would regard Stigler, like Friedman, as a highly accomplished positive economist of the first rank. Besides his highly regarded work on the microeconomics of markets, monopoly, and government regulation, Stigler has done a great deal of research on the economics profession. In one passage, Stigler actually calls for an economics of science:

> The history of science provides the information to investigate the behavior of sciences. For insufficient reasons the study of the behavior of sciences is labeled the sociology of science. The behavior of sciences has been investigated by sociologists – of whom the foremost is Robert Merton – but it has also been investigated by physicists such as Thomas Kuhn, by psychologists such as Edwin Boring, and in fact by a member or two of almost every discipline. One must be a mathematician to understand the evolution of mathematics and an economist to study the evolution of economics, and sociology puts its imperialistic title on this area of study only on the ground that sciences are practiced by human beings and therefore involve social behavior. In the same sense it would be possible and equally meritorious to describe as *the economics of science the economic organization and evolution of science* [italics added for emphasis].
>
> (Stigler 1982b: 112)

Stigler has contributed many pieces that clearly bring the Mertonian approach to the economics profession.[7] Merton is a sociologist and is one of the founding figures of the sociology of science.[8] Stigler's essays on the sociology of the economics profession have been collected into two volumes of selected works (Stigler 1982a, 1984). Stigler has also authored several pieces that retrospectively one might want to include in an economics of science (Stigler 1963, 1982b, 1986). The Stiglerian approach to an economics of science has been continued by two of his students Arthur Diamond (1988, 1994, 1995) and David Levy (1988).[9] The Stiglerian approach to an economics of science emphasizes economic aspects of the sociology of the economics profession. In this approach, there has been little emphasis on the systematic theoretical development of an economics of science and the consequential methodological and philosophical implications of an economics of science. Perhaps this is because of the infancy of this area of research. Furthermore, the economics of science presented here, while broadly compatible with the Stiglerian economic sociology of science, has been developed separately and independently of the contributions of Stigler and his students. Instead, Peirce's work and that of Rescher, Radnitzky, and Boland on the economic aspects of science have been some of the major influences on the economics of science which follow in this work.

As I make final revisions for publication, an awareness of a new subfield called the "economics of science" is beginning to emerge. This is a highly desirable phenomenon. Paula Stephan (1996) and Partha Dasgupta and Paul David (1994) have published recent surveys and there was a conference on "The Need for a New Economics of Science" in March 1997 at Notre Dame. The articles provide a review of the literature written in the Stigler–Merton tradition. For the Notre Dame conference, Esther-Mirjam Sent (1997) has authored a review essay which summarizes contributions from several disciplines and points of view. And Wade Hands (1997) has critically appraised the prospects for the application of economics to science and philosophy of science. Hopefully, these recent developments and the appearance of this book will do much to further the creation of the economics of science as a new subfield which ranges across many existing disciplines, but especially economics.

THE PROBLEM OF SELF-REFERENCE

An economics of science raises one of the most perplexing intellectual issues of the past century. An economics of science raises the problem of self-reference. Economic science as a discipline must be part of the subject matter of an economics of science, just like all other scientific disciplines. In intellectual history, there have been several notable instances of self-reference. They are the logical conundrum of reflexivity in mathematics, the liar's paradox in philosophy, the "limits of rationality" debate in philosophy of science, the reflexivity debate in sociology, and the theory of an evolutionary epistemology in philosophy of science. The first example, mathematical self-reference, is the type of analysis exemplified by Gödel's (1931) incompleteness theorems in which he mapped metamathematics into arithmetic. The second instance, an ancient liar's paradox, has been revisited by Russell (1902, 1907) and concerns the truth of statements from a self-professed liar, particularly those which make a claim to truthfulness.[10] The third instance of self-reference, the limits of rationality defense of empiricism, was offered by A. J. Ayer (1956) to defend empiricism as a standard of rationality even if the evidence for such a standard of rationality was insufficient. The fourth example refers to the reflexivity debate in contemporary sociology in which the sociology of science is being applied to sociology (Woolgar 1988, Ashmore 1989). The fifth example concerns David Hull's (1988) recent work developing an evolutionary theory of science with the theory of evolution in biology as a case study.

The question of self-reference is one of the most perplexing difficulties in all of Western thought. I believe there has been a tacit prohibition of this topic in contemporary economics and economic methodology. It may be nothing more than an aspect of the negative heuristic of a Lakatosian research program. The negative heuristic may function like a tariff protecting an infant industry. A new scientific research program may need several decades to demonstrate its fruitfulness before it is subjected to the most difficult and perplexing types of criticism. The negative heuristic may direct attention away from the most intractable issues. But sooner or later, the unresolved questions percolate to the surface. The degeneration of a research program and/or its maturity may create an environment in which the question of self-reference can be raised.

An economic appraisal of economic science bears a family resemblance to these well-known examples of self-reference outside of economics. Perhaps it is the mark of maturity when a domain of intellectual inquiry engages in reflective self-criticism. A mature discipline has less of a need to keep critics at bay than one which has recently emerged as a rival to entrenched ideas. Such considerations would apply to both internal and external critiques. Self-criticism as a concern no doubt emerges when the issues of scope and generality are raised at such an abstract level that they include the originating discipline itself. Sooner or later a field of study making claims to generality perhaps even universality must include itself. Otherwise universal claims must be significantly altered or perhaps abandoned if the discipline itself is admitted as an exception. If economic science is admitted as an exception to the laws of economics, then the issue of inconsistency would seem to emerge in economics. Economists would need to explain why economists escape the economic laws they seemingly so uniformly apply to others.

After constructing an economics of science, one can ask how far can an economic explanation of economics and other sciences be taken? The logical extreme would be that the rationality of science is completely explainable in terms of economic analysis and economic rationality – that economic science itself is primarily an economic phenomenon. The problem with such a position is that it would reduce all philosophies and methodologies of science to economics. Logically this would deprive economics of an independent philosophical or methodological standard of scientific objectivity. Objective knowledge would be impossible. I do not believe an economics of science should be taken this far. The alternative is to recognize that economics, including an economics of science, construed as rational maximizing behavior, is incomplete and cannot be universally applied – that it can add greatly to an understanding of professional scientific conduct, but not explain everything.

WHY AN ECONOMICS OF SCIENCE?

So far the reasons given for attempting an economics of science have been the following:

1 An economic perspective on science has not existed until quite recently. It is time for an economics of science to take its place alongside the other major approaches to studying science.
2 An economics of science is the best way to explore systematically and empirically the thesis that science is an economic phenomenon and that scientists are rational economic agents. Such an economics of science could help explain the consequences of resource scarcity and the relative incentive structures of science.

14

3 An economics of science could help provide a systematic perspective on misconduct in science and its significance relative to legitimate, normal science.

4 An economics of science could contribute to correcting the economic deficiencies of economic methodology which makes more use of traditional philosophy of science than economic analysis.

5 An economics of science essentially could function as an internal critique of mainstream economics and its limitations. This internal criticism would take two forms: (a) a critique of the substitutes argumentative structure of mainstream economics, and (b) an exploration of the problem of self-reference which occurs when a point of view is reflexively applied to itself.

6 An economics of science may serve a theoretical purpose as an epistemic microfoundation for economic processes and as a model of a self-corrective noncommercial market process.

Before moving to the substantive methodological, philosophical, and economics issues outlined above, two other purposes for an economics of science have appeared on the horizon as this work is being revised. One is a policy purpose and the other is an intellectual role. Given the recent large reductions in government funding for basic science, it now appears that a policy issue has emerged for an economics of science. The major funding agencies seem to have an interest in an economics of science as a framework for analyzing the allocation of funds to the various scientific disciplines and research projects. Whether an economics of science could succeed in such a pragmatic task remains to be seen. An economics of science may teach us much about how science functions, but it may also have something to say about the limits of scientific knowledge. If economics is considered a science, then an economics of science may face limitations about what can be known in trying to recognize good science before it has been done. Whether a government funding agency could select those scientific research project proposals which are most deserving of financial support is clearly an economic subject.

Another purpose which seems to be emerging is the positioning of an economics of science as a successor both to the growth of knowledge approach in philosophy of science and to the sociology of science of the past two decades or so. According to one perspective, the sociology of science has effectively come to dominate recent study of science. In the 1970s and 1980s, the more traditional approaches to the history and philosophy of science appear to have given way to a sociological, rhetorical-linguistic understanding of science. Wade Hands has noticed the seeming challenge which the sociology of science poses for philosophy of science:[11]

> During the last twenty years the sociology of scientific knowledge (SSK) has emerged as an influential new approach to the study of science. Unlike traditional philosophy of science which often emphasizes issues such as demarcation, appraisal, and the logic of scientific theory choice, the

15

sociology of scientific knowledge focuses on the inherently social nature of scientific inquiry. According to the SSK, science is practised in a social context, the products of scientific activity are the results of a social process, and scientific knowledge is socially constructed. . . . In other words: most of what philosophers have said about science is irrelevant, and science is fundamentally social.

(Hands 1994a: 75)

However, intellectually, SSK seems to have reached a dead end. The literature on the sociology of scientific knowledge seems to have become bogged down in the deconstruction of the rhetoric of groups, subgroups, and scientists in the scientific community. Such deconstruction seems to lead to the perspective that, once deconstructed, all scientific points of view are equally valid. What counts as success in science appears to be persuasiveness of an argument that may have little relation to actual scientific evidence. The SSK research program seems to have reached a view of science as intellectual anarchy. Philip Mirowski describes the controversy surrounding SSK in the following way:

As with so many other things, this has become all bound up and conflated in the minds of many with parallel cultural trends: political correctness, deconstruction, relativism, postmodernism, multiculturalism, and worse. When political circumstances such as the winding down of the cold war caught some physicists unawares, rapidly shrivelling their financial support from government agencies, they in turn began to lash out at what they saw as the naysayers threatening their livelihood. Some went so far as to blame certain representatives of SSK for having killed the Texas superconducting supercollider. Congress and the press then got worked up over what they considered to be fraud in science; suddenly, eminent scientists were being treated no better than Chicago ward-heelers.

(Mirowski 1995: 229)

In light of the apparent failure of SSK, some have headed toward economics. One work has already appeared. Philip Kitcher's (1993) *The Advancement of Science* uses economics to remedy some of the perceived excesses of the sociology of science. In his review of Kitcher, Mirowski writes these summary comments:

Kitcher posits an ideal rational actor who, under the tutelage of aeons of evolution, seeks the maximum personal advantage under the social constraints of the situation. Private vices become public virtues, and conflicting schemes are reconciled to a Pareto optimal outcome, which he identifies with a "socialized epistemology." And true to form, the eighth chapter is taken up with various recognizably neoclassical models . . .

I can just imagine some of my orthodox colleagues in economics finding their pulse start to race. "Science like a market!", they exclaim. Hasn't Kitcher heard of Chicago-style "economics of information" or "rational expectations", or recent game theory? Is he aware that Charles

16

Sanders Peirce was doing stuff like this more than a century ago (1879)? Why, there is even a fairly extensive modern literature on the "economics of science"! So he wants to demonstrate that science is efficient and progressive, does he? Move over, Philip; and out tumble all those economists happy as clams to deploy their rigorous "tools" on yet another social phenomenon. You want something, Doctor Pangloss? We've got it in 29 flavours and all at bargain basement rates.

(Mirowski 1995: 231)

While Mirowski's comments certainly dramatize the situation, an economics of science is now seen by some as a successor to both the older growth of knowledge approach of Popper, Lakatos, and Kuhn and the more recent SSK program.[12] Someone like Kitcher may see economics as an answer to recent controversy in the study of science. The perspective offered here aims to be more balanced. Although a systematic economics of science might remedy some of the problems of SSK and philosophy of science, it also could introduce other difficulties in wholly unexpected ways. Economists should not be so myopic. An economics of science no doubt comes with unexpected questions of its own. But the possibility of such difficulties should not stand in the way of the creation of an economics of science. It is much too soon to even begin to suggest that an economics of science would resolve most of the recent perplexities of either SSK or the older, more traditional history and philosophy of science.

In contrast to Kitcher's contribution, this economics of science has been created independently of the sociology of science. Such an economics of science embodies both promise and limitations. It may correct some of the deficiencies of SSK but introduce other intellectual problems in unexpected ways. Hopefully, an economics of science may counter to a significant degree the apparent negativism and subjectivity of recent research in the sociology of science. An economics of science may help narrow our conception of science conceived broadly as unstructured rhetorical anarchy among communities of scientists in favor of a more specific conception of science as a highly disciplined, pluralistic struggle in which resource scarcity brings a sense of objectivity to the understanding of the scientific enterprise. Intellectual anarchy in science implies an enormous waste of scarce resources devoted to too many points of view. Its opposite, intellectual monism in science implies an excessive waste of too many resources being devoted to a single point of view. Economic processes function more efficiently when alternatives are known and explicitly define the next best option. This is the notion of opportunity cost in economics. The same is true for science. To be efficient, science needs to avoid the extremes of anarchy and monism. Anarchy provides too many and monism provides too few critical alternatives for science to make progress. Pluralism means that rival theories, research projects, theories, and evidence are being created effectively defining epistemic opportunity cost, the next best alternative to the most widely accepted scientific point of view. This may be the ultimate contribution of an economics of science. From an economic point of view, science may need to be a small-numbers, pluralistic endeavor which continually devotes resources to a scientific point of view and at least one next best alternative. Perhaps this is an economic key to understanding scientific progress from an economic point of view.

THE STRUCTURE OF THIS BOOK

This book creates an economics of science in the following way. Formal development of an economics of science begins with conventional microeconomic analysis of misconduct in science. Misconduct concerns fraud, replication failure, and plagiarism of procedures, findings, and theories in science. Misconduct seems to be an obvious area where the traditional tools of the economist may find fruitful application. Chapter 2 deals with the problem of replication failure. Scientific results often cannot be reproduced. The microeconomics of the allocation of time is applied to provide an economic explanation of this phenomenon. Chapter 3 concerns fraud in science. There have been important cases where the standards of science have been deliberately breached for personal gain or prestige. A model of the economics of crime is reinterpreted and applied to some of the worst behavior of the scientist.

Although misconduct appears to be quite amenable to conventional economic analysis, the normal conduct of science could be more difficult to explain. Fortunately, one microeconomic model of normal scientific conduct already exists. More than a century ago, the American pragmatist, Charles Sanders Peirce, created an economics of research project selection. Chapter 4 presents and appraises Peirce's economic model of research project selection and philosopher Nicholas Rescher's cost-benefit interpretation of Peirce's model. Chapter 5 transforms Peirce's model into a cost-benefit model and incorporates Gerard's Radnitzky's cost-benefit approach to Popper's methodology of science. Topically the analysis in cost-benefit terms is extended from research project selection to an economic theory for choosing scientific facts, theories, and research programs or paradigms. Even scientific revolutions may be understandable from an economic point of view. The cost-benefit model is used for nonmarket situations where commercial market failure may be a problem.

In Chapter 6, the nonmarket focus is continued with an exploration of the notion of market failure in the competitive marketplace of ideas in science. This chapter presents William Bartley's concern for market failure in the marketplace of ideas and what he perceives as an unfortunate consequence, the neglect of Karl Popper's work by professional philosophers. Since Popper is so well known, Bartley's claim with regard to Popper is scrutinized and criticized in some detail. Questions of market failure can also be raised about the economics profession. Chapter 7 makes a similar argument about the dominance of Friedman's essay in economic methodology. If there is market failure in the economics profession, then the dominance of positive economics may be understood as an economic phenomenon. Chapter 8 presents and explores notions of a competitive marketplace of ideas, market failure, and the self-correctiveness of science in the context of market failure. Here it is argued that the marketplace of ideas is a metaphor for the self-correctiveness of science in the context of commercial market failure. Thus this common economic notion of science supports rather than conflicts with a cost-benefit model of the previous chapter. Of special interest are the contributions of Michael Polanyi, Nicholas Rescher, and Friedrich Hayek.

Cost-benefit analysis of the sort introduced in Chapter 5, explicitly extends the economics of science to nonmarket complexities such as organizations and incentive structures within organizations. Chapter 9 considers the organizational aspects of science and the metaphor of the marketplace of ideas in the context of an evolutionary view of the economy. Also asked is the question of the existence of science. Why do the unique organizational aspects of science largely exist outside the context of commercial markets and firms? In addressing this question, an alternative to the substitutes argumentative structure of the mainstream texts called the complements structure is hypothesized. The complements structure presupposes scarcity in the context of evolutionary indeterminism. Science, it is maintained, is a complement to commercial markets and firms and not a substitute for either.

Chapter 10 develops evolutionary conceptions of rationality for both economic and scientific activity. It is argued that the traditional maximizing conception of economic rationality needs to be considered as a special and limited case of a more general evolutionary conception of rationality. The last two chapters focus on aspects of the problem of self-reference. Chapter 11 is concerned with problems of self-reference in science and mathematics. The problem of induction, Gödel's incompleteness theorem, and falsification are reconsidered in the context of the problem of self-reference. Chapter 12, following Peirce's (1891) idea of the architecture of scientific and philosophical theories, creates a conceptual construct which I call the architecture of economic theory and method. A somewhat unexpected result is that an evolutionary economics of science is incompatible with the architecture of mainstream economic theory and method. This is especially true for the Walrasian, competitive equilibrium approach to economics.

CAVEATS AND INTERNAL CRITICISM

A few words of warning are needed at the outset of this inquiry. An economics of science is an inherently controversial topic, and raises issues of objectivity, corruption, and science failure. If the search for objective truth is contingent on resources and relative incentive structures, then truth may possess a character quite different than typically imagined. Scarcity in combination with the existence of economic incentives in science may make absolute scientific truth unattainable. Furthermore, if some scientists completely breach the rules of conduct for personal gain, then it is possible that the entire scientific process could be subverted by a few dishonest individuals. An economics of science must address these issues. I believe that there are real economic problems in science that have lead to widely publicized instances of misconduct in science. My personal view is that misconduct in science probably is no worse than in other areas of human conduct. An economic understanding of such misconduct, by acknowledging its pervasiveness, could enhance awareness, recognition, and detection, thereby strengthening the correctability of science.

Until quite recently, an economics of science mostly has been rejected by many in the intellectual world of academia. Most philosophers, except those noted, have long rejected an economic understanding of science. For decades if not centuries they have held that economic factors are external to science. Only factors which they deem internal to science are taken as relevant to an understanding of science. Academics other than philosophers and economists have not pursued an economics of science. Psychologists, philosophers, sociologists, rhetoricians, and historians of science have applied the insights of their disciplines to science, but they have not seen the need for an economics of science. Economists, except those noted above, have not seen the possibility of an economics of science either. Presently, application of economic ideas to science is casual and *ad hoc*. Often the application of economic ideas to economic science is taken as an opportunity to demonstrate cleverness and wit rather than a commitment to formal inquiry. The last group which has not embraced an economics of science comprises those from whom one might have expected such an approach. Economic methodologists are economists with an interest and specialization in applying the studies of science from the other disciplines to economics. Most methodologists, and the author includes himself, have focused on applying philosophy of science to economics. Some have begun to explore the implications of the sociology and rhetoric of science for an understanding of economics. But almost no one in economics has systematically explored or advocated an economics of science.

Another point of contention may be economic rationality. The choice of the premise of rationality as a starting point for an economics of science may be unacceptable to many, particularly those who find economic rationality quite limiting. Prevalent criticisms are that economic rationality concerns behavior rather than creative thought; that economic rationality is mechanical and the most significant things in life are not; that economic rationality pretends to be a general view of human action and it is not; and that economic rationality requires prodigious information processing capacity and skills and human beings possess them not. These are provocative criticisms of economic rationality, and some of them have been advanced by the author (Wible 1984b). Assuming economic rationality as a starting point should not be taken as evidence that criticisms of economic rationality, narrowly construed, have been dismissed or rejected. To the contrary, the views on economic rationality presented below are much more complex than a before-or-against duality would admit.

20

Views of economics and economic rationality presented in this work defy the convenient labels present on today's intellectual landscape. I consider myself a mainstream economist, but a dissident one. An economics of science is a vehicle for expressing simultaneous agreement and disagreement with mainstream economics. One way of expressing disagreement is by rejecting an idea and adopting an external rival. In economics, this leads to classification and categorization. He/she must be a Neoclassicist, Keynesian, Monetarist, Institutionalist, Austrian, or Marxist. I find these labels to be quite limiting and I prefer to take a different path. Another way of conveying disagreement is by provisionally adopting a point of view and following where it leads. This is internal criticism. Eventually, the problem of reflexive self-reference must be encountered. Such a strategy requires conditionally accepting a point of view and doing economics from that point of view. An internal strategy of criticism can be quite fruitful if pursued to its logical limits.

There are reasons for taking such a risky, internal strategy. Increasingly I believe a truly educated person is one who has the ability to suspend temporarily his/her own view of the world and take on an alternative. Obviously, attempting to see the world from someone else's point of view may evoke feelings of discomfort, alienation, and powerlessness. Conversation and debate in terms of someone else's conceptual framework puts the less experienced person at a disadvantage. But much can be learned from such an activity. Much can be gained from repeating the experience. Of course, placing oneself at a semantic and conceptual disadvantage in real discourse and argument requires a great deal of discipline, restraint, and awareness. It also requires reciprocation. At some point, the roles need to be reversed. The person with the upper hand needs to change places with the disadvantaged person. When conversation occurs in terms of a conceptual framework I have adopted, then I have the semantic upper hand and sense the exhilaration, authority, and power which comes with the subtle and superior command of abstract ideas. But I should not forget, the sense of "dis-ease" that may be felt by someone who is unfamiliar with my view of the world, my conceptual framework, my paradigm, etc. I am asking readers of this work to participate with me in this way. I am asking for proponents and opponents of an economic point of view of science to reconsider their positions. From potential proponents I ask for consideration of a domain of phenomena they have exempted from economic analysis – science. Until recently, almost nothing has been written about science from an economic point of view. From opponents of an economic view of science, I also ask a consideration of an economics of science. Paradoxically, many of their reservations about economics might find expression in economic form using economic analysis. Indeed we may find economic arguments for criticizing economics. I appeal to the idea of open-mindedness to keep this possibility alive. An economic criticism of science and economic science has a perplexing quality that we rarely see in current debates. An economics of science may be both supportive *and* critical of science and economic science. An economics of science may lead to

21

a new appreciation of the fertility of an economic point of view and also more clearly portray its limitations.

In this work, I make no claim to resolve the problem of self-reference. My task is to present an economics of science and secondarily consider self-reference in economics because it is an issue that cannot be skirted in creating an economics of science. Consideration of self-reference provides one of the best forums for presenting the inherent ambiguity of all conceptual frameworks in Western thought. Cultivation of the ability to step into an alternative world view also serves this purpose. One of my greatest disagreements with mainstream economics and some of its most significant rivals is the utter lack of an awareness of the inherent ambiguity of all conceptual frame works. As others have noticed, economists can be quite intolerant of their rivals. Perhaps intolerance is characteristic of all science and essential to scientific progress. What I desire for economics and all of the sciences has been characterized by William Bartley as an argumentative version of the golden rule – argue with others as you would have them argue with you. Self-reference gives this notion a new twist – apply standards to yourself that you adopt in arguing with others. For an economist, such consistency is the core of an economics of science. Economics must be used to understand science and economic science. Otherwise, economists might be charged with assuming that professional economic science is not an economic phenomenon. Who should listen to us if we as a profession endorsed such a position?

2

AN ECONOMIC THEORY OF
REPLICATION FAILURE

The founders of Economic Science constructed something more universal in its application than anything that they themselves claimed. . . . Economics brings into full view that conflict of choice which is one of the permanent characteristics of human existence. Your economist is a true tragedian.

(Robbins 1935: 86, 30)

If economic theory is correct, it should apply to the economics profession.
(Colander 1989: 148)

MISCONDUCT AS A POINT OF DEPARTURE

As a point of departure this economics of science begins with the general problem of misconduct in science. There are many other alternative aspects of science which could have been chosen as a starting point for an economics of science. Topics such as legitimate or normal science, scientific revolutions, market failure in science, the organizations and institutions of science, theory choice, and the rationality of science might have been chosen. Misconduct is the subject where this author first undertook an economic approach to science. That subject which initially drew my attention was the problem of replication failure in economics followed by that episode of fraud known as the Baltimore case.

There are several reasons for analyzing misconduct before rather than after the other aspects of science. First, it is better to begin with a problem which in many respects is easier than others. Difficult as it may be, an economic explanation of misconduct in science poses fewer obstacles than some of the other topics. Second, an economic analysis of misconduct in science could prepare the way for an economic understanding of important aspects of the legitimate, normal activities of science. Third, misconduct may be much more blatantly motivated by conventional desire for material and economic gain than legitimate, normal science. This is a subjective guess at this point, but those who commit misconduct may want the reputation, recognition, and resources which come from

23

being recognized as a first-rate scientist without expending the effort, resources, and time that are required to attain a legitimate record of scientific achievement. Their aims may be diverted from the traditional ends of fundamentally innovative scientific research to accumulating the means of scientific accomplishment such as a continuing stream of grants, laboratory facilities, research assistants, computer support, publications, and citations. The last reason for beginning with misconduct is to address the skeptics of an economics of science. Those in economics and other disciplines who think that an economics of science may not have much to say, might accept an economic understanding of misconduct in science. Thus this economics of science begins with misconduct because of a perceived amenability to economic analysis and with a less serious form of misconduct, replication failure.

REPLICATION FAILURE AS AN ECONOMIC PHENOMENON

Replication failure has recently been identified as a problem in the economics profession.[1] Certainly the problem is not limited to economics. Other scientific disciplines to varying degrees also may be subject to replication failure. An economic analysis of replication failure in the economics profession may be extended by analogy to other sciences. There may be no reason for preventing a general application of the economics of replication failure to all of the sciences. A starting premise is the conventional economic assumption that economists (and other scientists) are economically rational. Replication failure and a few other aspects of science may be explainable as the consequence of the rational scientist's allocation of time. Time-constrained scientists essentially are faced with a choice between professional activities which increase their income and prestige, and those which enhance the replicability of empirical research. In this context it is not surprising that replication suffers.

In the 1980s, the *Journal of Money Credit and Banking* (*JMCB*) with the support of the National Science Foundation initiated the first major study of the replicability of empirical results in a major mainstream economics journal.[2] This project was conducted by William Dewald, J. G. Thursby, and R. G. Anderson (1986). During a period of several years in the early 1980s, these authors requested that the data and programs be included with articles submitted for review to the *JMCB*. At a subsequent point in time, they attempted to replicate nine articles representative of those published in the *JMCB*. Using the items previously submitted by published authors, Dewald *et al.* found that replication of published empirical results is difficult to achieve. Their findings fall into three categories. First, less than half, or four of the nine articles were reproduced with the original techniques yielding results quite similar to those of the original authors. In another category were papers, whose findings were in fact duplicated, but with empirical techniques that differed substantially from those described in the published articles. In a third category were papers that could not be replicated or those in which the results obtained were remarkably different. In their summary, Dewald et al. conclude:

> The replication of research is an essential component of scientific methodology. Only through replication of the results of others can scientists unify the disparate findings of various researchers in a discipline into a defensible, consistent, coherent body of knowledge. . . . It would be embarrassing to reveal the findings of the Project save for our belief that the findings would be little different if articles and authors were selected from any other major economics journal. In private correspondence, the editor of another major journal (not the *AER*) confided that he shares our belief.
>
> (Dewald et al. 1986: 600, 601)

While one should not be too critical of the economics profession on the basis of one review of replicable research – indeed even the results of this study should be replicated by others – the reported results were explained informally in terms of economic incentives and constraints confronted by the individual economist: "replication – however valuable in the search for knowledge – does not fit within the 'puzzle-solving' paradigm which defines the reward structure in scientific research. Scientific and professional laurels are not awarded for replicating another scientist's findings" (Dewald et al. 1986: 587) and, "A single researcher faces high costs in time and money from undertaking replication of a study and finds no ready market place which correctly prices the social and individual value of the good" (Dewald et al. 1986: 589).

The preceding remarks suggest that an economist might allocate a larger proportion of time to producing new publishable results devoting relatively less time and effort to the tasks required for replication. This interpretation is supported further in one of the more interesting replication attempts by Dewald, Thursby, and Anderson. In their article, they report their efforts to replicate the large-scale macroeconometric model of Benjamin Friedman of Harvard University. Because of its complexity and scale, these authors were unable to reproduce any of Friedman's results. They attempted to transfer Friedman's large model and program from the IBM mainframe at Harvard to the one at Ohio State. The sheer magnitude of the effort required to transfer the model from one large computer to another led Dewald, Thursby, and Anderson to abandon the replication effort. To his credit, Friedman apparently contributed an enormous amount of time in preparing materials for this replication project. The authors report that: "Friedman estimated that the time and effort required to produce the manual and computer tapes [for the attempted replication] approximated that required to produce an additional article for a professional journal" (Dewald et al. 1986: 597). Friedman's estimate of the time involved in satisfying would-be replicators is the most direct evidence that there are substantial real economic costs associated with replication.[3]

For the sciences other than economics, there is a growing literature on the nature of replication and the associated problem of replication failure. Much of this research is broadly in agreement with Dewald *et al.*'s findings that replication is quite infrequent in science. The most detailed treatment is H. M. Collins' (1985) *Changing Order* which deals with the nature of replication in scientific practice. Collins provides three lengthy case studies from physics and psychology, and offers this overview of replication in science:

> Replication of others' findings and results is an activity that is rarely practised! Only in exceptional circumstances is there any reward to be gained from repeating another's work. Science reserves its highest honours for those who do things first, and a confirmation of another's work merely confirms the other is prizeworthy. A confirmation, if it is to be worth anything in its own right, must be done in an elegant new way or in a manner that will noticeably advance the state of the art. Thus, though scientists will cite replicability as their reason for adhering to belief in discoveries, they are infrequently uncertain enough to need, or to want, to press this idea to its experimental conclusions. For the vast majority of science replicability is an axiom rather than a matter of practice.
>
> (Collins 1985: 19)

In economics, Collins' work and the *JMCB* study have led two other authors, Mirowski and Sklivas (1991), to consider the degree of replication in econometrics. In econometrics, they argue that the focus is on innovative extensions of previous results. Consequently replication is infrequent:

> The reason why most people believe, however misguidedly, that the primary characteristic of science is the replicability of experiments is not that it is commonly encountered on a daily basis, but rather the scholarly journal presents experimental reports as if it were the case. "Replication" is an ideal of science; rarely is it an activity of scientific practice.
>
> If they do not replicate, what, then, do scientists do? A short flip answer would be that they generally "reproduce": that is, they convince each other and build on previous results. This is hardly sufficient as a general theory of science, but we are not that ambitious in this article.
>
> (Mirowski and Sklivas 1991: 154)

Other noteworthy works on replication or replication failure are Mulkay and Gilbert (1991), Rosenthal (1979), Smith (1970), and Campbell and Jackson (1979). Campbell and Jackson, who founded the journal *Replications in Social Psychology*, offer an overview of replication in science that is broadly compatible with the remarks of Collins and Mirowski and Sklivas above and the *JMCB* study of Dewald *et al.*:

> Unfortunately, there is a serious inconsistency between the verbal and behavioral commitment to replication research. The importance of

replication is often verbally espoused, but behavioral commitment (in terms of conducting and publishing replication research) may be nonexistent. The verbal commitment to replication as a foundation-stone of science, combined with the relative lack of behavioral enactment of a systematic program of replication research is an indication of a disparity between the ideal and the real. Ideally, replication is valued. Really, replication is not valued.

(Campbell and Jackson 1979: 3)

The preceding literature suggests that replication failure is a problem in many disciplines, not just economics. Apparently, replication is important in the rhetoric of most scientists, but it is often not fully implemented in routine scientific practice. The question at hand is whether an economic approach could help explain a more mixed picture of science; a picture of science which includes not only its most spectacular successes, but also a variety of research efforts which are routinely prone to replication failure. The task is to provide an explanation of science which incorporates both success and failure.

CONCEPTS OF REPLICATION IN SCIENCE

Before creating an economic model of replication failure, what is needed is a clear idea of what is meant by the term "replication". In the preceding literature, several concepts of replication were presented. What is needed before economic modeling is attempted is an analysis of various types of replication. Depending on whether the simplest idea of replication is included, the literature cited previously usually presents two or more types of replication. In the extreme, one contribution went so far as to provide a table of eight types of replication (Campbell and Jackson 1979: 5). And another, Collins (1985: 37), listed seven levels of determination in his theory of replication. While these elaborate discussions of the nature of replication are worthy of the reader's attention, they detract from the purpose at hand. For an economics of science, this literature suggests three useful categories of replication:

1 Direct replication (with or without detailed information)
2 Design replication
3 Conceptual "replication."

Direct replication is the idea that scientific investigations can be repeated by almost anyone of modest intelligence and experimental competence (Muma 1993). The original experiment or investigation is simply rerun in the same manner as was initially reported. There are other terms for this such as "mere" replication (Mulkay and Gilbert 1991: 155), and "literal" or "exact" replication (Campbell and Jackson 1979: 4). Direct replication is the concept most students encounter in the earliest stages of scientific education. Certainly the most basic results of the natural sciences are conveyed in laboratory settings where the student directly reruns the fundamental experiments of science. In Kuhnian terms, these basic experimental demonstrations serve as exemplars to give the student experience in obtaining experimental results. In this manner, a large proportion of high school and college science students learn the basic principles of science by replicating the results of the masters of bygone eras. Although a great deal is summarized in science texts for the students, it is the actual production of pure oxygen or hydrogen, it is the tangible experimentation with the chemical and electrical properties of metals, it is the actual movements of objects with measurable mass and velocity and the approximate replication of the laws of physics that are so convincing to the novice scientist. Such experimental demonstrations of the validity of laws of science persuade the student that she or he can replicate the most important results of science. If this fails, then it is the student whose competence is questioned rather than the laws of nature.

The study of Dewald *et al.* and the others quoted above maintain that direct replication rarely occurs in science.[4] On occasion direct replication is attempted without knowledge of experimental details which have been excluded from publication. But this sort of direct replication often fails. Reasons for this may be as follows. Science is more complex than mechanical reenactment of simple experiments. Also the process of inference and judgement is more difficult, less individual, and more social than a conception of direct replication would allow. It is very difficult to reproduce the results of an experiment without knowledge of what the researcher has done exactly. The published scientific article, which often is viewed as a condensed lab report, may not contain sufficient details for replication to occur. If this is the case, then it suggests specialized knowledge of the experimental situation is necessary. Increasingly, journals are requiring detailed information and the data to accompany a submitted research paper to facilitate replication with details. With adequate details and sufficient resources, one would hope that the results of scientific research could be directly replicated by a sufficiently motivated, specialized, and intellectually endowed researcher.

However, even when details are available, attempts to directly repeat an experiment or empirical study seem to be rare in the natural and social sciences. Instead another form of replication seems to emerge. Muma (1993) has called this type of study design replication. Design replication involves the use of an alternative experimental design which in theory might yield results similar to those reported in a previous study. One can imagine variations in the sample population, different investigating techniques, the use of a newer statistical package, new research assistants, or slightly modified circumstances for conducting a test. The goal is to obtain the same result with a different methodology. If the general results of a study hold up well under a wide variety of circumstances, then a scientific result is considered to have been replicated. A result which can be obtained from more than one experimental design is viewed as a stronger, more robust result than one which has been only directly replicated.

The last form of replication is conceptual "replication." Conceptual replication does not involve the actual repetition of previous experimental or empirical results. Rather a scientist takes a previous experiment or empirical study as a stepping stone for another investigation. The scientist imagines an application to a suitably related subject or pattern of phenomena. The researcher imagines a certain result which could hold hypothetically as long as the results of previous work can be taken as fact. The use of the word "replication" in the term "conceptual replication" is justified by the belief that the derived results of a new project likely would not hold if an earlier project was invalid and unreplicable. With conceptual replication, the results of one scientific study are chain-connected to another. The results of a prior study are taken as input into a subsequent study, but the assumed results of the previous study are not retested in any significant way. As long as the validity of the new study in this chain of inquiry remains intact, scientists move on to the next major step of scientific research as quickly as possible. Only if the validity of this chain of empirical inquiry is ruptured may replication and the degree of replication failure become an issue in the scientific community.

Further discussion of the nature of replication in science can be facilitated by conceiving of science as a series of related research projects represented in the following way:

$$RP_1 \rightarrow RP_2 \rightarrow RP_3 \rightarrow \ldots \rightarrow RP_N$$

Let RP_1 be the first research project in a new line of scientific inquiry. If RP_2 tries to repeat RP_1, in so far as that is possible, then RP_2 could be an attempted direct replication of RP_1. Because RP_2 would add little new knowledge to science, few direct replications seem to be undertaken as a routine matter in science. However, an experiment or study with a few design changes may offer the prospect of a small increment to our scientific knowledge. Let RP_3 be a study with design changes relative to RP_1 attempting to get the same results as RP_1 in a different way. This would be an attempted design replication. A third possibility is that another project RP_N might be a novel extension and application of RP_1 to a related but different type of subject. This would be a conceptual "replication." A conceptual replication assumes the validity of RP_1 in its domain of application, and uses the results of that investigation to establish a different experimental result. If RP_N succeeds as a research project and yields scientifically significant results, then RP_N serves to confirm and indirectly replicate RP_1. However, RP_N may in no way repeat the experimental details of RP_1. The "facts" generated by RP_1 have been used as inputs into another research project, RP_N. If RP_N gives good experimental results, then the facts of RP_1 have been replicated in a most circuitous and indirect fashion. As with design replication, the successful application of aspects of RP_1 to new phenomena tends to be regarded as strengthening the original line of research.

The point of conceptual replication is that despite the rhetoric of commitment to replication, genuine direct or design replication is often bypassed so that the scientist may focus on making an innovative contribution to science. The greater the innovative component of a proposed project, the more likely the researcher will pursue scientific investigations of that type. Direct replication promises little in the way of innovation to enhance a researcher's reputation. Design and conceptual replication allow the scientist to make a comparatively greater individual contribution to science. What appears to happen most often in science is that a sequence of studies occurs in which subsequent research depends in some important way on previous studies. Later studies often do not repeat the most important aspects of earlier studies. Rather, later studies are done conditionally assuming the validity of previous research. At some point, the chain of successful investigations fails. Conceptual replication failure occurs. This causes a reappraisal of the latest contributions. In the face of conceptual replication failure, direct or design replications may be attempted. It's at this point when the more mundane results get greater scrutiny. When simpler forms of replication are attempted in the context of a crisis due to conceptual replication failure, there may again be even more replication failures. Thus it is interesting that the most direct forms of replication and replication failure apparently appear when there is controversy.

It is in this context that the relative infrequency of direct and design replications must be understood. These types of replication often occur when some someone's research is under attack rather than as a routine part of science. An attempt by a rival scientist or graduate student to replicate the results of an important scientific paper is often taken as a hostile act. A direct replication may be seen as an act casting doubt on the competence of the original investigator. All of this suggests that actual replication as direct or design replication occurs less frequently in science than what one might expect based on the verbal significance placed on replication. The difficulties with direct replication have been further characterized in the following way as involving high costs for the researcher and the scientific community:

> Thus, from the point of view of a new entrant to empirical scientific research, replication must appear more costly and less rewarding than a strategy of extension and reproduction of an original empirical result. Replication is an inherently difficult procedure for the reasons discussed above, and if successful, has all manner of unattractive consequences. The new entrant could simply prove the originator right, which turns out a waste of time; or else he could prove the originator wrong, which creates further problems for the reporting process. A successful disconfirmation always implicitly calls into question the refereeing competence of the journal, and also makes inordinate demands upon journal editors to adjudicate the inevitable controversy which ensues between the originator and replicator about the nature of asymptotically satisfactory replication. Confrontations of these sorts are ended often only by recourse to third parties and further costly processes, if they can ever be said to be settled

conclusively. The payoff to replicators is intrinsically low: this is not an assumption, but rather an intrinsic feature of the social structure of science.

(Mirowski and Sklivas 1991: 154)

While some may deplore what appears to be so much replication failure in science, much of this may make sense from an economic point of view. Apparently, it is the economic incentives and constraints of science which push it away from the most to the least direct forms of replication. What usually happens is that previous scientific results get "tested" again when they are extended to new applications. Mostly it is only when this chain of extensions fails that the simpler forms of replication are attempted. Furthermore, if all research projects were directly replicated at least once and perhaps more often, then resources might be wasted and the pace of new scientific knowledge might be significantly diminished. Science as a systemic process makes varying use of a mix of all types of replication processes – direct, design, and conceptual replications – in order to make efficient use of the scarce resources of science. The economizing of resources thus exposes science to mistakes. At some point, these mistakes will be discovered and they will have to be corrected. From an economic point of view, there needs to be a balance between resources devoted to replication in its simpler forms and innovation. Attitudes and reward structures which are skewed toward innovation may set science up for replication failures of many types. But mistakes need to be corrected or they will impede scientific progress and innovation at some point. Viewing science as an economic social process with several complementary forms of replication activities places replication failure in a broader perspective. Replication failure in science may be an economic phenomenon.

AN ECONOMIC MODEL OF REPLICATION FAILURE

It should be clear from the preceding discussion of types of replication that Dewald *et al.* have identified at least two types of replication failure in economics. They found that it was difficult to do direct replications based only on information from the published articles in the *JMCB*. Greater success was obtained with direct replications when detailed knowledge was available. Some success was also achieved with design replications where a replicator got similar results using a modified methodological design. Due to the nature of the *JMCB* study, it appears that conceptual replications were not tried. Dewald *et al.*, however, would seem to agree that economic incentives fostered innovation in economic research at the expense of direct and design replications.

If there are economic incentives in science which favor innovation at the expense of the simpler forms of replication, an economic model of replication failure emerges as a possibility. In order to create an economic model of scientific choice, a widely accepted methodological criterion must be identified which

31

possesses important economic dimensions. As suggested by the project of Dewald *et al.*, one such criterion is replication. Replication takes time and imposes significant costs and unpleasant activities on replicators, their referees, and their journal editors. Replication is vitally important to any conception of science. Isolated instances of empirical validation are of little value to science. With replication in mind, Popper (1959: 86) has bluntly remarked: "Non-reproducible single occurrences are of no significance to science." Scientific results which cannot be duplicated at some point in a chain of successive research projects must be considered suspect. Empirical results that cannot be reproduced by peers of equivalent professional competence must be reappraised and perhaps rejected. The widespread existence of unreplicable "scientific" results would destroy interpersonal objectivity as the goal of scientific research. Without replication, empirical results become a private affair valid for one but not for others. This is the subjective state of affairs abhorred by most scientists.

An economic model capable of addressing significant economic aspects of replication and replication failure in science is the economic theory of the allocation of time created by Gary Becker (1965) and elaborated in Becker (1971: 45–8). Becker has created some of the most extraordinary applications of price theory in nontraditional transactional settings. Science is an idio-syncratic economic process and does not exhibit the exchange and ownership arrangements commonly seen in the conventional realm of the commercial economy. Similarly, economic science should qualify as human action replete with idiosyncratic exchange relationships because of its peculiar aims and institutional structures. The analysis of nontraditional economic relationships begins with a model of the household rather than science. Becker has developed a simultaneous consumption–production model of a household which is constrained by income, wealth (unearned income), and time. Households buy inputs which they use to produce the commodities they desire. A household's allocation of time between market and nonmarket activities is sensitive to the opportunity cost of time. As wages rise, time intensive processes of household production are replaced with less time intensive ones and the household's altered purchases of goods and services reflect this change.

I shall take a similar view of economic science. Following Becker, the economic scientist will be assumed to be a utility maximizer of commodities created by his/her own production processes. The scientist's production processes require the purchasing of inputs and the allocation of a fixed total amount of time to each "commodity" being produced. Specification of the economic scientist's utility function requires great care. The economist-scientist must be portrayed as someone who is sensitive to the standards of professional scientific conduct widely accepted among other positive economists, but who is also economically rational. Of course, ordinary commodities must also appear in the utility function. Becker (1971: 169–70) already has shown how households will allocate time among multiple occupations. As an extension of his joint consumption–production theory, rather simple modification of this analysis to tasks within an occupation will make the model suitable for the issue of replication in economic science.

What I would like to consider is the allocation of time by a first-rate professional economist between two important professional tasks: A_1 the production of *seemingly replicable articles* (SRAs) and A_2 those additional tasks and activities which ensure the replicability of the project making the resulting publications, *genuinely replicable articles* (GRAs).[5] GRAs would be research projects whose results could be repeated successfully if direct or design replications were undertaken assuming the availability of detailed information from previous projects.[6] SRAs would be those research projects, which on the surface look no different than GRAs, but whose replications would fail if they were replicated directly or with changes in design. If a complex professional and institutional environment can be imagined in which it is difficult and costly to distinguish between SRAs and GRAs in science, then it would be perfectly rational for the scientist to view both as goods and to begin the next project before tying up loose ends on the most recent one.[7] If the incentive and social structures of economic science require publication of apparently replicable results without providing a short-run process for distinguishing between those which are and those which are not replicable, then even the best and most rational of positive economists and scientists may produce results which no one can duplicate in practice.

The reason for distinguishing between activities A_1 and A_2 is economic. There are many aspects to scientific research which have the characteristics of fresh tomatoes or highly perishable fish. Computer software, hardware, and programmers change from one project to another. Research assistants come and go. Electronic data sources may be revised continuously. Human recollections of past activities may dim and fade. Time and resources must be devoted to the preservation of these ephemeral aspects of scientific research. Otherwise projects which are repeatable directly or in design may not be so in practice. While this issue may not be so important for the natural sciences, it is of extreme importance to economics. Economic behavior seems to change rapidly at certain periods in history. When such change occurs, we need to know whether the apparently reported changes in human behavior are actually in the phenomena and the data or whether they are a cumulative reflection of many marginal changes in research technique.

The preceding considerations imply that there is an implicit but widely understood incentive structure which emphasizes apparent innovation at the expense of the simpler forms of replication. Dewald *et al.* (1986: 587) conclude that "replication . . . does not fit within . . . the reward structure in scientific research." An economic interpretation of their comment would be that direct or design replication is rewarded less than seemingly more innovative contributions. This means that the economist could view his actual wage, w, as a weighted average of two wages: w_1 a higher wage perceived as a reward for research thought to be quite innovative and w_2, a lower wage for any minimal level of replication activities undertaken by the professional economist.[8] Although it is possible that some might not undertake any replication activities, I would argue that this would be extreme. Some minimal level of replication, perhaps just a small fraction of the published articles, would seem to be necessary to enhance or maintain a professional reputation. An empirical economist who had no replicable research, would seem to be open to the possibility of career-threatening criticism. One would suspect that some activities and efforts of the scientist would be directed toward preservation of the records and trail of evidence. In order to avoid the high costs associated with a dispute stemming from a highly public replication failure, some self-protective measures would be appropriate for the scientist. What is at issue is how and to what extent the scientist balances the quest for innovative scientific discovery with costly self-protective activities that facilitate replication in the face of potentially hostile opposition. This is most likely a trial and error process in which the scientist balances innovation possible from the next project against the likelihood of mistakes from an ongoing project.

Keeping in mind the preceding comments, the professional economist's utility function is defined to include: Z_1, SRAs; Z_2, GRAs; and Z_3 all other commodities and activities entering this economist's preference function. The utility function is represented as:

$$U = U(Z_1, Z_2, Z_3) \tag{1}$$

In equation (1) it is assumed that the positive economist is "economically rational" and that SRAs and GRAs are goods. Furthermore the indifference curves characterizing the utility function are assumed to be negatively sloped and convex to the origin.

The items which enter the economically rational economist's utility function are produced by the allocation of time and by the purchase of appropriate inputs. Inputs and outputs are related with fixed coefficient production functions. The production functions show the time, b_i, and the material input, a_i, required to produce each GRA, SRA, or each unit of consumption goods.[9] The minimum appropriate time horizon for the economically rational economist's optimization problem is taken to be a year.[10]

The optimization problem facing the economist then can be formulated as a constrained maximization process. The economist's utility function is maximized with respect to a single, joint resource constraint by formulating the appropriate Lagrangian, L:

$$L = U(Z_1, Z_2, Z_{3)} - \lambda \, (p_1 x_1 + p_2 x_2 + p_3 x_3 + (w_1 + w_2)t_3 \\ + w_1 t_2 + w_2 t_1 - (w_1 + w_2)t - v) \tag{2}$$

The resource constant is formed by combining the usual income constraint with a total time constraint. In order to have a single constraint, time must be convertible to income in the current period. This means that w must be adjustable in the current period.

While the mathematics of maximization is well known to all economists, this version of Becker's allocation of time model has some unique features that deserve further elaboration. This will permit greater attention being given to the role of time in scientific decision-making. In order to facilitate further analysis, the resource constraint in the Lagrangian needs to be reformulated using outputs rather than inputs. Once important substitutions are made, the budget constraint can be formulated in terms of the outputs and the input coefficients from the production function.[11] Presented in the usual way the joint income, time, and budget constraint takes the following form:

$$Z_2 = -\frac{P_1}{P_2} Z_1 - \frac{P_3}{P_2} Z_3 + \frac{(w_1 + w_2) \, t + v}{P_2}$$

The Ps are shadow prices which incorporate the input prices, the wage rates w_1 and w_2, and the production coefficients for the purchased inputs (as) and for time (bs). The shadow prices are defined as follows:

$$P_1 = p_1 a_1 + w_2 b_1$$
$$P_2 = p_2 a_2 + w_1 b_2$$
$$P_3 = p_3 a_3 + w_1 b_3 + w_2 b_3$$

The role of time and other inputs in the model can be analyzed by comparing P_1 and P_2. Consider the material inputs first. The spirit of the research on replication failure by Dewald et al. suggests that for most cases there is no difference in the material resources required for SRAs and GRAs. The major difference is the time taken to ensure replication. Typically this means taking additional time to preserve the records of the research as it is carried out by the researcher. An exception to this assumption might be Benjamin Friedman's macro model which could require extensive nonlabor resources for any replication effort. Thus in most cases it seems reasonable to assume that material input prices and quantities are identical for SRAs and GRAs or that $p_1 = p_2$ and $a_1 = a_2$. Turning from the material to the time inputs, if Dewald et al. are correct in their observations that replication takes a lot of time, then the time input for GRAs is much larger than for SRAs or $b_2 > b_1$. If this is the case and $w_1 > w_2$, then $P_2 > P_1$. This means that the slope of the joint budget constraint is $-(P_1/P_2)$ and less than one in absolute value.

The slope of the joint budget constraint being less than one in absolute value illustrates the most important features of the model: (1) the implicit reward structure of science valuing SRAs as much as GRAs so that $w_1 > w_2$, and (2) the fact that replication activities take time or $b_2 > b_1$. Both of these features of the problem make the implicit price of GRAs higher than for SRAs or $P_2 > P_1$. The joint resource constraint implies that there is a significant real opportunity cost associated with the preservation of the records of scientific research in economics. The total number of articles published by the individual will be lower, the more time is devoted to such preservation activities.

The complete optimization problem facing the economically rational positive economist is graphically depicted in Figure 2.1. The optimum is found where the preference map is tangent to the income–time constraint at point A. Point A is clearly superior to point B which represents the maximum number of articles which could be produced by this economist in an average year. This is due to the fact that the positive economist must produce some GRAs or his reputation will suffer. The methodological significance of point A should not be underestimated. It suggests that an economist or scientist who perceives both GRAs and SRAs as goods will produce *both* types of articles. In a complex scientific environment in which it is difficult to distinguish between GRAs and SRAs, research will be created which cannot be duplicated. This theoretical result is quite consistent with the Dewald, Thursby, and Anderson project. If the reputation of the economist's or scientist's employer depends on maximizing the joint total of Z_1 and Z_2, then any increase in w is likely to be associated more with SRAs than GRAs, hence with w_1. This whole process could be quite tacit and subjective. The economist can be conceived as rationally responding to the incentive structures and implicit contracts in his/her transactional setting even if a great deal of that structure has not been formally elaborated.[12] In this analysis, attention is restricted solely to the *best case* situation when the SRAs could have become GRAs – if the positive economist had only taken the time to preserve important aspects of his/her research program.

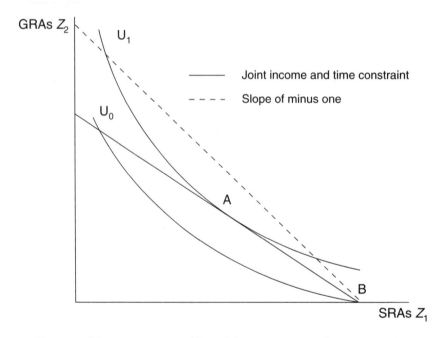

Figure 2.1 The optimization problem of the time-constrained positive economist

SOME EXTENSIONS AND APPLICATIONS OF THE MODEL

The allocation of time model portrays some of the most important features of replication failure in economics as described by Dewald, Thursby, and Anderson. In the context of a complex scientific and institutional setting, economically rational scientists respond to the implicit reward structure of their discipline and produce both replicable and unreplicable research. A methodological purist might decry such a result. Such a purist would maintain that only GRAs should be produced by the true scientist. A methodologically pure solution could be obtained if the optimum of the scientific economist were a corner solution on the GRA axis. Such a solution would represent a mix of all GRAs and no SRAs. Thus a methodologically pure solution would stand in sharp contrast to the solution depicted in Figure 2.1.

The methodologically pure result can be obtained in several other ways from a more general taxonomy of preferences structures. Besides the possibility of a corner solution resulting from negatively sloped indifference curves like those assumed in the preceding allocation of time model, other possibilities for the pure result include: (1) straight-line indifference curves, (2) positively sloped indifference curves, and (3) lexicographic preferences.[13] Straight-line indifference maps deal with neuter preferences.[14] SRA neuter preferences imply a situation in which more nonreplicable research leaves the utility of the scientist unaffected. In this case, the preference map would be composed of horizontal lines. Only more truly reproducible research would make the scientist better off. This type of scientist would produce only replicable research because the optimum would be on the GRA axis. Positively sloped indifference curves present similar issues as neuter preferences. For the method-ologically pure result to occur, the indifference curves must slope upward to the right on the GRA–SRA plane and increase in steepness. Here SRAs are actually a "bad" and GRAs are a "good." Optimization would occur as a corner solution on the GRA axis. No unreplicable research would be produced by an economist with such preferences. The major point is that, in this case, the "pure" positive economist not only produces no unreproducible work, but the production of unreplicable work would actually make him worse off. Research products that do not measure up to widely espoused standards of professional conduct accepted by most scientific economists would be a source of disaffection.

Lexicographic preferences provide yet another way to obtain the method-ologically pure result. Lexicographic preferences involve bundles of goods being ordered like the words in a dictionary. Bundles are ordered by the first item in the bundle, then by the second, followed by the third, etc. For the scientific economist, all combinations of GRAs and SRAs would be ordered first by the number of GRAs and then second, when the number of GRAs are the same, by the number of SRAs. Lexicographic preferences cannot be represented by indifference curves. All points on the GRA–SRA plane would be ranked. The ordering required for the methodologically pure result would be more GRAs preferred to less and fewer SRAs preferred to more. Consider Figure 2.2. Bundles A, B, and C can be ranked by the preceding criteria. Bundle A is preferred to B because A has more GRAs. Bundle B is preferred to C because it has fewer SRAs even though C represents more total publications and an equal number of GRAs. The methodologically pure economist facing a budget constraint would end up at D and would prefer to publish fewer articles if it is known that quality is at stake. The lexicographic approach to understanding the behavior of economists is more elaborately developed by Peter Earl (1983, 1988). Earl's treatment is more in the satisfying style and draws on the work of H. A. Simon, while the preceding presentation searches for preference structures that would yield methodologically pure results when the positive economist is confronted with a joint income and time constraint.

The stark contrast between the methodologically preferred corner solutions and the allocation of time solution to the optimization problem facing the positive economist, may overstate the problem of replication failure. Professional development may lessen the incidence of replication failure if learning occurs. Learning itself is difficult to incorporate into a static utility model of scientific choice. However, the consequences of learning can be approximated. Suppose

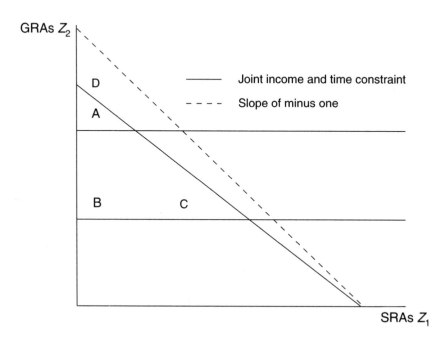

Figure 2.2 Lexicographic preferences of a methodologically pure economist (A is preferred to B which is preferred to C)

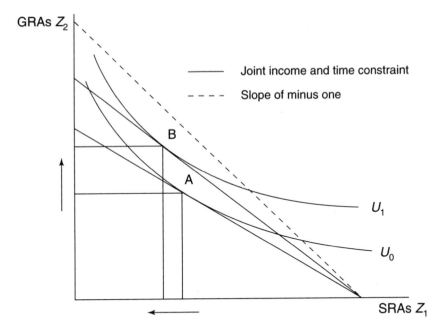

GRAs Z_2

Joint income and time constraint

- - - - Slope of minus one

B

A

U_1

U_0

SRAs Z_1

Figure 2.3 A methodologically preferred change in article output

that we have an economist whose professional skills have matured so that the preservation efforts required to ensure replication have become more efficient. In the model, this consequence would imply that the time input required for replication is now less or b_2 has fallen. If this is the case, then the joint resource budget constraint will rotate upward to the right. This represents a reduction in the shadow price of a GRA, or P_2 falls. As with a fall in price in ordinary consumer theory, the situation now facing the transactor presents unexploited opportunities. The mix of articles being produced by the positive economist or scientist could stay the same, move toward SRAs, or move toward GRAs. The latter situation is represented in Figure 2.3. Here the joint budget constraint rotates to the right, but not past the benchmark line with a slope of minus one.

A shift in the mix of research output toward GRAs is methodologically preferred because it represents a reduction in unreplicable research and a concomitant rise in reproducible work. Economically this could be achieved as a consequence of a "substitution" effect as the shadow price of a GRA falls. The result would be even more pronounced if the substitution effect were supplemented with a negative rather than a positive "income" effect. This would suggest that for most economists SRAs are "inferior" goods and would be produced less as replication efficiency increases.[15]

Besides this extension of the model, there are two interesting applications which further reinforce the fruitfulness of the notion that scientific economists are economically rational. The first application concerns the impact of promotion and tenure requirements on the young scientist and the second considers the optimization problem of the pure theorist.

Tenure and promotion requirements are an important aspect of the institutional structure of economic science. The allocation-of-time approach to scientific decision-making in economics can be further illustrated by analyzing these requirements. It is not uncommon for such requirements to specify an annual publication rate as a minimal criterion of scholarly achievement. A publication rate minimum can be represented as a line with a slope of minus one. In Figure 2.4, let TT represent a minimal annual publication requirement which does not distinguish between GRAs and SRAs but is merely concerned with the total annual number of articles produced in ranked journals. As depicted, it is clear that such a requirement can have a negative impact on economic science. The individual who is subject to such a requirement of necessity creates more SRAs by moving from point A to point B. Thus tenure requirements can have an adverse impact on the quality of research done by the younger members of the profession. Besides this negative scientific externality, point B also represents a lower level of individual well-being. Minimal publication rate requirements may make both the profession and individual positive economist worse off.[16]

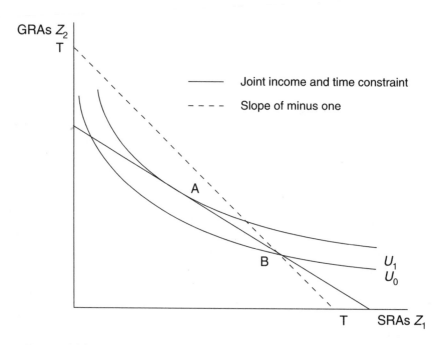

Figure 2.4 The negative methodological impact of a publication rate requirement on the economically rational positive economist

Although the preceding model has been developed only for empirical research, similar considerations could be made for pure theoretical research. Pure theoretical research involves minimal replication time relative to empirical research because it merely requires the reworking of the equations or the checking of the validity of each step in the proof of a theorem or lemma. Z_1 and Z_2 could be redefined as pure theoretical contributions and as path-breaking applied empirical research respectively. If the profession rewards Z_1, pure theory, more highly than Z_2, empirical research, and if Z_2 is more time-consuming to replicate than Z_1, then an economically rational economist or scientist might produce both types of research. One can even conceive of a corner solution for certain individuals who produce only pure theoretical research. If more pure theoretical research could be produced by some individuals in a given unit of time, then it is perfectly rational for an individual with theoretical talents to completely ignore empirical research. Such a theoretician could be represented by a corner solution at a point which achieves a publication rate maximum like point A in Figure 2.5. Thus if we allow theoretical specialization in economic science, then it is certainly possible that a pure theoretician will produce more articles than similarly situated empirical researchers for whom replication, even at a minimal level, is more time intensive.

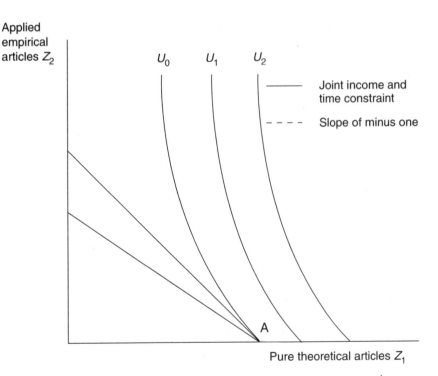

Figure 2.5 The optimization problem of the time-constrained pure theorist

41

CONCLUSIONS

Replication is a recurrent problem in the economics profession and in science. An economic perspective suggests that rational scientists will produce some research which results in replication failure. Scientists respond rationally to the rewards and costs of doing scientific research in the context of the complex social processes of scientific discovery. If they have worked carefully and professionally, scientists as individuals seem to take the replicability of their research for granted, even though they may have begun the next piece of research before the latest one has been completed fully. As a social process, replication is more complicated than the individualist accounts. Science seems to function as a series of chain-connected research projects in which subsequent projects presuppose the validity of earlier projects without fully or directly replicating previous projects. At some point this chain of connected research projects suffers a major failure. In the scientific process, the detection of error is as much a social as an individual process. It is in the face of a major scientific failure that resources are devoted to the more direct forms of replication. Consequently, until a major failure or problem is encountered in scientific investigation, the economic structures of science seem to emphasize innovation at the expense of direct or design replications.

After an initial consideration of the problem of replication failure in economics and other sciences, the analysis began with an economic model of scientific choice. The model focused on a dimension of science often ignored by the epistemologist – the role of time. Scientific research takes time and the replication of research takes even more time. Utilizing a Becker-type allocation of time model, the professional scientist was considered to be an economic agent whose choices and behavior was sensitive to the opportunity cost of time. Because of the opportunity cost of time, the model suggested that the rational scientist would produce both replicable and unreplicable research. In part this may be due to the complexities and informational asymmetries which have constituted the idiosyncratic environment of all the sciences for the past few decades. An extension of the model suggested how replication could be less of an issue for the profession. If unreplicable research is considered to be an "inferior" good by the maturing economist, then the mix of research output could shift toward more reproducible results as a professional scientific career unfolds. Beyond this extension, there were two other applications of the model. One application implied that promotion and tenure criteria could increase replication failure among younger members of the profession. Another application considered the case of a pure theorist. But the major inference from the preceding analysis is that replication failure is an economically rational consequence of the existing reward and cost structures of science considered as a complex social process.

3

AN ECONOMIC THEORY OF FRAUD IN SCIENCE

Discussion of fraud in science is becoming a cottage industry in need of an environmental impact report. Fraud is devastating to science; it undermines the basic respect for the literature on which the rapidity of scientific advance depends. It must be rooted out wherever and whenever it is discovered.

(Koshland 1988b: 585)

The current interest in scientific misconduct is not focused on honest errors in experimentation or in interpretation of data. It deals rather with how scientists perform their work, how they deal with each other and with the public, how they report their findings, and what self-imposed principles govern these activities. Fraud, misrepresentation, theft, plagiarism, and intentional injury to others by individual scientists threaten the credibility of the scientific process.

(Friedmann 1992: 19)

FRAUD AS AN ECONOMIC PHENOMENON

An economic view of replication failure in science suggests that error and mistakes are a constant aspect of the scientific endeavor. Mixed in with a continuous record of sustainable and replicable achievements in science are those experiments or empirical investigations which cannot be duplicated. An economic theory of replication failure implies that the continuous presence of faulty research is a by-product of scarce resources being focused on a quest for innovative discoveries. This mixed picture of science as an economic process which encompasses both success and failure can be taken one step further with a consideration of a more reprehensible form of misconduct in science – the problem of fraud. As with replication failure, one might suspect that an economic theory of science would suggest that fraud is always possible in science. Those very aspects of science which lead to the most spectacular and innovative discoveries may set the stage for fraud in science. In economics, outright fraud is somewhat difficult to document because economists make heavy use of data

43

collected by government agencies. Difficulty with documentation does not mean that it does not occur. Confronted with such difficulties, the question of fraud in science means that we must turn to other sciences. As a matter of principle, the problem of fraud should not be viewed as being confined to those disciplines where the worst instances of fraud in science have occurred. An economic analysis of fraud in science should apply to all of the sciences to some degree.

As with replication failure, fraud in science can be understood as an economic phenomenon. Although there may be other productive and insightful disciplinary approaches to fraud, an economic one needs to be developed as well. Fraud in this context is the deliberate violation of scientific principle for personal material gain and professional advancement. Fraud consists of intentional misreporting of results, falsification of data, complete fabrication of unperformed experiments, deception of colleagues, and threats of retaliation and revenge directed at whistle-blowers. In our society such actions have not been criminalized unless misuse of public funds is involved nor has provision been made for civil penalties. As a legal matter, these actions mostly have not been defined as fraud. Yet anyone who is committed to science recognizes how damaging these activities can be. I call these activities fraud because they are a perversion of science. Almost no one who has an interest in the subject of fraud has a conceptual framework capable of characterizing alternative forms of misconduct in science. Scientists tend to insulate themselves from the significance of the problem while the journalists tend to see it everywhere. An economic approach raises the possibility of systematically categorizing different forms of misconduct with some being almost routine in nature and others as being extraordinary and "criminal" in nature. Fraud is the main point of focus in this chapter, but replication failure, the subject of the previous chapter, is considered briefly in order to contrast fraud with another form of misconduct considered less serious.

RECENT EPISODES OF FRAUD IN SCIENCE

The prospect of fraud in science may seem surprising to most practising scientists. Scientists seem to take their commitment to scientific principles as a matter of professional and personal integrity. Such sensitivities are also extended to colleagues. In this type of high-minded environment, few scientists actively suspect or look for egregious violations of scientific principle. However, cases of unambiguous fraud have shaken the scientific establishment. There is the case of Cyril Burt in psychology and several troublesome cases in biomedical research during the 1980s. These biomedical cases have been the focus of a congressional investigation headed by Representative John Dingell.[1]

Before his death, Sir Cyril Burt was one of the most respected figures in educational psychology. A year before his death, the American Psychological Association gave him its Thorndike award for achievement. This is the first time this award was given to a foreigner (Hearnshaw 1979: 226). Burt's reputation remained intact during his lifetime. There were several episodes when his research was attacked by those who disagreed with its political implications. Only after his death were charges raised concerning the validity and integrity of his research.[2] Throughout his lifetime Burt's research was considered the most important work concerning sources of human intelligence – heredity versus environment (Broad and Wade 1982: 206 ff.). Burt's work clearly supported the notion that heredity was the major factor in determining intelligence. This conclusion was based on observations of many pairs of identical and fraternal twins who had been separated during some part of their lifetime. Identical twins were most appealing because they inherit identical genetic material from their parents, while nonidentical twins do not. Burt claimed to have administered an identical intelligence test to dozens of sets of twins during his service as an educational psychologist in London. He reported a correlation coefficient of .771 in many of his published studies concerning the results of his intelligence test administered to many pairs of twins.

The year after his death, psychologist Leonard Kamin began circulating various papers in manuscript that were critical of Burt's work. Kamin (1974) questioned the scientific validity of Burt's work. Points made by Kamin were that the original data seemed nonexistent, Burt's methods were subject to bias, and that the .771 correlation coefficient was invariant for many different sample sizes. Leslie Hearnshaw, Burt's official biographer reports that the same correlation coefficient was reported in more than twenty different studies:

> The fourth criticism, relating to the invariance of many of the correlations, however, was decisive. Although the sizes of Burt's samples of MZ twins, DZ twins, and siblings all changed from one report to another, many of his correlations, some twenty in all, did not. They remained constant to three places of decimals. This was wholly incredible. For example, the correlation for the group tests of intelligence for MZ twins reared apart was 0.771 for 21 pairs in 1955, and for 53 pairs in 1966; and that for MZ twins reared together was 0.944 for 83 pairs in 1955, and for 95 pairs in 1966. An occasional coincidence might have been acceptable, but not twenty such coincidences in a table of sixty correlations. There was obviously something wrong with Burt's work. Kamin made no further accusation.

> (Hearnshaw 1979: 233–4)

In his initial monograph on the subject, Kamin restrained his criticism of Burt, only rejecting the scientific validity of his work. Charges of fraud were not made at this time. Hearnshaw (1979: 235) records that it was *The Times* of London that raised the charges of fraud implying that Burt's correlation coefficients were obtained by working backwards – that the data were calculated to yield the .771 correlation coefficient. Hearnshaw had been chosen to eulogize Burt at his funeral and maintains that he was quite sympathetic with Burt's views on psychology. Furthermore, Hearnshaw was chosen by Burt's sister to be his official biographer.[3] After his lengthy investigation into the issue of fraud, Hearnshaw came to the conclusion that Burt had deliberately deceived his peers in the scientific community:[4]

> The charges of fraud no doubt brought Burt far greater public attention after his death than his achievements ever brought him during his lifetime. The evidence reviewed earlier in this book has shown beyond reasonable doubt that these charges were true: Burt did deceive the scientific community on matters of moment, and even after the utilisation of his data by others to substantiate conclusions of social significance, he never issued disclaimers. He committed a grave offense against the tacitly accepted codes of scientific ethics. Such lapses may be more common than we care to admit, but in a man of Burt's standing they were scandalous and hard to forgive.
>
> (Hearnshaw 1979: 318–19)

Other than Burt's case, most of the major recent cases of fraud appear to be in the biomedical field. Consideration of cases is limited to the 1980s. Among others, there are five cases that have gained varying degrees of attention by scientists and the public at large. A brief summary of these cases is found in Table 3.1.

In the early 1980s, the case of John Darsee, a young cardiologist, began to emerge.[5] Darsee was a protégé of Eugene Braunwald at Harvard Medical School. At the time, Braunwald was a preeminent American cardiologist. Some dimensions of the Darsee affair are astounding. While at Harvard during a two-year period, Darsee published nearly one hundred papers and abstracts. This constitutes an enormous level of productivity – four publications per month. His high rate of publication apparently put him in high regard with his mentor, Braunwald. However, other young researchers in Braunwald's laboratory became suspicious. They decided to monitor Darsee's research activities. Some of them began to observe his methods for obtaining data. Late at night they discovered that he had falsified the raw data for an experiment which was later published. At this point the information was taken to Darsee's supervisors. Darsee was confronted with a charge of fraud for this experiment. However, Darsee's peers suspected that he was systematically faking most of his research and that almost all of Darsee's publications might be affected. Braunwald viewed the matter differently, thinking that it was an isolated incident. Apparently Braunwald still viewed Darsee as the best young research associate with whom he had ever worked. At the institutional level, Harvard reacted by merely suspending Darsee for five months allowing him to continue his research at Braunwald's lab. Harvard did not notify the National Institutes of Health (NIH) about the original case of faked data. During the five-month period of suspension, NIH began to suspect irregularities in data reported by Darsee for another study. When this second prospective change of fraud was known, Harvard Medical School appointed a committee to investigate these incidents. Both NIH and

Table 3.1 Some recent cases of known or suspected fraud in science

Case	Date	Nature of case	References
1 Cyril Burt (University College London)	1943(?)–1966	Created data to support the theory that heredity is the dominant factor in creating human intelligence.	Hearnshaw (1979) Kamin (1974) Eysenck and Kamin (1981)
2 John Darsee (Harvard Medical School)	1981	Darsee forged the raw data for an experiment that was later published. Other studies by Darsee also were questioned. His field of research was cardiology. NIH barred him from receiving federal research funds for ten years.	Broad and Wade (1982) Budiansky (1983b) Stewart and Feder (1987b) Braunwald (1987)
3 Steven E. Breuning (University of Pittsburgh)	1983	His research concerned the effect of psychoactive drugs on the behavior and mental disposition of the retarded. He was the first scientist criminally indicted for fraud.	Holden (1986) Anderson (1988a) Gosselin (1988)
4 Joseph Cort (Mt Sinai Medical School, NYC)	1983	Cort admitted fabricating data in two scientific papers regarding the reduced side effects of a blood-clotting agent.	Budiansky (1983a)
5 Claudio Milanese and N. E. Richardson (Harvard's Dana Farber Cancer Institute)	1986	Milanese manipulated data regarding the function of T-cell activities in the immune system. The lab work could not be reproduced. Milanese *et al.* (1986b).	Culliton (1986)
6 Thereza Imanishi-Kari and David Baltimore (MIT and Tufts)	1984-96	A research assistant alleged that the data for an experiment on the transmission of genes and the functioning of the immunological system were misrepresented when published in *Cell*. Charges reversed in 1996.	Culliton (1988a) Culliton (1988b) Foreman and Howe (1996)

Congress later found fault with the manner and speed with which Harvard handled the incident.[6] Harvard apparently took the attitude that fraud is extremely rare in science, because science has internal processes which would discover cheating. Because of what they viewed as the high likelihood of discovery, Harvard officials were slow to respond to the Darsee case and slow to systematically investigate the extent of forgery in Darsee's many studies.[7]

In another notorious case, Stephen Breuning formerly of the University of Pittsburgh, conducted research on the role of drugs in altering the behavior of the mentally retarded.[8] Breuning was one of a handful of investigators doing research in this field. His research affected the way physicians and institutions treated their patients. In 1983, Robert Sprague, who had formerly hired Breuning as a research associate, began to question Breuning's work. Sprague thought Breuning's results were too good, and that the reliability of his ratings were "impossibly high" (Holden 1986: 1488). Sprague asked to review Breuning's work. Breuning responded with a new study supporting his previous results. With this information, Sprague investigated the background of the new study directly contacting the institution where the research had been conducted. Sprague contacted the director of psychology at the institution where Breuning supposedly conducted his study. The director reported that he had no knowledge of Breuning's investigation. Eventually, Sprague gave the results of his inquiry to the National Institute of Mental Health (NIMH). NIMH investigated both Breuning and Sprague. In 1988, a criminal indictment was brought against Breuning for submitting false research results supporting a grant application to NIMH. He was later convicted of fraud (Anderson 1988c).

In another case that has not drawn widespread attention, Dr Joseph Cort, a former researcher at Mt Sinai hospital in New York City has admitted fabricating data in two different scientific papers (Budiansky 1983a). Cort's research dealt with hormones that increase the ability of the blood to clot. One of the hormones has significant side effects. Cort's claims for significant reduction of side effects were greatly exaggerated. A committee appointed to investigate the affair by Mt Sinai, concluded that the research was fabricated. Apparently, Cort admitted to the committee that one of the variations of the clotting factor had not been synthesized. Furthermore, the committee found no evidence to support the claim that a second variation of the clotting factor had been synthesized. Apparently only three of the five forms of the clotting hormone that Cort supposedly synthesized, were in fact created by Cort. Subsequently Mt Sinai retracted the published articles based on the fabricated data.

The case of John Darsee is not the only recent case of scientific misconduct to occur at Harvard (Culliton 1986). In the Spring of 1985, researchers at Harvard's Dana-Farber Cancer Institute reported the discovery of a new molecule which would stimulate the development of cells in the immune system. The discovery would have been useful in the treatment of both cancer and AIDS. Claudio Milanese and a graduate student, Neil Richardson, conducted the research in the laboratory of Ellis Reinherz. Their study was published in *Science* (Milanese *et* *al.*1988a). When Milanese returned to Italy, other researchers in Reinherz's lab were unable to continue his experiments. Later Milanese admitted that he manipulated the data. Then in November 1988, Milanese retracted the paper and apologized to the scientific community (Milanese *et al.* 1988b: 1056).

Most recently there is a case involving Nobel Laureate David Baltimore. Baltimore was not the principal investigator, but because he is so well known the case is known generally as the Baltimore case. The controversy concerns an article published in *Cell*, (Weaver *et al.* 1986). The principal author of the paper was Thereza Imanishi-Kari who at the time was affiliated with the Massachusetts Institute of Technology (MIT).[9] The paper describes research in the area of immunology and serology. The data concern the transmission of genes and the functioning of the immunological system in an experiment done with mice. A post-doctoral student, Margot O'Toole maintained that the data in the paper were inconsistent with laboratory records. O'Toole pressed the issue with her superiors until an internal investigation was begun. After two internal reviews, both committees decided that the issue was a misinterpretation rather than a misrepresentation of the data (Culliton 1988a: 240). In 1990, Baltimore left MIT to assume the presidency of Rockefeller University in New York City. The Congressional investigation into allegations of fraud continued. The Secret Service found that the data had been fabricated and one of the coauthors, Imanishi-Kari, was implicated. Later a federal prosecutor decided that while the charges of fraud had merit, it would be difficult to successfully proceed with a criminal trial. During this affair, Baltimore was faulted for defending the integrity of his coauthor despite the evidence that fraud had been committed. Baltimore's position created such a controversy that he was forced to resign the presidency of Rockefeller University.[10]

The matter might have died at this point. However, a former MIT graduate student in Imanishi-Kari's lab brought O'Toole's complaints to the attention of two researchers at the National Institutes of Health ([Maddox] 1987). Walter Stewart and Ned Feder (1986) have taken to themselves the task of investigating charges of fraud in the biological sciences. O'Toole's basic complaint is that the conclusions in the paper are contradicted by the actual records (Culliton 1988a: 240). Stewart and Feder basically support O'Toole's claim and have written a manuscript criticizing the paper as originally published. Furthermore, the dispute has been the subject of a Congressional investigation (Anderson 1988b). Stewart and Feder have testified before Congress giving their views of the matter. The hearings have been widely covered in the press. From these and other proceedings, the conclusion has emerged that this episode involved fraud. Baltimore has conceded that errors have been made but seems to vacillate on the issue of fraud. Most recently, in June of 1996, a review board found Imanishi-Kari not guilty of misconduct. The Research and Integrity Panel of the Department of Health and Human Services reversed the findings of the Office of Research Integrity from that same department. In 1994, the Office of Research Integrity had declared that data had been falsified (Foreman and Howe 1996).

The preceding cases of fraud or alleged fraud have been widely discussed in the press, in professional journals, in Congress, and on television.[11] However, these cases provide no indication of the scope and depth of the problem of fraud in science. Federal agencies give thousands of grants per year amounting to billions of dollars of funded scientific investigations. Private foundations add to this amount. In their book, *Betrayers of the Truth* published in 1982, William Broad and Nicholas Wade report on thirty-four cases of known or suspected fraud that have come to their attention. They make no claim that their list is exhaustive. What is unusual about their list is that it includes some of the great figures of science: Ptolemy, Galileo, Newton, Bernoulli, Dalton, Mendel, and Millikan among others. A second source on the magnitude of fraud is Stewart and Feder. They have gained a reputation as watchdogs against fraud in bio-medical research. They report that they receive about two phone calls per week or approximately 100 complaints per year alleging some degree of misconduct (Stewart and Feder 1988). Other evidence reported about the magnitude of fraud comes from the press. A recent article in the *Boston Globe* reports that 102 cases of misconduct were reported to the National Institutes of Health during a recent six-year time span (Gosselin 1988: 28). Thus the phenomenon of science fraud exists. It is difficult to judge the magnitude of the problem; although it certainly damages the reputation of science.[12]

AN ECONOMIC APPROACH TO FRAUD IN SCIENCE

While almost no one knows the true extent of the problem, fraud in science is a potentially significant if not explosive issue. The incidents summarized in Table 3.1 have done extensive short-term damage to the reputation of science. On the one side, scientists, particularly the editors of journals tend to minimize the extent of fraud. On the other hand, lay people such as journalists tend to dramatize the issue categorizing many forms of misconduct and unintended error as fraud. Daniel Koshland, editor of *Science*, comments:

> Journalists must distinguish between fraud, sloppiness, and differences of opinion. When an accusation of fraud is made, if the evidence appears weak or the charge exaggerated a careful journalist should be alerted to probe more deeply. . . . Scientists respect integrity, scholarship, and good judgement as much as they abhor fraud, sloppiness, and poor judgement, but these are very different phenomena. Those who mix them together in uncritical ways may decrease our chances of eliminating true fraud, may damage reputations unfairly, and may diminish enthusiasm for healthy differences of opinion at the cutting edge of science.
>
> (Koshland 1988b: 585)

Concern with the impact of fraud on the scientific community has drawn the attention of the American Association for the Advancement of Science. They have initiated a project on scientific fraud and misconduct with the American

Bar Association. The authors of one of the reports on misconduct have this to say about misconduct in science:

> Congress, the media, federal agencies, and the scientific community have all spent a considerable amount of time in the past several years investigating, debating, and seeking solutions and preventive approaches to fraud and misconduct in science. Few would argue that such ethical misbehavior is widespread among scientists. Yet most observers agree that – even if the incidence is low – the matter must be acknowledged and dealt with effectively.
>
> (Teich and Frankel 1992: 1)

In another editorial in *Science*, Koshland again considered the issue of misconduct and remarked that:

> Those who expect progress without mistakes do not understand progress. When mistakes do occur, whether by fraud, sloppiness, or honest error, it is essential that they be corrected as rapidly as possible, and retractions, however embarrassing, must be made. In a smaller and cozier world, deviations from high standards of scholarship were dealt with informally; today's scientists need to realize that errors must be handled more formally, and in full view of an anxious public. In complex problems of fraud, misconduct, or error, scientists will need to develop procedures that nonscientists will find thorough, objective, and fair. Otherwise, the case will be made that lay persons must themselves be the judges, a potential nightmare when complex science is involved.
>
> (Koshland 1988c: 637)

Besides more attention to ascertain the empirical dimensions of the problem, what is needed is a framework which separates fraud from lesser forms of misconduct in science – some excusable, others inexcusable. Those disciplines which have been taken as basic for studying science such as the history, philosophy, sociology, and psychology of science no doubt may have important things to say about the nature of fraud in science. What I propose to do is bring the insights of conventional economic analysis to bear on this important issue of fraud.

As a starting point, two general categories of misconduct in science – replication failure and fraud – have been proposed. As defined in the previous chapter, the term "replication failure" referred to those scientific research results which could not be repeated because the incentives of science favored innovation rather than replication. The basic argument was that time is scarce and scientists are rewarded for innovation. The argument was that scientists allocate their time to the more rewarding, innovative research rather than carefully preserving the details of past research essential for replication. In contrast, fraud is different. Fraud is defined as a deliberate, egregious breach of scientific principles solely for personal material gain and professional advancement.

51

Obviously, someone accused of fraud would immediately attempt to hide behind the less serious charge of replication failure. Besides replication failure, fraud involves the deliberate falsification of data, complete or partial fabrication of research projects, and knowingly providing the results of such activities to the scientific community at large through the normal processes of peer evaluation and publication.

Fraud is an entirely different matter than replication failure. The allocation of time model for replication failure envisions scientists who are fundamentally committed to implementing the principles of science. But at the fringe, their commitment is eroded by the pressures of time and scientific competition. Fraud is just the reverse. Fraud envisions scientists who are bent on perverting the principles of science and at the fringe creating the appearance of conformity in order to cover up their breaches of scientific principle. Obviously, the allocation of time model could handle fraud. Rather than conceptualizing a division of occupational tasks devoted to replication versus innovation, the division of time could be fraudulent versus legitimate activities. Fraudulent research obviously could be time saving and present the possibility of professional advancement. However, the allocation of time model does not really do justice to certain aspects of fraud. Replication failure may be mostly an unwitting activity while fraud is deliberate and calculated. Although fraud may shade into replication failure in certain situations, in the cases of recent biomedical fraud and the Cyril Burt affair, an intention to deceive one's peers is obviously present.[13] Insider knowledge of how science is practiced, that the work of respected colleagues is rarely questioned, is used by the perpetrator of fraud to mask the nature of his/her misdeeds.

A model of fraud capable of addressing some of the more distinguishing aspects of fraud can be found in the economics of crime literature.[14] Once again the path-breaking work was done by Gary Becker (1968) in his famous essay "Crime and Punishment: An Economic Approach." However, an approach more suitable for my purpose is an economic approach to crime which includes the role of uncertainty.[15] Isaac Ehrlich (1973) has adapted Becker's approach to crime so that it can be interpreted as decision-making under uncertainty. I will outline my interpretation of Ehrlich's model applying it to fraud in science rather than crime in general.[16] The model envisions a scientist who produces both legitimate and fraudulent research. Fraudulent research is perpetrated because of the potential for material gain. However, there is also the possibility of being discovered. If the fraud is discovered, then the rewards of scientific work would be significantly reduced. The traditional model of choice under uncertainty involves an estimate of the expected utility of two mutually exclusive outcomes. One activity would be chosen over another on the basis of expected utility. However, legitimate and fraudulent activities may not be mutually exclusive or even identifiable before experiments are done and repeated. For fraud in science, the issue is the optimal mix between fraudulent and illegitimate activities.

Most of the mathematics will be left to the appendix at the end of this chapter. An outline of the model, its assumptions, and conclusions are presented here. Consider two types of activities in science: fraudulent activities, f, and legitimate activities, l. The model assumes no training costs and no entry costs for either activity, no costs of movement between the two activities, and that the returns to f and l are monotonically increasing functions of time worked.[17] Fraudulent activities are risky because the returns depend on two different states of the world – success or discovery. If discovered and punished, some explicit or implicit penalty will be paid for the fraudulent activities. Relatively simple equations can be used to elaborate. Let R_l and R_f be the pecuniary returns to legitimate and fraudulent activities with each being a function of the time worked. Thus:

$$R_l = W_l(t_l),\qquad\qquad(1a)$$

$$R_f = W_f(t_f),\qquad\qquad(1b)$$

Furthermore, suppose that the individual has a utility function

$$U_i = U(X_i, t_c),\qquad\qquad(2)$$

where i is the state of the world, X_i is a composite market good representing wealth and the income earned from f and l in state i, t_c is the amount of time given to nonmarket, consumption activities, and U is an indirect utility function. Given the preceding definitions and equations, there are two possible states of the world denoted by two different levels of consumption or material well-being: X_d, the level of consumption available if fraud is discovered and X_s, the level of consumption if the fraud is successful and goes undetected. X_d and X_s are defined as:

$$X_d = A + R_l + R_f - F_f,\qquad\qquad(3a)$$

$$X_s = A + R_l + R_f,\qquad\qquad(3b)$$

where A is the market value of the individual's current assets and F_f is an explicit or implicit penalty associated with the discovery of fraud. If P_f is defined as the probability of the fraud being detected, then $l - P_f$ is the probability of not being discovered. Expected utility is defined as:

$$EU(X_i, t_c) = (1 - P_f)U(X_s, t_c) + P_f U(X_d, t_c)\qquad\qquad(4)$$

The modeling of individual choice under uncertainty is the problem of maximizing expected utility with respect to t_f, t_l, and t_c subject to wealth and time constraints.

Equation (4) is to be maximized subject to the wealth constraints (1a) and (1b) and a time constraint:

$$t_o = t_f + t_l + t_c$$

and other restrictions:

$t_f \geq 0$; $t_l \geq 0$; $t_c \geq 0$.

Solution of the model requires that the Kuhn-Tucker first order optimality conditions must be met. The first order conditions describe the individual's optimal allocation of time between fraudulent and legitimate activities in science. From the first order conditions, it can be shown that the allocation of time must satisfy the following equation:

$$-\frac{R_f' - R_l'}{R_f' - F_f' - R_l'} = \frac{P_f U'(X_d)}{(1 - P_f) U'(X_s)} \tag{5}$$

R_f', R_l', and F_f' are the derivatives with respect to time for income from fraud, income from legitimate activities, and the penalty for fraud. The term on the right-hand side of (5) is the slope of an indifference curve and represents a weighted marginal rate of substitution between consumption in two different states of the world, discovery and successful elusion of charges of fraud. The term on the left-hand side essentially represents an opportunity boundary.

The optimizing solution can be depicted graphically as in Figure 3.1. The indifference curve is U_0 and the opportunity boundary is AB. The opportunity boundary is defined only for that portion between points A and D. This is due to the peculiar nature of this situation under conditions of uncertainty. The $X_s X_d$

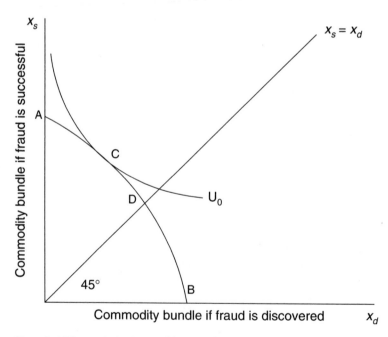

Figure 3.1 The optimization problem confronting the fraudulent scientist under uncertainty

plane represents possible states of the world but only X_s or X_d will in fact occur. Take point C for example. The individual's fraudulent activities will either be discovered or they will not. If undiscovered X_s will occur and $X_s > X_d$. The difference between X_s and X_d is the penalty associated with known fraud. Thus the individual chooses to add fraudulent activities to his mix of professional tasks not knowing in advance whether discovery will occur. The individual must take a genuine risk hoping for X_s but realizing there is a possibility the outcome will be X_d. There is only one solution where fraud will not be committed. If the point of optimization were at D, then $X_s = X_d$ and the penalty for fraud must be interpreted as being nonexistent because the fraud would not occur.

Reconsidering the first order condition describing the individual scientist's optimization under uncertainty, equation (5) has additional behavioral implications. The more negative or the greater the slope becomes in absolute value, the less fraud will be committed by the individual. This will occur if the probability of being discovered, P_p, increases, or if the penalty F_f associated with time spent in illegitimate activities increases. Either of these reduces the incentive to engage in fraudulent activities in science. If the marginal return to fraudulent activities increases relative to legitimate activities, then the individual would be expected to increase the proportion of time spent on illegitimate activities. It is possible that a person who spent no time on fraudulent activities would do so if the return to those activities increased. This is illustrated in Figure 3.2. At point A, the individual commits no fraud and there is no possible penalty associated with his activities. However, a rise in the rate of return to fraud will cause the boundary to rotate because command over goods and services will be greater if evasion is successful. At point B, the individual scientist devotes a portion of his time to illegitimate activities. At B, $X_s > X_d$. Obviously the individual believes that there is little risk of discovery.

Economic models of fraud and replication failure suggest that misconduct in science can be understood from an economic point of view. However, the primary motivation of individual behavior in science may not be economic incentives. Daniel Koshland remarks: "Science is a low-paying profession. The reason that scientists, who are a fairly intelligent group, put up with this situation is the psychic bonus, the belief that we are conquering difficult problems crucial to the future of mankind" (Koshland 1988a: 241). But science is affected by material and pecuniary incentives. Science must make provision for the economic sustenance of scientists. At the margin, scientists may slant their mix of professional activities towards those that increase their material well-being and professional status. This may cause replication failure. In the extreme, a few individuals take this process beyond the bounds of science. They take advantage of the integrity of their colleagues and the processes of peer review. They deliberately take a calculated risk to commit fraud. An economic approach suggests that misconduct may always be part of the landscape of science. Replication failure may be prominent but not dominant. Fraud should be much rarer than replication failure. Just as we should not expect any real society, no

The value of the economic models of scientific misconduct is that they add conventional economic analysis to the tool kit of the methodologist. Perhaps a great deal of what scientists and economists do can be explained on economic grounds. If economic incentives play an important role in economics and all sciences, then no purely philosophical, methodological, or social-psychological model of science will be adequate. Perhaps methodologists need to add economic theory and techniques of empirical appraisal to their repertoire of research skills. Furthermore, the models of fraud and replication failure raise an important intellectual issue. The models present a conflict between the economic rationality of science as expressed in optimization theory and the scientific rationality of the sciences as embodied in methodological notions requiring empirical replication – like falsification, verification, confirmation, etc. The economic models suggest that some apparently scientific results in economics and other sciences may fail to meet the accepted high standards of science. Limited science failure is a distinct possibility for economic reasons.

One should also keep in mind that while meaningful issues can be discussed from an economic viewpoint, an economic perspective may suffer from inherent limitations. Taken to an extreme, an economic view point would suggest that science is mostly an economic activity. My arguments in this and the previous chapter should not be taken to this extreme. Whether science has a more funda-mental economic dimension is something which requires further consideration in the next few chapters.

MATHEMATICAL APPENDIX: THE EHRLICH MODEL OF CHOICE UNDER UNCERTAINTY

Isaac Ehrlich's (1973) model of illegitimate activities in the context of un-certainty has been adapted for the problem of fraud in science. The problem is to determine the optimal mix of fraudulent and legitimate activities; f and l. The model makes the following assumptions: (1) no training costs, (2) no entry costs, (3) no costs of movement between two activities, and (4) returns to fraud-ulent and legitimate activities are monotonically increasing. These assumptions imply that highly trained scientists are under consideration. Inadequately trained scientists would not have the appropriate professional and technical knowledge to commit fraud.

The pecuniary returns to f and l are defined by the following equations:

$$R_l = W_l(t_l), \tag{1a}$$

and

$$R_f = W_f(t_f), \tag{1b}$$

where t_l and t_f are the time spent in each activity. Furthermore, suppose that the individual has a utility function

$$U_i = U(X_i, t_c), \tag{2}$$

where i is the state of the world, X_i is a composite market good representing wealth and the income earned from f and l in state i; t_c is the amount of time given to nonmarket, consumption activities; and U is an indirect utility function. Given the preceding definitions and equations, there are two possible states of the world denoted by two different levels of consumption or material well-being. X_d is the level of consumption available if fraud is discovered and X_s is the level of consumption if the fraud is successful and goes undetected. X_d and X_s are defined as:

$$X_d = A + R_l + R_f - F_f, \tag{3a}$$

and

$$X_s = A + R_l + R_f, \tag{3b}$$

where A is the market value of the individual's current assets and F_f is an explicit or implicit penalty associated with the discovery of fraud. If P_f is defined as the probability of the fraud being detected, then $1 - P_f$ is the probability of not being discovered. Expected utility is defined as:

$$EU(X_i, t_c) = (1 - P_f)U(X_s, t_c) + P_f U(X_d, t_c) \tag{4}$$

The modeling of individual choice under uncertainty is the problem of maximizing expected utility with respect to t_f, t_l, and t_c subject to wealth and time constraints. Equation (4) is to be maximized subject to the wealth constraints (1a) and (1b) and a time constraint:

$$t_o = t_f + t_l + t_c$$

and other restrictions:

$$t_f \geq 0; \ t_l \geq 0; \ t_c \geq 0.$$

Solution of the model requires that the Kuhn-Tucker first order optimality conditions must be met. This requires formulation of the function:

$$F(X_i, t_f, t_l, t_c, \lambda) = EU(X_i, t_c) - \lambda(t_f + t_l + t_c - t_o) \tag{5}$$

Solution of the model requires that the following first order conditions must be met:

$$\frac{\partial EU}{\partial t_f} - \lambda = 0, \tag{6a}$$

$$\frac{\partial EU}{\partial t_l} - \lambda = 0, \tag{6b}$$

$$\frac{\partial EU}{\partial t_c} - \lambda = 0, \tag{6c}$$

Additional Kuhn-Tucker conditions are:

$$\lambda(t_f + t_l + t_c - t_0) = 0 \tag{6d}$$

and

$$t_f + t_l + t_c - t_0 \leq 0. \tag{6e}$$

Substituting the right-hand side of (4) into (5), the preceding first order conditions become:

$$\frac{\partial EU}{\partial t_l} = (1 - P_f) \frac{\partial U}{\partial X_s} \frac{\partial X_s}{\partial t_l} + P_f \frac{\partial U}{\partial X_d} \frac{\partial X_d}{\partial t_l} - \lambda = 0, \tag{7a}$$

$$\frac{\partial EU}{\partial t_f} = (1 - P_f) \frac{\partial U}{\partial X_s} \frac{\partial X_s}{\partial t_f} + P_f \frac{\partial U}{\partial X_d} \frac{\partial X_d}{\partial t_f} - \lambda = 0, \tag{7b}$$

$$\frac{\partial EU}{\partial t_c} = (1 - P_f) \frac{\partial U}{\partial t_c} + P_f \frac{\partial U}{\partial t_c} - \lambda = 0. \tag{7c}$$

Since we are most interested in the allocation of time between f and l, equations (7a) and (7b) will be developed in detail. Equations (7a) and (7b) require the solutions of the following partials calculated from (3a), (3b) and (1a) and (1b):

$$\frac{\partial X_s}{\partial t_l} = \frac{dR_l}{dt_l} = R'_l, \tag{8a}$$

$$\frac{\partial X_s}{\partial t_f} = \frac{dR_f}{dt_f} = R'_f, \tag{8b}$$

$$\frac{\partial X_d}{\partial t_l} = \frac{dR_l}{dt_l} = R'_l, \tag{8c}$$

$$\frac{\partial X_d}{\partial t_f} = \frac{dR_f}{dt_f} - \frac{dF_f}{dt_f} = R'_f - F'_f. \tag{8d}$$

Equations (8a) and (8c) should be substituted into (7a) and (8b) and (8d) into (7b). By setting (7a) equal to (7b) and making the preceding substitutions we have:

$$(1 - P_f)U'(X_s)R'_l + P_f U'(X_d)R'_l = (1 - P_f)U'(X_s)R'_f$$
$$+ P_f U(X_d)(R'_f - F'_f). \tag{9}$$

Equation (9) can be further simplified by combining terms with the same variables. Thus:

$$(1 - P_f)U'(X_s)(R'_l - R'_f) = P_f U'(X_d)(R'_f - F'_f - R'_l),$$

or,

$$\frac{R'_f - R'_l}{R'_f - F'_f - R'_l} = \frac{P_f U'(X_d)}{(1 - P_f)U'(X_s)} \tag{10}$$

Equation (10) is the same as equation (5) in the text and forms the basis of the analysis. One would expect that $R'_f > R'_l$ and that $R'_f > F'_f + R'_l$. Under these conditions the slope of the opportunity boundary implicit in the left-hand side of (10) is negative.

4

PEIRCE'S ECONOMICS OF
RESEARCH PROJECT
SELECTION

Economical science is particularly profitable to science; and that of all the branches of economy, the economy of research is perhaps the most profitable.

(Peirce [1902b] 1985: 1038)

The methodology of inductive practice is, in Peirce's view, pivotally dependent on the intelligent deployment of economic considerations from the very outset.

(Rescher 1978a: 66)

RESEARCH PROJECT SELECTION AS AN ECONOMIC PROBLEM

The previous two chapters have examined scientific misconduct from an economic point of view. While misconduct in science can be explained as an economic phenomenon, the legitimate, normal activities of science pose a much greater challenge. As with an economic analysis of misconduct, I will continue to assume that the scientist is economically rational. But this is the last chapter that will make use of the traditional, narrowly interpreted assumption that economic rationality is mere optimizing behavior. Subsequent analysis implicitly and then explicitly broadens the notion of economic rationality. In this chapter, I turn my attention to an economic theory of research project selection in science.

In the previous comments, it has been remarked that an economic theory of legitimate, normal science poses a much more difficult challenge than an economic understanding of misconduct. The hope was that an economic understanding of misconduct would pave the way to an economic theory of legitimate science. In previous chapters, the economic models of fraud and replication failure were utility maximizing models from microeconomics. The models were recognizable as being different versions of the theory that rational individuals optimize their sense of material and psychic well-being. For an economist, the models do not have to be literally identical to realize that they both come from the same theory. The model of fraud is more complex than the allocation of time model used for replication failure. But they both substantively embody the same theory of individual rational behavior.

With regard to legitimate science, it would be useful to create an optimizing model of normal scientific behavior. Hopefully, such a model would be of the same genre or family of models as those for replication failure and fraud, and clearly be identifiable as exemplifying the same optimizing theory of the individual that is found in neoclassical microeconomics. At this point, we must remember that an optimizing model of the conduct of the scientist as an individual does not imply that science as a social economic process is a mechanical equilibrium process. Rather than taking existing microeconomic models and modifying them with special applications to science, another approach could be taken. An economic model of the economics of scientific research has existed for over a century and has languished in relative obscurity. The model is clearly a neoclassical microeconomic model and the author is an eminent evolutionary philosopher. Any modern economist would recognize that this model of science bears a family resemblance to those for fraud and replication failure and thus comes from the same theory of individual behavior. The author of this model is of sufficient eminence that the model deserves scrutiny on its own terms without attempting to reconstruct it in a modern form. Thus the work of the previous two chapters on the economics of science concerning fraud and replication failure is "extended" to legitimate, normal science by reconsidering an important contribution authored almost twelve decades ago.

More than a century ago, the brilliant founding thinker of American pragmatism, Charles Sanders Peirce, proposed an economic approach to scientific research project selection. Peirce's proposal is found in his piece titled, "Note on the Theory of the Economy of Research" (1879). Historically, Peirce's Note may be seen as inaugurating an economic approach to science, an economics of science. In the Note, Peirce developed a cost-constrained utility model for choosing among alternative research projects. The model is a neoclassical microeconomic model like those of fraud and replication failure in the previous two chapters. The purpose of this chapter is to present and appraise Peirce's suggestion for an economics of research project selection in science as a way of extending an economics of science from misconduct to legitimate, normal science. Peirce's proposal mostly has been overlooked by the economics profession and philosophy of science. A case can be made that the Note was possibly the first piece of modern scientific research in all of economics. This claim is based on the novelty of the method of argument, the graphical techniques, and the ratio of the marginal utilities found in the Note. The Note is also significant for making economic factors a central part of a theory of scientific inference, something which contemporary economic methodologists and philosophers still have not done except for a few notable exceptions. And it has been used by philosopher Nicholas Rescher to interpret and criticize Karl Popper's notion of falsification. With regard to these issues, Peirce's model assumes that scientists are economically rational. Yet Peirce was an evolutionary philosopher who created an evolutionary metaphysics. Peirce is thus an example of how a model of rational economic behavior can be assumed in the broader context of an evolutionary view of the world.

THE ROLE OF ECONOMICS IN PEIRCE'S THOUGHT

Charles Sanders Peirce was the founder of pragmatism. Philosopher Philip Wiener writes that Peirce was "the most versatile, profound, and original philosopher that the United States has ever produced" (Wiener 1958: ix). Pragmatism was the distinctly American school of philosophy that sought to extend the experimental mindset of science to all of life.[1] Such a mindset was Peirce's prescription for making our thoughts and ideas clear.[2] Economics played a role in this process of clarifying ideas. Economic considerations were to be used in narrowing the number of hypotheses to be considered for actual testing. Peirce's pragmatism was expanded and reinterpreted by William James and John Dewey. But Peirce's economy of research was neglected and probably had little impact on the subsequent development of pragmatism. Other than founding pragmatism, Peirce made important contributions to mathematics, statistics, geodesy, symbolic logic, and scientific inference. These achievements are well known and widely recognized by contemporary scholars in these fields. But Peirce's economic contributions have been virtually ignored by economists. On the personal side, Peirce was a difficult man. He was something of a grating and eccentric personality.[3] Consequently, it was difficult for him to retain a university position. For most of his life, he worked for a government agency called the US Coast Survey. Peirce's project for an economics of research is included in his annual report of 1876, which was printed and published as the Note in 1879 (Peirce 1879).

Until quite recently, in the modern economics literature the only place that I have seen Peirce's interest in economics referenced is in a compendium of essays documenting the emergence of mathematical economics. In Baumol and Goldfeld's *Precursor's in Mathematical Economics: An Anthology*, the entry for Peirce is nothing more than a short letter.[4] Neither the Note nor other comments by Peirce on the economy of research or political economy are included. In the anthology, Baumol and Goldfeld (1968) note that A. A. Cournot had published *Researches into the Mathematical Principles of the Theory of Wealth* in 1838.[5] It was the most advanced work in mathematical economics in that period of time. What is found in Peirce's letter are comments on Cournot. The letter was written to the astronomer Simon Newcomb (Peirce [1871a] 1962: 186–7). Newcomb also had an interest in political economy which resulted in a handbook many years later called *Principles of Political Economy* (1886).[6] Peirce's letter contains a few simple equations concerning profit maximization using calculus. In the letter, Peirce inferred that the results of profit maximization are dependent on whether there is unlimited competition or not. He concluded that: "This is all in Cournot."[7]

But Peirce's interest in economics is much broader and more fundamental than what the Note and the letter to Newcomb would suggest. His interest in economics took three separate but complementary directions. First, Peirce had an abiding concern for creating a general mathematical political economy. Second, as part of his general evolutionism, Peirce recognized the economic function of the conscious mind and of scientific theories. Third, Peirce conceived of the economy of research as one of the major aspects of his theory of inference.

Peirce's interest in the political economy of his time vastly transcended the characterization of his thought as being merely interested in Cournot as portrayed in the Baumol and Goldfeld volume. For Peirce, Cournot's project for mathematically formulating economic ideas stimulated a vision for creating a mathematical political economy. The equations in Peirce's letter to Newcomb were intended to be a first step toward a mathematical political economy. Peirce had an enduring interest in creating a mathematical political economy. This aim is what drove his interest in mainstream political economy. Another economist who interested Peirce was David Ricardo.[8] What interested Peirce was the logical structure of the theory of rent in Ricardo's *Principles* (Peirce [1893, 1897] 1960). Peirce thought that Ricardo's conceptualization of political economy made it more amenable to mathematical representation. Besides Ricardo, Cournot, and Newcomb, Peirce was aware of the economic contributions of Malthus, J. S. Mill, Charles Babbage, and possibly Irving Fisher.[9] Additionally, Peirce's father, Benjamin Peirce, a professor of mathematics at Harvard and the foremost American mathematician of his time, also had a keen interest in a mathematical political economy. Apparently, Peirce and his father collaborated in giving at least one public lecture on mathematical political economy in 1871.[10]

Besides mathematical political economy, the second major area of Peirce's interest in economics was the economic function of mind and scientific theories. A similar point of view can be found in John Dewey's philosophy.[11] In the context of an uncertain, evolutionary world, Peirce recognized the economic function of conscious thought and of scientific theories. To be effective, thoughts and theories must distil meaning and information and represent them in an efficacious way. Peirce believed science to be an area of human thought where the economic function of the mind reached its most general form. Peirce ([1896] 1960: 48) referenced the writings of the physicist Ernst Mach who developed this "instrumental" view of consciousness and science much more elaborately than Pierce. Mach's views on the economy of science and thought are found in two widely circulated late nineteenth-century works.[12]

Having briefly considered Peirce's concern for mathematical political economy and the economy of thought, the third aspect of his interest in economics can now be addressed. Of the three areas constituting Peirce's interest in economics, the one which he developed to the highest extent was his economy of research. Economic aspects of research were an explicit part of Peirce's theory of inference. The nature of scientific inference was a lifelong concern of Peirce's. The initial phase of inference was a process which Peirce called abduction. Abduction is the use of known facts to formulate as many alternative hypotheses as could be imagined by the investigator. By an economics of research, Peirce meant that a hypothesis which was less costly to investigate than others, should be investigated first. This assumed a similar level of benefit among the hypotheses being compared. One can imagine researchers ranking alternative research projects by cost. Peirce would have the investigator choose the research project which was least costly. Such an economics of science implies that the scientist has some knowledge about the costs of doing research one way rather than another. This seems to suggest something like an economic abduction about the relative costs of alternative research methods as a supplement to the more basic abductive process involved in creating scientific hypotheses. The scientist would have general information about the cost of doing the investigation and should use this sort of economic knowledge in the selection of research topics.

Peirce's "Note on the Economy of Research" is by far the most sophisticated contribution he has made to economics. The Note was written relatively early in his career. After writing the Note, Peirce continued to make the economy of research an integral part of his theory of science. He repeatedly returned to this theme in his discussions of the nature of scientific inference. Several are worth quoting. In a comment written in 1896 titled, "The Economy of Research," by the editors of the *Collected Papers*, Peirce restated the theory originally introduced in the Note:

> There is a doctrine of the Economies of Research. One or two of its principles are easily made out. The value of knowledge is, for the purposes of science, in one sense absolute. It is not to be measured, it may be said, in money; on one sense that is true. But knowledge that leads to other knowledge is more valuable in proportion to the trouble it saves in the way of expenditure to get that other knowledge. Having a certain fund of energy, time, money, etc., all of which are merchantable articles to spend upon research, the question is how much is to be allowed to each investigation; and *for us* the value of that investigation is the amount of money it will pay us to spend upon it. *Relatively*, therefore, knowledge, even of a purely scientific kind, has a money value.
>
> This value increases with the fullness and precision of the information, but plainly it increases slower and slower as the knowledge becomes fuller and more precise. The cost of the information also increases with its fullness and accuracy, and increases faster and faster the more accurate it is. It therefore may be the case that it does not pay to get *any* information on a given subject; but, at any rate, it *must* be true that it does not pay (in any given state of science) to push the investigation beyond a certain point in fullness or precision.
>
> If we have a number of studies in which we are interested, we should commence with the most remunerative and carry that forward until it

becomes not more than equally remunerative with the commencement of another; carry both forward at such rates that they are equally remunerative until each is no more remunerative than a third, and so on [original emphasis].

(Peirce [1896] 1960: 49)

In 1901, Peirce again returned to his concern with economic issues of research. Peirce wrote a long essay approaching the length of a short monograph on the methodology of interpreting ancient manuscripts. This essay is titled, "On the Logic of Drawing History from Ancient Documents especially from Testimonies." In this essay Peirce considers again the nature of hypothetical inference. "Economical considerations" play a fundamental role in his conception of inference:

Now economy, in general, depends upon three kinds of factors; cost; the value of the thing proposed, in itself; and its effect upon other projects. Under the head of cost, if a hypothesis can be put to the test of experiment with very little expense of any kind, that should be regarded as a recommendation for giving it precedence in the inductive procedure. For even if it be barely admissible for other reasons, still it may clear the ground to have disposed of it. In the beginning of the wonderful reasonings by which the cuneiform inscriptions were made legible, one or two hypotheses which were never considered likely were taken up and soon refuted with great advantage.

(Peirce [1901] 1985: 754)

One of the last discussions of the economics of research by Peirce is contained in his 1902 grant application to the Carnegie Institution. The purpose of the request was to pull together many of his disparate writings into a coherent set of memoirs which would form a unified system of logic. The economy of research was to have an important role in the unified logic. At this point in his life, Peirce was destitute. He had lost his job with the Coast Survey. He was unable to find an academic position anywhere in the United States. Peirce survived with financial support orchestrated by his good friend William James and by his paid reviews and articles for various magazines and publications. In the grant application, proposed memoir number twenty-eight was titled "On the Economics of Research." In this piece, Peirce restated many of the themes already introduced above:

Many years ago I published a little paper on the Economy of Research, in which I considered this problem. Somebody furnished a fund to be expended upon research without restrictions. What sort of researches should it be expended upon? My answer, to which I still adhere, was this. Researches for which men have been trained, instruments procured, and a plant established, should be continued while these conditions subsist. But the new money should mainly go to opening up new fields; because

66

new fields will probably be more profitable, and at any rate, will be profitable longer.

I shall remark in the course of the memoir that economical science is particularly profitable to science; and that of all the branches of economy, the economy of research is perhaps the most profitable; that logical methodeutic and logic in general are specially valuable for science, costing little beyond the energies of the researcher, and helping the economy of every other science.

(Peirce [1902b] 1985: 1038)

PEIRCE'S ECONOMIC MODEL OF RESEARCH PROJECT SELECTION

In the "Note on the Theory of the Economy of Research," Peirce proposed an economic theory of research project selection in science.[13] The theory is much more rigorously developed than the intuitive summaries Peirce provided in later years. Its argumentation is so rigorous that it could be the first truly modern scientific piece in all of economics. Peirce's theory of the economy of science is premised on the idea that resources can be used to increase the precision of measurement.[14] The theory is based on the idea that resources can be expended to reduce probable error in science. Probable error is a nineteenth-century term dealing with the precision of a statistical estimator in scientific inquiry. It is a precursor to the notion of a confidence interval. The first paragraph of Peirce's Note introduces the notion of probable error and reads as follows:

When a research is of a quantitative nature, the progress of it is marked by the diminution of the probable error. The results of nonquantitative researches also have an inexactitude or indeterminacy which is analogous to the probable error of quantitative determinations. To this inexactitude, although it be not numerically expressed, the term "probable error" may be conveniently extended.

(Peirce [1879] 1967: 643)

The second paragraph of the Note restates the concern with probable error as an economic problem:

The doctrine of economy, in general, treats of the relations between utility and cost. That branch of it which relates to research considers the relations between the utility and the cost of diminishing the probable error of our knowledge. Its main problem is, how, with a given expenditure of money, time, and energy, to obtain the most valuable addition to our knowledge.

(Peirce [1879] 1967: 643)

In the main body of the essay, Peirce focused on the allocation of additional resources to established, ongoing research. Once the basic expenditures of a project have been made, Peirce maintained that additional expenditures would improve the accuracy of knowledge, but the benefits would begin to diminish:

> We thus see that when an investigation is commenced, after the initial expenses are once paid, at little cost we improve our knowledge, and improvement then is especially valuable; but as the investigation goes on, additions to our knowledge cost more and more, and, at the same time, are of less and less worth. . . . All the sciences exhibit the same phenomenon, and so does life.

(Peirce [1879] 1967: 644)

In "Economy of Research," Peirce followed a method of argument which any contemporary economist would recognize. Peirce created a mathematical model of the choices facing the researcher. The model anticipated many developments in modern microeconomics. Peirce theorized that the total utility of a series of research projects should be maximized subject to a limitation on total cost. He represented total cost and total utility as follows:

$$\Sigma_i \int V_i s_i \cdot ds_i \qquad (1)$$

$$\Sigma_i \int U_i r_i \cdot dr_i \qquad (2)$$

In these equations, V and U are functional symbols regarding the cost and utility of individual research projects and r is probable error. V is positively related to s, the reciprocal of probable error, and U is positively related to the "diminution" of probable error. As Peirce uses the notation, Vs today would be written as $V(s)$ meaning that cost is a function of variable s and Ur would be written as $U(r)$, meaning that U is a function of r. An index number i is used to designate each of the many alternative research projects under consideration. The integral of $V_1 s_1$ would represent the cost of the first research project, the integral of $V_2 s_2$ the second research project, and the integral of $V_i s_i$ the cost of the ith research project. The index number works in the same way for the utility of the research projects.

In the total cost function, equation (1), Peirce defines s to be the reciprocal of probable error, $s = 1/r$, and $V_i s_i$ to represent the cost of reducing probable error for any research project. One of the integrals represents the cost of reducing probable error for an individual research project. The total cost of reducing the probable error of all research projects is represented by the summation over the cost of all i research projects. In Peirce's theory, the cost of research rises as probable error is reduced. Peirce also speculates that cost, $V_i s_i$, is a linear, proportional function of s and that its integral is a quadratic function of s.

In the total utility function, equation (2), r represents the probable error of the research project and $U_i r_i$ is the utility resulting from reducing the probable error of the results. Again, just one of the integrals represents the utility of reducing probable error for an individual research project. The total utility of reducing the probable error of all research projects is represented by the summation over all of the research projects. Here Peirce also speculates about the functional form of the utility equation. He asserts that utility, $U_i r_i$, is a quadratic function of probable error.

Since Peirce's theory is developed in terms of a multiple project model, the theory requires a decision criterion comparing one project to another. In order for the total utility of all research projects being considered to be maximized subject to a total budget or cost constraint, the relative value of one project must be compared to another. To solve this problem, Peirce created a ratio of the marginal utility of a project to its marginal cost. He called this ratio the "economic urgency" of the research project. Although he did not use the terms marginal utility and marginal cost, Peirce wrote: "Let $Ur\ dr$ denote the infinitesimal utility of any infinitesimal diminution, dr of r. Let $Vs\ ds$ denote the infinitesimal cost of any infinitesimal increase, ds, of s" (Peirce [1879] 1967: 643). In modern terminology, $Ur\ dr$ would be the marginal utility of reducing probable error and $Vs\ ds$ would be the marginal cost for decreasing the probable error of any one research project. Economic urgency for a single research project is denoted with the variable y as follows:

$$y = \frac{Ur \cdot dr}{Vs \cdot ds} \tag{3}$$

A ratio of economic urgency for every research project is designated as y_i. At this point, Peirce restates the maximization problem of the economy of research with the following equations:

$$C = x_1 + x_2 + x_3 + etc. \tag{4}$$

$$y_1 = y_2 = y_3 = etc. \tag{5}$$

where C is the total amount that can be spent on all projects and x_i is the cost of an individual project. Equation (4) is an aggregate budget constraint for all projects undertaken by the researcher and equation (5) governs the optimal allocation of funds to each research project. It means that the marginal utility per dollar spent on reducing probable error in each research project should be equalized across all research projects in order to maximize the value of research from this series of scientific research projects. Peirce was writing before the development of modern price theory with indifference curve analysis and its technical vocabulary. Concerning economic urgency, the ratio of marginal utility to marginal cost, Peirce commented:

> When the investigation has been carried to a certain point this fraction will be reduced to the same value which it has for another research, and the two must then be carried on together, until finally, we shall be carrying on, at once, researches into a great number of questions, with such relative energies as to keep the urgency-fraction of equal values for all of them. When new and promising problems arise they should receive our attention to the exclusion of the old ones, until their urgency becomes no

greater than that of others. It will be remarked that our ignorance of a question is a consideration which has between three and four times the economic importance of either the specific value of the solution or the cost of the investigation in deciding upon its urgency.

(Peirce [1879] 1967: 645)

At a later point in the grant application to the Carnegie Institution, Peirce summarized the implications of the preceding model in the following way:

Research must contrive to do business at a profit; by which I mean that it must produce more effective scientific energy than it expends. No doubt it already does so. But it would do well to become conscious of its economical position and contrive ways of living upon it.

(Peirce [1902b] 1985: 1038)

Having developed his theory for the most general, multiple research project case with mathematics, Peirce proceeded to simplify with the special case when two projects are under simultaneous consideration. The two-project case allows Peirce to graphically portray his theory of the economy of research. Peirce's illustration is reproduced as Figure 4.1. The total cost of two projects is on the horizontal axis. The ratio of economic urgency, of marginal utility to marginal cost, is represented on the vertical axis by Y_1 and Y_2. The graph of the first research project is represented in the usual way by curve $S_1 T_1$. The representation of the second project is reversed and read backwards from the $X_2 O_2$ origin. Curve $S_2 T_2$ represents the second project. For both projects, the ratio of marginal utility to marginal cost for reducing probable error decreases as more funds are expended on each project. At the intersection point of the two curves, P, the ratios for the two projects are equal. Peirce projected a line from P to the horizontal axis which established how additional funds should be allocated to

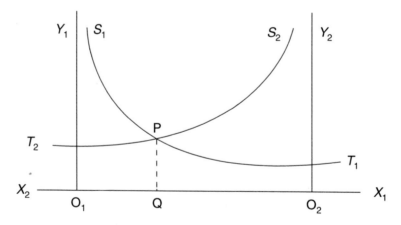

Figure 4.1 Peirce's graphical portrayal of the economy of research

the two projects. As Peirce portrayed it, greater additional funding should be allocated to the second project than the first.

THE NOTION OF PROBABLE ERROR AND THE EARLIEST CORRECT USAGE OF THE LOGIC OF STATISTICAL INFERENCE

The notion of probable error as Peirce used it is now no longer current in modern science. An understanding of probable error is central in understanding Peirce's analysis of the economics of research project selection both in the Note and in subsequent comments. As mentioned previously, the term "probable error" is a precursor of the notion of a confidence interval. Fortunately, Peirce's use of probable error has already been analyzed and interpreted in a work on the history of statistics (Hacking 1990). This work argues that Peirce was the first to correctly formulate the logic of modern scientific inference using probable error. If this is so, then the Note is a significant illustration of Peirce's path-breaking understanding of modern statistical inference.

According to Ian Hacking (1990: 209), the standard use of the term "probable error" arose from astronomy. In an informal way, astronomers used probable error to mean that a measure of a position was within a given error of the true value half of the time. Or as Robert Dorfman has written: "It is a measure of the accuracy of an estimate equal to the range around the true value within which it has a 50–50 probability of lying."[15] We already know that Peirce corresponded with the astronomer Simon Newcomb, that he was employed by the Harvard Observatory, and that Peirce's father was a consulting astronomer.[16] So it is not surprising that Peirce made use of a statistical concept developed by astronomers. Hacking describes Peirce's use of probable error in the following way:

> Peirce had a model for this kind of argument, based on the standard practices of astronomers, the "probable error". The probable error divides measurements into two equal classes. If the errors are Normally distributed, then in the long run half the measurements will err in excess of the probable error, and half will be more exact. But what does this amount to?
>
> (Hacking 1990: 209)

Relating probable error to more modern statistical terminology, Hacking answers the question just raised. Peirce's use of probable error apparently provides the core of the modern theory of confidence intervals:

> Peirce is original in understanding the logic of the situation. Readers familiar with the logic of statistical inference will have noticed that Peirce was providing the core of the rationale of the theory of confidence intervals and of hypothesis-testing advanced by Jerzy Neyman and E.S. Pearson in the 1930s, which is still, for many, the preferred route in

statistics. As usual, I am unconcerned with Peirce the precursor. Neyman did not learn anything from Peirce. Still, there is a certain line of filiation. The first modern statement of the rationale of confidence intervals was given not by Neyman but by the Harvard statistician E.B. Wilson. Wilson had been a pupil of Peirce's cousin B.O. Peirce, and was a lifelong admirer of the family. He was one of the few readers of C.S. Peirce on errors of observation, and wrote a paper about it. He had the right perspective as regards predecessors. . . . But it appears that only Peirce, Wilson and then Neyman got clear about the logical principles of this type of reasoning.

(Hacking 1990: 210)

Based on Hacking's appraisal, Peirce was the first to formulate the principles of statistical inference in a modern way with the idea of probable error. Probable error is a precursor to the more modern notion of a confidence interval. A confidence interval is a more explicit measure of the precision of a statistical estimator than the variance or calculated standard error of the estimator.[17] The confidence interval gives an interval of parameter values that likely contain the true mean. A 95 per cent confidence interval means that there is a 95 per cent probability that the interval covers the true mean. It does not give the probability that the true mean is in the interval. The true mean is a constant. The probability is zero or one that the true mean is in the confidence interval. The endpoints of the confidence interval are random variables to which probability can apply. The true mean is not a random variable. Additionally, Peirce's probable error appears to be the statistical opposite of the confidence interval. Rather than giving the degree of our confidence in an estimator, probable error gives the opposite. Thus probable error is equivalent to one minus the confidence interval.[18] The probable error of a 95 per cent confidence interval apparently would be 5 per cent.

The precision of an estimator as captured in the confidence interval is multi-dimensional. It involves the width of the confidence interval, the percentage level of interpretation, and sample size. For example, for a given sample size a 95 per cent confidence interval would have wider endpoints than a 90 per cent or 50 per cent confidence interval. A 50 per cent confidence interval would be quite small. With repeated sampling, the 50 per cent confidence interval means that only half of the time would the interval contain the true value of the parameter being estimated. Thus a higher level of confidence means wider or less precise endpoints to the interval. If we want a high degree of confidence without widening the endpoints of the interval, then the sample size would need to be increased. Econometrician Jan Kmenta has expressed some of these matters in the following way:

We should realize that the higher the level of confidence, the wider the corresponding confidence interval and, therefore, the less useful is the information about the precision of the estimator. . . . On the other hand, narrower confidence intervals will be associated with lower levels of confidence. . . . Obviously, given the level of confidence, a shorter interval is more desirable than a longer one.

(Kmenta 1971: 187–8).

In his critical interpretation of the significance of Peirce's work on statistical inference, Hacking does not specifically discuss the Note. This was unnecessary because Peirce had written frequently on both astronomy and statistical inference before he authored the Note. The Note was not Peirce's first piece to use the notion of probable error.[19] Nor does Hacking discuss the economic aspects of statistical inference as Peirce did. Yet it is clear that Peirce continually conceived of statistical inference as having an important economic dimension that was crucial in the selection of those hypotheses which should be tested. It is also clear that Peirce's Note embodied the degree of sophistication regarding statistical inference that Hacking saw in Peirce's other writings.

Peirce's Note calls attention to the economic aspects of statistical sampling. These economic aspects of sampling likely are known to every well trained statistician and econometrician. I suspect that the economic aspects of sampling are part of the common sense of graduate instruction in statistical inference.[20] With regard to statistical inference, Peirce's economy of research implies the following view of empirical research: that the value of scientific research depends on the degree of its precision; that the level of precision depends on sample size; and that sample size depends on costs of observation relative to available resources. None of this may be new to anyone experienced in the field of statistics. What is significant is that Peirce not only created a formal model of the economics of research and sampling, he also is the first to have correctly conceived of the logic of modern scientific inference.

PEIRCE'S NOTE AS THE FIRST SCIENTIFIC PIECE IN ECONOMICS

Beyond the statistical and economic implications of Peirce's economy of research project selection, another significant claim regarding the novelty of Peirce's Note can be made. A case can be made for claiming that Peirce's "Note on the Theory of the Economy of Research" is very modern and certainly among the first truly scientific piece in all of economics. The general context for this claim is the Baumol and Goldfeld (1968) anthology of writings of the precursors of mathematical economics. Peirce's Note can be directly compared with the contributions in the anthology. I believe that any economist who would read Peirce's essay would recognize it as the most modern and scientific of all of the early mathematical writings in economics. There are three specific aspects of Peirce's essay which make it an extremely innovative piece in economics compared to the mathematical economics of his time and in light of contributions which would come in the early part of the twentieth century. First, the method of argument which appears in the essay is novel. Second, the representation of

73

the argument with a special two-case graph was extraordinary for its time. Third, Peirce's development of the economic implications of his theory with ratios of marginal utilities was nothing less than path-breaking.[21]

The method of presenting scientific arguments in modern economics journals is known as the hypothetico-deductive method. This is the method for structuring the typical scientific article found in all of the major journals in economics. In brief, the hypothetico-deductive method requires the following: a clear analytical statement of a theory with mathematical equations or logical propositions that are independent of evidence or observation; the derivation of observable implications of the theory, and the testing of these implications in some appropriate manner. In philosophy of science, the origin of this method is traced to logical positivism. Logical positivists created the method in response to the reconceptualization of mathematics and logic formulated in Bertrand Russell and A. N. Whitehead's *Principia Mathematica*.[22]

What is extraordinary is that Peirce's essay exhibits the same structure of logical inference that the positivists created decades or perhaps a half century later. Peirce's Note is developed in exactly the manner of a modern theoretical journal article in economics. The sophistication of his Note rivals that of theoretical pieces authored during that innovative period which G. L. S. Shackle (1967) has called the years of high theory in economics during the 1920s and 1930s. Further evidence of the modernity of Peirce's method of scientific inference can be found in other writings of Peirce. It is not difficult to find an analysis of inference that is quite similar to the hypothetico-deductive method. One of these is an essay of Peirce's called "What is a Leading Principle?" In this piece, Peirce clearly maintained a logical theory of inference:

> Such a process is called an *inference*; the antecedent judgement is called the *premiss*; the consequent judgement, the *conclusion*; the habit of thought, which determined the passage from the one to the other (when formulated as a proposition), the *leading principle*. . . . A habit of inference may be formulated in a proposition which shall state that every proposition *c*, related in a given general way to any true proposition *p* is true. Such a proposition is called the *leading principle* of the class of inferences whose validity it implies [original emphasis].
>
> (Peirce [1880] 1955: 130, 131)

In a peculiar way, the novelty of Peirce's method of inference is apparent in the opinion of Simon Newcomb. Newcomb did not fully comprehend Peirce's method of inference. In 1889, Peirce was still working for the Coast Survey and attempting to finish a report of the results of the pendulum experiments. Peirce sent his report to the superintendent who sent it to Newcomb for appraisal. Newcomb wrote a lengthy letter recommending rejection of the report as a publication of the Survey:

> A remarkable feature of the presentation is the inversion of the logical order throughout the whole paper. The system of the author seems to be

to give first concluded results, then the method by which these results were obtained, then the formulae and principles on which these methods rest, then the derivation of these formulae, then the data on which the derivations rests and so on until the original observations are reached. The human mind cannot follow a course of such reasoning in this way, and the first thing to be done with the paper is to reconstruct it in logical order.
(Newcomb letter of April 28, 1890 in Brent 1993: 197)

Peirce's Note clearly embodies the method of inference proposed by Peirce in his concept of a leading principle. Peirce started with a mathematical statement of the theory and derived implications from the statement of the theory. Unlike his gravimetric research, Peirce did not have experimental evidence to support his conclusions about the economics of research. Nevertheless, Peirce did believe that his own experience with experimental science gave some empirical validity to his call for an economics of research. His method of drawing inferences in the Note is as modern as anything now being published in modern economics journals.

The second innovative aspect of Peirce's essay is the graph that he created for the two case version of his economy of research. Graphs tend to be deleted from modern scientific articles in economics, but this was not always the case. And graphs are extremely useful in classroom instruction and in textbooks. The graph represented as Figure 4.1 is a reproduction of the one from the version of the Note published by the Coast Survey in 1879. While this may not seem significant, and I easily could have glossed over it, it must be noted that Peirce had an extremely keen interest in graphical representations of scientific work. Peirce created a projection of the earth which was still in use for some navigational purposes during World War II.[23] Peirce also drew the graphs for his father's lecture on mathematical political economy in 1871. Peirce either actually drew or supervised preparation of the graph that is presented in the Coast Survey version of the Note. Again in the context of the essays in the Baumol and Goldfeld volume, there is nothing which can compare with the representational sophistication of the graph which Peirce created in the Note. Furthermore, although a similar graph can be found in Jevons' *Theory of Political Economy* (1957: 97), Peirce's graphical representation is somewhat more advanced. In his figure, Jevons placed the marginal utility of two goods on the vertical axes and the quantities purchased on the horizontal axis. In contrast, Peirce put the ratio of the marginal utility per dollar of cost on the vertical axes and the dollars to be spent on the horizontal axis.

A third innovative aspect of Peirce's Note concerns the manner in which he developed utility theory. Again, I turn to an early work in mathematical economics in the Baumol and Goldfeld volume. In discussing the contribution of W. E. Johnson on the theory of utility curves which was written in 1913, Baumol and Goldfeld present criteria for assessing the theoretical advances represented in the piece. One criterion is particularly relevant to Peirce's Note.

One of the innovations was "an explicit analysis of utility which uses only the ratios of marginal utilities and hence is free from considerations of cardinal utility" (Baumol and Goldfeld 1968: 96). Again scrutiny of Peirce's Note with this criterion in mind suggests how thoroughly modern the Note is. In the Note, Peirce made no mention of actually measuring utility. The implications of his theory have no dependence on cardinal utility. As Johnson did in 1913, the Note, written as early as 1876, depended only on ordinal utility. The fundamental conclusions of Peirce's theory of the economy of research depend only on the ratios of the marginal utility of funds spent on rival research projects. This is the equation which I have designated as equation (5). A version of equation (5) appears in virtually every discussion of consumer theory in all of the principles texts I have ever encountered. Peirce appears to have been among the first to create this representation and formalization of utility theory. Again this suggests how truly innovative Peirce's Note in fact is.

NICHOLAS RESCHER ON PEIRCE'S ECONOMY OF RESEARCH

Perhaps the only philosopher to take seriously Peirce's project regarding the economy of research is Nicholas Rescher (1976, 1978a, 1978b, 1989, 1996).[24] Rescher believes that the importance of Peirce's ideas on an economic theory of science have been overlooked. Rescher maintains that Peirce's theory is something like cost-benefit analysis:[25]

> Peirce proposed to construe the economic process at issue as the sort of balance of assets and liabilities that we today would call cost-benefit analysis. On the side of benefits, he was prepared to consider a wide variety of factors: closeness of fit to data, explanatory value, novelty, simplicity, accuracy of detail, precision, parsimony, concordance with other accepted theories, even antecedent likelihood and intuitive appeal. But in the liability column, there sit those hard-faced factors of "the dismal science": time, effort, energy, and last but not least, crass old money.
>
> (Rescher 1978a: 69)

Behind Peirce's economy of research Rescher (1978a: 25 ff.) asserts is a geographic exploration model of science. This geographic model entails a finite physical world with a discernable and slowly changing nature. If studied long enough, scientific opinion would converge to a single view or theory of that world. According to Rescher (1978a: 26), with the geographic model Peirce thought of science in two stages: a preliminary stage of searching for the structure of qualitative relationships and a secondary stage of quantitative refinement. The preliminary stage was noncumulative but the secondary stage was a cumulative phase of increasing quantitative precision. During the first stage, there is disagreement regarding the content of a theory. In the second phase, given appropriate theoretical development, knowledge is increasingly refined. Scientific progress ultimately becomes a matter of exactness and detail. In the context of a geographic model of the phenomena being investigated, an economic approach makes a lot of sense. Additional resources could bring us closer to the truth. This is a situation ideally suited for economic analysis.

Rescher believes that the geographic exploration model of scientific progress which Peirce apparently assumed is flawed. Referring to the work of T. S. Kuhn (1970) and others who critiqued positivism, Rescher denies that all scientific progress can be understood as a process of cumulative accretion. The geographic model is misleading. Rescher believes that scientific progress is more a matter of changing the theoretical framework than filling in a "crossword puzzle" (Rescher 1978b: 29). On this narrower point, I am in agreement with Rescher.

Rescher's characterization of a geographic model of science behind Peirce's Note and his economics of science needs some amendment. This may be too restrictive an interpretation of Peirce. It is true that Peirce spent much of his professional scientific career attempting to measure the differential pull of the earth's gravity in various locations in the United States and Europe. It is also understandable how the number of locations and the quality of the instruments for measuring gravity would be affected by the availability of economic resources. Apparently, Peirce was continually involved with efforts to fund more observations and the purchase of more accurate pendulums to enhance the quality of his measurements. Peirce wanted to be known as one of the best scientists in the world in measuring the earth's gravity. But it is also quite apparent that the fundamental notion of statistical inference in the Note, probable error, came from Peirce's extensive work in astronomy, not from geology. Furthermore, it quite significant that Peirce continued to apply his economic vision of hypothesis formation outside the domains of both astronomy and geology. Peirce thought that economic dimensions of inquiry were just as relevant in other domains such as the interpretation of ancient manuscripts. His most extensive elaboration of the economy of research is found in discussion of the logic of interpreting ancient manuscripts. Certainly this is an area more open to diversity than the fundamental measurements of the earth's gravity. Economic issues may need to be raised for research projects in more complex domains than geology and astronomy.

In a recent work, Rescher continues to expand on ideas concerning the economic dimensions of scientific research first encountered with Peirce. What Rescher contributes is an awareness that economic concerns continuously affect science.[26] He believes that no conception of science can be complete if the economic dimensions of science are ignored. In his conclusion to his recent book *Cognitive Economy*, Rescher clearly portrays economics as central to an understanding of science:

> For inquiry – in science and elsewhere – is a human activity which, like any other, requires the expenditures of effort and energy in a way that endows the enterprise with an unavoidable economic dimension.

Economic factors shape and condition our cognitive proceedings in so fundamental a way that they demand explicit attention.

(Rescher 1989: 150)

RESCHER'S PEIRCEAN INTERPRETATION OF KARL POPPER

Few economists may know of the significance of Peirce's philosophy and fewer still are aware of the economic aspects of his theory of science. Karl Popper is the philosopher of science typically recognized as having most influenced modern economics and methodology (Caldwell 1991). Popper's reputation in economics is due mostly to his idea of falsification. Yet there are connections between Peirce and Popper. Popper (1972b) has recognized the influence of Peirce in his adoption of an indeterminist interpretation of physics and Einstein's work. Both Popper and Peirce are evolutionary indeterminists. Beyond these similarities, there is another connection. Nicholas Rescher has applied the economics of research project selection from Peirce's work to Popper's widely influential notion of falsification. Rescher discusses falsification as one of several aspects of the problem of induction which can be resolved or enhanced in the context of an economic framework.[27] Rescher portrays Popper's methodology of falsification as an example of philosophy of science without economics. Like other philosophers, Popper makes no mention of the economic dimensions of scientific research. Implicitly, the assumption seemingly would be that science is nearly costless so that economic factors can be ignored. Furthermore, no attention is given either to increasing costs or the opportunity costs faced by the researcher in attempting to falsify scientific theories.

According to Rescher, Popper presents an evolutionary methodology of inquiry in his *Objective Knowledge* published in 1972.[28] Popper portrays falsification in science as evolutionary competition among rival theories arbitrated by falsifying episodes and evidence generated by experiment and observation. Of course Popper was aware that falsification was no simple matter (Popper 1959: 86). More was required to reject a theory than disconfirming evidence. A better theory was required before one theory would be rejected for another (Popper 1965: 215–50). A better theory is the one which is most fit to survive the testing of both proponents and opponents. Between rival theories there is an evolutionary process of elimination through trial and error.

More specifically, Rescher summarizes Popper's methodology of falsification as containing three main elements (Rescher 1978a: 53): (1) a realization that the number of plausible hypotheses is infinite, (2) an awareness that science is a process of trial and error in eliminating alternative hypotheses, and (3) a sense that the process of eliminating hypotheses (falsification) is blind. The third element of Popper's methodology is the one which Rescher maintains is improved by reference to Peirce and economic considerations. Rescher does not believe that falsification is a "matter of blind, random groping" (Rescher 1978a:

53). Rescher asserts that Popper faces a real dilemma. If falsification operates among all conceivable or even proposed hypotheses, then there would never be sufficient time and resources for such a task. Popper's random and blind conception of the growth of scientific knowledge could not be carried out by humans with real resource constraints. Thus Rescher holds that Popper's theory of the growth of knowledge is incomplete because it does not explain the "rate and structure of scientific progress" (Rescher 1978a: 52).

In Rescher's (1978a: 65) view, the problem with Popperian falsification is underdetermination. There are an infinite number of potential hypotheses and a finite body of empirical knowledge. Criteria of some sort must be used to select which hypotheses are going to be tested. Otherwise the task of falsification would be impossible. When Rescher (1978a: 51–63) applies economics to Popper's methodology for eliminating hypotheses, he maintains that it solves the underdetermination problem. Rescher maintains that there are just too many possible hypotheses to be considered with Popper's methodology. He believes there are almost an infinite number of hypotheses for scientific investigation. The researcher faces an impossible task. Faced with numerous hypothetical alternatives that could exhaust lifetimes, Rescher turns to economics. In the face of underdetermination, Rescher turns to Peirce and his economy of research. Rescher, taking his cue from Peirce's economy of research, believes that scientists should use economic criteria in deciding which hypotheses should be tested and subject to possible falsification. Using a cost-benefit metaphor, that hypothesis should be tested which offers the greatest net benefit to science. If two hypotheses are equal on grounds other than economics and if one involves much less time and resource expenditure than the other, then the least costly hypothesis should be tested. Rescher offers a general economic interpretation of his critique of Popper and falsification:

> The point is that our economically oriented approach is wholly undogmatic regarding generality preference. We replace Popper's purely logical concern for universality-for-its-own-sake with an economico-methodological concern for universality-relative-to-cost. If we take this economic line and do sensible decision making on the basis of the seemingly reasonable economic precept, "Maximize generality subject to the constraints of affordability," then our basic concern is one of cost-benefit analysis, seeking to optimize returns subject to resource-outlays.
>
> (Rescher 1978a: 83)

Judged from the vantage point of an economist, Rescher's critique of Popper and the Peircean economic corrective seem to make a lot of sense.[29] For an economist it is hard to imagine that science is unaffected by scarcity and incentives. Certainly the intellectual merits of the underdetermination problem require evaluation from philosophers. However, without an economic dimension, Popper's method and those of other philosophers of science seem to be at such a high level of abstraction that they become dissociated from the conduct of real day-to-day science. Rescher's and Peirce's contributions make the fact that real science is done in an economic environment important for philosophy of science.[30]

Rescher should be given credit for seeing the intellectual significance of Peirce's economic approach to research project selection. What is of the utmost significance is that Rescher is concerned with an economic dimension of scientific research which economists and philosophers have ignored almost entirely. Using a cost-benefit interpretation of Peirce's model, Rescher legitimately raises economic issues regarding the nature of science. He correctly calls attention to the notion of opportunity cost which he sees as being quite relevant to the selection of research projects. Most methodology and philosophy of science is conceived without reference to constraints, incentives, and markets. It reminds one of the state of economics texts several decades ago when increases in consumption and production were presented as having no impact on resource costs or the environment. For Peirce and Rescher, philosophy of science is seriously deficient if its economic dimensions are ignored. They focus on an economic dimension of science which is fundamentally important to understanding science – the role of economic factors in research project selection. Following the precedent established by Peirce, Rescher asserts that the fundamental propositions of economics apply to science. Economists may find some minor basis for quibbling about issues of detail, but the main point is one that every economist must take seriously. Scarcity is universal and science is no exception to the "laws of economics."

All of this makes a great deal of sense to an economist. Rescher maintains that hypotheses should be tested to the maximum degree that resources allow. But there is one issue regarding Peirce and Popper that must be raised. The issue concerns the originality of the idea of falsification. Generally, the creation of the notion of falsification is attributed to Karl Popper, and I have no doubt that Popper should be credited with authorship in this case. Like so many of Peirce's intellectual contributions that were authored and then lost for so long, Peirce appears to have had an awareness of essential aspects of falsification. Peirce and his eccentric lifestyle must be given a great deal of the responsibility for obscuring many of his own contributions for so long. In the 1902 grant application to the Carnegie Institution, Peirce appears to have stumbled onto the idea of falsification:

> The true presuppositions of logic are merely *hopes*; and as such, when we consider their consequences collectively, we cannot condemn scepticism as to how far they may be borne out by facts. But when we come down to specific cases, these hopes are so completely justified that the smallest conflict with them suffices to condemn the doctrine that involves that conflict. This is one of the places where logic comes in contact with ethics [original emphasis].

> (Peirce [1902b] 1985: 1028–30)

Regarding this passage Brent (1993: 281) comments parenthetically, "compare Karl Popper's doctrine of falsification." And concerning another of Peirce's papers Brent remarks: "To read Popper or Carl Hempel on the logic of science after reading the 'Illustrations' shows how little has been added to the model first proposed by Peirce over a century ago" (Brent 1993: 117).

CONCLUSIONS

In this chapter, Peirce's microeconomic model of research project selection in science has been reconsidered and cast as a stepping stone in the creation of an economics of science. Peirce's model helps us move beyond economic analysis of the problems of misconduct in science. His economics of research project selection essentially allows us to take the first step towards the creation of an economic theory of legitimate, normal science. Peirce's Note appears to be based on the same theory of rational, optimizing behavior as those of fraud and replication failure. His model embodies the notion that resources must be used to increase the precision of scientific observation and research. Peirce maintained that research dollars should be allocated to those projects whose increased precision is most valued by science.

Peirce's "Note on the Theory of the Economy of Research" is truly extraordinary. It is extremely unfortunate that it has been thoroughly neglected by the economics profession for more than century. A case can be made that the Note was among the first pieces of modern scientific research in all of economics. This claim is based on the novelty of the method of argument, the graphical techniques, and the ratio of the marginal utilities found in the Note. The Note is also significant for making economic factors a central part of a theory of scientific inference, something which contemporary economic methodologists and philosophers still have not done except for a few notable exceptions. And the Note also has been used to criticize and reformulate the idea of falsification. Philosopher Nicholas Rescher has interpreted and extended Peirce's economic interpretation of science to Karl Popper's notion of falsification. Rescher argues that falsification needs to be supplemented with economic criteria. Together, the unprecedented contributions of the Note, Peirce's subsequent comments on the economy of research, and his prescient ideas about scientific inference constitute a Peircean vision of science. His message is that science requires an explicit understanding of the economic factors of science.

Peirce's essay may be path-breaking for economics in a way that cannot be directly inferred from the Note or a more generalized Peircean vision of science. Except for similarities with a Marshallian perspective, a Peircean vision of economics is different from anything apparent in economics today. Mainstream economists in recent decades have tended to associate optimization and equilibrium theory with a Walrasian, mechanistic vision of economic activity. And the most prominent evolutionary economists of our time, the American Institutionalists, have tended to reject optimization and equilibrium as relevant theoretical constructs. Like the Institutionalists, Peirce rejected the mechanism that flourished in physics and in other disciplines during his lifetime. Peirce was an evolutionary indeterminist. Like the mainstream economists, Peirce saw optimization theory as a useful tool of economic analysis. For Peirce, optimization took place in the context of a more general evolutionary view of the world. Peirce's vision of political economy was that of a mathematical theory assumed in the broader context of an evolutionary view of the world with an economy of research as an integral part of the conception of scientific inference.

5

A COST-BENEFIT APPROACH TO RESEARCH PROJECT SELECTION, POPPER'S METHODOLOGY, AND SCIENTIFIC PROGRESS

Popper's entire philosophy of science is simply *an application of the method of neoclassical economic theory*. The possibility of such an incredible conclusion only exemplifies the problems which await anyone interpreting Popper's writings on the topic [emphasis added].

(Hands 1985: 85–6)

A COST-BENEFIT LOGIC OF SCIENCE

This economics of science began with economic models of misconduct and then turned to economic analysis of the normal, legitimate activities of the scientist. The transition from misconduct to legitimate science was facilitated by focusing on Peirce's contributions to the economics of science. Peirce proposed an economics of research project selection using a utility model which was later interpreted as a cost-benefit approach to research project selection. This cost-benefit interpretation of Peirce was extended to the philosophy of Karl Popper as a critique of neglected economic aspects of falsification by Nicholas Rescher. However, quite independently of Rescher's critique, a cost-benefit interpretation of Popper has been articulated by another philosopher. Philosopher Gerard Radnitzky (1987a, 1987b) has proposed a cost-benefit interpretation of Popper's methodology which is a much broader than a critical reappraisal of falsification. Radnitzky's cost-benefit elaboration of Popper extends beyond falsification to the selection of facts and theories in science.

A cost-benefit model of such broad scope as Radnitzky's again raises questions about Popper's methodology of science. In this chapter, Peirce's conception of an economics of research is reformulated as a cost-benefit model. This reformulated cost-benefit theory is used to consider Popper's methodology and other aspects of science from a cost-benefit perspective.

RADNITZKY'S COST-BENEFIT INTERPRETATION OF POPPER

Gerard Radnitzky (1987a, 1987b) has created an economic interpretation of Popper's methodology which is complementary to Rescher's interpretation of Popper. Rather than elaborating an economic view of falsification and research project selection, Radnitzky focuses on the choice of theories and facts. The title of two of his articles, "The 'Economic' Approach to the Philosophy of Science" and "Cost-Benefit Thinking in the Methodology of Research" convey the nature of his point of view (Radnitzky 1987a, 1987b). The core of his economic approach is cost-benefit thinking as a methodology of research. Radnitzky maintains that cost-benefit thinking is implicit in Popper's methodology: "Popperian methodology may be viewed as an application of the economic approach to epistemic situations" and *"Popper's methodology can be seen as a special case of the application of the CBA-frame to espistemic (sic) situations"* (Radnitzky 1987b: 160; 1987a: 298; italics in original).

At the center of Radnitzky's conception of Popper's methodology is a cost-benefit theory of rationality. Radnitzky creates a philosophical theory of rationality. His theory consists of six requirements or postulates that constitute a rationality principle and seven corresponding initial conditions that translate the rationality principle from logic to historical human behavior.[1] Radnitzky's fourth requirement is clearly economic, asserting that an implicit or explicit cost-benefit analysis is a part of all rational behavior including the behavior of scientists. According to Radnitzky, rational action involves choice. Choice in turn implies a weighing of costs and benefits: "Man is a chooser. *All* rational choices involve the weighing up of benefits and costs, [and] rest upon the 'opportunity cost' principle" [original emphasis] (Radnitzky 1987a: 285).

Rather than focusing on the selection of research projects as do Peirce and Rescher, Radnitzky (1987a: 296 ff.) is concerned with the rational choice between rival sets of facts and theories. He distinguishes between universal and basic statements in science. Universal statements are the most general and abstract statements of a theory. Basic statements are the "facts" of science. Basic statements are observation reports that tell us what is happening, and when and where it is happening.

Consider how basic facts are chosen by the scientist. Radnitzky asks whether the acceptance or rejection of basic statements in science is a rational process. He recognizes that most scientists accept or reject basic statements with a felt sense of near certainty. He believes this is methodologically irrelevant. What is important is whether the logic of the decision can be reconstructed using cost-benefit analysis. Radnitzky (1987a: 307) maintains that the decision to rethink or reappraise the basic facts of science share the major characteristics of an investment decision. If there is positive value to rechecking the basic facts, then the scientist will begin to criticize the basic statements or facts of his scientific discipline. As mentioned previously, replication failure may be an occasion for reconsidering the facts. For whatever the reason, a reconsideration of the facts may entail a degree of self-criticism if the researcher has been one of the creative forces behind the universal and basic statements which constitute the current state of his field of scientific inquiry. Radnitzky's own words describe the process of selecting facts in cost-benefit terms:

> *The decision process may be suitably reconstructed as a cost-benefit assay*, in which account is taken of the costs involved, in particular, the opportunity costs of the rechecking. When it has been decided that a statement is unproblematic at the moment, the estimated utility of an additional rechecking diminishes drastically and may perhaps, in some cases drop to zero [original emphasis].
>
> (Radnitzky 1987a: 303)

So that there is no misunderstanding, Radnitzky rephrases the process for selecting facts and asks whether a falsified fact, a falsified basic statement, would be retained as part of science:

> The methodological reconstruction of this case – *guided by the cost-benefit frame* – shows that the valuation of the *costs* is *objective*, and that, in the case under discussion, *the costs of defending the falsified basic statement b_d constitute costs in an objective sense* and that these costs would be unbearably high.
>
> (Radnitzky 1987a: 304)

After arguing that cost-benefit analysis is an implicit part of the rational appraisal of the fundamental facts or basic statements of science, Radnitzky (1987a: 308) next turns to the appraisal of competing theories. For the preference of one theory over another to be rational, the decision must be based on objective grounds. Radnitzky believes that there are costs to defending a theory. Since the costs of defending competing theories are not identical, one of the theories will have an advantage over the other. Radnitzky believes that such cost differences are objective and that eventually they will lead to a change in which a new theory is accepted. Radnitzky summarizes the choice between rival theories in cost-benefit terms:

> The cost of defending a falsified theory or a theory for which the balance sheets of successes and failures is less good than that of its competitors is evaluated objectively. This case, incidentally, illustrates that the concept of cost may be useful even if we cannot measure costs. These costs are opportunity costs in the wide sense, i.e., in the sense of *epistemic resources foregone*, resources which would have been available if one had opted for the competitor of the theory. . . . In rational theory preference a *cost-benefit analysis* has to be used [original emphasis].
>
> (Radnitzky 1987a: 319)

A COST-BENEFIT MODEL OF RESEARCH PROJECT SELECTION

While Peirce's model is a utility model of research project selection, Radnitzky advocates a cost-benefit approach for explaining the selection of facts and theories. If we are to have a theoretically consistent approach to science, then all of these problems should be addressed from the same type of theory. Utility theory is by no means exhausted and may yield further insights regarding the economic dimensions of scientific inquiry. However, I am in essential agreement with Radnitzky's cost-benefit approach and Rescher's cost-benefit rhetoric of science. They imply that the choices facing the scientist are more like those found with an investment problem rather than a consumption decision. Is the scientist more like a producer who intermittently faces the implementation of large-scale strategic decisions or, like the consumer who continually and marginally modifies a bundle of household purchases in a piecemeal fashion? I believe that science can be better understood from production than consumption theory.

For economists, the differences between production and consumption are quite important. These differences may enhance an economic understanding of science. Cost-benefit analysis is an extension of investment analysis from the theory of the firm. Production involves the creation of goods and the use of inputs like capital and labor in discrete amounts. The discrete, lumpiness of production in the short run could lead to a revision of the criteria of research project selection found in the utility model of Peirce. In this section, the main task is to reformulate Peirce's utility approach to research project selection using cost-benefit analysis. In the next section, this approach will be extended to the selection of facts and theories so that we may analytically reformulate Radnitzky's interpretation of Popper.

Because cost-benefit analysis occupies such a prime role in the rhetoric and philosophy of Rescher and Radnitzky and their economic interpretations of Peirce and Popper, the time has come to move beyond both utility theory and philosophical analysis. Let us create a cost-benefit model of research project selection as another approach to the underdetermination problem.[2] Doubts about this approach can be momentarily and provisionally suspended because difficulties inherent in cost-benefit analysis will be encountered subsequently. A cost-benefit model of research project selection emulates the theory of investment in the private sector.[3] In the private sector, a firm undertakes investment in conformity with certain well-established rules. The firm makes a multiperiod calculation of the value of each rival project. Calculation of net present value requires estimation of the revenues generated from a project in each time period and an approximation of the initial cost of putting the project in place. Because the revenue stream occurs over time, future revenues must be discounted to the present. This requires that a discount rate must be assumed. Once the appropriate rate is acquired, then the present value for the investment project can be calculated. A firm should initiate an investment project if its net present value is positive and if there is no other project with a greater net present value. In the public sector, a similar multiperiod formulation of the investment decision can be made and constitutes cost-benefit analysis. Its limits will be discussed in conjunction with the cost-benefit theory of science.

In the United States, cost-benefit analysis became prominent in the 1960s with the growth of government programs during the administration of President Lyndon Johnson.[4] Government expanded at an unprecedented rate for a peacetime economy. Many government projects were initiated. Cost-benefit analysis was proposed as an analytical framework for comparing alternative projects and considering their relative net benefits. The government version of cost-benefit analysis was called the Planning Programming Budgeting System (PPBS). It consisted of five major elements: a careful specification of objectives, analysis of output, measurement of costs, comparison with alternatives, and an attempt to establish common modes of analysis throughout government. In practice PPBS did not work very well. Measurement of costs and benefits is not straightforward because of various types of market failure. The categorization of cost and benefits is often quite arbitrary, and competing political agencies and bureaucracies may have quite different and inherently incomparable missions and objectives.[5]

In science, the Peircean problem of allocating funds to alternative projects also could be represented as a multiperiod cost-benefit problem. Research projects in science produce benefits for society which can be obtained only by utilizing scarce resources. As in the business sector, the benefits of a scientific project may extend into the future. However, its costs may extend over the lifetime of the project rather than being concentrated in the initial period. Scarce resources and any unwanted by-products of scientific investigation constitute the costs of scientific research. A cost-benefit model takes the following general form:

$$NPV = Z_0 - C_0 + \frac{Z_1 - C_1}{(1 + i)^1} + \ldots + \frac{(Z_n - C_n)}{(1 + i)^n} \tag{1}$$

where Z_i are the benefits from scientific research, C_i are the costs of a research project and its final product, and i is a discount factor.[6] In the domain of scientific research, the benefits of scientific research may come from several sources. These sources may be any eventual direct marketable benefits to the public, the value of any indirect external benefits to the public, and whatever value the project may have in enhancing scientific knowledge as valued by the scientific community. Among the costs of a research project would be the value of labor used in the project and in any subsequent production of products from the project, the implicit rental value of the laboratory or other equipment costs associated with implementing the project, the cost of formal statistical interpretation of the data, the cost of publishing the results, the manufacturing costs of commercial production of any new product resulting from the research, and any external costs associated with the research and the manufacture of the resulting product. Furthermore, there ought to be a variable capturing the time dimension of the project signifying that time is a finite resource.

Consider the two project scenario suggested in Peirce's "Economy of Research." Rather than using utility theory, analyze the two-project scenario with a cost-benefit model. Following the investment analogy with the private sector, a research project is a plausible candidate for the scientist if its net present value is positive and if there is no other project with a greater net present value. This criterion is thought to be superior to other decision rules which have had a degree of prominence in the cost-benefit literature.[7] All of the benefits and costs of the two projects would have to be estimated. Assuming a relevant discount factor, then the net present values of the two would need to be compared. Analytically, the decision for the individual scientist can be represented in the following way:

$$NPV_I > NPV_{II} > 0 \qquad\qquad (2)$$

where I and II represent the two projects. Assuming that both projects have a positive net present value, then project I with the higher net present value supposedly would be chosen. If there are sufficient funds, both projects could be chosen. This criterion is different than the criterion for allocating funds among alternative projects in utility theory. Here the projects are rank-ordered. Consequently the decision criterion is discrete rather than continuous. An equality of marginal conditions for the multiproject decision like that of Peirce's model as found in equation (5) in Chapter 4 is unlikely. In this regard, cost-benefit analysis may be more appropriate for science than utility theory. But there are difficulties which must be considered before the conclusions of a cost-benefit comparison are accepted fully. These difficulties are essential for understanding positions that Radnitzky takes regarding the application of cost-benefit analysis to Popper and to science.[8]

The very existence of cost-benefit analysis as a theory of public expenditures is due to a significant economic problem, market failure. If markets could be used to organize all of economic life, then nonmarket organizations like government would have no purpose.[9] Since markets do fail, government decision makers are faced with making economic decisions in an environment disconnected to some degree from the market process. Markets may fail because the conditions for their existence preclude their establishment or they may fail because of externalities. Total market failure provides the opportunity for government and other nonmarket organizations and institutions to be created. Partial market failure occurs with externalities and raises the prospect of corrective government intervention. Externalities occur when there are third-party spillover effects not accruing to the buyer and seller in the marketplace. A public sector investment decision should include estimates of positive and negative externalities because externalities typically are not part of the calculations of the private sector.

There is another difficulty with the nonmarket nature of a cost-benefit decision rule. For investment decisions in the private sector, most of the data constituting the raw material for the present value calculation are determined in the market. The estimate of the initial cost of a firm's investment project and its product prices are largely based on existing and expected future market prices. In the public sector, much of the data which enters the cost-benefit framework is not market based. To the extent that materials and resources must be purchased from the private sector, the cost of public projects may be market related. But if government is the only purchaser of a resource for which there would not otherwise be a market, the prices paid are more government than market determined. On the benefits side, estimates are often made of external costs which the private sector no longer has to bear. These estimates of necessity contain a degree of arbitrariness because there is no market to serve as a reference point for a meaningful comparison.[10]

In science, many decision processes may be further removed from the market than public sector decisions in government.[11] Science consists of projects intended to develop evidence for testing the fundamental theories of science. It would be hard to place a market value on the worth of evidence in furthering scientific progress. While current research costs could be known quite accurately, present and future benefits may be partly unimaginable and thus difficult to estimate. Knowing whether end-products could be created which lead to the appearance of new markets may be nothing more than a guess. For science it is appropriate to ask whether a cost-benefit model has any hope of being estimated in any objective, quantifiable way.

Another major problem concerns the discount factor which enters the denominator of the multiperiod present value calculations. In the private sector it is appropriate to use a market rate of interest with a term to maturity which approximates the lifespan of the investment project. But this may be inappropriate for the public sector. If the private sector values returns near the present more than those in the distant future, then it may be inappropriate to use the market rate of interest.

Similarly for science, its remoteness from the market has important implications for the rate of discount used for science in equation (1). A discount factor for science should be used which is different than a corresponding market rate of interest for a private sector project or the discount factor used for the appraisal of government projects. The time horizon of professional scientists may exceed those of bureaucrats in government agencies and those decision makers in the private sector. Other things being equal, it is hard to tell whether a higher or lower discount rate should be used for science. On the one hand, because scientific research projects are most likely more uncertain than investment projects in the private sector, perhaps a larger rate of discount should be used. On the other hand, the net benefits of scientific research may be grossly understated so that a lower discount factor might be necessary.[12] A lower discount factor would raise the estimate of the net present value of a research project.

When a firm in the private sector makes a mistake, market processes force a correction and if the mistaken investment decision is significant, then the firm exits from the industry. When a government agency fails, it may be difficult to terminate the agency and redirect spending toward other purposes.[13] Government agencies largely escape the discipline of the marketplace. If basic science is even further removed from the market than bureaucratic agencies, then it may be even more difficult to control spending on wasteful projects in science. One would expect that research projects which no longer have scientific merit would be eliminated on purely scientific grounds such as replication failure or competition from a superior alternative. But if science is really further removed from the marketplace than public agencies and if the scientific evidence is complex and ambiguous, then the problem of wasteful spending in science may be greater than it is for government agencies.

Cost-benefit analysis has not revolutionized the process of public sector choice to the extent originally imagined. Political and ideological competition seems to play a more definitive role in determining the size and distribution of government funds among alternative projects. Yet cost-benefit analysis for all of its deficiencies remains the most rational analytical framework for conceiving of the choices available to government agencies. Perhaps it may help us understand choices available to scientists as well. But cost-benefit analysis may not revolutionize analysis of choice in science any more than it has in the public sector.[14]

A COST-BENEFIT APPROACH TO THE SELECTION OF FACTS, THEORIES, AND RESEARCH PROGRAMS

While Peirce and Rescher apply economic analysis to the problem of selecting the next research project, Radnitzky applies cost-benefit analysis to two other issues – the choice of facts and theories by scientists. The model developed in equations (1) and (2) is a cost-benefit reformulation inspired by Peirce's utility approach to research project selection, by Rescher's cost-benefit interpretation of Peirce, and by Radnitzky's cost-benefit interpretation of Popper. Let us attempt to extend the analytical framework of the cost-benefit model from research project selection to the choice of facts and theories. In this way, we can both expand and critique Radnitzky's use of cost-benefit analysis as a fundamental aspect of philosophy of science.

What Radnitzky apparently wants to address is the logic of the situation facing an individual scientist in evaluating his professional research commitment. Should the scientist accept the facts and theories of the research program in which he works or those of the next best alternative? As an individual, each researcher must make such a decision and periodically reevaluate it. At issue is whether cost-benefit analysis can be used to represent the choices confronted by the individual scientist. Radnitzky (1987a: 286) is aware of the difficulties of applying cost-benefit analysis to actual government expenditures. The literature on cost-benefit analysis written by economists is full of an awareness of the conceptual and empirical limitations of the theory. The level of awareness of the limitations of the methods of positive economic science by those in public finance is as sophisticated as any methodologist could author.

Rather than evaluating the net present value of just one research project versus another for the scientist's own research activities as Peirce did, the scientist must make a judgement about the value of research being done by peers in his own research program and in its nearest rival. Here I am using the idea of a research program as elaborated by Imre Lakatos (1978a). Consider the scientist's selection of facts. One possibility would be to represent a researcher's valuation of the "facts" in rival research programs as the summation of the value of all the facts for every research project in each program. We have already recognized the subjective and arbitrary aspects inherent in cost-benefit analysis, so that these considerations still hold.[15] Let every research project known to an individual researcher be represented with a cost-benefit model like equation (1). The total value of the research program for an individual would be the sum of the net present values of all known research projects. An individual scientist's valuation of the research in one research program could be represented as:

$$V_{RPI} = \sum_{i=1}^{n} NPV_I^i (F_I^i) \tag{3}$$

The valuation of an alternative research program would be:

$$V_{RPII} = \sum_{k=1}^{l} NPV_{II}^k (F_{II}^k) \tag{4}$$

A formal estimate of the subjective valuation of the collective facts in one rival research program versus another by one scientist follows in the subsequent equation:

$$V_{RPI} (F_I^i) > V_{RPII}^k (F_{II}^k) \tag{5}$$

where F_I^i and F_{II}^k represent the facts from each research program. Equation (5) assumes that there are two rival research programs, I and II, that there are n research projects in research program I and k research projects in research program II, and that the net present value of all of the facts in both programs is given a qualitative, subjective appraisal by an individual scientist. The logic of the situation is that the scientist chooses the research program with the greater aggregate net present value of facts as valued by the scientist.

The problem of theory preference could be given a similar reformulation. Radnitzky maintains that the researcher chooses one theory over another based on the individual's appraisal of the relative net benefits of a theory. He calls this the epistemic costs and benefits of choosing one theory rather than another. Thus the researcher faces a choice of rival theories between two commensurable research programs. If similarly defined Ts are substituted for the Fs in equations (3) and (4) above, Radnitzky's point can be stated more formally as:

$$V_{RPI} (T_I^i) > V_{RPII}^k (T_{II}^k) \tag{6}$$

91

where T_I^i and T_{II}^k represent theories of each program. Again equation (6) takes the comparative net present value of the theories of each research program as generated from a summation of research projects in each research program and as valued by an individual scientist. The individual would decide to adopt theoretical framework I or II based on a subjective appraisal of which research program's theories has the greater aggregate net present value.

One problem with the preceding representation of these choices facing the scientist is that facts and theories are interrelated issues. Facts and theories may be not as separable as the two preceding equations imply. Kuhn (1970) and Lakatos (1978a) have argued that facts are impregnated with theoretical ideas. Perhaps a better way to represent the problem would be to recognize that the appraisal of facts and theories must be done together. This inseparability can be represented in the following equation:

$$V_{RPI}\left(F_I^i\left(T_I^i\right)\right) > V_{RPII}\left(F_{II}^k\left(T_{II}^k\right)\right) \tag{7}$$

where the F and T variables are defined in the same way as above. Equation (7) portrays a subjective aggregate comparison of the value of both the facts and the theories as they are embodied in specific research projects in one research program relative to another. The researcher considers the facts and theories to be interrelated and chooses that research program whose research projects in aggregate have a greater net present value than the next best alternative research program. Although facts have a theoretical dimension, they are generally thought to be at a lower level of abstraction. Consequently, facts are represented as being a function of the theoretical framework rather than conversely.

Because of the complexity of science and the subjectivity of the cost estimates faced by individual scientists in attempting to make the type of comparative judgement implied by equation (7), it is certainly possible, if not likely, that rational individuals may favor rival research programs. Rational scientists may value those research projects in their own research program more highly than an antagonist would. The converse is also true. An antagonist likely would value familiar research more highly. If we allow that reasonable individuals can place different values on alternative appraisals of both the facts and theories, then intelligent, rational individuals may support different theories and research programs. Thus Radnitzky's cost-benefit logic of science could account for pluralism in science, so that there is never just one approach or school of thought in science.

Expanding on Radnitzky's cost-benefit conception of facts and theories in science, one research program would be abandoned for another if an alternative delivers more of what a scientist values. At the factual level what a scientist wants is accuracy, comprehensiveness, robustness, relevance, descriptiveness, congruence with theory, etc. At the theoretical level, what a scientist desires is generality, rigor, relevance, scope, etc. A better research program apparently is one which is easier to defend factually, theoretically, and by implication economically, where it becomes easier to marshall resources for one view of science rather than for a rival. Evidently, competition among rival research programs has a significant economic dimension. A research program facing escalating costs and diminishing benefits would find it difficult to dominate a rival with decreasing costs and increasing returns.

AN APPRAISAL OF RADNITZKY'S COST-BENEFIT INTERPRETATION OF POPPER

Radnitzky claims that he is merely elaborating an economic approach already implicit in Popper's thought. This claim needs to be considered carefully. Radnitzky (1987b: 161) uses the following statement by Popper to support his cost-benefit interpretation of Popper's methodology. In comparing the methodologies of the social sciences, Popper claimed he is emulating economics: "The main point here was an attempt *to generalize the method of economic theory (marginal utility theory) so as to become applicable to the other theoretical-social sciences*" [original emphasis] (Popper 1976: 117–18).[16] As with others, it appears that Radnitzky clouds the distinction between utility and production theory. Radnitzky's cost-benefit economic interpretation of Popper's method is not based on utility theory *per se*. Obviously, there are economic dimensions to all human behavior because of the scarcity of both material resources and time. But whether Popper's methodology constitutes an economic approach to science is not settled by one quotation from Popper. I believe that Radnitzky's economic approach to philosophy of science extends way beyond anything which Popper might have had in mind. The fact that the methodological choices the researcher faces can be represented formally as economic decision criteria like equations (5), (6), or (7), highlights the creative nature of Radnitzky's contribution.

The nature of Popper's appeal to economics and the adequacy of Radnitzky's economic interpretation of Popper can be appraised by reconsidering the debate over the methodological unity of the social and natural sciences. An economic approach to science provides a new context for debating the methodological unity of the sciences. Recently there has been some disagreement concerning Popper's position on the methodological unity of the natural and social sciences. Do they share the same methods? Popper seems to want to have it both ways.[17] One interpreter, Hands (1985) has hypothesized that there are two different Poppers: Popper$_n$ for the natural sciences and Popper$_s$ for the social sciences. Apparently Popper$_n$ maintains that the natural sciences are falsifiable, predictive sciences concerned with phenomena governed by natural law while Popper$_s$ holds that the social sciences eschew prediction and falsification aiming to explain the logic of a social situation and/or the unintended consequences of social action. Furthermore, Popper$_s$ the situational determinist, apparently has a high regard for economics particularly utility theory. What utility theory formalizes is the logic of the transactional situation facing ordinary buyers and sellers. Social science for Popper would be a generalization of the method of utility theory, reconstructing the logic of the situation facing a human agent.

Popper's regard for economics needs reappraisal. Upon encountering the economic approaches to science of Peirce, Rescher, and particularly Radnitzky, it is clear that Popper's situational determinism is not an "economic approach" as an economist understands that term.[18] Popper wants the form without the content. Popper$_j$, the situational determinist's economic approach, really contains no economics as economists know it. Otherwise the economic approaches of Peirce, Rescher, and Radnitzky would be unnecessary. And Rescher has argued that the methodology of Popper$_n$, falsification, leads to the underdetermination problem which requires an economic remedy. Thus in Popper's methodology, for either Popper$_s$ or Popper$_n$, there is no concern for scarcity and thus little economic content. From Popper we deserve an answer to some of the following questions. If it is not scarcity, what is it that determines the logic of the situation facing a scientist? If there is a logic of choice in science separate from scarcity, what are the factors which determine this logic? Furthermore, as an economist one can ask why scarcity should be excluded from a theory of science particularly if it espouses an economic approach? Why exclude scarcity from the logic of the situation of science if utility theory is so important to Popper?[19]

At some levels, the economic approaches of Peirce, Rescher, and Radnitzky provide some clues. They are much more directly economic in nature than Popper's situational determinism. Peirce, Rescher, and Radnitzky do recognize that scarcity is a fundamental factor affecting the growth of scientific knowledge. Furthermore, they make no distinction between an economics of the natural sciences versus an economics of the social sciences. Indeed, the economic approaches of Peirce, Rescher, and Radnitzky are applied to the natural sciences like physics, astronomy, and geography. If the social sciences were inherently and fundamentally different from the natural sciences, then one would expect to discover this in some economic way. Ultimately two different economics of science would be needed. The equations summarizing the choices facing individual scientists like (5), (6), and (7) in some important way would need to be different for the natural and social sciences. No matter how these questions are broached, an answer requires a more direct economic approach to science than is found in Popper's writings. Radnitzky's work is much more economic than anything Popper had in mind.

Radnitzky's economic vision of science is comprehensive and extensive. Radnitzky argues for an economic interpretation of the following: (1) all rational problem-solving in human behavior, (2) a cost-benefit logic of scientific rationality, (3) a cost-benefit logic for selecting facts, (4) a cost-benefit logic for selecting among rival theories, and (5) an economic, cost-benefit reinterpretation of Popper's methodology of science. Furthermore, Peirce and Rescher advocate an economic theory of research project selection. These economic interpretations of science have an obvious appeal to an economist. They imply that the path toward understanding human knowledge must encounter economics. One can hardly be an economist and object to this position. If as an economist one believes that the creation and dissemination of knowledge and information is centrally vital to understanding economic processes, then it seems inconsistent to exclude science from a conception of information-creating economic activity.

CONCLUSIONS

An economics of science requires an economic theory of the normal, legitimate conduct of science. An economic theory of science limited to misconduct would not be much of an economics of science. Following the suggestions of philosophers, a cost-benefit theory of the legitimate activities of science has been proposed. Peirce's utility model of research project selection was reformulated as a cost-benefit model. Then the model was further extended to the selection of facts, theories, and research programs by individual scientists. This demonstrates that an economics of science can address some of the major issues of science considered in recent philosophy of science.

What is so interesting about a cost-benefit approach to science is that analysis of the sort Rescher used to critique Karl Popper's methodology of science has also been used to reinterpret Popper on a much broader scale. Gerard Radnitzky has maintained that Popper's methodology is essentially a cost-benefit logic of science – that Popper's methodology is an economic approach to science. Radnitzky's cost-benefit interpretation of Popper appears to be wholly independent of Rescher's cost-benefit critique of Popper. A cost-benefit interpretation of Popper's methodology raises a question regarding the methodological unity of the sciences. Do the natural and social sciences share the same or possess different methodologies of science? An economic, cost-benefit approach to science provides a new way to raise this concern for the methodological unity of the sciences. Also cost-benefit analysis explicitly recognizes the problem of market failure. If the processes of conventional commercial markets were at work, cost-benefit analysis would be unnecessary. Cost-benefit analysis implies that we are perhaps far removed from the self-corrective forces of the market-place.

6

MARKET FAILURE IN THE MARKETPLACE OF IDEAS

The cases of Karl Popper and the economics profession

Epistemology must seek better to understand the expansions and the contractions, the booms and the slumps, in the generation of knowledge. It must seek to identify what contributes to the growth of knowledge, and what stands in its way. It must seek to understand the principles under-lying the competition of ideas in the marketplace of ideas, and to identify ideas and institutions that do, and that could, contribute to such a competitive market, and those that hinder it . . .

There is little hope of accelerating the advancement of learning and the growth of knowledge until it is more widely acknowledged . . . that individuals working in educational institutions are as self-interested as businessmen, but that the organisational framework in which they operate – the network of incentives, constraints, and sanctions – tends to work against public benefit, and does so just because educational and professional institutions work contrary to market principles.

(Bartley 1990: 93, 100)

MARKET FAILURE IN SCIENCE AND PHILOSOPHY

The creation of an economic theory of science, regardless of how it is received by philosophers and even economists, is itself an event of some importance. Unless an economist follows most other philosophers, historians, and sociologists of science and maintains that economic aspects of science are external to science, an economist can hardly ignore an economic theory of science.[1] An economics of science is now emerging in the many aspects of science that can be understood from an economic point of view. So far the key aspects of an economics of science are: (1) optimizing theories of misconduct, and (2) a cost-benefit theory of the selection of research projects, facts, theories, and research programs. Cost-benefit theory is an economic approach to decision-making outside the domain of the commercial marketplace. Its application to science inherently raises the issue of market failure in the domain of science. Widespread market failure in science raises reservations regarding the competitiveness of science.

Market failure in science is one of the major arguments in the late William Bartley's (1990) *Unfathomed Knowledge, Unmeasured Wealth: On Universities and the Wealth of Nations* (*UKUW*). Also found in *UKUW* are several other themes consistent with an economic cost-benefit interpretation of science. Among them are an economic interpretation of epistemology, an economic critique of universities in retarding the growth of scientific knowledge, and an economic critique of intellectual bias in science and philosophy of science. More specifically, as an example of bias, Bartley asserts that Popper's methodology of science has been neglected by philosophers and philosophy of science. This apparent bias against Popper is explained by Bartley as a consequence of market failure in the marketplace of ideas. Bias can be effective in retarding worthwhile contributions only if the economic and social circumstances in scientific and academic circles permit lesser quality ideas to prevail over better ones. Such bias can be analyzed with a cost-benefit approach to research projects and research programs in science.

The economic reasoning behind Bartley's argument concerning the neglect of Popper's contributions is impeccable. Wherever markets fail, adverse consequences often result. However, Bartley's selection of Popper as a case study of market failure in the marketplace of ideas may be misplaced. It may be that science and universities can be mostly characterized as arenas of market failure in the marketplace of ideas. But it also could be the case that Karl Popper is not the best instance on which to rest the argument. Popper is one of the best-known philosophers of science of our time. Popper seems hardly the figure one would choose as an example of the adverse consequences of market failure in academia. Indeed if market failure is to be expected, then one would expect a handful of figures to dominate the disciplines and subdisciplines of science. In this context, it is possible that the situation is the reverse of what Bartley has described. In the reverse situation, Popper would be the beneficiary rather than the victim of intellectual discrimination in the marketplace of ideas constituting science and studies of science.

After considering the plausibility of Bartley's economic defense of Popper, concern with market failure in science and academia is then directed toward economics. Bartley's economic critique of science invites application to the discipline of economics. Like philosophy, the largest segment of the economics profession practices their trade in academic institutions. If a cost-benefit economics of science leads to criticism of the noncompetitive institutional structure of science, then economics as a discipline cannot be exempted from Bartley's critique. Otherwise, why should Bartley's economics of knowledge be taken seriously if it does not apply to economic science?

BARTLEY'S ECONOMIC CRITIQUE OF SCIENCE AND UNIVERSITIES

William Bartley has presented an economic critique of science and universities in his *UKUW*. In this work, Bartley makes broader claims than I have hitherto made for an economics of science. Bartley asserts that epistemology is a branch of economics and that Karl Popper's work on methodology and philosophy of science has been neglected by professional philosophers and philosophers of science. Apparently, Popper has been enormously influential with scientists and a segment in philosophy of science, but not with philosophers in general. Bartley believes there is a reason for the neglect of Popper. He maintains an economic theory of universities would explain why Popper is a threat to entrenched disciplines in universities. That discipline which has triumphed in explaining universities and science is sociology. Bartley argues that a sociological under-standing of universities and science works to shield professors and researchers from competition. A sociological understanding of science ostensibly is in the self-interest of those who are already entrenched in universities. Apparently their self-interest is the prime force behind the neglect of Popper by sociologists of science and by most philosophers.

Bartley maintains that an important attribute of scientific knowledge is the unknowable nature of its infinite consequences. This is "unfathomable knowledge." When new ideas and hypotheses are created and eventually accepted as scientific theories, the conclusions, implications, and subsequent theories which may result years, decades, and centuries into the future simply cannot be known now. Bartley remarks: "All knowledge is born, and forever dwells, behind a veil that is never shed. After their birth, bodies of knowledge remain forever unfathomed and unfathomable. They remain forever pregnant with consequences that are malleable only within limits. They are autonomous" (Bartley 1990: 32). Unfathomed knowledge is an aspect of evolutionary episte-mology. The outcome of the evolutionary production of knowledge is objective knowledge. Objective knowledge is knowledge which is known by individual subjects and is independent of any particular individual consciousness. Objective knowledge, in Bartley's view, is a manifestation of spontaneous order in the sense in which Hayek uses the term. A spontaneous order is a pattern which emerges from the actions of intelligent human beings, but the order in the pattern was not conceived or designed by any particular individual. Such emergent order is a reflection but not a product of consciousness and intelligence. The best example of a spontaneous order is Hayek's (1948) theory of the market as a competitive process for guiding economic decisions.

The sociology of knowledge is criticized by Bartley as that discipline which most importantly ignores the unfathomable nature of knowledge. Sociology of knowledge aims to explain that all knowledge is a consequence of special interests so that political and social conditions can be explained as a consequence of personal or group interests. Bartley asserts that Marx was an ancestor of the sociology of knowledge. The aim of the sociology of knowledge is to create an awareness of society so that individuals may intervene and change society. What such an approach ignores, in Bartley's view, is that society is a matrix of spontaneous orders, not created by an individual consciousness. No one can foresee the future consequences of any attempts to alter a spontaneous order, because such consequences, viewed *ex ante*, are unfathomable.

In place of a sociology of knowledge, Bartley would like to create an economic epistemology, which he calls "ecology." Ecology would be part of a larger undertaking encompassing economics, epistemology, biology, evolutionary theory, and general systems theory. The task of ecology would be to investigate the conditions of organismic growth. Bartley's remarks on economics and epistemology are surprising:

> The central concern of that branch of philosophy known as epistemology or the theory of knowledge should be the growth of knowledge. This means that the theory of knowledge is a branch of economics.
>
> That this should be so is not surprising. After all the first economist, Adam Smith, was a professor of philosophy; and undergraduate programs in "Philosophy, Politics and Economics" still play a major role in British universities. But *why* should this be so? It is so simply because knowledge is a form of wealth – indeed, perhaps its most valuable form. Economics and epistemology are both concerned with growth and contraction in wealth, and are further connected in that knowledge often, if not always, advances arm in arm with increase in other forms of wealth, and retreats when wealth declines. Knowledge is a primary component of capital – which makes epistemology the economics of knowledge. To investigate how this particular form of wealth is discovered, augmented, transformed, and transmitted is the business of both epistemology and economics [original emphasis].
>
> (Bartley 1990: 89)

In arguing for an economic approach to the creation of knowledge, Bartley (1990: 91, 136 ff.) rejects much of what is now known as neoclassical economics. In particular, econometrics and general equilibrium theory are dismissed for not being concerned with either the growth of knowledge or wealth. By economics Bartley seems to have Hayekian economics and public choice theory in mind.

Bartley conceives of an economics of knowledge as a genuine free market of ideas.[2] The free market implies the right to supply and to receive ideas. Bartley recognizes that this is not an unlimited right, because freedom entails the right to ignore specific ideas by directing one's attention where the individual desires. Again, the economic point needs to be kept in mind that more ideas come our way than we can rationally assimilate. Somehow the opportunity cost of time demands that we restrict and direct our attention. Attention is our most scarce cognitive and epistemic resource according to H. A. Simon (1978).

Beyond the opportunity cost of time, however, Bartley maintains that the marketplace of ideas is limited by entrenched positions. The entrenchment is so deep and pervasive that the free market of ideas ceases to exist:

> I *was taught* as a student that the university is a marketplace of ideas where new ideas are welcome and falsehoods can be challenged without recrimination, where standards of gentlemanly discourse, honour, honesty and courtesy prevail, where one can – indeed, is expected to – think boldly and ambitiously and deeply. The veil of deception woven by these great ideals is so strong (as also in the church) that many students not only learn these things, but actually *experience* life at the university in this way.
>
> I *learnt* as a professor that matters and manners were very different: that reigning doctrines or fashions or ideologies (the words hardly matter) govern research and appointments in many fields, especially in the arts but also in some sciences, and that most of these ideologies have been in power for many decades, stifling much genuine innovation [original emphasis].
>
> (Bartley 1990: xvi)

Like the economy itself, the marketplace of ideas is both creative and destructive. For Bartley knowledge is created and it can be lost. Markets are particularly useful in directing attention to error. The detection of error is the "dismal" function of the marketplace (Bartley 1990: 29). Where the market functions less well, errors are harder to detect. In the context of market failure, the growth of knowledge slows down, stops, or perhaps can even be reversed. For Bartley this is also true of the marketplace of ideas. If the detection of error is hampered by a restricted marketplace of ideas, then science and universities may cease to make progress.

The essence of Bartley's argument seems to be that without a free market, false philosophies dominate social circumstances that are far removed from the error-detecting influence of the marketplace of ideas. Universities are complex and highly sophisticated organizations marked by the absence of a competitive spontaneous order and dominated by false ideologies and scientistic pseudo-scientific disciplines. Of course sociology is castigated as a scientistic discipline, so is much of economics, particularly macroeconomics, and psychology. Bartley broadens his argument and maintains that most creativity occurs outside the university. Literature and music are added to the list of human activities that are stifled by the university setting.

Bartley's criticism of universities extends to the sociologically oriented work of Thomas Kuhn. Bartley focuses on an inconsistency which he sees in attitudes held by many academicians. Thomas Kuhn's (1970) *The Structure of Scientific Revolutions* is one of the most cited works of the past several decades. Kuhn portrays science as progressing without any important role for the free market. Yet many in the academic community conceive of the intellectual environment as a free market of ideas. Bartley sees the emphasis on paradigms and research programs coming from Kuhn and the sociology of knowledge as incompatible with free markets. Bartley believes that this inconsistency effectively defends universities and the disciplines they house from criticism that ultimately leads to stagnation:

> Kuhn's sociology of knowledge is incompatible with a free market of ideas. . . . Analogies have often been drawn between a free market in ideas and free markets in goods and services. Yet intellectuals tend to dislike such comparisons. They see the free market in ideas as something on a higher plane, qualitatively different from free markets in commodities and the like. Many of them indeed even hate the marketplace as traditionally conceived, and would want nothing to do, even analogically, with a free market in coal, housing, fish, or petroleum . . .
>
> Many people praise Kuhn not only for having realistically described life in the various scientific disciplines, *but also for having appreciated that it could not be otherwise.*
>
> What sort of report does Kuhn give? Is it of a marketplace of ideas? Hardly. Kuhn reports milieu in which nothing resembling a market operates, and he ignores economic explanations almost entirely. Kuhn might have investigated institutions of learning from an economic rather than a sociological point of view, but he did not. Both Kuhn and Wittgenstein . . . have created philosophies which justify and rationalise entrenchment and reduce competition.
>
> Our universities are in the midst of an intellectual slump: they are, in terms of the generation of new knowledge, in a depression [original emphasis].
>
> (Bartley 1990: 96, 104, 120)

While Kuhn has triumphed in the university setting, Popper supposedly has been given a quite different reception. Although Bartley has been a critic of Popper's and at times parted company with him, he regards Popper as one of the most creative philosophers of the century. Yet according to Bartley, Popper and his contributions have not been accepted by the philosophy profession. Apparently, academic philosophy in the university setting has stagnated and does not recognize that Popper has offered solutions for some of its most funda- mental problems. Summarizing the response of the philosophical community, Bartley writes:

> Many will not mention or cite him, yet scrupulously cite two of his students who publicly disagreed with him on minor points: Lakatos and Feyerabend. It is a way of dealing with some of the issues without mentioning the hated name of Popper. One can make a career as an opponent of Popper's ideas, but not as a proponent of them. He is "fair game": one may say anything about him – and steal any of his ideas, or those of his followers – with impunity.
>
> (Bartley 1990: 193)

Thus Bartley sees Popper and the apparent lack of acceptance of his brilliant contributions as an example of all that is wrong with philosophy and the sociology of knowledge. His prescription is an economic epistemology of unfathomed knowledge, spontaneous order, and a free marketplace of ideas.[3] An implication seems to be that an economic epistemology, if accepted by those on university campuses, would facilitate the acceptance of Popper as an important figure in twentieth-century thought and would lead to an antagonistic reappraisal of Kuhn's work on the sociology of scientific revolutions.

MARKET FAILURE IN THE MARKETPLACE OF IDEAS AND PHILOSOPHY OF SCIENCE: THE CASE OF KARL POPPER

Bartley's contributions to philosophy of science present an opportunity to reconsider the scope of competition in science. His economics of knowledge is as explicitly and directly economic as the economic approaches of Radnitzky, Polanyi, and Hayek, but not those of Peirce and Rescher. With regard to competition, Bartley merges the metaphorical notion of a marketplace of ideas with Hayek's notion of economic competition as a spontaneous order. At its best, science would be highly competitive in a self-corrective sense. He also recognizes that the production of knowledge is a form of capital formation. Essentially Bartley implies that knowledge or "scientific capital" must be created before specific technologies are embodied within capital goods. Knowledge is a more fundamental form of capital than the capital stock. I believe this is an important expansion of the idea of capital and shows that the production of knowledge lies behind the production processes of the economy.

Bartley's criticism of science and universities is quite similar in some respects to the perspective which emerges from the cost-benefit approach to science suggested by Rescher and Radnitzky and more fully developed in the cost-benefit model of Chapter 5. The pervasive insight of the cost-benefit approach to science is market failure and the remoteness of science from the marketplace. Cost-benefit analysis would not be necessary if the market were universally a successful organizer of economic activity. But government and science are far removed from the marketplace. Cost-benefit analysis is an attempt to re-formulate market-oriented decision criteria so they can be applied to decisions outside of the domain of the market. In many respects, cost-benefit analysis is an example of the substitutes argumentative structure of mainstream economics extended to science. Bartley makes the same point as Rescher and Radnitzky and the cost-benefit model – that universities are far removed from the marketplace and as a consequence market failure is pervasive in the academic scientific research establishment. Bartley's emphasis on knowledge as a form of capital is also consistent with the investment outlook of cost-benefit theory. His economic approach to knowledge recognizes the inherent limitations of the market. In addition, Bartley reformulates the idea of market failure so that it applies to the marketplace of ideas. There is market failure in the free marketplace of ideas. In Bartley's view, this is lamentable. He believes that it is possible to correct some of the failure with institutional changes designed to increase the competitiveness of science. Bartley argues for a return to a competitive marketplace of ideas.

Because there is market failure in the marketplace of ideas, Bartley sees two specific consequences.[4] First he believes that universities are no longer creative places for research and development. Bartley maintains that there is more creativity in producing knowledge outside of the university where the marketplace of ideas is closer to the real market. Second, there is another form of market failure with the growth of knowledge process in an academic setting. An effective bias against better ideas is essentially a form of market failure in the marketplace of ideas. Specifically, for Bartley the neglect of Popper by professional philosophers is an instance of market failure in philosophy. Bartley (1990: 165) believes that Popper is one of the most creative philosophers of the twentieth century. Philosophy is mostly done in universities, and unlike research and development, is difficult to move to nonuniversity settings that are closer to the marketplace. If Popper has made contributions as significant as Bartley believes, then imperfections in the intellectual marketplace are an appropriate economic explanation of his neglect by his professional peers.

The argument is elaborately embellished by Bartley. Brief quotations provide a summary of the content and texture of his economic critique of professional philosophy:

> In consequence of his *de facto* exclusion from the philosophical profession, Popper and his followers are not true participants in the contemporary professional dialogue woven by these two schools (positivism and Wittgensteinian philosophy). Rather, he has ruined the dialog, and this is deeply resented. To point out that he is not recognized is not to say that he has been unheeded. If he is on the right track, then the majority of professional philosophers the world over have wasted or are wasting their careers. And they know it.
>
> (Bartley 1990: 196)

> Those who inhabit the world of ideas face an ecological crisis – a crisis whose resolution demands a confrontation with and a rethinking of the entire question of community. Separated as it is from the wider culture by its own professional organisation, the "intellectual community" threatens to dissolve, and indeed has for the most part dissolved, into a loosely federated band of guilds (which act like interest groups or lobbies, but are more feudal in their organisation and in the sensibility of their members) of "disciplinary" craftsmen – *federated* less by a common tradition or shared values as by the need to exert concerted pressure to gain financial support [original emphasis].
>
> (Bartley 1990: 201)

103

There is simply not one market of ideas, there are many markets of ideas. Even in commerce, it is not always easy to determine just what is the market in which particular products compete. The irony here is that Popper's thought is excluded from a market or econoniche in which it first developed and which it could transform: namely professional philosophy.

(Bartley 1990: 201)

At another point, Bartley reports a remark that Popper made to him which supports his critical view of professional philosophy: "Here I am being showered with honours as no professional philosophers before me; yet three generations of professional philosophers know nothing about my work" (Popper as told by Bartley 1990: 200).

An economic reformulation of Popper being neglected can be fashioned from the cost-benefit approach of an economics of science. In the context of market imperfections and failure, philosophers can be viewed as economic agents. Each philosopher must estimate the opportunity costs and benefits of specific intellectual commitments on the basis of incomplete information. A philosopher considering whether to write about Popper would estimate the costs and benefits of including an explicit Popperian dimension in his next project. This decision could be modeled using equations (1) and (2) from Chapter 5 and explicitly formulated as the following decision criterion:

$$NPV_{-KP} > NPV_{KP} \qquad (1)$$

Equation (1) means that a philosophical research project excluding Popper's ideas (project $-KP$) has a greater present value than one including his contributions (project KP). A philosopher whose decisions could be approximated with equation (1) would choose a research project which ignores Popper's contributions to philosophy of science. The result from equation (1) for individual research projects can be generalized to the research program level. If individual projects of a non-Popperian research program are valued less than Popperian ones, then this result will likely hold at the research program level. As in the previous chapter, if we represent the summed present value of the projects as the present value of the research program, then the corresponding result at the research program level would be as follows:

$$V_{RP\ -KP} > V_{RP\ KP} \qquad (2)$$

The preceding quotation of Bartley implying that many philosophers are wasting their careers if Popper is right would be the reverse of the inequalities of equations (1) and (2).

Further explanation of the decision to neglect Popper would concern the nature of the information on which the present value comparison is based. The individualized decision envisioned in the cost-benefit model and equations is impossible to implement with complete and accurate information. Such information is unfathomable to use Bartley's caricature. Additional information must come from the community of science. The judgements of peers may substitute for information that might be too costly to obtain or justify in any other way. Dependence on the judgement of others because of the cost and complexity of providing reasonable substitutes means that certain influential points of view may dominate a discipline. Because of cost considerations and the judgmental, peer-based substitutes for information, it is likely that the decisions made by individual philosophers will cluster around one or a small number of dominant positions or research programs. If the inclusion of Popper reduces the value of the philosopher's next paper or book below the next best alternative because of peer-based influences, then the Popperian project would be avoided.

Again it needs to be emphasized that it is costly for an individual researcher to provide his/her own estimates of all the costs and benefits of a Popperian research project. An individual must rely on collegially generated judgmental substitutes to fill in the informational gaps. Given the near impossibility of complete information, this is the economic thing to do. The market cannot work in the marketplace of ideas because the corrective information necessary for revising individual decisions in the direction of a hypothetical free market simply does not exist. But it may also mean that the research of certain individuals can be unfairly criticized as being unworthy for considerable periods of time.

These considerations lead to a view of science which parallels oligopoly theory to some extent. Science has had long periods of dominance by a reigning paradigm or research program, punctuated by periods of revolutionary change when another paradigm or research program becomes dominant. Science is pluralistic. All of the paradigms or research programs could have existed before a scientific revolution and they could exist after a revolution. But what matters is that the "industry leader" has changed. This change can be understood using cost-benefit logic. As the economic fundamentals of science change so that one program becomes more costly to defend than another, rational scientists change their minds and their commitments. Consequently, research programs and perhaps paradigms rise and fall. Organizational innovations or regulatory interventions by government to alter this process may not be readily apparent or perhaps even desirable. Corrective adjustments in the marketplace of ideas where significant market failure occurs may take decades or centuries.

A CRITIQUE OF BARTLEY'S DEFENSE OF POPPER

In theoretical terms, Bartley may be headed in the right direction with his analysis of market failure in the marketplace of ideas. However, Bartley's economic defense of Popper as a victim of bias exercised in the context of market failure needs to be reappraised. From an analytical point of view, a more complete statement of bias would recognize that some theories and their proponents are given too much attention in science and academia while other

105

theories and theorists are given too little notice. For Bartley to assert that Popper has been given too little attention means that the opposite argument also needs to be appraised. In order to accept Bartley's defense of Popper, we must first look at the opposite hypothesis that a great deal of attention has been devoted to Popper's work. If this alternative hypothesis were accepted, then it would seem that Bartley's defense of Popper would collapse. For either case, too little or too much notice given to Popper, our attention needs to be directed to the consequences of market failure in the marketplace of ideas. The economics is the same in both situations, but the conclusions with regard to Popper's status may differ.

For anyone familiar with philosophy of science, Popper presents an image somewhat contrary to the one drawn by Bartley. Popper has been one of the best known philosophers of science of the past half century or so. In economics, Popper may still be the most widely recognized name from philosophy of science because he is most often associated by the rank and file with the idea of falsification which is found in Friedman's essay on positive economic methodology. Outside of economics in the other social sciences and in philosophy, the name of Popper is widely recognized. Indeed perhaps it is the case that Popper has been the beneficiary rather than the victim of market failure in the marketplace of ideas.

Keeping in mind the problems of market failure in the sciences and those disciplines which specialize in the study of science, the task of observing the relative significance of one person's contributions is considered. One common way of estimating the relative prominence of someone's work is with citations. Citations can be a useful device for approximating the significance of one's publications in influencing the ideas of others. Of course citation numbers may embody certain problems and some of these problems may be due to the market failure issues already considered. Thus citations could be a biased measure of contributions to the marketplace of ideas. Someone who is cited a great deal may be the beneficiary of market failure in science and philosophy, while others whose contributions deserve more frequent citation suffer in relative obscurity. Another possible bias may be that citations capture a short- rather than a long-term impact of an individual's contributions to a discipline or subdiscipline. The sixteen-year time span for the four years used below may not adequately capture the long-run importance of certain contributions to science or philosophy. A third possible bias is that citations may either be favorable or unfavorable. A citation may either accept a previous contribution and build on it or critically reject or reconstruct an earlier contribution. Also it is quite possible that the sciences mostly build on previous work while philosophy and its subdisciplines are more critical in nature. From Chapter 2, it appeared that most scientific research is not repeated or received in a critical or hostile manner because scientists seemed to be biased in favor of finding the next innovative discovery. This was an aspect of the problem of replication failure. Perhaps science and philosophy of science are fundamentally different in this regard.

Keeping these difficulties with citations in mind, some evidence on these matters can be found in the *Social Sciences Citations Index* (*SSCI*). This index not only records references in the social sciences and economics, it also includes scholarly journals for the discipline of philosophy. Rather than spending a great deal of time counting references over many years, what is needed is a rough estimate of the relative magnitude of citations to Popper's work. Such an estimate would help us either appraise Bartley's claim that Popper's meritorious contributions have been unduly neglected or establish its opposite that Popper is quite well known. The approximate number of citations to Popper can be compared with those of a few other philosophers and some noted economists. For the economists, Chicago Nobel prize winners such as Stigler, Friedman, Becker, and Ronald Coase may provide a frame of reference. For philosophy, philosophy of science, and sociology, Kuhn, Wittgenstein, R. K. Merton, Bartley, Kant, Rorty, Foucault, Dewey, Feyerabend, and Lakatos were chosen. Freud and Marx were also put on the list because of their long-term influence on philosophy, economics, and the other social sciences and because of Popper's strong opposition to their most important ideas. Again economics typically emphasizes relative rather than absolute valuation, so here the interest is how citations to Popper's work compare to those of other well-known figures.

In order to appraise Bartley's claim that Popper's contributions have been rejected not on the basis of intrinsic merit, but rather because of a contrary exercise of market power in a flawed marketplace of ideas, a rough estimate of Popper's influence on the marketplace of ideas was used. Since Popper is so well known, it does seem strange to hear the claim that he is not cited frequently or that Lakatos and Feyerabend are often cited instead. As a rough estimate of the number of citations, the amount of column space in the *SSCI* was measured for each of the individuals mentioned in the previous paragraph for the years 1979, 1984, 1989, and 1994. The aim was not to provide a database for formal scientific inference on these issues. Rather, the purpose was to gather enough descriptive evidence to evaluate Bartley's claims about the neglect of Popper. The data as collected by the author can be found in Table 6.1.[5] For each of the years surveyed, several columns of citations to Popper's work is found. If there are three or four citations per centimeter of column length, then there were hundreds of citations to Popper for each of the years cited.

With regard to each of the years surveyed, some specific comparisons are possible. In 1979, Popper trailed only Freud, Marx, and Milton Friedman in the amount of space devoted to cataloging citations. Also in that same year, Popper's citations exceeded those of Kuhn, Merton, and Dewey by a small margin. A similar pattern seems to emerge for 1984 where the relative rankings of citation space do not appear to have changed in any qualitative way from 1979. However, in 1989, there is one major change to note. In that year, space given to Michael Foulcalt's citations exceeds the space devoted to Popper. By 1994, other qualitative changes appear. In 1994, citation space devoted to Popper appears to have dropped by 20 to 25 per cent and citation space

Table 6.1 Citation space devoted to well-known figures in the history of Western thought for the years 1979, 1984, 1989, and 1994

Name	1979	1984	1989	1994
Philosophers				
Bartley	3.0	2.0	3.0	2.0
Dewey	77.5	66.0	73.0	72.0
Feyerabend	26.5	27.0	21.0	10.5
Foucault	51.5	62.0	124.0	149.5
Freud	447.0	358.5	531.0	497.5
Kant	59.0	66.5	59.0	69.5
Kuhn	95.5	82.5	85.5	75.5
Lakatos	29.0	25.5	23.0	18.0
Merton	102.5	78.0	82.0	59.0
Popper	105.0	108.0	87.0	67.0
Rorty	4.0	13.0	34.5	85.0
Wittgenstein	52.0	38.0	53.5	52.0
Economists				
Becker	67.5	77.5	N.A.	20.0
Coase	26.0	31.5	45.0	52.5
Friedman	126.0	132.0	119.0	110.5
Keynes	61.5	82.0	61.0	65.0
Marx	319.5	329.0	259.5	111.5
Stigler	68.0	86.5	77.0	69.5

Note: Citation space as measured in centimeters in the *Social Sciences Citations Index* for the years indicated. On average a centimeter represents three or four citations. Data collected by the author.

given to Rorty and Dewey surpasses what had been given to Popper. However, citation space for Popper still continues at a high level even if it is somewhat diminished.

With regard to all of the years surveyed, some general observations may be in order. With regard to the economists, Popper has done quite well with citations except in comparison to Friedman and he does not trail Friedman by much. For each of the four years surveyed, citation space devoted to Popper exceeds that of the other Nobel prize winning economists such as Stigler, Becker, and Coase. Popper also exceeds reference space given to John Maynard Keynes who is often recognized as the most influential economist of the past century. This is quite an achievement when it is recognized that there are many more economics than philosophy journals. With regard to the philosophers, Popper's citations exceed those of Lakatos and Feyerabend by a factor of four or five to one. Furthermore, Bartley identifies Ludwig Wittgenstein as a chief philosophical rival of Popper. Ironically, Popper's citations take up a great deal more space in every year surveyed than what was given to Wittgenstein.

The preceding descriptive evidence suggests that Popper has fared well in the marketplace of ideas even if there are inherent problems in citation data. For much of his career, Popper appears to have been one of the most cited of living philosophers and perhaps one of the most cited figures of all time. One could make a case that Friedman, Freud, and Marx are not philosophers and have influenced thinking and theorizing in academic disciplines many times larger and with many more journals than all of philosophy, philosophy of science, and the other subdisciplines specializing in the study of science combined. Relative to the number of persons in relevant disciplines and subdisciplines who might potentially be influenced, it could be argued that the proportionate impact of Popper is greater than that of Friedman, Freud, and Marx. Such a strong conclusion would counter Bartley's claim that Popper has not fared well in the marketplace of ideas. But the stronger claim would take a much more sophisticated parsing of the relevant evidence than what could be attempted here.

There is one aspect of Popper's claims which might have a degree of validity. Popper's claim as reported to Bartley, is not that he is not well known or well cited, but rather that professional philosophers do not recognize his work sufficiently. Again, the aim here has been to refute Bartley's broader claim that Popper is not well cited in the marketplace of ideas. It may be the case that citations to Popper's ideas are disproportionately found in philosophy of science, the social sciences, and in the subdisciplines specializing in the study of science rather than in philosophy. Thus Popper's point about the distribution of citations may show some prejudice from philosophy in general. Again, the issues were not explored with formal purposes of statistical inference in mind, but the distribution of citations for others such as Kuhn, Lakatos, and Feyerabend did not appear to be a whole lot different than Popper's. In this regard, it may be that Popper has been more favorably treated in relative terms by the professional philosophers and their journals than someone like Kuhn or some of the others.

The preceding considerations suggest a review of equations (1) and (2) which provided a cost-benefit interpretation of Bartley's view of the neglect of Popper. Equation (1) portrays Bartley's claims about Popperian research projects being less valued than others and equation (2) generalizes Bartley's view to the level of a research program. If Bartley's view is correct, as a research program of interrelated if not chain connected research projects, the Popperian research program appears to be valued less than its rivals. However, the pattern of citations noted previously with Popper faring quite well in relation to others, may or may not cause us to rethink the inequalities in the preceding equations. It depends on the nature and quality of the citations to Popper's work. If the large amount of citation space given to Popper is an indication of the positive regard of his work and Bartley is wrong, then the inequalities in equations (1) and (2) would need to be reversed. Popperian research projects and a Popperian research program would be highly valued. However, if most of the citations reference Popper's work in a negative, critical way, then there would be no need to reverse the inequalities. Thus it is possible that Popper's work is well cited, but not widely accepted. Popper's may be cited as an interesting alternative which is not pursued or followed further.

From an economics of science point of view, it appears that Bartley has the economic analysis correct. Market failure in the marketplace of ideas could bias citations so that some are overcited and others are undercited given the inherent merit of their contributions. However, with regard to Popper, Bartley seems to have gotten it backwards, If anything, Popper appears to be over rather than undercited. Thus an economic appraisal of Bartley's *UKUW* is somewhat mixed. The economic analysis appears to be plausible, but the application to the case of Karl Popper does not seem supportable empirically and raises many questions and objections.

MARKET FAILURE AND THE ECONOMICS PROFESSION: THE CASE OF FREE MARKET ECONOMICS

Bartley's economic approach to knowledge has implications for the discipline of economics. This is the issue of self-reference again. If there is market failure in the marketplace of ideas in science and in universities, then one can ask if such market failure affects economics. If market failure is so severe in university philosophy and sociology that intellectual concentration is likely and citations patterns can be seriously distorted, then is it not possible that such imperfections are present in all disciplines including economics?[6] An economics of science cannot exempt economics from such an inquiry. If an economic approach to knowledge points to the imperfections of the growth of knowledge process in general, then economic science might suffer similar internal imperfections. Other disciplines may suffer the same fate.

Because of market imperfections in science and the marketplace of ideas, one would expect that there would be one or a few dominant positions in economics. Sciences are complex and their futures are unfathomable. Information is costly to obtain so the best available substitutes need to be found. The professional commitments that economists must make will be based on incomplete, asymmetrical, impacted information, and judgmental substitutes for information. Under these conditions, it is possible that something like a paradox is encountered. The commitment to a market-oriented conception of economics could be the consequence of market failure within the economics profession. If there really is no free market in the world of ideas as Bartley suggests, then the success of free market economics in the economy may not be justifiable by its success in the intellectual domain of ideas among professional economists. The free market of ideas can serve as a justification of free market economics only if economic science itself is free of significant market imperfections.

As with the discipline of philosophy and the case of Popper, the effect of market imperfections in the marketplace of ideas in economics could be formulated with an individualistic decision-making criterion. In cost-benefit terms, the decision could be represented as follows:

$$NPV_{FME} > NPV_{-FME} \qquad (3)$$

Equation (3) means that because of market imperfections in economic science, research projects emphasizing the free market economic (*FME*) position would be valued more highly than those which recognize market imperfections (*-FME*). The relative success of rival positions would be a factor in the subjective cost-benefit valuations of potential research projects by its individual adherents. Generalized from the level of individual research projects to research programs, the corresponding result would be:

$$V_{RP\ FME} > V_{RP\ -FME} \qquad (4)$$

If this valuation were the consequence of market imperfections in science, then it would be economically rational to commit oneself to a research program that minimizes an awareness of market imperfections. Consequently, free market economics could dominate in economic science because it is the beneficiary of market imperfections within the economics profession. Free market economics has been particularly effective in competing for resources for its practitioners. Rivals do exist such as Institutional, Keynesian, Post-Keynesian, Monetarist, Austrian, and Marxian economics. But they have been less successful in garnering the same level of support exhibited by mainstream neoclassical economics. Because of the economic dominance of free market economics in an imperfect marketplace of ideas, research projects in free market economics may have a higher net present value than projects contemplated in a rival program, regardless of their intellectual merits.

As a case in point consider Keynes and Keynesian economics. It can be argued that Keynes and Keynesian economics in recent decades have been neglected as a consequence of dominance of neoclassical economics which pays little attention to the problem of systemic market imperfections. Keynes and Keynesian economics imply that market failure and imperfections in the economy are of fundamental importance in understanding capitalism. At the theoretical level, Walrasian equilibrium economics emphasizing the perfect functioning of competitive auction markets has reigned supreme in much of the mainstream economic literature. Thus Keynes and Keynesian economics may themselves be victims of market failure and imperfections in the marketplace of ideas that give dominant reign to free market economics.[7] My personal judgement is that Institutional economics has been rejected to a greater extent than Keynesian economics and Monetarism to a lesser extent. Market imperfections within economic science have allowed resources to flow to research projects and programs asserting the efficiency of the marketplace.

Another case of apparent failure in the marketplace of ideas in economics is understanding the Great Depression. In the interpretation of economic history, the Keynesian and to a lesser extent the Monetarist interpretations of the Great Depression have been accepted less well than the New Classical view. From a Keynesian view, the Great Depression may be that historical episode which best epitomizes the breakdown of the economy conceived as a competitive market process. The Great Depression is an example of general, systemic market failure.

Monetarists locate the blame for the Depression with government and the Federal Reserve rather than the failure of markets in the private sector. An economics-of-knowledge point of view suggests a merging of the Keynesian and Monetarist perspectives. Before the Depression, monetary and financial processes facilitated the production of and substitutes for economic knowledge. Furthermore, financial markets and institutions provided substitutes for unfathomable information which would otherwise be infinitely costly to obtain. During the Great Depression, the collapse of the banking system and financial markets, regardless of the cause, destroyed some of the better substitutes for unfathomable economic information. Speculation in financial markets was a market imperfection that subverted and degraded the epistemic processes of financial markets. From an economics of knowledge point of view, the Great Depression represented the fundamental breakdown and destruction of knowledge producing processes and their substitutes in the economy.

The alternative view of the Great Depression denies the failure of markets and competition and minimizes the significance of the failure of Federal Reserve policy.[8] It has become increasingly dominant. The most extreme position is that of the New Classicals. In their view, the Great Depression represents an unusual example of corrective equilibrium forces at work rather than market failure. The economy is viewed as being on an oscillating equilibrium path so that business cycles, even recessions, are viewed as part of an equilibrating adjustment process of the economy. The Great Depression was nothing more than an extreme form of equilibrium adjustment that is observed once or twice a century. Versions of the Great Depression as an equilibrium process are now widely accepted in the profession, although there is no unanimity on the subject.

While I have indicated my individual bias and view regarding the consequence of market failure within the economics profession, I believe the issues transcend any particular conception or ideological position at any particular time in history. Using rhetoric from oligopoly theory, some day the dominant paradigm or research program in economics will be something other than Walrasian neoclassical microeconomics and the New Classical macroeconomics. There will be another dominant position with lesser rivals attempting to replace it. But the fundamental intellectual issues raised by an economic theory of science focusing on market imperfections in the marketplace of ideas will still remain. How are resources essential for creating a critical alternative to a dominant position in science obtained? Since there may be too much emphasis on conforming to an existing dominant position in science or philosophy, the resource question is a significant issue. A criticism cannot have the opportunity to succeed if there are no resources devoted to it. Organized rival research programs or schools of thought might provide the material resources essential for real criticism. Perhaps this is why some form of pluralism may be healthy for science. Otherwise the exercise of dissent would be denied the vital resources necessary for focusing on the errors of a rival research program.

It is logically possible that free market economics is true for the economy and for the free marketplace of ideas. It is also logically possible that free market economics is false both in the economy and in the marketplace of ideas. A third possibility is that one may be true while the other is false. But such a distinction creates a dichotomy between science and the economy which we have tried to break down in this essay. Intellectual capital is required for constructing the economy. Ideas are necessary for producing and acquiring tangible goods and resources and for creating intangible organizations, attributes, and values of ordinary economic affairs. Science helps us create intellectual capital for the economy. Philosophy of science helps us create intellectual capital for science. The creation of all capital seems to be an economic process fraught with imperfections, especially the growth of knowledge in science and in economic science. Science is an economic phenomenon. Scarcity affects science. Science is far removed from the ideal of competition found in economics texts. Perhaps the texts need to be revised to incorporate an economics of science.

CONCLUSIONS

William Bartley has argued that market failure persists in the marketplace of ideas for science and philosophy. Bartley further maintains that scientists and academics are driven by self-interest, and he argues for an economic ecology of knowledge. The pervasiveness of market failure in the marketplace of ideas means that intellectual, cultural, and sociological biases may determine decision-making in science, philosophy, and academia rather than truth. In Bartley's view, merit is often sacrificed because of the errors due to market failure in the marketplace of ideas. The case Bartley chose as an example of bias prevailing over merit is the supposed neglect of Karl Popper's work. However, Popper ranks among some of the more highly cited figures of the past few decades. Only if citations were almost exclusively negative and critical would Bartley's portrayal of the neglect of Popper have an element of truth to it. On the whole, Popper appears to be the beneficiary of market failure in the marketplace of ideas with his work being over rather than undercited.

While Bartley's economic analysis of market failure in the scientific, philosophical, and academic marketplace of ideas seems largely correct even if his case in point is not, there are other disciplines which might exhibit market failure. After considering the case of Popper, attention was directed to the case of free market economics in the economics profession. The thesis that free markets enhance social welfare better than other alternatives has dominated economics for decades if not centuries. The dominance of such a position could be a consequence of market failure within the discipline of economic science. It may be that market failure within the economics profession has created a relative reward structure which encourages novice economists to pursue research in support of free markets. Thus the preeminence of free market economics may be the result of market failure in the marketplace of ideas which constitutes the

7

MARKET FAILURE IN THE MARKETPLACE OF IDEAS
The case of Friedman's essay

Friedman's essay "The Methodology of Positive Economics" has been the source of much debate amongst economists since it appeared in 1953. It would not be claiming too much to say that it is the most cited, if not actually read, work on economic methodology.

(Pheby 1988: 84)

So famous is Friedman's thesis that it has even become the subject of widely disseminated jokes. O'Brien . . . says that students at Belfast University told him the following story (I heard the same story told at a party of economists in Bangkok four years earlier): "An economist, an engineer and a chemist were stranded together on a desert island with a large tin of ham but no tin-opener. After various unsuccessful exercises in applied science by the engineer and the chemist aimed at opening the tin, they turned in irritation to the economist who all the while had been wearing a superior smile. 'What would you do?', they asked. 'Let us assume we have a tin-opener', came the unruffled reply."

(Blaug 1980: 103, n. 24)

MARKET FAILURE IN ECONOMIC METHODOLOGY

In Western thought the notion has existed that competition in the market-place of ideas enhances truth and discourages falsehood and error. As Bartley has noted, many intellectuals and scientists have maintained such a position. However, it is quite possible that imperfections exist in such a competitive marketplace of ideas. Some theories and ideas may get emphasized too much and others too little. The episodes of Popper in philosophy and the dominance of free market economics in economics are cases in point. They appear to be unfairly advantaged in an uncompetitive marketplace of ideas which surrounds science. Furthermore, other imperfections in science such as misconduct in science were the subject of Chapters 2 and 3. The implicit incentives within science, which mostly encourage innovation, may also lead to replication failure and a small number of deviant scientists may intentionally deceive their peers thus committing fraud. Inefficiencies, such as misconduct and market failure in science may lead to a thoroughly revised vision of the nature of science compared to the contributions of other approaches to science.

Besides the cases of Popper and the dominance of free market economics, there may be another significant case of possible market failure in the marketplace of ideas. It is another example illustrating the degree of competitiveness of ideas within the discipline of economics. Consider Milton Friedman's essay on scientific method in economics. For half a century, virtually all economists, if they have read anything in economic methodology have read Friedman's "Methodology of Positive Economics." What is truly astonishing is that Friedman's essay was authored prior to many major changes in philosophy of science, yet it has managed to survive unprecedented innovations in conceptions of science outside of the economics profession. It has been interpreted and reinterpreted as much as any one piece in all of economics. Friedman's essay has a record of survival that is unmatched by any other piece of literature in economics. The persistent dominance of the essay suggests the possibility of some sort of market failure in the marketplace of ideas in economics. An account of the dominance of Friedman's essay begins with a summary of the essay. Then the interpretations of the essay are related to recent innovations in philosophy of science. Following this, the dominance of Friedman's essay is restated in terms of an economics of science. Perhaps an economic, cost-benefit explanation can be given for the dominance of Friedman's essay in economic methodology.

FRIEDMAN'S ESSAY

Milton Friedman's essay, "Methodology of Positive Economics," has dominated economics more than any other view of science in the English-speaking world. This dominance has been noted by two well-published economic methodologists, Mark Blaug and Bruce Caldwell. Blaug (1976: 149) has stated that Friedman's essay is "the one article on methodology that virtually every economist has read at some stage of his career." And Caldwell has remarked that:

> Milton Friedman's "The Methodology of Positive Economics," ... is probably the best known piece of methodological writing in economics. It is also a marketing masterpiece. Never before has one short article on methodology been able to generate so much controversy. It has been reviewed often, usually negatively. Yet ironically, the methodological prescriptions advanced in his essay have become widely accepted among many working economists. And this has happened without Friedman ever having directly responded to his critics!
>
> (Caldwell 1982: 173)

In the essay, Friedman conceives of economics as having two major branches, positive and normative economics. This distinction has a long history in the

116

development of economic thought (Hutchison 1964: 23–50). In the essay, Friedman, quotes J. N. Keynes characterization of positive and normative economics from his *The Scope and Method of Political Economy*:

> As the terms are here used, a *positive science* may be defined as a body of systematized knowledge concerning what is; a *normative* or *regulative science* as a body of systematized knowledge relating to criteria of what ought to be, and concerned therefore with the ideal as distinguished from the actual; an *art* as a system of rules for the attainment of a given end. The object of a positive science is the establishment of *uniformities*, of a normative science the determination of *ideals*, of an art the formulation of *precepts* [original emphasis].
>
> (Keynes [1917] 1963: 34–5)

Following Friedman and Keynes, positive economic science is the domain of objective economic science. Predictions about the consequences of any change in economic circumstances relate to positive economics. Normative economics concerns policy judgements based on value judgements. Presumably, it is positive economics which most concerns Friedman.

For Friedman, a major aim of positive economic science is the development of theories that can be tested against the evidence. A theory is composed of two elements: one is a deductive, linguistic component and the other is an inductive, generalizing or abstracting component. When viewed as a language, theories are logical filing devices and must be consistent and coherent. When viewed as inductive generalizations, theories are abstractions based on prior knowledge of the data. Theories and hypotheses must arise out of the data "to assure that a hypothesis explains what it set out to explain" (Friedman 1953: 12). Furthermore, the same data potentially may be used as a basis for an inductive generalization and as a test of this generalization: "The facts that serve as a test of the implication of a hypothesis might equally well have been among the raw material used to construct it, and conversely" (Friedman 1953: 13).

In the essay, Friedman asserts that economic theories need to be tested against appropriate evidence. One sort of test is the predictions of the theory: "A theory is to be judged by its predictive power for the class of phenomena which it is intended to 'explain'" (Friedman 1953: 8). A few sentences later, Friedman turns the discussion of evidence and prediction to ideas that sound a lot like falsification. This is where Friedman's essay sounds most like Popper. But there are no references to any of the relevant philosophical literature of the period on falsification. With regard to the discovery of countermanding evidence Friedman asserts that:

> The hypothesis is rejected if its predictions are contradicted. . . . it is accepted if its predictions are not contradicted; great confidence is attached to it if it has survived many opportunities for contradiction. Factual evidence can never "prove" a hypothesis; it can only fail to disprove

it, which is what we generally mean when we say, somewhat inexactly, that the hypothesis has been "confirmed" by experience.

(Friedman 1953: 9)

Friedman then proceeds to develop one of his most controversial positions. He maintains that really significant theories are unrealistic because of the view of abstract, inductive generalizations. Such abstract generalizations might even seem descriptively false. Friedman maintains that:

> Truly important and significant hypotheses will be found to have 'assumptions' that are wildly inaccurate descriptive representations of reality, and in general, the more significant the theory, the more unrealistic the assumptions. . . . To be important, therefore, a hypothesis must be descriptively false in its assumptions.

(Friedman 1953: 14)

What Friedman wishes to refute is the widely held notion that the validity of a theory can be determined by the realism of its assumptions. He distinguishes between the specification of assumptions as part of the analytical aspect of a theory and the actual empirical determination of the circumstances for which a theory is valid. The experimental circumstances under which a theory may result in valid predictions cannot be analytically specified as part of the theory.

What Friedman is really after with the preceding considerations is a defense of economic rationality as a competitive, maximizing process. Since most transactors do not self-consciously maximize, one of the most fundamental assumptions of economic theory seems blatantly unrealistic. Friedman is suggesting that economic theory should not be considered unrealistic, just because the assumption of rationality is intuitively unrealistic. He defends this contention by considering (in his view) a similar hypothesis. The alternative hypothesis is that leaves behave "as if" they seek to maximize the amount of sunlight they receive. This hypothesis is acceptable even though we usually think of leaves and plants as unconscious, having no internal sense of deliberation. Scientists do not reject this maximizing theory in the case of leaves merely because it seems unrealistic. Similarly, prediction or the failure to falsify becomes the only relevant concern for testing the realism of economic theories based on maximization in positive economics.

This concern for not interpreting rationality as an attribute of the internal state of mind of the transactor may be the most positivistic aspect of positive economics. Logical positivism, as a philosophy of science, is characterized by an aversion to mentalistic concepts; they are pseudoscientific issues. By maintaining that rationality should not be interpreted realistically and mentalistically, Friedman is very close to the position of the logical positivists. For Friedman, rationality is a counter factual behavioral assumption which is of great instrumental value. It greatly reduces the concepts needed to predict the behavior of leaves, economic transactors, or even billiard players. Again, in Friedman's words:

It seems not at all unreasonable that excellent predictions would be yielded by the hypothesis that the billiard player made his shots as if he knew the complicated mathematical formulas that would give the optimum directions of travel. . . . Our confidence in this hypothesis is not based on the belief that billiard players, even expert ones, can or do go through the process described [original emphasis].

(Friedman 1953: 21)

Other than rationality, Friedman was also defending the theory of economic competition. In the same way that rationality as an optimizing process was being criticized for being unrealistic, the theory of competition was similarly being attacked. Friedman admitted that many circumstances in the economy violated the assumptions of competition. On the basis of the realism of the assumptions, few if any real-world situations would conform to the theory of competition. Rather than literally interpreting the assumptions of the theory, Friedman advocated a weaker criterion. All that was required was that economic activity behave "as if" it were competitive. Then the theory of competition could be tested on the basis of its predictions and not its assumptions. Friedman also took great care to distance his theory of competition from the Walrasian perfect competition which Hayek found so offensive. Friedman repeatedly alluded to Alfred Marshall's theory of competition. Marshall's approach is much more amenable to an evolutionary view of transactor and market behavior than is the Walrasian approach.[1]

INNOVATION IN PHILOSOPHY OF SCIENCE AND FRIEDMAN'S ESSAY

Other than the testimonies of various economists, there is another way to demonstrate the dominance of Friedman's essay in economic methodology. Since Friedman's essay first appeared in 1953, there have been significant, if not revolutionary changes in philosophy of science. Until recently, these innovations have not significantly altered the primacy of Friedman's essay as a methodological essay in economics. The revolution in philosophy of science is one I would associate with the works of Popper, Kuhn, and Lakatos in the 1960s and early 1970s. This is a question of dating the revolution. As far as substantive content, this revolution rejected positivism and more sophisticated, less rigid versions of empiricism that emanated from positivism. Other philosophers preceded, accompanied, and succeeded Popper, Kuhn, and Lakatos in their rejection of positivism and related conceptions of empiricist science. And newer philosophies of science have appeared that are critical of the contributions of Popper, Kuhn, and Lakatos.

One way of characterizing the innovations in philosophy of science is what some philosophers call a shift in a metatheory. Popper, Weimer, Bartley and others have noted the existence of a metatheory. A metatheory exists when many philosophies or conceptual frameworks share some common ways of conceiving of the role of theories in the search for knowledge. Empiricism as a metatheory means that all varieties of empiricism exhibit a common logical and epistemological structure. All variations of empiricism require that knowledge be justified in some way even if the presumption of empirical justification cannot be justified. Weimer has called this a justificationist metatheory of knowledge.[2] This use of justificationism seems quite close to another categorization scheme found in D. N. McCloskey's (1985) *Rhetoric of Economics* called modernism. Following McCloskey's analysis, all of the justificationist varieties of empiricism are modernist. Modernism is the belief that knowledge can have secure foundations and that science is the best example of knowledge with a secure foundation.

By way of contrast, a new metatheory seems to be emerging in recent philosophy of science and in other disciplines concerned with the nature of human knowledge. The search for a secure foundation to knowledge appears to have been abandoned. A nonjustificational metatheory has emerged as a critical approach to epistemology. It is clearly post-modernist in McCloskey's use of that term. It is critical because no uniquely authoritative criterion is offered as the rational criterion or justification of knowledge as is found in all justificationist epistemologies. Although criteria of empirical status may still be used in science, we now know that the nonempirical disciplines of logic and mathematics incorporate unprovable and hence arbitrary assumptions. In other words, a logical model of truth and certainty is itself unprovable and uncertain. Furthermore, nonjustificationist philosophers of science like Kuhn and Lakatos have added additional dimensions to our understanding of scientific activity. No longer is the analysis of science confined to hypothetical statements of fact. Lakatos has extended analysis of science to research programs and Kuhn to paradigms and world views. Since Kuhn and Lakatos, others such as Laudan, Merton, Hull, and Toulmin have continued this trend. The progressiveness of a research program or paradigm cannot be reduced to something so narrow as a single, monolithic authoritative criterion of theory appraisal like verification, falsification, or prediction.

The alternative metatheories of science are summarized in Tables 7.1 and 7.2. These tables need to be read as a rough outline of recent innovation in philosophy of science and economic methodology. They are quite suggestive and many of the entries would need much more qualification than could be given here. An overly simplified outline of intellectual change in philosophy of science is needed in order to show the tremendous variety of interpretations of Friedman's essay. The justificationist, modernist philosophies of science are presented in Table 7.1 and the nonjustificational, post-modern conceptions of science can be found in Table 7.2. Justificationist philosophies of science take the concept of truth and proof from logic and mathematics as a model of how true knowledge is to be obtained. Neojustificationsts differ marginally from justificationists in that they are aware of the problems associated with induction; but believe that

Table 7.1 The justificationist metatheory and philosophies of science as they relate to interpretations of Friedmanian positive economics

Metatheory of science	General epistemological focus	A philosophy of science within the metatheory	Epistemological criterion of philosophy science	Representative philosophers	Economists supporting, criticizing (*) or rejecting (**) positive economics in relation to this view of science
Justificationist	Logical justification of knowledge claims	Classical empiricism	Inductive generalization	J. S. Mill J. N. Keynes	McCloskey * Wible *
		Logical positivism	Verification	Carnap, Russell Schlick, Wittgenstein	Hollis and Nell ** Wilber and Wisman *
		Falsificationism	Falsification	Popper of LSD	Bear and Orr, Blaug *
	Probabilistic justifications of scientific success (neojustificationist)	Confirmationism	Probabilistic confirmation of hypotheses	Hempel, Nagel Carnap, Ayer	Caldwell * Tarascio and Caldwell *
		Conventionalism	Failure to probabilistically reject hypotheses	Duhem R. A. Fisher J. M. Keynes	Rotwein McCloskey *
		Instrumentalism	Prediction	Bridgeman Boring	Boland * Hollis and Nell **

Table 7.2 The nonjustificationist metatheory and philosophies of science as they relate to interpretations of Friedmanian positive economics

Metatheory of science	General epistemological focus	A philosophy of science within the metatheory	Epistemological criterion of philosophy science	Representative philosophers	Economists supporting, criticizing (*) or rejecting (**) positive economics in relation to this view of science
Nonjustificationist	Processive evolutionary growth of knowledge	Critical fallibilism	Growth of knowledge through research programs, demi's, invisible colleges	Popper Lakatos Hull Toulmin	Blaug * Caldwell ** Mason * Backhouse *
		Sociological-psychological fallibilism	Growth of knowledge through puzzle solving and paradigm shifts	Kuhn Polanyi Weimer	Hands ** Coats ** Redman * Pheby **
		Rhetorical fallibilism	Growth of knowledge through discourse, argument, persuasion	Dewey Rorty Prelli	Hirsch and de Marchi * McCloskey ** Klamer * Samuels * Mäki *
		Economic fallibilism	Growth of knowledge altered by economic conditions of science	Peirce Rescher Bartley Radnitzky	Boland *, Mayer * Hands *, Diamond * Wible *, Levy* Mirowski *

some sort of empirical justification is the best route to scientific progress, even if that belief cannot be justified.

These extraordinary innovations in philosophy of science and related disciplines, as portrayed in schematic fashion in Tables 7.1 and 7.2, have drawn the attention of many economists and methodologists. Initially, rather than dealing directly with the philosophical problems, economists focused their concern on Friedman's essay. Each time an innovative position was created in philosophy of science, someone in economics reinterpreted Friedman's essay. Many of the interpretations were favorable. Others were unfavorable. The overall result is that Friedman's essay has been reappraised in light of every innovation in philosophy of science over the past few decades. The specific debates are summarized in the excellent contributions of others and it is not part of my objective to present a new synthesis of these methodological debates in economics or to review Friedman's essay. The bare outlines of this literature is summarized in the far right columns of Tables 7.1 and 7.2.

Mostly Friedman's essay has been interpreted as a variation of one of the justificationist philosophies of science as summarized in Table 7.1. However, the most recent and most detailed interpretation associates Friedman's methodology with John Dewey's instrumentalism. There is some uncertainty whether to categorize Dewey as a sophisticated neojustificationist or as a nonjustificationist. If we approach the issue with a liberal spirit and grant the richest interpretation as the basis for interpreting Dewey, then it is conceivable that Friedman's essay might contain the seeds of a nonjustificational methodology of economic science. It must be acknowledged that this is an extremely controversial issue in light of the Chicago School's emphasis on empiricism. Popperians like Boland have essentially attributed a neojustificationist view to Friedman's essay. My point is not to take a philosophical position with regard to Friedman's essay, but rather to use the debate over the philosophy and metatheory of science behind Friedman's essay to argue for a nonjustificational, post-modern economics of science and to illustrate the functioning of the marketplace of ideas in science.

BOLAND'S DEFENSE OF FRIEDMAN'S ESSAY

No matter what one may think about Friedman's essay, it has had an extraordinary run. It has made few references either to the broader philosophical literature in philosophy of science or to the more narrowly focused economic methodological literature which preceded it. The essay raised many issues of a philosophical nature about the scientific status of economics. It also used many general philosophical terms about scientific inquiry which are not always mutually consistent. These apparent inconsistencies in Friedman's essay were the subject of a vigorous defense more than a decade ago by Lawrence Boland.

In his "A Critique of Friedman's Critics," Boland (1979) attempts to refute Friedman's detractors and reinterprets the essay as a coherent instrumentalist conception of economic science. Boland has the reputation as being one of the foremost Popperian methodologists in economics. Whether he agrees with Bartley's thesis that there is significant failure in the marketplace of ideas is not known to me. The following is not meant to imply either that Boland supports or opposes the notion of a competitive marketplace of ideas. My point is the narrower one, that one of the best defenses of Friedman's essay is the one that Boland has already made.

Boland's defense of Friedman's essay develops four main arguments. The first is that all of the critics have misinterpreted Friedman's essay:

> Milton Friedman's essay, "Methodology of Positive Economics," is considered authoritative by almost every textbook writer who wishes to discuss the methodology of economics. Nevertheless, virtually all the journal articles that have been written about that essay have been very critical. This is a rather unusual situation. The critics condemn Friedman's essay, but virtually all the textbooks praise it. *Every* critic of Friedman's essay has been wrong [original emphasis].
>
> (Boland 1979: 503)

In Boland's view, the basis of much of the criticism of Friedman's essay is premised on an erroneous philosophy of science. Table 7.1 helps to illustrate what has happened. One of the easiest ways to misinterpret Friedman's essay is to mistakenly identify it as logical positivism. Some critics simply have taken the essay as the economic analogue of Vienna Circle positivism. Since philosophers have found significant flaws in logical positivism decades ago, this interpretation makes it easy to reject Friedman's essay. The rejection proceeds like this: Philosophers have rejected logical positivism, Friedman's methodology is a version of logical positivism, therefore Friedman's essay should be rejected. Similar types of arguments have been made with regard to Karl Popper's philosophy of science. Mark Blaug, a methodologist at the London School of Economics, has adopted a Popperian conception of science as reformulated by the late Imre Lakatos. Blaug (1976: 149) claims that Friedman is "Popper-with-a-twist" in economics. For those who find flaws with Popper's approach to science, Blaug's interpretation presents an opportunity to criticize if not reject Friedman as a Popperian.

Boland maintains that criticisms of the sort outlined above are all wrong. He argues that a clear and correct conception of science is behind Friedman's essay. It is instrumentalism:[3]

> The fundamental reason why all of the critics are wrong is that their criticisms are not based on a clear, correct, or even fair understanding of his essay. Friedman simply does not make the mistakes he is accused of making. His methodological position is both logically sound and unambiguously based on a coherent philosophy of science – Instrumentalism.
>
> (Boland 1979: 503)[4]

This is the second main argument in defense of Friedman's essay.

Boland's third major argument concerns the logic of Friedman's defense of his essay. Rather that presenting a few necessary arguments that could be refuted thus contradicting Friedman's methodology, Friedman's methodology presents many sufficient arguments. This is a disjunctive type of argument. Effective criticism of one argument in favor of an instrumentalist positive economics leaves many other arguments still supporting the theory. This makes it extremely difficult to criticize the essay. Boland depicts the dilemma faced by critics of Friedman's essay:

> Instrumentalism presents certain obstacles to every critic. When instrumentalists argue by offering a long series of reasons, each of which is sufficient for their conclusions, it puts the entire onus on the critic to refute each and every reason . . . [and] In order to defeat a pure disjunctive argument, one must refute every assumption – clearly a monumental task [original emphasis].
>
> (Boland 1979: 521, 506).

The last argument that Boland presents is a self-referential defense of Friedman's essay. Boland maintains that in addition to the other arguments Friedman uses, he also defends his views with an instrumental argument. In other words, an instrumentalist positive economic methodology is defended instrumentally:

> Any effective criticism must deal properly with Friedman's instrumentalism. Presenting a criticism that ignores his instrumentalism will always lead to irrelevant critiques such as those of Koopmans, Rotwein, and De Alessi. None of these critics seems willing to straightforwardly criticize instrumentalism. . . . Friedman makes this all the more difficult by giving us, likewise, an instrumentalist argument in support of instrumentalism itself. Thus, refuting or otherwise successfully criticizing only some of Friedman's reasons will never defeat his view. Since Friedman never explicitly claims that his argument is intended to be a logically sufficient defense of instrumentalism, one cannot expect to gain even by refuting its "sufficiency." Yet it would be fair to do so, since "sufficiency," is the only logical idea that instrumentalism uses. Such a refutation, however, is unlikely, since it would seem to require a solution to the problem of induction. . . . The repeated attempts to refute Friedman's methodology have failed, I think, because instrumentalism is its own defense, and its *only* defense [original emphasis].
>
> (Boland 1979: 521, 522)

FRIEDMAN'S ESSAY: A CASE FOR MARKET FAILURE IN THE MARKETPLACE OF IDEAS

From the perspective of an economics of science, the issue presented by the many dissimilar interpretations of Friedman's essay is whether these episodes and

Boland's defense illustrate efficiency or failure in the marketplace of ideas. Friedman has always defended free, competitive markets in the commercial economy, and he has argued that discretionary intervention in the economy by government creates more harm than it does good in correcting market failure. Friedman's Chicago colleagues Stigler, Hayek, and Coase have written extensively about free markets in the realm of ideas. And Friedman (1981) has written about the harm of government intervention in the form of grantsmanship in distorting the direction of scientific research.

One explanation of the dominance of Friedman's essay in economic methodology for so long could be efficiency in the competitive marketplace of ideas in economics. This would be a consistent Chicago view extended from goods and service markets to ideas. Therefore, the repeated success of Friedman's essay could be viewed as a consequence of a competitive scientific debate within economics. A competitive economic defense would be that Friedman's essay had more value as a guide to doing economic science than any of his rivals. Each time the essay was criticized by a rival, the superior value of Friedman's essay as a guide to economic science was demonstrated by the failure to dislodge Friedman's essay. One strategy might be to link Boland's defense of Friedman with the thesis of efficiency in the marketplace of ideas. From Boland's (1979) piece, one could argue that Friedman's essay, despite so many reinterpretations, embodies a coherent methodology of economics and that Friedman's critics have all been wrong. On this basis, one possibly might conclude that the marketplace of ideas worked quite well. Weaker positions were voiced but did not prevail. The better view of economic science, Friedman's essay, repeatedly vanquished inferior alternatives.

Another reading of Boland's defense of Friedman could take the contrary position of market failure. The opposite point of view would be that there is very little intellectual competition among alternative views on economic methodology and science. For example, consider the nature of criticism and countercriticism in the debates over Friedman's essay. To criticize Friedman and effectively compete against his ideas, one would have to have a clear and accurate understanding of his essay. Boland argues that none of Friedman's rivals correctly interpreted his methodological and philosophical position. This position is instrumentalism. Boland is aware of Popper's criticisms of instrumentalism and would not categorize himself as an instrumentalist. However, Boland's assessment of Friedman's rivals is that they have not legitimately challenged the inherent instrumentalism of Friedman's methodology. For competition to take place, the rivals would have had to consider the issues posed by instrumentalism. Since instrumentalism was not addressed, there was very little genuine competition in this small sector of the marketplace of ideas.[5]

If this market failure interpretation of Boland's defense of Friedman's essay is taken as the more valid one, then the dominance of Friedman's essay as a conception of science can be explained in exactly the same way as the pervasive influence of Popper in philosophy of science in the previous chapter.

Imperfections in the scientific marketplace of ideas could create an environment in which judgmental substitutes for information are relied upon. Desired empirical knowledge upon which an informed decision could be made simply does not exist. The full value of Friedman's positive economics as a way of doing economic science would be known only when it has been replaced by a better alternative some time in the future. In the mean time, choices have to be made.

In the context of an economics of science, the decision of the individual scientist is portrayed as a cost-benefit choice among rival alternatives. Cost-benefit analysis implies an economic situation fraught with imperfections because we are so far removed from the stabilizing forces of competitive commercial markets. The reasoning of a cost-benefit economics of science fosters an awareness of the noncommercial market character of science. Outside the realm of commercial markets, it is difficult for market processes to work well. Economists expect market failure outside of the domain of the commercial marketplace. The cost-benefit approach to decision making was created to provide an economic framework for nonmarket decisions in the domain of public finance. The use of the cost-benefit approach implies a judgement that science requires an awareness of nonmarket processes and problems like that found in public finance.

As was done previously, let us represent the choice of a research program by a young economist at the outset of a career using cost-benefit theory. What novice economists have to do is estimate the value of a career as portrayed in Friedman's essay versus the next best alternative. An estimate of such relative values would be highly subjective, incorporating minimal information, and making use of judgmental substitutes for absent information. Friedman's essay could be viewed as an attempt to clarify his conception of science so that it increases the value of a Friedmanesque research program in the economics profession. A young scientist would choose to be a Friedmanian positive economist if (in his or her subjective estimate and using all of any extremely scarce facts) the net present value of this career path was greater than that of an alternative. This can be represented as:

$$V_{RP\ PE} > V_{RP\ -PE} \qquad (1)$$

Equation (1) means that a research program comprised of research projects consistent with a Friedmanian view of positive economic science is judged to have more value than a research program of projects from another vision of economic science. If the majority of young economists make such a decision, then a positive economic conception of economic science would become widely adopted. If there is market failure in the marketplace of ideas in economics, then career path decisions of the sort suggested by an economics of science in equation (1) may not be very efficient. Patterns of bias could emerge in economics just like those identified in philosophy and philosophy of science in the previous chapter. In economics the existence of market failure could be responsible for the dominance of Friedman's methodological essay.

An awareness of the noncompetitive nature of the marketplace of ideas was also found in Bartley's critique of universities and scientific disciplines. Recall that Bartley has characterized science in universities as exhibiting significant imperfections in the marketplace of ideas. Universities have become bastions of false philosophies and ideologies. Apparently, intellectuals despise commercial markets. Bartley also holds that the incentive structures of scientific disciplines work to discourage competition. The choice of research topics and appointments to new positions work to favor an entrenched or dominant position in science. Those in control of a dominant position in science act in their self-interest to maintain the dominance of their own school of inquiry. Bartley asserts that the existing organizational structures of science work against the public good. All of this suppresses innovation in science.

Now we must consider the case for the dominance of Friedman's essay as a consequence of market failure in the marketplace of ideas. If Bartley's view of academic science is correct, then the discipline of economics should not be an exception to the pervasive market failures that he has identified. The dominance of the essay could be the consequence of the incentive structures within economics and economic methodology discouraging competition. Choices of research topics could work to entrench positive economic science as the dominant conception of that discipline. Like other scientists, those in key positions in the economics profession could act in their self-interest to maintain the supremacy of positive economic science. If Bartley is correct, organizational structures and ideas such as those which dominate economic science may not work for the public good. Thus whatever else it may represent, Table 7.1 (and to a lesser extent Table 7.2) could represent a pattern of dominance by Friedman's essay in economic methodology which works to suppress innovation in economic science.

FRIEDMAN'S SOMEWHAT UNWARRANTED DOMINANCE OF TWO SIMILAR METHODOLOGICAL RIVALS: DEWEY AND SAMUELSON

The categorization scheme represented in Tables 7.1 and 7.2 is the most recent manifestation of a search for the most plausible interpretation of Friedman's essay. For this author, the search began when I was a graduate student taking philosophy of science classes at the same time I was enrolled in economic theory. At that time, as someone relatively new to a complex discipline, I simply wanted to know about positive economics. What was the view of science that I was supposed to practice when I finished my graduate training? Naively, I assumed that an essay like Friedman's (which all of my professors told me to read) would have a coherent philosophy of science behind it. This is the same attitude that existed with regard to math, statistics, and computers. If I wanted to know more than the economics department could offer about these subjects, then a few courses in these other departments would give added skill and a better understanding of these tools. What I found when I took philosophy of science outside of the economics department was shocking. It appeared that Friedman's essay was dated and had no coherent philosophy of science behind it. Friedman's essay seemed impossible to locate philosophically. An excursion into philosophy of science was troubling rather than helpful in searching for a coherent understanding of Friedman's essay.

At times I was tempted to write to Friedman and simply ask him if there was an identifiable philosophical position behind his essay. Thoughts of the well-known game show, *To Tell the Truth*, crossed my mind. If only the true or best interpretation of Friedman's essay would stand up and reveal itself. A letter seemed a good solution to my quest. About that time, Lawrence Boland published his widely read interpretation of Friedman's essay. As noted in the previous section, Boland's essay also presented a scathing critique of Friedman's critics. He also claimed that a coherent methodological position was behind Friedman's essay. Boland asserted that despite some ambiguities Friedman's essay is best interpreted as an instrumentalist methodology of economic science. As an instrumentalist, Friedman does not care about deep philosophical issues like the problem of induction or even truth. If induction is not a solvable problem, then it is hard to know whether economic theories are indeed true in any absolute sense. In an important sense, Boland's interpretation portrays Friedman as a believer in intellectual specialization. Intractable philosophical issues should be left to the philosophers and economists should practice science as positive economists until the philosophical issues are closer to philosophical resolution. Boland (1981) also portrays Friedman's essay as a shorter-run version of Karl Popper's philosophy of science. Policy issues of the sort that an economist would study with data are not the types of issues which are addressed well by Popper's philosophy of science. For Boland, Friedman's essay can be interpreted as the economic methodological analogue of a Popperian approach to economic science.

Boland's instrumentalist interpretation of Friedman's essay as an instrumentalist methodology of science within the broader context of a Popperian philosophy of science was quite helpful for a time. Popper was the most widely read philosopher of science in economics and Friedman's essay was the most widely read methodological piece so it seemed "natural" to interpret Friedman in light of Popper. Boland was quite convincing in arguing that Popper's scathing criticisms of instrumentalism should not apply to Friedman's essay. But there was one unresolved problem or two with the instrumentalist interpretation of Friedman's essay which Boland did not consider. In his essay, Friedman criticizes the methodological positions of the American institutionalists, particularly those of Thorstein Veblen. Friedman's essay reads as though it is a rejection of the dominant school of economics at the time he was writing his essay. The problem is that the institutionalists also call their methodology of science "instrumentalism," emphasizing the philosophy of the American pragmatist John Dewey. Dewey called his philosophy "instrumentalism" to distinguish it from the contributions of Charles Peirce and William James. Thus it appears that Friedman via Boland is once again embracing a conception of science which he appeared to reject in his essay.

To remedy this apparent contradiction, Abraham Hirsch and Neil de Marchi wrote a long book, *Milton Friedman*, claiming that the Deweyian position was the instrumentalist position behind Friedman's work. After reading Boland's interpretation of Friedman's essay, this author wrote a long piece claiming that Friedman's instrumentalism was a special case of Dewey's (Wible 1984a). Hirsch and de Marchi (1990: 6) criticized me for relying too much on Boland's view. They broadened the scope of inquiry about Friedman beyond the methodological essay. Hirsch and de Marchi claimed that any interpretation of Friedman's essay needed to be supplemented with an awareness of the way Friedman actually conducted economic research. In this broader context, Hirsch and de Marchi concluded that Friedman is more of a Deweyian instrumentalist than a Popperian.

Interpreting Friedman's essay as an instrumentalist methodology of economics raises another concern other than those related to the philosophies of Popper and Dewey. One of the sharpest attacks of Friedman's essay in earlier methodological debates in economics was criticism from Paul Samuelson. Samuelson aimed his attention at what he called the "F-Twist." The F-Twist concerns the unrealistic assumptions of competition and rationality as maximization. For Friedman these assumptions are valid as long as theories incorporating these assumptions yield good predictions of future economic events. Samuelson then attempted to criticize Friedman's essay on its own terms by making unrealistic assumptions about Friedman's methodology. Samuelson ends with the "prediction" that Chicago methodology exists to explain away objections to Chicago economics.

What is intriguing about all of this is that Samuelson's criticism of Friedman's positive economics makes it appear as though methodology could make a difference to economic theory. If Friedman's methodology is correct, then it would seem to support Chicago's conservative economic positions. If Samuelson's critique of Friedman is correct, then the more liberal positions of Cambridge could possibly exhibit superiority. However, if Friedman's essay is given an instrumentalist interpretation of either variety, then the methodological differences between Friedman and Samuelson almost disappear. In his *Foundations of Economic Analysis*, Samuelson (1947) adopted a view of science known as operational behaviorism. Operational behaviorism dominated both physics and psychology at Harvard during the 1940s. Operational behaviorism is an instrumentalist approach to science. Meaningful scientific statements were those that prescribed a sequence of measuring operations for observing the consequences of a theory.[6]

With hindsight it appears that reinterpretation of Friedman's essay as an instrumentalist philosophy of science may help to clarify the concepts behind positive economics. However the instrumentalist interpretation raises a question about what was really going on in economics. While there are important differences among the views of Friedman, Dewey, and Samuelson, their methodologies in retrospect appear more similar than different. These differences are important and others have explored the details of these differences at great length. I refer the reader to the excellent writings of Boland and Frazer and to Hirsch and de Marchi. But from a metatheoretical perspective, the methodologies of Friedman, Dewey, and Samuelson appear more similar than different. In retrospect, what was all the fuss really about? Perhaps an economics of science perspective can shed some light on this matter.

Indeed if we return to Table 7.1 summarizing the many reinterpretations of Friedman's essay, it is difficult not to conclude that failure exists in the marketplace of ideas in economics. The pattern of dominance is nothing short of astonishing. Friedman's essay is sufficiently flawed from a philosophical point of view that its success cannot be accounted for on philosophical grounds.[7] The coherence of an instrumentalist version of positive economic science, I attribute to Boland not Friedman. Similarly, if Friedman's views are at all similar to Dewey's, then this broader identification of the methodology of positive economics with Dewey must be attributed to Hirsch and de Marchi. Furthermore, the creative interpretations of the literature surrounding Friedman's essay by Boland, Hirsch, and de Marchi would not have been necessary unless significant imperfections existed in the marketplace of ideas in economics and methodology. Lastly, the differences between Friedman and Samuelson on methodology appear to be less significant than they once were. Friedman's essay is not the competitive homogenous methodological product interpreted and accepted in the same way by all economists as many textbook authors would have us believe. Nor can the failures of rival positions be accounted for on philosophical grounds. Some of them were not all that different from Friedman's position to the extent they can be categorized as instrumentalist-like methodologies of science. Imperfections in the marketplace of ideas would present an environment in which one view of economic science could dominate another. The dominance of Friedman's methodological essay can be understood from an economic point of view. Ideas markets are very different from goods and service markets. In science, ideas markets take a long time to adjust. This allows a flawed view of science to dominate a scientific discipline over both similar and dissimilar conceptions of that science. The dominance of positive economic methodology and Friedman's essay can be understood as an economic phenomenon.[8]

Since Boland and Hirsch and de Marchi authored their instrumentalist interpretations of Friedman's essay, methodologists have almost stopped reinterpreting Friedman's essay as new ideas about science emerge in many difficult disciplines. McCloskey's *Rhetoric of Economics* is a good example of this trend, It made almost no effort in discussing Friedman's essay. As Friedman's essay slowly passes from the scene, the question naturally arises concerning a new conception of science. What conception of science will replace Friedman's "The Methodology of Positive Economics" in texts, in graduate instruction, and in professional discourse? Perhaps it should come as no surprise that I would argue for an nonjustificationist, post-modern economics of science.

CONCLUSIONS

Economists because of their professional training in the virtues of free, competitive markets for goods and services, tend also to believe in a free competitive marketplace of ideas. But an economics of science gives economic reasons for reconsidering this instinctive position regarding the marketplace of ideas. The marketplace of ideas is far removed from the commercial marketplace. There are difficulties in extending the traditional theory of competition from goods and services to ideas. The nonmarket setting of science creates an environment in which intellectually dominant schools of thought emerge which perpetuate their own survival. In this chapter, I have suggested that the dominance of Friedman's essay is another example of significant imperfections in the marketplace of ideas. Friedman's essay has been difficult to interpret in a consistent and coherent way. The most coherent interpretations of Friedman's essay by Lawrence Boland and by Hirsch and de Marchi are truly remarkable. But the necessity of their interpretations and the sheer defensiveness of their works would not have been forthcoming or necessary in a more competitive marketplace of ideas in economics.

My interpretation of the dominance of Friedman's essay does not resolve all of the ambiguities surrounding Friedman's essay. The debate, in my view, has been conducted in the context of significant imperfections in the economics discipline. But Table 7.1 also shows how quickly philosophy of science has corrected its own errors. Some economists will hold that Friedman's essay really is intellectually superior to all of the proposed philosophical substitutes. Thus, in their view, intellectual progress was enhanced by the dominance of Friedman's essay. Other economists will take the opposite view that all of the philosophical views of science were superior to Friedman's essay at every stage of the debate. I cannot settle such a dispute. My point is that an economics of science may allow for a coherent understanding of the dominance of Friedman's essay whether that essay was right, wrong, or flawed. The debate over Friedman's essay is itself an economic phenomenon. It is from the perspective of an economics of science that broader questions can be raised about the nature of positive economic methodology. The marketplace of ideas in economics exhibits significant imperfections. Economic science is not a competitive marketplace of ideas. What is needed in place of Friedman's essay is an economics of science.

8

SELF-CORRECTIVE SCIENCE IN THE CONTEXT OF MARKET FAILURE

The marketplace of ideas is not really a market

The community of scientists is organised in a way which resembles certain features of a body politic and works according to economic principles similar to those by which the production of material goods is regulated. . . . Such self-coordination of independent initiatives leads to a joint result which is unpremeditated by any of those who bring it about. Their coordination is guided as by an "invisible hand" toward the joint discovery of a hidden system of things.

(Polanyi 1962b: 54 and 55)

A more subtle objection to methodological discussion is that it is unnecessary. Those doing substantive research are driven, as if by an invisible hand, to do their work as well as it can be done. But the invisible hand works its wonders only when there is a market in which producers sell their wares. If the standards that govern production are set, not by consumers, but by the producers themselves, the invisible hand is moribund. More specifically, as I will argue. . . . the self-interest of economists biases their methodological choices.

(Mayer 1993: 4)

MARKETS, SELF-CORRECTIVENESS, AND SCIENCE

In the literature on the nature of science, the theme of market failure in science is really quite recent. In Chapter 6, we saw that William Bartley (1990) has criticized universities and the discipline of philosophy on the basis of market failure in the marketplace of ideas. In Chapter 7, another case of apparent intellectual dominance has been Milton Friedman's essay on positive economic methodology, which has dominated thinking about the nature of economic science for almost half a century. Thomas Kuhn (1970) has depicted science as being dominated for long periods of time by normal science, where normal science is characterized by one or a few points of view which prevail over a large number of less well supported competing points of view. These portrayals of market failure in science suggest that the dominance of academic and scientific disciplines by one or a small number of schools of thought is the norm rather than the exception.

Other than market failure, the theme of misconduct in science was the topic of Chapters 2 and 3 applying microeconomics to the problems of replication failure and fraud in science. The chapter on replication failure was an application of Becker's well-known theory of the allocation of time. Scientists were portrayed as being sensitive to the opportunity cost of time. If they placed more emphasis on the next innovative piece of research rather than tedious activities permitting the replication of their empirical results, replication failure often would result. The chapter on fraud in science applied an expected utility model from the economics of crime literature to recent problems of misconduct in the biomedical area. Under conditions of uncertainty, some deviant scientists take a rational, calculated gamble and deliberately deceive, fabricate, and falsify important aspects of scientific research.

On the surface, economic thinking with regard to science may lead to a dismal conclusion. Because science is a nonmarket activity, economic theory would suggest that market failure and perhaps misconduct is a problem for science. If market failure and misconduct are problematic, then an economic point of view would place science in a very unfavorable light. However, such a negative portrayal of science is much too extreme. One reason for creating an economic approach to science is to avoid either extreme pessimism or myopia. An economic point of view which suggested that science was often self-corrective in the context of market failure would go a long way toward providing a balanced view of science as an economic process. The general view would be that of an autonomous error-correcting social process in the very long run and a flawed economic and organizational process in the short run.

Since I have previously dealt with the issues of misconduct and market failure in the marketplace of ideas, in this chapter I will be concerned with assertions of the self-correctiveness of science. The chapter reviews in some detail two lines of thought and the views of three prominent thinkers who have argued for the self-correctiveness of science. The last part of the chapter considers aspects of the substantive intellectual and economic issues raised by this literature. I will first explore historical aspects of the basic notion of the self-correctiveness of science. Second, I will consider the origins of the conception of a competitive marketplace of ideas. Then I will explore the ideas of three individuals who provide a framework for thinking about science as a self-corrective process which is far removed from the commercial marketplace. The contributions of F. A. Hayek, Michael Polanyi, and Nicholas Rescher provide a portrayal of how science could be self-corrective in the context of market failure. Their contributions imply that the marketplace of ideas is not really a market. In the last substantive part of the chapter, I argue that science should be viewed as a partially endogenized economic process which can be further interpreted as the economic opposite of competitive auction markets.

NONECONOMIC CONCEPTIONS OF THE SELF-CORRECTIVENESS OF SCIENCE

The negative implications of an economic analysis of both misconduct and market failure in science can be balanced with the views of those who essentially suggest that science surmounts these problems. In contrast to concerns with market failure and misconduct, a large number of observers and commentators of science have advanced an entirely different conception of science than the market failure interpretation. Historical figures like Priestley and Peirce, contemporary philosophers like Polanyi and Rescher, and economists like Blaug, Stigler, and Hayek have in different ways asserted the self-corrective nature of science. They have maintained that science is a self-corrective marketplace of ideas.

In contrast to the awareness of market failure in the marketplace of ideas which comes from the recent literature on the history, sociology, and philosophy of science, there is a long history to the notion of the self-correctiveness of science. From a longer-run point of view, it is striking that scientists, philosophers, and economists continually have asserted the fundamental self-correctiveness of science. These notions of self-correctiveness typically are couched in terms of the appraisal of evidence, hypotheses, and theories. In his monograph, *Methodological Pragmatism*, Nicholas Rescher has written extensively about the self-corrective nature of science.[1] He has traced the notion of self-corrective science to Peirce in the nineteenth century and to Joseph Priestley in the eighteenth century. During Priestley's time, scientists took a mathematical model of successive approximation as their example of the self-correctiveness of science. Priestley expressed the self-correctiveness of science in the following words:

> Hypotheses, while they are considered merely as such, lead persons to try a variety of experiments, in order to ascertain them. These new facts serve to correct the hypothesis which gave occasion to them. The theory, thus corrected, serves to discover more new facts, which, as before, bring the theory still nearer to the truth. In this progressive state, or method of approximation, things continue.
> (Priestley 1767: 381 as quoted in Rescher 1977: 168)

Rescher (1977: 168) has argued that Priestley's method implied an automatic procedure of moving from guesswork to an answer which approaches correctness with each successive stage of refinement. Priestley's conception of scientific method was that an hypothesis could lead to many experiments thus creating new evidence. It was new evidence or facts which redirected science. Notice that there was nothing economic about Priestley's conception of the self-correctiveness of science.

In comparison to Priestley, Charles Peirce's conception of the self-correctiveness of science was quite different. Priestley's mechanical view of scientific method implied a short-run view of the self-correctiveness of science. In contrast, Peirce took a long-run view and held that science would ultimately reach truth in the long run as scientific opinion converged to one view of truth which Peirce called the final opinion. One of Peirce's most significant statements on truth is found in his well-known essay "How to Make Our Ideas Clear:"

> All the followers of science are animated by a cheerful hope that the processes of investigation, if only pushed far enough, will give one certain solution to each question to which they apply it. . . . So with all scientific research. Different minds may set out with the most antagonistic view, but the progress of investigation carries then by a force outside of themselves to one and the same conclusion. . . . This great hope is embodied in the conception of truth and reality. The opinion which is fated to be ultimately agreed to by all who investigate, is what we mean by truth, and the object represented in this opinion is real.
>
> (Peirce [1878] 1955: 38)

Peirce's position is that in the long run, the self-correctiveness of science would lead to the truth. No mention is made of economic factors influencing this final opinion. Apparently the economics of research project selection so elegantly expressed by Peirce in his "Note on the Theory of the Economy of Research" was ignored in his conception of truth.

Economists have also maintained that science is self-corrective. An attitude of an economist which is quite similar to Rescher's is that of Mark Blaug. Indeed, one of the strongest assertions of the correctability of science that I have encountered has been penned by Blaug:

> Science, for all its shortcomings, is the only self-questioning and self-correcting ideological system that man has yet devised; despite intellectual inertia, despite built-in conservatism, and despite the closing of ranks to keep heretics at bay, the scientific community remains loyal to the ideal of intellectual competition in which no weapons other than evidence and argument are permitted. Individual scientists sometime fall short of those ideals but, nevertheless, the scientific community as a whole is the paradigm case of the open society.
>
> (Blaug 1980: 45–6)

What Blaug's position adds to the ideas of self-correctiveness of Priestley and Peirce is the idea of competition. Some of this may be implicit in Peirce, but it is clear in Blaug's comments. It is not a matter of one theory being judged with regard to evidence. Theories compete against one another. Before the fact, it may be difficult to imagine what theories may compete against each other. Theories thought to be completely irrelevant to a subject of investigation may take a surprising turn and reveal evidence that is wholly unanticipated. After the fact it is easier to understand why one theory displaced another. But the nature and outcome of the competition among theories is difficult to foresee. In an attempt to appraise theoretical development in economics, Blaug portrays progress in economics as competition between theories:

> None of these questions can be fruitfully discussed if all that is available to us is a single theory. Scientific theories can only be meaningfully assessed in terms of competing hypotheses for the simple reason that methodology provides no absolute standard to which all theories must conform: what it does provide are criteria in terms of which theories may be ranked as more or less promising.
>
> (Blaug 1980: 159)

For Blaug, the self-correctiveness of science is the ability to rank the existing alternative theories.[2] Some theories are better than others. Over time some theories survive and others do not. This is how science makes progress. It is surprising that Blaug makes no mention of the invisible-hand mechanisms of the commercial marketplace or the marketplace of ideas. The self-correctability of science is located in a conception of how evidence impacts an appraisal of scientific theories and in the rivalry of competing scientific theories. Science apparently is self-corrective in spite of the flaws in its self-adjustment processes. While economic resources are necessary to generate facts and for theories to compete, the processes of the self-correctability of science are not those of self-correctable commercial market processes.

THE NONECONOMIC ORIGIN OF THE MARKETPLACE OF IDEAS

Besides all of the many assertions of the self-correctiveness of science by Peirce, Priestley, Rescher, Blaug and others, there is another domain of thought which also contributes to an optimistic outlook regarding the adjustment processes of science. Closely related to, but independent of, the notion of self-correctiveness in science is the idea of a competitive marketplace of ideas. The idea can be traced to the works of John Milton in the 1600s. One of the earliest references to the truth-enhancing role of competition among ideas comes from Milton's *Areopagitica* written in 1644. It is one of the first writings on freedom of speech and the role of such freedom in revealing error. *Areopagitica* is not an economic treatise. *Areopagitica* contains Milton's arguments for freedom of the press which were addressed to the British Parliament. In that period of time, Parliament maintained that many false, scandalous, seditious, and libellous works were being published in an unchecked way by independent private printing shops. These works raised the specter of political and social instability. In 1643, Parliament became concerned about the publication of so many books opposing existing religious and political practices. Consequently, an order was passed requiring that all printed works must be licensed by Parliament. Also in that same year, Milton was married but his wife left him after a few weeks of marriage. Milton wrote a tract on divorce which claimed that divorce was a private matter which should be permitted for individuals who deem themselves incompatible. This tract on divorce was published without the appropriate license from Parliament. It had an incendiary effect in his time and proceedings against Milton were begun. Milton's response to the order of Parliament and to the proceedings against him resulted in *Areopagitica*.

The title of Milton's work is based on the practices for censoring books in ancient Athens. Mostly, in classical Greek antiquity, books were not censored except for one or two notable exceptions. There is the case of an ancient Greek who wrote a work doubting the existence of the gods. These views offended those in authority. Milton ([1644] 1952: 384) recounts that "the books of Protagoras were by the judges of Areopagus commanded to be burnt." Milton also directed attention at practices other than those of the Greeks. Other episodes of censorship before his time were reprised for the benefit of Parliament. Milton's historical point was that book publishing was largely unregulated until Parliament passed this licensing act. His main intellectual arguments were that truth would result from the free and open encounter of opposing ideas and that censorship and regulation would protect falsehood and error. Regarding freedom of expression Milton wrote: "Give me the liberty to know, to utter, and to argue freely according to conscience, above all liberties" (Milton [1644] 1952: 410). Concerning the clash among conflicting ideas, Milton argued that ideas which appear to be quite opposing should be left to play against each other:

> And now the time . . . to write and speak what may help to the further discussion of matters in agitation. The temple of Janus with his two controversial faces might now not unsignificantly be set open. And though all the winds of doctrine were let loose to play upon the earth, so Truth be in the field, we do injuriously, by licensing and prohibiting, to misdoubt her strength. Let her and Falsehood grapple; who ever knew Truth put to the worse, in a free and open encounter?
>
> (Milton [1644] 1952: 409)

Regarding the negative effects of censorship, Milton wrote that error likely would be protected by government regulation: "For who knows not that Truth is strong, next to the Almighty? She needs no policies, nor stratagems, nor licensings to make her victorious; those are the shifts and the defences that error uses against her power" (Milton [1644] 1952: 409). While Milton did not actually use the term "marketplace of ideas," it is clear from the preceding quotations that all of the essential ingredients are present. Truth benefits from the free open exchange of ideas while government regulation serves to protect falsehood and error. Furthermore, the free expression of ideas is considered the most fundamental aspect of liberty.[3]

During the Middle Ages, another example of a free marketplace of ideas emerged. One of the major consequences in the practice of the free expression of ideas was the university. The university originated as something like a marketplace of ideas where arguments could be presented and debated. In his inaugural address to the rectorship of the University of Berlin in 1877, Hermann von Helmholtz provided his view of the origin of universities:

> The European Universities of the Middle Age had their origin as free private unions of their students, who came together under the influence of celebrated teachers, and themselves arranged their own affairs. . . . Such a free confederation of independent men, in which teachers as well as taught were brought together by no other interest than that of love of science; some by the desire of discovering the treasure of mental culture which antiquity had bequeathed, others endeavouring to kindle in a new generation the ideal enthusiasm which had animated their lives. Such was the origin of Universities, based, in the conception, and in the plan of their organisation, upon the most perfect freedom.
>
> (Helmholtz 1895: 240–1)

From Milton's defense of liberty and Helmholtz's conception of the university as a free association of individuals having a love of science and ideas, I turn to much more recent conceptions of the marketplace of ideas by two well-known economists. In recent years, concern for a free marketplace of ideas has been explored by the late George Stigler and Ronald Coase. In his essay, "The Intellectual and the Market Place," Stigler (1963) characterizes the attitude of intellectuals toward the commercial marketplace. He maintains that intellectuals are a luxury for any society. The growth of the modern, productive economy supports the existence of an expensive class of intellectuals. Yet, most intellectuals contemptuously disregard the commercial marketplace. According to Stigler, most intellectuals have no desire to know more of the world of business, while those in business may wish to know more of the world of the intellectual.

In advance of his discussion of the domain of ideas, Stigler provides a brief characterization of the economy as a competitive system of private, voluntary contracts. Competition is what drives the system, but there are imperfections in this system. Even where there is economic concentration, sufficient rivals exist so that the coercive power that any one firm might have in the marketplace is diminished. Apparently, the degree of monopoly power is overstated in Stigler's view. Having characterized the world of commerce, Stigler turns to a similar characterization of the realm of ideas. The intellectual world, despite its differences from the commercial realm and despite episodes of misconduct, is an imperfectly competitive marketplace of ideas:

> The intellectual world, and I speak not exclusively of scholarship, is also a voluntary system. Its central credo is that opinions are to be formed through free discussion on the basis of full disclosure of evidence. Fraud and coercion are equally repugnant to the scholar. The freedom of thought is preserved by the open competition of scholars and ideas. Authority, the equivalent of monopoly power, is the great enemy of freedom of inquiry.

139

Competition in scholarship is in some ways more violent than in business; the law sets limits on the disparagement of a rival's product, unless it is done in a book review in a learned journal.

(Stigler 1963: 5)

After Stigler, one of the more in-depth examinations of the marketplace of ideas was done by Ronald Coase. Coase's (1974) widely cited essay is titled, "The Market for Goods and the Market for Ideas." In the essay, Coase does not go through comparative arguments establishing parallels between the commercial marketplace and the marketplace of ideas. His main point is an observation that the relationship of government to the market is very different for ideas than for goods and services. Government regulation of goods and service markets is widely accepted because the government plays an important role in constructing and enforcing the rules of the marketplace. Coase maintains that it is in the self-interest of intellectuals to support regulation in the market for goods and services but to oppose it in the market for ideas. In contrast, the market for ideas is often thought to be off limits to government interference. In the United States, this prohibition has taken the form of the First Amendment to the Constitution guaranteeing freedom of speech, writing, and religious belief.

While the First Amendment provides significant protection to the marketplace of ideas in the United States, its scope has encountered limitations. Although there is unfettered freedom of the press and of religious belief, Coase believes that government regulation is present in other aspects of the marketplace of ideas. New communications technologies have been created to disseminate ideas. But First Amendment protection has not necessarily followed. His explanation for this is self-interest. Broadcasting is one area which has not been extended the protection of the freedom of the press. Coase notes that the newspaper component of the news industry has gone to great lengths to protect their freedom from government intervention. However, print journalists seem to have little or no concern for similar protection for broadcast journalism. Coase also calls our attention to the fact that education is an important component of the marketplace for ideas. There is extensive regulation of education which in part is an extension of the government financing needed to support education. Such government financing is again in the self-interest of intellectuals who would benefit as teachers and professors. This ambivalence to the regulatory role of government in ideas markets leads Coase to question the consistency and wisdom of our attitudes toward government:[4]

We have to decide whether the government is as incompetent as is generally assumed in the market for ideas, in which case we would want to decrease government intervention in the market for goods, or whether it is as efficient as it is generally assumed to be in the market for goods, in which case we would want to increase government regulation in the market for ideas.

(Coase 1974: 390)

POLANYI'S NONMARKET, SELF-CORRECTIVE
REPUBLIC OF SCIENCE

In the preceding two sections, ideas about the self-correctiveness of science and the value of a competitive marketplace of ideas were presented. The optimism expressed in those sections stands in sharp contrast to the themes of misconduct and market failure resulting from systematic application of economic theory to science. But there is a middle ground between these two extreme points of view. Theoretically, one solution would be to suggest a separate, nonmarket process of self-correctiveness in science which is quite different than the forces which stabilize a commercial market economy. In this regard, an analogy often is made which mixes the metaphors implying that science is a self-corrective marketplace of ideas. However, if the basis of the self-correctiveness of science is entirely different than for commercial markets, then the analogy remains a metaphor. This means that the marketplace of ideas is not really a market as an economist typically understands that term. Two eminent scholars have taken such an approach to science. Michael Polanyi and Friedrich Hayek separately have developed a nonmarket conception of the correctiveness of science. I consider Polanyi's contribution in this section and Hayek's in the next.

Most scientists believe that science is self-corrective, highly competitive, and rational. One way of interpreting this self-correctiveness is a comparison with another self-corrective social process – the economy. Together these beliefs in self-correctiveness, competition, and the rationality of science encompass some of the fundamental ingredients of an economic theory of competition. In the domain of science, this conception of competition is known as the competitive marketplace of ideas. The metaphor of the marketplace of ideas suggests that science is an invisible-hand process which is in some respects similar to markets in the economy. In his piece "The Republic of Science," Polanyi compares the self-coordination of science with markets:[5]

> What I have said here about the highest possible coordination of individual scientific efforts by a process of self-coordination may recall the self-coordination achieved by producers and consumers operating in a market. It was, indeed, with this in mind that I spoke of "the invisible hand" guiding the coordination of independent initiatives to a maximum advancement of science, just as Adam Smith invoked the "invisible hand" to describe the achievement of greatest joint material satisfaction when the independent producers and consumers are guided by the prices of goods in a market.
>
> (Polanyi 1962b: 56)

Polanyi's most fundamental premise is that there is a general principle of mutual self-adjustment in society with science and commercial markets being separate instances of this more general principle of self-coordination:

> I am suggesting, in fact, that the coordinating functions of the market are

but a special case of coordination by mutual adjustment. In the case of science, adjustment takes place by taking note of the published results of other scientists; while in the case of the market, mutual adjustment is mediated by a system of prices broadcasting current exchange relations, which make supply meet demand.

(Polanyi 1962b: 56)

In science, coordination is different than in the market. The locus of coordination is an information exchange process. In the economy, relative market prices convey an extensive amount of information. In science, the equivalent of the informational exchange of the market is a process of mutual observation. Each scientist needs to observe the research of others. Polanyi illustrates with a simple example – putting together a giant jigsaw puzzle. He imagines one way of attempting to solve the puzzle would be to divide the pieces among a number of individuals who have been hired to help solve the puzzle. Then each puzzle solver would be told to try to solve the puzzle individually and in isolation from the others. Polanyi believes that this method would be quite ineffective. Each individual would have only a few of the pieces that would fit together. Another method might be to provide duplicates of the puzzle, so that each puzzle solver would have all of the pieces. An even better method according to Polanyi would be to have everyone work together on the puzzle:

The only way the assistants can effectively cooperate and surpass by far what any single one of them could do, is to let them work on putting the puzzle together in sight of the others, so that every time a piece of it is fitted in by one helper, all the others will immediately watch out for the next step that becomes possible in consequence. We have here in a nutshell the way in which a series of independent initiatives are organized to a joint achievement by mutually adjusting themselves at every successive stage to the situation created by all the others who are acting likewise.

(Polanyi 1962b: 55)

Moving beyond the puzzle-solving and invisible-hand metaphors, Polanyi inquires in more detail regarding the self-coordination of science. In science, there are several aspects of the process of self-coordination that transcend the previous metaphors. First, the publication of research results is vital to science. Publication serves to distribute information among scientists. This gives individual researchers an opportunity to respond to the situation created by the published results of other scientists. Second, scientific merit plays an important role in coordinating science. Scientific merit affects the choice of problems which the scientist will consider. Merit depends on plausibility of a problem, the estimated value of the resolution of this problem to science, and the originality of the contribution that the scientist may offer in resolving the problem under consideration. Third, authority plays a pivotal role in coordinating science.

142

Authority comes in the guise of professional standards, authoritative individual scientists, and in networks of overlapping competencies. Authority has a dialectical quality. It encourages conformity to the existing standards of inquiry in the scientific community. It also encourages originality and dissent. In this regard Polanyi (1962b: 58–9) remarks: "The authority of scientific opinion enforces the teachings of science in general, for the very purpose of fostering their subversion in particular points."

Polanyi's republic of science is not perfect. The spontaneous self-coordination of science leaves room for error and misconduct of the worst sort. The authority of the scientific community must exercise some censorship to weed out the most abnormal forms of conduct in the community:

> Scientific publications are continuously beset by cranks, frauds and bunglers whose contributions must be rejected if journals are not to be swamped by them. This censorship will not only eliminate obvious absurdities but must often refuse publication merely because the conclusions of a paper appear to be unsound in the light of current scientific knowledge.
>
> (Polanyi 1962b: 57)

In another passage, Polanyi considers the allocation of research dollars among the different sciences in a manner that is quite reminiscent of Peirce's "Note on the Theory of the Economy of Research." Polanyi's piece does not have the mathematical formalism of Peirce's essay, but the conclusions are quite consistent with Peirce's. Polanyi uses the concept of scientific merit to discuss the rational allocation of funds among the various branches of science:

> If the minimum merit by which a contribution would be qualified for acceptance by journals were much lower in one branch of science than another, this would clearly cause too much effort to be spent on the former branch as compared with the latter. Such is in fact the principle which underlies the rational distribution of grants for the pursuit of research. Subsidies should be curtailed in areas where their yields in terms of scientific merit tend to be low, and should be channelled instead to the growing points of science, where increased financial means may be expected to produce a work of higher scientific value. . . . So long as each allocation follows the guidance of scientific opinion, by giving preference to the most promising scientists and subjects, the distribution of grants will automatically yield the maximum advantage for the advancement of science as a whole.
>
> (Polanyi 1962b: 60–1)

Polanyi concludes his portrayal of science as a spontaneous order with a metaphor. He maintains that the "Republic of Science is a Society of Explorers" (Polanyi 1962b: 72). It is an association of independent explorers who combine to move towards achievements that are unknown to them. Exploration is governed by rules serving the traditional authority of science. However, there is a self-renewing quality to the authority, since the continued existence of science depends on the creativity and originality of its participants. The authority of the scientific community is mostly nonhierarchical. The authority of scientific opinion is between scientists, not that of one scientist over another. Polanyi's republic of science searches for the truth. The republic may coalesce into a leading position which he calls a "dominant orthodoxy." Because science aims for truth, it ensures the right of dissent. Orthodoxy can be opposed on the grounds of truth, but not on any arbitrary basis whatsoever. Intellectual anarchy and barbarism are rejected but not pluralism. Pluralism may be necessary for further scientific progress as long as opposition is premised on a mutual search for truth.

From an economic point of view, Polanyi's republic of science helps in some ways but leaves some unanswered questions. Polanyi clearly portrays two different self-corrective processes for science and for commercial markets. Prices mediate markets while published results of scientific research make science self-adjusting. An independent self-corrective process of mutual adjustment in science is one way to remedy the problems of science that emanate from an economic analysis of misconduct and market failure in science. But this puzzle-solving process leaves an important economic question unanswered. Science depends on resources to support the careers of those involved, their avenues of communication, their publications, their laboratory instruments, etc. Nowhere does Polanyi discuss whether the flow of resources will be adequate to support his vision of science as a self-correcting, puzzle-solving exploration. If the economic basis of science erodes, then in some way one would expect that it would negatively impact the autonomous, noneconomic self-correctiveness of science. Is it possible that the economic substratum supporting science of all types could work so poorly that science mostly fails? Polanyi's general optimism with regard to science suggests that he views science failure as a minor problem, although he does not pose the issue as an economic problem.

HAYEK'S THEORY OF SCIENCE AS A NONCOMMERCIAL, RULE-GOVERNED ORDER

Michael Polanyi's puzzle-solving republic of explorers is not the only way one could advance the thesis of the self-correctiveness of science in the face of misconduct and market failure in science. An economist who has created a similar vision of science and the economy is F. A. Hayek. Perhaps because Hayek is an economist, the economic content of Hayek's views are richer and more complex. Hayek advances a conception of the self-correctiveness of science which is literally quite different to the self-correctiveness of the commercial marketplace.

The vision of society as an array of institutions governed by imperfect invisible-hand processes is most clearly found in the writings of F. A. Hayek.

Not only is the economy viewed as a self-corrective competitive marketplace of ideas, but also law, human behavior, political institutions, and even the mind are also viewed as self-corrective spontaneous orders. Hayek's theory of the competitive, commercial marketplace is an application of a general theory of how ideas are constructed and, once constructed, how they compete in our complex world and economy. The general thrust of Hayek's writings on the institutions of society is that they all constitute growth of knowledge processes in the context of scarcity and ignorance. Hayek has written a great deal about science mostly on rather narrow methodological topics. His view of institutions as means for dealing with epistemic scarcity suggests that it is equally applicable to science. Hayek implies this in certain passages. Although Hayek has not created an economic theory of science, a theory of science as a spontaneous, imperfectly competitive marketplace of ideas is ripe for plucking from Hayek's writings on competition and the institutions of society.

For Hayek, competition is a process for discovering knowledge. This is true whether the process is a game, a commercial business, a test, an exam in a university setting, or even science. Most conceptions of competition – whether they refer to the economy, to science, to games, or to any other process of creative activity – exist to produce knowledge that would otherwise not be available. Competitive processes produce knowledge that cannot be obtained in any other way. Hayek's view is found most clearly in his essay on the subject, "Competition as a Discovery Procedure":

> *Wherever* the use of competition can be rationally justified, it is on the ground that we do not know in advance the facts that determine the actions of competitors. In sports or examinations, no less than in the award of government contracts or of prizes for poetry, it would clearly be pointless to arrange for competition, if we were certain beforehand who would do best. As indicated in the title of this lecture, I propose to consider competition as a procedure for the discovery of such facts as, without resort to it, would not be known to anyone, or at least would not be utilised [original emphasis].
>
> (Hayek [1968] 1978: 179)

Like most mainstream economists, Hayek extols the virtues of a market system of economic organization. A market system has superior information-creating qualities. In the mainstream neoclassical view, the informational superiority of the market is attributed to prices. Prices are the fundamental informational ingredients of the market process. Prices and price changes are taken as givens to which economic agents must respond. Prices play an important role in Hayek's view, but they are not the most fundamental level of information in the economy.

In his essay, "The Use of Knowledge in Society," Hayek presents a view of the price system which I have not seen repeated elsewhere. For Hayek, the most fundamental level of knowledge in the economy is the common-sense knowledge that individual agents discover in their particular economic situations. Hayek's phrase for this is "knowledge of particular circumstances of time and place" (Hayek 1948: 80). Everyone has knowledge of their own situation which would be difficult for others to discover at that moment in time. Some of this peculiar knowledge could be of economic value:

> To know of and put to use a machine not fully employed, or somebody's skill which could be better utilized, or to be aware of a surplus stock which can be drawn upon during an interruption of supplies, is socially quite as useful as the knowledge of better alternative techniques. The shipper who earns his living from using otherwise empty or half-filled journeys of tramp-steamers, or the estate agent whose whole knowledge is almost exclusively one of temporary opportunities, or the *arbitrageur* who gains from local differences of commodity prices – are performing eminently useful functions based on special knowledge of circumstances of the fleeting moment not known to others.
>
> (Hayek 1948: 80)

It is this qualitative, idiosyncratic information discovered and produced by ordinary economic agents which is the most basic form of information in the economic system according to Hayek. The problem of the economy is to create a mechanism to convey some of the more significant attributes of these discovered economic situations facing many transactors. The price system is a mechanism which distills some of the most important characteristics of unique, particular economic situations and represents them in a form that they can be understood by others. The market is like a laboratory instrument that provides a few important indicators of an unknown phenomenon or activity being studied. In this regard, Hayek describes:

> The price system as a kind of machinery for registering change, or a system of telecommunications which enables individual producers to watch merely the movement of a few pointers, as an engineer might watch the hands of a few dials, in order to adjust their activities to changes of which they may never know more than is reflected in the price movement.
>
> (Hayek 1948: 87)

In another essay, Hayek likens the process of economic competition to a process of exploration of the unknown. Competition is a process for discovering "new ways of doing things better than they have been done before" (Hayek 1946: 101). In yet another passage, Hayek portrays competition as prospecting. Individuals search for unused economic opportunities that, when discovered, may be emulated by others (Hayek [1968] 1978: 188).

For Hayek, the market is just one of many types of self-organizing process in society. He calls them spontaneous orders. A spontaneous order is a pattern characteristic of a self-regulating system that is independent of any individual mind or consciously structured plan. At one point, Hayek uses the term "cosmos" to describe a spontaneous order in comparison to the planned order of a humanly designed organization:

> While we have the terms "arrangement" or "organization" to describe *made* order, we have no single distinctive word to describe an order which has formed *spontaneously*. The ancient Greeks were more fortunate in this respect. An arrangement produced by man deliberately putting the elements in their place or assigning them distinctive tasks they called *taxis*, while an order which existed or formed itself independent of any human will directed to that end they called *cosmos*. Though they generally confined the latter term to the order of nature, it seems equally appropriate for a spontaneous social order and has often, though never systematically, been used for that purpose [original emphasis].
>
> (Hayek [1967] 1978: 73)

For Hayek, what social theory should discover is patterns of spontaneous order. Again I quote from Hayek's writings to find the clearest statements of his position:

> But while the order of the physical environment is given to us independently of human will, the order of our social environment is partly, but only partly, the result of human design. The temptation to regard it all as the intended product of human action is one of the main sources of error. The insight is that *not all order that results from the interplay of human actions is the result of design* is indeed the beginning of social theory. . . . All deliberate efforts to bring about a social order by arrangement or organisation . . . take place within a more comprehensive spontaneous order which is not the result of such design [original emphasis].
>
> (Hayek [1967] 1978: 73)

What Hayek seems to be saying is that competition in the economy and elsewhere takes place in the context of a cosmos of spontaneous order. The patterns of interaction among the competitors is unplanned although it is impacted by the conscious efforts of the competitors. Such a competitive cosmos makes better use of the information possessed and being discovered by each of the competitive participants, than could any humanly designed organization structured on the basis of authority.

Hayek's theory is that all social processes are imperfectly competitive, information-creating and ordering processes. He makes no exception anywhere for science. Taking Hayek's view of society as a cosmos of competitive knowledge creating processes and applying it to science would result in a conception of science as a process. Science is a competitive cosmos or a spontaneous, self-correcting order for discovering new fundamental knowledge about the properties of our world. Economic competition and scientific inquiry are both discovery processes. Economic competition and scientific competition differ in the type of facts they attempt to ascertain or discover. In economic competition, the facts

147

are relative to a particular circumstance or situation. Commercial economic knowledge for Hayek is idiosyncratic information about particular times, places, and circumstances. On the other hand, scientific knowledge concerns "'general facts,' which are regularities of events" (Hayek [1968] 1978: 181).

Hayek's conception of science as a cosmos or a competitive spontaneous order like the market and other social processes leaves one problem unresolved – the self-correctiveness of science. Hayek has an unusual understanding of the knowledge in the market as situational, particular information in specific economic circumstances. Prices are constructed indicators of relative scarcity about these unique situations. Although prices are not the most basic level of knowledge in the economy, price changes provide an indicator for economic agents to alter their practices and decisions. Price changes provide an indication that something must be different. As economic agents respond to variations in relative prices, the economy moves in a self-corrective direction. For science to be self-corrective, there must be something in science which provides the equivalent of the indicator function of changes in market prices. For Hayek, the self-correctiveness of science is located in evidence and methodological rules. Methodological rules require that a scientist search for and publicize evidence that can be reviewed by other scientists. Methodological rules specify part of the process by which the participants of a process mutually adjust their activities to each other in response to relevant evidence. Competitive behavior in science is rule-governed. The rules of science are typically what constitutes the various methodologies of science. Individual scientists honor methodological rules and the results of evidence as part of their commitment and desire to be part of a scientific community. Rules capture some of the authority of the scientific community at any given moment in history. Rules and evidence provide authority in science but this is not authoritarian because membership in a scientific discipline is not imposed. Rather it is a choice that an individual makes as the best use of their occupational efforts. Methodological rules are not static and unchanging. Methodological rules of science provide a provisional sense of authority in science and they can be challenged and changed. The rules of science are not absolute, they change in an evolutionary, adaptive fashion and there is room for mistakes.[6]

Throughout his life, Hayek focused on one mistake which he thought pervaded the social sciences. Hayek objected to the straightforward application of the methods of the natural sciences to the study of social phenomena. He called this scientism (Hayek 1942). Taken one step further, the scientistic attitude held that questions about alternative government policies could be resolved using the methods of the natural sciences. In the extreme, this culminated in the so-called scientific socialism. Hayek rejected both central planning and the day-to-day, short-run government intervention pursued in Western Europe and North America. Hayek denied that such choices could be decided using the methods of the natural sciences.

Hayek's thesis about scientism is an implicit admission of an important limitation on the self-correctiveness of science. If the methods of the natural sciences could be applied to social phenomena in a time horizon matching the needs of politicians and bureaucrats, then government could proceed by policies informed step by step with the methods of science. A denial of this possibility constitutes a rejection of the short-run correctability of science. Hayek objected to the application of science to the management practices of government because he maintained that individual social events were unpredictable. Instead Hayek advocated a search for patterns in social phenomena and an "explanation of the principle" behind such patterns.

Hayek believed that the modern social sciences had become dominated by a scientistic mindset. If this is true and scientism really is a form of error with regard to real science, then a truly self-correcting social science must at some point repudiate the scientistic attitude. In economics, Hayek opposed Keynesian economics as a scientistic approach to economic policy. From the late 1940s through the 1970s, Keynesian economists envisioned intervention in the economy on the basis of scientifically justified changes in policy. Changes in monetary policy and/or fiscal policy were to be based on the most recent evidence available from large-scale, multiple equation econometric models of the economy. The Keynesian policy of fine-tuning aggregate economic activity with measured changes in monetary and fiscal policy was challenged and ultimately abandoned in a debate with a resurgent conservative classical vision of the economy. The challenge to Keynesian economics from the New Classical economics lead to a rejection of extreme policy activism. Although it was not Hayek's critique which lead to a rejection of the scientistic attitude in Keynesian economics, this modification of the Keynesian position surely is consistent with a longer-run vision of the nature and limits of the self-correctability of scientific knowledge.

The irony of all of this is that the New Classical school was in a different way more scientistic than Keynesian economics. The New Classicals set out to demonstrate theoretically and empirically the flawed inferiority of Keynesian macroeconomics. However, the theoretical general equilibrium core of New Classical economics, although still pedagogically important, has been replaced with theoretical exploration now focusing on the macroeconomic implications of imperfect competition and economic growth. New Classical economics has not been so much as rejected as bypassed. The interests of professional economists have turned elsewhere. Again, the abandonment of the extreme scientism of the New Classical school can be seen as self-correcting and progressive from the vantage point of a Hayekian vision of economic science and economic processes.[7]

As with Polanyi's puzzle-solving republic of science, Hayek's self-ordering cosmos of science helps with some issues but raises others. In Hayek's conception of science, the locus of self-correctiveness is found in methodological rule-governed inquiry. Methodological rules govern the way evidence is created and interpreted as supporting one theory and not another. But if Hayek's rule-governed cosmos of science uses economic resources, then the problems of market failure may undermine the otherwise self-corrective generation of new evidence and theories in science. Hayek himself continually worried about this prospect with the flawed view of science known as scientism. Evidently those with scientistic pretensions of the social sciences emulating the natural sciences were able to outcompete opposing views and dominate the social sciences for decades at a time. They essentially formed an intellectual cartel largely excluding their rivals. Economics is a good example where scientistic attitudes associated with Friedman's essay dominated economics for decades. Scientistic points of view of several varieties – the neoclassical, the Keynesian, and the New Classical – controlled the largest share of resources in the economics profession for quite some time. Market failure in the form of scientific intellectual mono-polies dampened the diversity and possible progress of economic science. In spite of all of this, Hayek was still optimistic that science would be self-corrective.

RESCHER'S LOGARITHMIC RETARDATION THEORY AND SCIENTIFIC PROGRESS

While Polanyi and Hayek each provide a theory of how science can be self-corrective, their characterizations of the self-correctiveness of science are largely noneconomic. For Polanyi, the mutual self-adjustment is located in puzzle-solving and for Hayek methodological rules help to make science self-corrective. In their views, the self-correctiveness of science is located in some noneconomic processes of appraising evidence, hypotheses, and theories. Additionally, both Polanyi and Hayek allow for significant problems and flaws in their vision of self-corrective science to the extent that science may go in an erroneous direction for decades. However, neither Polanyi nor Hayek have theorized that there may be economic aspects of the self-correctiveness of science. There is one economic view which partially remedies this deficiency. Nicholas Rescher (1978b) has written a long book on the economics of the natural sciences called *Scientific Progress*. In this book, Rescher considers what impact economic resource constraints may have on the nature of scientific progress and thus on its self-correctiveness.

In other books, Rescher (1977, 1978a) had already raised the question of the self-correctiveness of science from a Peircean perspective. Recall that Peirce had maintained that scientific opinion would converge in the long run to one view of truth which he called the final opinion. Rescher's position differs from Peirce in the following way. Rescher is skeptical of Peirce's idea that science will be self-corrective in the sense that it leads inevitably to more accurate answers that are taken to be closer approximations to the truth. There may be serious errors with current positions in science. These errors will be corrected with scientific progress. Science is self-correcting in the sense that errors will be corrected by more science. These could be incremental revisions of the existing framework of science. Or they could be wholesale rejections of existing science and replaced by some unknown or even unimagined theory. Science is self-corrective in the sense that *"science is autonomous"* [original emphasis] (Rescher 1977: 171).

With the Peircean origins of his economic philosophy of science clearly identified, the most significant contribution in Rescher's work on the self-correctiveness of science is *Scientific Progress*. The theme of scientific progress is an important one because the idea became quite controversial in the aftermath of T. S. Kuhn's *The Structure of Scientific Revolutions*. Kuhn at one point maintained that science progressed by scientific revolutions as one paradigm replaced another. This notion has been criticized because of the thesis of incommensurability also advanced by Kuhn. If paradigms are incommensurable, then objective comparisons between successive paradigms are impossible. If there is no basis for comparing successive paradigms, then it is difficult to conclude whether progress or self-correction has taken place. This questioning of the objective basis of science has continued with more recent analysis of science emphasizing the rhetoric, discourse, and deconstruction of science. But Rescher rejects the extreme incommensurability position. In *Scientific Progress*, Rescher argues that science does advance and that the advance of science depends crucially on the technology and availability of resources for observation. Because observation is escalating in complexity and cost, Rescher asserts that scientific progress occurs at a decelerating rate. There is a logarithmic retardation to scientific progress due to the effect of scarcity on the cost of observation.

Scientific Progress is divided into five major parts.[8] The first part consists of four chapters providing background for Rescher's logarithmic deceleration thesis regarding scientific progress. There are five possible theories regarding the future of scientific progress and four suggest an end to scientific progress. They are termed the *fin de siècle* view. This general view was prominent in the late nineteenth century. Progress in physics and other natural sciences was thought to be approaching a natural limit and science was perceived as nearing a completed state. The fifth theory asserts the potential limitlessness of science. Rescher's retardation thesis is one version of the view that the future of science may be unlimited. An unlimited future for science is not based on the quantitative or qualitative infinity of nature. Either of these views of nature would imply the limitlessness of science. In particular, the thesis that nature is composed of an endless hierarchy of levels of physical order would imply the unending nature of science. Instead, Rescher adopts a narrower position premised on the scientist's ability to create new theoretical constructs. The potential limitlessness of science is based on the human ability to conceive and theorize about the world. Theories as hierarchically nested conceptual structures can be created, altered and improved. In principle, there needs to be no end to the theoretical conceptualizing and reconceptualizing of our world.[9]

The second major part of *Scientific Progress* concerns the deceleration of scientific progress. Scientific research escalates in cost. One of the first to call attention to the increasing cost of scientific research was the physicist Max Planck. Rescher calls this aspect of science, *Planck's Principle of Increasing Effort.*

This principle is used by Rescher to explain a puzzle with regard to scientific progress. Even though effort and resources have grown exponentially, Rescher asserts that first-rate innovation in science has increased at a constant rate. In the absence of Planck's Principle, one would have expected an exponential increase in scientific findings. But cost escalation can explain why there has been no acceleration of scientific progress. New resources have been necessary just to keep up the current pace. At another point Rescher cleverly reformulates the point. He argues that the number of truly significant results in science are not proportionally related to the total number of results. Instead he suggest that important results are the square root of total results. This gives added support to his thesis regarding the logarithmic deceleration of science.

Part three of *Scientific Progress* elaborates the cost escalation of science by focusing on the technological dependency of science. Rescher maintains that the really major advances in science are new conceptual perspectives, new problems, or new ways of posing old problems. However, scientific progress is never exclusively conceptual. Progress at some point must depend on new facts. It is the new facts that depend on the existing level of technology and the resources that can be devoted to implementing that technology. Rescher envisions a stratified hierarchy of technological levels of observation. Each level corresponds to state of the art technology for a generation. A new generation of technology typically alters and improves observational performance by one or more orders of magnitude. Initially, when a new level of technology is implemented, scientific discovery and progress come rather easily and quickly. As the easiest discoveries are made, the rate of progress slows down suggesting a saturation effect quite similar to the economic idea of diminishing returns. The rate of progress can accelerate only if a new technology is created which expands the scientist's powers of observation. But here again an economic problem is encountered. New generations of technology escalate in complexity and in cost.

In part four of *Scientific Progress*, Rescher likens the movement through higher levels of technology to an arms race against nature. He envisions discontinuous leaps in performance and cost as technology improves from one generation to the next. Since cost increases by orders of magnitude from one technological level to the next and resources are limited, Rescher concludes that it will take longer and longer to reach the next stage of technological development. With the constant resource flow of a zero growth world, escalating technological complexity means that we must wait longer for each new period of significant scientific progress. Part five is the last part of *Scientific Progress*. Here Rescher raises the issue that there may be questions for which we will never have sufficient resources to provide adequate answers. For economic reasons, some things will be forever beyond human knowledge.

Like Polanyi and Hayek, Rescher maintains that science is mostly self-corrective and that there are serious problems with the self-correctiveness of science and its ability to make progress. Unlike Polanyi and Hayek, Rescher presents an elaborate portrayal of the economic aspects of the self-correctiveness of science. Progress and self-correctiveness in science depend on new observations and new observations are dependent on technology. Technology improves in discontinuous stages which increase in cost at an accelerating rate. Given a constant flow of resources and cost escalation due to the nature of improvements in observational technology, Rescher concludes that scientific progress will decelerate. This is inherently an economic argument making economic aspects a central part of a conception of the self-correctiveness of science. Rescher does not suggest that the economic aspects of the self-correctiveness of science function like markets. However, like Polanyi and Hayek, Rescher does not ask whether his vision of the self-correctiveness of science is impeded by market failure and misconduct. He does not analyze whether economic concentration by a dominant school of theory would further decrease the decelerating growth of science. It is also quite possible that market failure may lead to a resource flow which is less than the steady-state constant flow of resources assumed in his thesis of the logarithmic retardation of scientific progress.

PARTIALLY ENDOGENIZING SCIENCE AS AN ECONOMIC PROCESS

At this point I return to a consideration of the themes of this chapter restating them in the form of an economic puzzle of science. The puzzle goes something like this: Science clearly lacks the self-corrective stabilizing forces of commercial markets, yet the notion of a competitive marketplace of ideas asserts the competitive self-correctiveness of science. How can science be both self-corrective and a domain of misconduct and market failure? Polanyi, Hayek, and Rescher have each provided part of an answer. Polanyi and Hayek theorize that science and the market economy constitute distinct adjustment processes. In the economy, Polanyi and Hayek both emphasize the role of prices in facilitating corrective adjustments. In science, Polanyi emphasizes mutually observed puzzle solving and Hayek emphasizes methodological rules in relation to theories and evidence as the core of the adjustment process (Butos 1987). These are aspects of a non-economic invisible-hand process which allow science to be self-corrective, and Rescher has called attention to the escalating cost of observational technology as a reason for the deceleration of scientific progress and self-correctiveness in science.

None of these eminent scholars have analyzed fully the self-correctiveness of science as an economic process. Rescher comes the closest with an economic analysis of why scientific progress slows down. An analysis of the self-correctiveness would aim to translate the essential ideas of the self-correctiveness of science into economic terms. One of the main problems is that the time horizon of most conceptions of economic processes are much shorter than those of science. The very idea of stabilizing market adjustments connotes a much shorter period of time than the amount of time required for adjustment processes in science. Even if the average length of the business cycle is used as a longer estimate of the time necessary for a market economy to stabilize, the adjustments processes of science would seem to be of much greater duration. Science typically occurs beyond the time horizon used in most economic theories. Another problem is the public good nature of scientific theories and research where it is difficult for the discoverers of a breakthrough to capture a significant share of the benefits of their work. A third problem is that science is far removed from the demand for its product resulting in science being dominated more by the producers than the ultimate consumers.

However, beyond these economic difficulties, there is another problem with the solutions offered by Hayek and Polanyi. In theorizing that science and the market are separate distinct corrective processes, Hayek and Polanyi come quite close to fully exogenizing science as a noneconomic process. Unfortunately, this is contrary to the very idea of conceiving of science as an economic process. For decades, if not centuries, philosophers, sociologists, historians, and others have asserted that economic functions are external to an understanding of science. In their view, the rationality of science apparently was unaffected by economic motives and circumstances. In opposition to this approach, an economic view of science has been developed which leads initially to an emphasis on misconduct and market failure in science. However, to remedy the inherent pessimism of a conception of science focused on its flaws, the contributions of Hayek, Polanyi, and Rescher have been presented. In a nutshell, the antidote to the dismal portrayal of science from an economic point of view comes quite close to abandoning the economics of science we sought to embrace.

My solution to this dilemma is to reject extremes. Science is neither fully endogenous in the economy nor fully exogenous. To state it positively, science is a partially endogenized economic process. My point can be made more clearly with regard to three conceptual distinctions in Figure 8.1. Figure 8.1 contains three sets of conceptual distinctions: one for science, one for the economy, and another for markets. Conceptual distinction I was the one discussed above categorizing internal and external factors that affect science. Typically, it has been the logic and methodology of scientific inference which has been taken as internal to science. External factors have been those in the social environment of science such as history, sociology, psychology, and economics. The presumption was that a theory of science should be addressed to the internal aspects of science. It is this distinction which explains in large part why there has been so little research on the economic aspects of science. Conceptual distinction II appears in a lot of economic research on the economics of organizations and institutions. This distinctions dichotomizes economics into market and non-market processes. Conceptual distinction III is the categorization scheme in the contributions of Polanyi and Hayek. They see both markets and science as self-corrective processes with the self-correctiveness of science justifying the metaphor that science is a competitive marketplace of ideas.

The solution I offer is to identify conceptual distinction III with conceptual

Figure 8.1 Three conceptual distinctions concerning science and the economy

distinction II rather than I. Conceptual distinction I is rejected because it would associate the marketplace of ideas with an internal, noneconomic logic and methodology of scientific inference and it would associate commercial markets with factors external to science. This interpretation would make all economic factors external to science. If conceptual distinction III is related to II, this suggests that science is mostly a nonmarket economic process. In this view, a great deal of economics that economists have done on market failure and the creation of organizations, institutions, and contracts as a response to market failure would be associated with science conceived as a self-corrective process. For long periods of time, institutions and organizational processes have evolved which permit a great deal of economic autonomy for the scientific community. Science as a nonmarket social and institutional process has evolved so that it functions in a nonmarket manner. The self-corrective processes of science work best in scientific terms when they are far removed from the influences of commercial markets. But any attempt to create a social process which is largely independent of market forces is itself an economic decision. Furthermore, science is a resource-using process. Thus the attempt to isolate science from economic forces ultimately must be incomplete and partial.

Rather than conceiving of science as an exception to economic processes, an alternative would be to expand our vision of economics. To the major markets and sectors of the economy we could add science. One often used characterization of the economy is the four-sector model from macroeconomics. This is shown in Table 8.1. In addition to the usual sectors of goods, money, bonds (financial markets), and labor, science could be added as another fundamental economic process. In an economic sense, science is a peculiar and unique process. Science is about as far as one can get from the conventions of the commercial marketplace. But there is still much that can be learned from science. Nonmarket activities need to resolve economic problems otherwise their functions are hampered or they cease to exist. Science may be a window on economic aspects of social processes far removed from the commercial marketplace. Indeed, I might go so far as to suggest that science be considered the economic opposite of competitive auction markets like the bond and stock markets. Thus science might have much to teach us about the economics of nonmarket processes in society.

Table 8.1 The major sectors or markets of the economy including science as a partially endogenized economic process

Speed of adjustment	Sector	Example	Adjustment horizon
Slowest	Science	Science in universities and research labs	Months, years, decades
	Labor and capital goods	Unions and career ladders Machine tools	Months, years
	Goods	Consumer goods and services	Days, weeks, months, years
	Money	Cash management practices	Days, weeks, months
Fastest	Bonds	Auction markets in finance, commodities, and foreign exchange	Moment by moment, days.

Furthermore, I suggest that science be conceived as having an extremely long-term adjustment process which historically has been mostly self-corrective in the long run, but not in the short run. The correctiveness of science allows for many flaws such as intellectual monopolies, market failure, and misconduct in the short run. Additionally, the past progressiveness and self-correctiveness of science gives good reasons for optimism. Progress, though likely, is not inevitable and the possibility of failure for prolonged periods is ever present. Also, it must be realized that the sort of self-correctiveness that an economist has in mind typically does not occur in science. Scientists and economists use the words self-correctiveness in a remarkably different way. Science is not self-corrective in the same fashion as commercial markets. There may be shadow prices in the minds of each scientist for doing one thing rather than another, but they are much more subjective and have a wide degree of dispersion compared to the relative prices which occur in commercial market processes. The fact that the self-correctiveness occurs at all in science is therefore all the more remarkable when it is realized how deep and pervasive the nature of market failure is in science.

CONCLUSIONS

In this chapter I have contrasted the optimism of those who maintain that science is a self-corrective marketplace of ideas with the more critical awareness which comes from a more analytical application of economics to science. Initially, an economics of science implies that misconduct and market failure should be significant problems in science. However, the position which I have suggested attempts to avoid the extremes of conceiving of science as being either completely economic or noneconomic. Science has been portrayed as a partially endogenized, nonmarket economic process. The allocation of resources and incomes to scientists and to certain lines of research has important flaws, particularly in the short run. But there is no reason to expect the incidence of misconduct and market failure in science to be worse than it is in other nonmarket processes such as government and nonprofit organizations. In the long run, science is mostly self-corrective surpassing both the problems of misconduct and market failure.

To support these conclusions, some of the more detailed statements of the self-correctiveness of science and the marketplace of ideas have been explored. In most cases, the self-correctiveness of science has been asserted with an explicit awareness that science faces serious problems. Polanyi has drawn a picture of the spontaneous, self-corrective nature of science which also corrects for serious problems such as fraud and bungling. Hayek is aware of a major flaw in the application of scientific methods to the social sciences which he has labeled as scientism. And Rescher views the advancement of science as slowing to a logarithmic rate of retardation because of resource constraints and cost escalation. Despite the flaws of science, Polanyi, Hayek, and Rescher still assert that science is self-corrective. Polanyi likens the problem of coordination in science to the public solving of a puzzle. Hayek sees science as a market-like process with rule-governed evidential inquiry replacing the price system as the locus of self-correctiveness. Rescher focuses on new observations that come from the next technological breakthrough. Science typically is viewed as being self-corrective in spite of failure in the marketplace of ideas and problems of misconduct such as fraud and replication failure. If one can conclude that science is indeed self-corrective in spite of market failure, this would lead to a new level of appreciation for the processes, institutions, and the organizational arrangements of science. Science may be the economic opposite of auction markets. As such, science could take its place alongside the major sectors and markets of the economy as an altogether different category of economic activity thus expanding our conception of the nature of economic activity.

9

ON THE ECONOMIC
ORGANIZATION OF SCIENCE,
THE FIRM, AND THE
MARKETPLACE

I submit that the full range of organizational innovations that mark the development of the economic institutions of capitalism over the past 150 years warrant reassessment in transactions cost terms. . . . Every exchange relation qualifies.

(Williamson 1985: 17)

Whatever is true of people in general had better apply to scientists as well. Scientists are people. One cannot claim simultaneously that people in general cannot sustain long-term widespread altruistic behavior and that scientists can, without offering some explanation for this peculiar state of affairs. Why are scientists so special? Because no one yet has suggested that any unique features of science as a social institution are due to the peculiar genetic makeup of scientists, the only plausible answer must lie in the peculiar structure of science as a social institution.

(Hull 1988: 304)

FROM COST-BENEFIT THEORY AND MARKET FAILURE
TO THE ECONOMIC ORGANIZATION OF SCIENCE

This economics of science portrays science as an imperfect process with the potential for both astounding success and abysmal failure. Science is mostly a self-corrective process, but nevertheless a potential for failure is always present. Besides the examples of misconduct noted in earlier chapters, the cases of Popper, free market economics, and Friedman's essay raise a concern for market failure in the scientific marketplace of ideas. A myopic conception of science as a competitive process that inevitably and without question leads to progress and truth needs significant amendment. An economics of science that encompasses scientific progress and also misconduct and market failure in the marketplace of ideas can provide such amendments. Market failure in the marketplace of ideas raises a concern for the organizational and institutional structure of science. If there is significant market failure in the marketplace of ideas and if it

158

is undesirable for government to intervene and correct market failure in the domain of science, then there must be other organizations, institutions, and processes which contribute to the self-correctiveness of science.

Science is an array of organizations and processes for producing fundamental knowledge about the nature of the world. Science is far removed from the commercial marketplace. The institutions and organizations of science are unique. They are different than anything else observed in either the private or public sector of the economy. From an economic point of view, this uniqueness of science as an economic process requires explanation. If science is not organized like a competitive industry or firm, then how is it organized? In this chapter, I consider science as a production process for creating the most fundamental capital that human beings can produce – epistemic capital. Science produces intellectual capital in the form of scientific theories. I ask why science needs peculiar institutions and processes unlike any others in the economy and society. In economic terms, the question is: Why does science exist as a separate economic entity? Why are its institutions and organizations so unique?

SCIENCE AS AN ANOMALY TO THE SUBSTITUTES THEORY OF INSTITUTIONS IN MAINSTREAM ECONOMICS

Mainstream economics, particularly neoclassical economics is often characterized as having no theory of institutions. This characterization is based on a half-truth and therefore is quite misleading. While it is true that institutions play an insignificant role in competitive equilibrium models in economic analysis, a theory of institutions pervades modern mainstream economics. I believe it is important to identify and elaborate the theory of institutions in mainstream economics because it has not been clearly and succinctly characterized elsewhere. I would like to argue that a substitutes theory of institutions has emerged in recent decades in economics. This substitutes theory can be characterized broadly with the following propositions: that markets and other institutions are essential for economic activity (institutional pluralism), that the market is primary, and that other institutions are secondary to the market. This theory has emerged in two related but different domains of inquiry. First, in the domain of political economy, an argumentative conceptual structure relating government and the economy has appeared. A *substitutes argumentative structure* gradually has evolved which assumes that government is a substitute for the market. Second, in an ancillary literature on production and business organization, a substitutes approach to understanding the firm has been created. To form the core of a more complete theory, a substitutes theory of institutions would integrate the substitutes argumentative structure of government and the marketplace with the substitutes literature on the firm and the marketplace. A substitutes theory of institutions would assume that firms, government, and other forms of organized economic activity, are deviations from and substitutes for competitive markets. With regard to science, this theory of institutions will be both helpful and limiting. Eventually, I want to criticize this theory. But there is much to learn from this theory.

The substitutes argumentative structure regarding government and the market economy is portrayed in Table 9.1. It can be found piecemeal in virtually every mainstream economics text and professional journal. In professional journals, the complex demands of scientific inference require formal modes of expression which obscure the broad, overarching arguments found in the discipline. In textbooks, this argumentative structure is more readily apparent, although no text explicitly presents it. And this argumentative structure has both stimulated and inhibited scientific progress in economics.

Table 9.1 The substitutes argumentative structure of most mainstream economics texts: sequence of argument

	Microeconomics issues	*Macroeconomics issues*
I Market efficiency	Competitive efficiency of markets	Classical, self-adjusting, noninflationary full employment economy.
II Market failure	Externalities Economic concentration Poverty Market instability	Recession Depression Stagflation Financial crisis and panics

III Government intervention	Public goods provision
	Antitrust policy and regulation
	Welfare programs
	Minimum wage laws
		Stabilization policies:
		  Monetary policy
		  Fiscal policy
		Regulation of financial institutions and markets
		Tax law revision

IV Government failure	Public choice as rational corruption Vote-maximizing politicians Voting paradox	Inflation and unemployment Pro-cyclical policies Political business cycle Long and variable policy lags Rational expectations
V Institutional change	Deregulation Welfare reform Reduction in the size of government	Monetary policy rule Balanced budget amendment Incomes policy Competitiveness/industrial policy

What the substitutes argumentative structure of economics presents is an ahistorical, evolutionary story regarding the efficacy of competition and attempts to correct the side effects of free markets with government intervention. This argumentative structure presents possible successive stages of institutional change. These qualitative stages require the lapse of real historical time. The very nature of the stages of analysis suggests a limitation in application to an advanced capitalist economy. With reference to Table 9.1, the substitutes argumentative structure of recent economics unfolds with the presumption that competitive markets are the most efficient organizers of economic activity. Often there is little if any justification given for taking competitive markets as a point of departure for economic analysis. But competition is often flawed. If there is a little "sand in the machinery" of the market, then the story of competition is modified to allow for informational failures and other categories of market failure.[1] Markets are efficient, but they do fail. The reasons are now well known in economic theory. There are externalities at the micro level such as pollution, free-rider behavior, moral hazard, and adverse selection. There are uncapturable benefits such as positive neighborhood effects. And the macro economy appears to be subject to episodes of recession and stagflation. The possibility of market failure, raises the issue of correctability. If we know how markets function, and if we know how they fail, then perhaps some form of intervention might remedy the worst cases of market failure. Most government policy of the past few decades appears to be justified on the basis that a free market economy can be improved on the basis of well-structured government policies.

Conservatives have disagreed with the argument that government should substitute for the market where it fails. One form of conservative criticism extends the substitutes argumentative structure with another argument. If the market can fail, then perhaps government intervention can also fail. Government may fail adequately to carry out the well-intentioned policies aimed at reversing the most painful aspects of unfettered capitalism. The failure of government may be due to a difference between theory and the real world. Perhaps interventionist theories work well in texts and in the classroom, but not in the real world of commerce. In fact, contemporary conservativism has advanced the argument that government failure is worse than the market failure which the government intervention was designed to correct. Contemporary liberals of course disagree with the appraisal of the conservatives. Liberals, however, have come to recognize that there are significant instances of government failure and that the case for a large role of government in the economy is not as clear as it once was.

The last level of the substitutes argumentative structure is one which calls for institutional change. Institutional change may be necessary if discretionary intervention by government is unworkable and if market failure is particularly severe implying that the rules of the game need to be significantly altered. Liberals and conservatives of course disagree on the nature and level of institutional change. Proposals by conservatives are quite fundamental and tantamount to a constitutional-level restructuring of the relationship of government and the economy. Liberals tend to see institutional change at this level as unnecessary, preferring to alter the nature and substance of government regulation, programs, and policies. An important change in the debate over the past few years concerns the timing and duration of any institutional changes. Longer-run changes in the relationship of government and the economy are thought to be much more effective than short-run or temporary changes. In large part, this is a consequence of Milton Friedman's permanent income hypothesis which stimulated extensive research on the relationship between income and consumption and the ability of the government to alter consumption patterns with tax policy. Permanent or longer-run changes in tax policy have a more immediate and stronger effect than shorter or temporary changes in policy. This result appears to be generalizable to other areas of the relationship between government and the economy such as education, monetary policy, and regulatory policy. Thus the broad outline of the substitutes argumentative structure proceeds from market efficiency to market failure, to government intervention, to government failure, and finally to institutional change at the constitutional level. Constitutional change includes explicit constitutional amendments for economic purposes and implicit changes such as changes in the rules governing the conduct of economic policies.

The substitutes argumentative structure is a remarkable intellectual structure and mainstream economics has made significant advances in theory and application. But there are exceptions to the substitutes argument that even the most mainstream of economists would recognize. Government is not the only organizational alternative to the market. A theory of just the marketplace and its relationship to government is hardly a complete theory of institutions. From an economist's perspective, other significant entities are missing. One of the most notable is the firm. The substitutes argumentative structure ignores the firm. A theory of markets would require nothing more than individual households. Firms are not essential to a mainstream theory of a market-based economy. To be sure, a theory of the firm as a profit–wealth maximizing entity does exist and significant resources have been devoted to developing this theory of the firm. But the firm is a glaring omission from the substitutes argumentative structure which pervades modern mainstream economics.

In conventional mainstream economics, the firm is treated as a black box. Its internal structure and character largely are ignored. The emphasis is on externally observable behavior in the marketplace. Typically the firm is characterized technologically as a production function which responds in a mechanistic way to the opportunities for profit apparent in both product and resource markets.[2] Given technology and the possibility of borrowing through financial markets or institutions, the firm is viewed as carrying out a straightforward process for optimizing its present value. Jensen and Meckling encapsulate the traditional view of the firm:

> While the literature of economics is replete with references to the "theory of the firm," the material generally subsumed under that heading is not a

theory of the firm but actually a theory of markets in which firms are important actors. The firm is a "black box" operated so as to meet the relevant marginal conditions with respect to inputs and outputs, thereby maximizing profits, or more accurately, present value.

(Jensen and Meckling 1976: 82–3)

While this view of firms prevails in almost all of the textbooks, it leads to a problem – the problem of the firm. If markets are universally assumed to be the most efficient organizational arrangement and do not require the presence of firms for confronting scarcity, then why do firms exist at all?[3]

Beyond the traditional theory of the firm as a profit-maximizing entity, another theory has developed to address the question of why firms exist. This theory is not included in most micro theory texts and course materials. Most often firms (like households) are presupposed as an essential individualist building block of the economy without further explanation. The existence question of firms is never raised. A theory aiming to explain the existence of firms has been developed and can be seen as a variation of the substitutes argument. The theory that government substitutes for markets when they fail to organize economic activity efficiently can be extended to firms. Firms may come into existence to remedy significant aspects of market failure.

Together the substitutes argumentative structure of mainstream political economy and the substitutes conception of the firm would suggest the broad outlines of a *substitutes* theory of institutions in economics. A substitutes theory of institutions would assume that other forms of organized economic activity are, like the government and the firm, derivatives of and substitutes for competitive markets. Figure 9.1 depicts the substitutes theory of economic organization. The preeminence of the assumptions of scarcity and markets is exhibited by their position to the far left. Markets are designated as the best solution to the problem of scarcity. Of course markets fail.[4] Other institutional structures come into existence to compensate for the inadequacies of markets. In this view, these other institutional arrangements no doubt would not exist if markets were universally successful in organizing human activity. Nonmarket

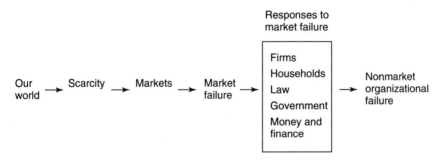

Figure 9.1 The substitutes theory of economic organization

163

organizations are viewed as an attempt to emulate the ordering of the market-place – an extension of the marketplace by nonmarket means. Each of the nonmarket organizational substitutes for the market may fail. In some cases, the failure of the nonmarket institutions may be worse than the market failure it was designed to correct.[5]

What I want to do is further extend the substitutes theory of institutions from government to the firm and then to science. Like the existence of the firm, the existence of science is an anomaly for the mainstream substitutes approach to economic theory and institutions. Other than the inadequate metaphor categorizing science as a competitive marketplace of ideas, there is no main-stream economic theory of science and its institutions. In modern mainstream economics, the theory of institutions is a substitutes theory. My criticism is that mainstream economics needs a complements theory of institutions. My test case is science. It is possible to view the organizations and institutions of science as a substitute for other structures, but this view is limited and inadequate. A substitutes theory of science would be limited by the limitations of a substitutes theory of institutions. A complements theory of science would yield a much more comprehensive economic understanding of science and its peculiar organizational arrangements.

WHY DO FIRMS EXIST? THE SUBSTITUTES VIEW

Why does science exist? There are well-known philosophical answers to this question. Science exists to discover truth regarding unknown, significant aspects about ourselves and the world in which we live. And science exists to enhance our lives by resolving problems that reduce the pain and suffering of humanity. No matter how laudable these answers may be, from an economic perspective they are not satisfactory. They make no mention of the economic dimensions of science. The economic world of most economists consists of households and firms interacting in a commercial marketplace. Additionally government, a legal system, and foreign and financial sectors make for a more complete vision of the economic world. However, conspicuous by its absence is science. Science is rarely included in the economic universe. Check almost any text – introductory, intermediate, or graduate – and verify that science is not an economic topic. Even more significantly, check every monograph and collection of readings on economic methodology and see that the economic dimensions of science have been largely ignored by economic methodologists. They even fail to include the economic notion of science as a competitive marketplace of ideas. To be sure, economics is discussed and the issue of economics being a science is raised, but not science as an economic subject. So I come back to this question: Why does science exist? Why isn't the work of science encompassed within the scope of economic theories of the house-hold, the firm, and the marketplace or other entities typically found in an economist's world?

Before an answer to "Why does science exist?" can be given, two other important questions will be raised. The first is: Why do firms exist? The second is: Why do markets exist? Presently there is a well-developed literature on the existence of the firm. But this literature presupposes the existence and primacy of markets. Regarding markets, there is a vast literature on efficiency as the economic function of the commercial marketplace, but there is very little on why markets uniquely resolve the efficiency question. The question of why science exists may be answered more easily after the efficiency rationale for the existence of markets and firms is more fully explored. So I begin with the recent literature on the existence and nature of the firm, ask why markets exist, raise questions regarding the economic nature of science, and then explore aspects of the economic organization of science.

Why do firms exist?[6] This is a question skirted by the substitutes argumentative structure which pervades almost all of the pedagogical literature in the economics profession. Consider the most basic assumptions of economic analysis. In mainstream economics, the fundamental assumptions of economic theory appear to postulate the existence of scarcity and markets but not firms. Scarcity is a substantive proposition about the nature of the real world. It specifies a fundamental limitation of resources, incomes, and products available for human consumption and production. Markets help us cope with scarcity. Furthermore, markets can function without firms. Thus the scarcity-coping role of markets can be achieved without firms.

The absence of the firm from the substitutes argumentative structure of mainstream economics constitutes an anomaly providing an opportunity for theoretical innovation. One answer to this puzzle regarding the existence of firms has been set forth by a group of economists whose views are known as the New Institutional Economics (NIE). The New Institutional Economics is recognized as originating with Ronald Coase's (1937) influential and highly regarded work on transactions cost. Coase developed a transactions cost theory for understanding the firm and the role of property rights in the marketplace. Others who have made significant contributions are Armen Alchian, Harold Demsetz, Kenneth Arrow, and Oliver Williamson among many others. Alchian and Demsetz (1972) have specifically focused on the firm as a facilitator of team production. Arrow (1969) has emphasized the need for nonmarket alternatives to the market as a response to risk. And Williamson (1985), synthesizing almost all of the NIE literature, has taken the view that the firm is a contractual coalition serving as a governance structure for extremely complex economic processes.

Coase's theory of the firm first appeared in 1937 in his now well-known essay, "The Nature of the Firm."[7] In that essay, Coase seeks to answer the question of why there is any organization other than the price system for organizing economic activity. Comparing the roles of the firm and the market, Coase asks: "But in view of the fact that it is usually argued that co-ordination will be done by the price mechanism, why is such organisation necessary? Why are there these 'islands of conscious power'?" (Coase 1937: 333). Before answering the question, Coase goes on to observe that "the distinguishing mark of the firm is the supersession of the price mechanism," and that the entrepreneur not just the price system is a coordinator of economic activity (1937: 334).

In creating a theory supporting the existence of the firm, Coase first asserts that there are several types of transactions costs associated with using the marketplace. The first type are informational. They are costs associated with acquiring an awareness of relative prices. These costs may be reduced due to the emergence of specialists who keep track of what's going on in particular markets and industries. Another category of costs are negotiating costs concerned with initiating and analyzing contracts. Negotiating costs may be reduced when a firm internalizes production processes which would require a numerous array of contracts if production were alternatively organized by individuals. A third cost or disadvantage of the marketplace is risk. Some individuals may find short-term contracts undesirable. The organizational structure of the firm may allow individuals who prefer longer-term security arrangements a reduced exposure to short-term risk.

At this point Coase is ready to set forth his answer regarding the existence of firms. Firms exist because they organize production more efficiently than the marketplace. Firms economize on information, differential risk aversion, and negotiation costs. Coase summarizes the argument:

> We may sum up this section of the argument by saying that the operation of a market costs something and by forming an organisation and allowing some authority (an "entrepreneur") to direct the resources, certain market-ing costs are saved. The entrepreneur has to carry out his function at less cost, taking into account the fact that he may get factors of production at a lower price than the market transactions which he supersedes, because it is always possible to revert to the open market if he fails to do this.
>
> (Coase 1937: 338)

The theory of the firm inaugurated by Coase was significantly expanded by Armen Alchian and Harold Demsetz (1972). To Coase's explanation of the firm as a transactions cost-minimizing entity, Alchian and Demsetz added the nature of team production. The unique feature of the firm is its status as a centralized contractual agent in facilitating a team productive process. There are problems associated with team production that can be resolved more efficiently within the firm than in the marketplace.

According to Alchian and Demsetz (1972: 778), there are two key demands placed on an economic organization like the firm: measuring and controlling productivity and rewards. Neither of these tasks are addressed in the traditional theory of the firm nor in Coase's article. Team production makes these tasks more difficult. With team production, the marginal products of individual workers are not separable. The inseparability of the productive contribution of one person from another creates a situation conducive to shirking. One of the roles of the firm is to create an agent who can effectively monitor both team

166

production and shirking. The role of the owner is one for which incentives exist for enhancing both team productivity and for deterring shirking. The residual claimant status of the owner ensures that the owner is a better monitor of productivity and shirking than the workers hired by the owner. Thus the firm exists because owners face incentives that allow them to more effectively manage team production than if it occurred in the vertically unorganized setting of the marketplace.[8]

Among the most prominent of recent publications to the NIE theory of the firm are those of Oliver Williamson. Williamson considers Coase and Arrow to be two of his most influential teachers. Williamson's most important works are his *Markets and Hierarchies* (1975) and *The Economic Institutions of Capitalism* (1985). Furthermore Williamson has authored numerous articles dealing with many of the intricate arrangements constituting the internal structure and functions of the firm. While Coase has focused attention on the firm as a more efficient arrangement for reducing several types of transactions costs and Alchian and Demsetz (1972) have expanded the theory to include the difficulties of team production, Williamson primarily has viewed the firm as an array of efficient institutional arrangements. Technology, while important, is a secondary aspect for explaining the organizational nature of the firm. The firm is a transactions cost-minimizing, contractual coalition. Transactions costs are broadly defined as the costs encountered in organizing the production and marketing of complex goods and services in a modern industrial economy and society (Williamson 1990: 67).

Besides viewing Coase, Arrow, Alchian, and Demsetz as important precursors of his work, Williamson also notes the influence of the ideas of John R. Commons (1934) and Friedrich Hayek (1948). What particularly interests Williamson (1975: 3) is that Commons made the transaction rather than the individual the unit of analysis in his economics. In Common's view, order had to be created from disharmony and conflict among individuals. The benefits of efficiency could never be obtained unless there were "working rules" to govern the collective action required in the modern corporation. Regarding Hayek, Williamson (1975: 4–5, 1991: 160) has focused on his theory of the market as a spontaneous governance structure that reflects human planning and design, but one where the apparent order and design is not the consequence of a single, rational and conscious mind. Because much of the knowledge in the market system is idiosyncratic and specialized rather than general and standardized, the market is a continuously evolving spontaneous ordering mechanism. Hayek (1948) apparently believes that a spontaneously ordering marketplace is necessary to complement the neurophysiological limits on human information processing and decision-making. These limits have been denoted as bounded rationality by H. A. Simon (1978) and Williamson. In Williamson's (1991: 173) view, the firm facilitates the neurophysiological limits of human decision-making, not just the marketplace. Bounded rationality is at work within the firm and in the marketplace as well.

What emerges from the NIE theory of the firm is a conception of the firm as a transactions cost-minimizing contractual coalition for organizing complex, team-oriented production processes. This is an important contribution. But this awareness of the NIE position is incomplete. It fails to address one of the most significant aspects of this theory of economic organization. The NIE conception of the firm has taken an unnecessarily restrictive position regarding the firm and the marketplace. While there are two possible versions of institutional pluralism, it has taken what I have previously identified as a substitutes position. The issue is significant because it concerns the status of the market relative to other institutions in the economy. A complements position emphasizes the necessity of the market as one among a whole array of institutions necessary for an efficient and growing economy. A substitutes position gives preeminence to the market above all other institutions. Furthermore, there is the possibility that the substitutes position can be masked as a complements position. Even in the complements approach to institutions, there is a sense in which institutions substitute for one another. Institutions are always growing or contracting even in a complements position. Institutions viewed most fundamentally as complements for each other may be "substitutes at the margin." An expansion of the market could come with the diminution of government. Or the scope of economic activity organized within the firm could come at the expense of both the market and government.

At this point a question can be raised about the theory of institutions in the NIE literature previously summarized. Is the theory being developed a substitutes theory of institutions or the complements theory with organizational substitution at the margin?[9] Quotations from the previous literature will clearly identify the theory as a substitutes theory of institutions. In Coase's article on "The Nature of the Firm," the substitutes position can be seen clearly:

> The "integrating force in a differentiated economy" already exists in the form of the price mechanism. It is perhaps the main achievement of economic science that it has shown that there is no reason to suppose that specialization must lead to chaos. . . . What has to be explained is why one integrating force (the entrepreneur) should be substituted for another integrating force (the price mechanism).
>
> (Coase 1937: 344)[10]

In a 1963 article, Kenneth Arrow intimates that nonmarket organizational structures exist to substitute for the market:

> I propose here the view that, when the market fails to achieve an optimal state, society will, to some extent at least, recognize the gap, and non-market social institutions will arise attempting to bridge it. . . . The doctrine that society will seek to achieve optimality by nonmarket means if it cannot achieve them in the market is not novel.
>
> (Arrow 1963: 947)

168

In their classic article, Alchian and Demsetz clearly depict markets and firms as substitutes. They view firms as internal markets which compete with public markets: "The firm can be considered a privately owned market; if so, we could consider the firm and the ordinary market as competing types of markets, competition between private proprietary markets and public or communal markets" (Alchian and Demsetz 1972: 795). Most recently the conception of the firm as a substitute for the market can be seen in Oliver Williamson's extensive writings. In one place, Williamson (paraphrasing von Clausewitz) remarks that the firm is a continuation of the market by other means:[11]

> I submit that hierarchy is much more than a continuation of market mechanisms. In very much the same way as "War is not merely a political act, but also a political instrument, a continuation of political relations ... *by other means*" ... so likewise is hierarchy not merely a contractual act, but also a contractual instrument, a continuation of market relations *by other means*.
>
> (Williamson 1991: 162)

In another place, in Williamson's *Economic Institutions of Capitalism*, one can find perhaps the most definitive statement of the substitutes position. In his most systematic and comprehensive theoretical treatise, Williamson states that it is useful to assume that markets have a primary existence to other organizations:

> Recall further that the parties to the transactions so described have the option of crafting governance structures responsive to their contracting needs. Only as market-mediated contracts break down are the transactions in question removed from markets and organized internally. The presumption that "in the beginning there were markets" informs this perspective.
>
> (Williamson 1985: 87)[12]

The substitutes conception of economic institutions is a remarkable achievement. In addition to positive economic methodology and the formalization of economic theory, the substitutes conception may be one of the most significant intellectual structures contributing to the dominance of mainstream economic science over the past half century or so. The substitutes view embodies a broad strategic program for expanding the domain of mainstream scientific research in the economics profession. If a mainstream economist had wanted to conceive an adaptive, expansive vision of mainstream economics which would grow at the expense of its most significant rivals such as Marxist, Austrian, and Institutionalist economics, I can imagine no better way than following the substitutes conception of economic science. I am not suggesting a conspiracy of any sort. With the substitutes view, I am merely retrospectively identifying an emergent and enormously effective succession of arguments for dominating the growth of economic science.

WHY DOES SCIENCE EXIST? THE SUBSTITUTES VIEW

Having set forth reasons for the existence of the firm, the case of another organizational structure arises. There is another important resource-intensive set of arrangements which strictly speaking are not dominated by firms or markets. An economic theory would be incomplete if it did not encompass this particular realm of economic activity. The activity which I have in mind is science. Science is a resource-using endeavor which is influenced by the market and occasionally conducted within firms and even households, but science mostly lies outside of traditionally conceived economic activity. Although there are incentives and rewards and maximizing behavior in science, I do not believe that science is predominantly or completely an extension of the marketplace by other means. This does not mean that we cannot better understand important aspects of science by an analogy with the marketplace. In particular, the subject matter of Chapters 2 and 3, misconduct in science such as fraud and replication failure, can be understood if we assume that scientists behave as if they are rational economic agents in a hypothetical marketplace. Some normal conduct in science may also be partly explainable from a substitutes perspective.

A theory of science as a corrective substitute for market and firm failure is a possibility. A conception of science as an economic enterprise could begin with the substitutes literature of economic organization in NIE. The expectation is that this approach would be both fruitful and incomplete. The functions of nonmarket organizations highlighted in the contributions of Coase, Alchian, Demsetz, and Williamson no doubt are important in science as well. The issue is to what extent science can be thought of as an extension of the marketplace by other means.[13] To the limited extent that science is an extension of the market, then the most important aspects of the substitutes position could be incorporated into the complements position.

Returning to Coase's article on the firm, I ask the same questions he asked to see if they make sense for science. The issue raised by Coase was the puzzle of the firm: Why is there an organizational structure like the firm if the price system is universally the most efficient organizer of economic activity? In light of the NIE theory of the firm, the puzzle of the firm can now be restated as the puzzle of science. If markets and firms are the most efficient organizers of economic activity, then why does science exist? Why does science as a unique array of organizations exist as an alternative to the price system, and why are there islands of conscious power other than firms called scientific disciplines? The NIE view that firms save on transactions cost and substitute for markets must apply to science. The organizational structures of science apparently must reduce search, negotiation, and risk aversion costs in ways that cannot be achieved through markets and firms. Scientific research is a complex activity. Information is asymmetric, idiosyncratic, technical, and impacted. Understanding what science is about requires years of professional education and practice. The peculiar organizational structures of a scientific discipline no doubt perform more efficiently many of the same functions that hierarchically ordered firms do in the context of ordinary commerce in reducing the inherent transactions costs of science. Evidently the organizational structures of the firm would not sufficiently reduce the transactions costs of science so that firms cannot be the principle organizational structure of science. Kenneth Arrow's application of many of these ideas to the medical profession illustrates how the organizational structures of science may reduce transactions costs for those involved in medicine:

> I wish to repeat here what has been suggested above in several places: that the failure of the market to insure against uncertainties has created many social institutions in which the usual assumptions of the market are to some extent contradicted. The medical profession is only one example, though in many respects an extreme one. All professions share the same properties. . . . The logic and limitations of ideal competitive behavior under uncertainty force us to recognize the incomplete description of reality supplied by the impersonal price system.
>
> (Arrow 1963: 967)

Moving from Coase to Alchian and Demsetz, the issue of team production becomes a point of focus. For Alchian and Demsetz, the owner of the firm possesses a unique set of incentives which lead him to be more concerned with measuring productivity and shirking than the workers. Consider the role of teamwork in science. Science is not typically organized as a business and does not have a capitalist organizational structure (stockholders). But significant teamwork does exist in science. Ownership of ideas, theories, and empirical discoveries is highly developed in the sense that innovations are credited to their discoverers. Teams of discoverers gain ownership through multiple authorship. This is increasingly important in science. Fundamental scientific findings and innovations require extensive cooperation by highly specialized researchers. Direct economic gain and the ownership of those gains is not a fundamental motivation for the scientist. Productivity and shirking in science may be less important in science because individual scientists retain authorship over their discoveries and contributions even in a multiple authorship arrangement.

Oliver Williamson's conception of the firm and the marketplace as rival governance structures which minimize transactions costs obviously applies to science. Williamson (1985) theorizes that hierarchical nonmarket organizations substitute for the market because of asset specificity, the neurophysiological limits of bounded rationality, and complex, idiosyncratic circumstances, situations, and products. Whatever the organizational structures of science may be, from a Williamsonian perspective they would exist to reduce the transactions cost of pursuing science. In his view, science would be a nexus of explicit and implicit contracts which minimize transactions costs and constitute the governance structure of science. These characteristics are also quite descriptive of science. Organizations in science may not be as hierarchically ordered as the firm, but the unique organizational arrangements of science may solve many of the same problems.[14] Science would be viewed as a rich array of cost-minimizing governance structures which substitute for the marketplace, and even for firms.

While the substitutes theory of the NIE theory of the firm may yield many new insights regarding the nature of science, the market orientation of this perspective may not take us far enough. The primacy of the marketplace makes little sense in the case of science. I believe that we are so far removed from the domain of the real marketplace that viewing science as a substitute for the market makes limited sense. The transactions organized within science apparently would almost never take place within the commercial marketplace and firms. Markets for the things which scientists produce as scientists would rarely, if ever, be formed spontaneously. Given such difficulties, another array of spontaneous arrangements evolved to form the modern scientific disciplines.

WHY DO MARKETS EXIST? THE COMPLEMENTS VIEW

The substitutes theory of NIE is an important contribution from which I have learned a great deal. But it presupposes the primacy of markets as efficient organizers of economic activity without further explanation. There is another view of the relationship of firms and the marketplace which I shall call the complements position. The complements position is broadly characterized by the following propositions: that many institutions may be necessary for a more complete view of economic activity (institutional pluralism) and that no institution plays a preeminent role surpassing that of all other institutions. While the market and the firm are among the most significant institutions of society, neither is primary. The success of the marketplace and firms are intertwined with those of other institutions. Like the substitutes theory of NIE, the complements position begins by presupposing scarcity as a fundamental and pervasive material limitation on human behavior. However, the primacy of the market is reconsidered as a subject of inquiry rather than a presumption. The question posed by Coase regarding firms is now asked of markets: Why do markets exist?[15] The answer which I propose for this question will also be suggested for firms and for other institutional arrangements like science.

In the history of economics, there is a precedent for a complements theory of institutions. The "old" institutionalist school rooted in the ideas of Thorstein Veblen and John Dewey could be characterized as embracing a complements approach to institutions. However, even the old institutionalists have not characterized their differences with mainstream economics as I have in terms of substitutes and complements.[16] The old institutionalists tend to portray mainstream theory in a pejorative way as equilibrium theory without institutions except for the marketplace. In contrast, a complements theory would partially endogenize institutions other than the market. Economic forces affect all institutions even if they are not commercialized or dominated by market processes. A complements theory of institutions would partially endogenize science. Thus science could be viewed as a test case of the problems encountered with endogenizing any institution in the context of economic (but not necessarily commercial market) processes.

A complements theory of economic organization, while still assuming scarcity, replaces the primacy of markets with an assumption about the nature of the world – indeterminism. Indeterminism is the thesis that disorder, chaos, and evolutionary change are more fundamental than order, pattern, and natural law. Indeterminism implies fundamental uncertainty. Indeterminism does not deny that there are high levels of order and pattern in our world, both in natural phenomena and in human behavior and in society. Indeterminism means that all order and pattern have been created either by natural or human causes and that order and pattern are still being created and evolving.[17]

Of what significance is indeterminism to economics? Evolutionary indeterminism as a principle assumption of economic science would significantly enhance our understanding of the economic universe.[18] Indeterminism compounds the problem of scarcity. Scarcity in economics typically means a limitation on resources and time. Scarcity is primarily material and chronological. But in an evolutionary world, scarcity acquires an epistemological dimension. As our world and our economy change, knowledge of existing circumstances becomes dated. Things which are known acquire a dimension of obsolescence and things which are new and not yet known by all may be difficult to anticipate and imagine. In an indeterministic world and economy, there exists the continuous creation, destruction, and annihilation of knowledge. The epistemic structure of society and the economy is quite fragile. Fundamental uncertainty exists.[19] A situation of epistemic scarcity is created.[20] Thus the two fundamental assumptions of a complements theory of economic organization would be epistemic scarcity (uncertainty) and indeterminism as compared to scarcity and markets for the traditional mainstream approach.

In a world characterized by epistemic scarcity, the creation of knowledge and information becomes a task of paramount significance. Anything which enhances order and pattern-reducing uncertainty and the specter and degree of chaos may find a place in human affairs. Markets exist to enhance and inform us of otherwise unknown instances of economic order and pattern in our world. The price system helps identify important similarities characterizing multitudes of otherwise idiosyncratic, unique, and unstandardized economic processes. The price system is an instrument which allows us to monitor economic activity in the way that a Geiger counter helps us meter radioactivity.[21] The difference is that a Geiger counter, in principle, can be conceived and created by one individual while the price system cannot.

Because epistemic scarcity is pervasive, markets are not adequate in all cases to reduce the inherent chaos in human affairs to a functional level. Apparently, there is market failure. But markets are not the only way to cope with epistemic scarcity. Nonmarket organizational structures also offer significant opportunities for reducing epistemic scarcity. Authoritarian hierarchical structures can be an "effective" way of dealing with epistemic scarcity. Authoritarian political regimes allow one individual to impose order on others. Such an imposed order may by either insidious or benevolent, but dehumanizing in either case. Epistemic scarcity can be ameliorated by entities other than markets, firms, and dictators. If we view economic agents as being at sea regarding epistemic scarcity, anything which enhances order and pattern in economic behavior might spontaneously evolve to cope with the problem of indeterminacy. Other hierarchically structured organizations can be seen as information ordering and enhancing innovations. Households with children have an inherent hierarchical order due to the succession of generations. Government and our legal system can be viewed as hierarchical structures which complement those mentioned above. Even and perhaps especially the existence of money, accounting, and the financial sector contribute to the epistemic ordering and reordering of the economy and society.[22]

A complements theory of economic organization is schematically portrayed in Figure 9.2. Evolutionary indeterminism is taken as a fundamental assumption characterizing the nature of the world in which we live. In such a world, epistemic scarcity and uncertainty are pervasive. Confronting a chaotic world, many spontaneous hierarchical responses appear, not just markets and firms. Individuals in isolation may simply repeat many behaviors. Habitual behaviors are really hierarchically organized, repetitive personal actions which would pattern our lives even in a Robinson Crusoe existence. The epistemic cost-reducing aspects of individual habits should not be underestimated. Repetition of any behavior or phenomenon must be a fundamental source of all knowledge and information. Repetitive behavior may appear in the context of an unstructured marketplace or in the context of other hierarchically structured entities like businesses, households, courts, government, and financial institutions.[23] Of course personal habits are far from sufficient for managing the chaotic indeterminism of the world in which live.

In the complements view, a variety of qualitatively differentiated organizations are essential for resolving epistemic scarcity. Humanity cannot depend on

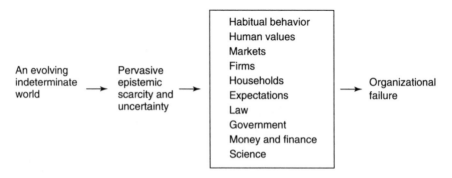

Figure 9.2 The complements theory of economic organization

just one institution like the market or even the primacy of one institution among others. We cannot put all of our organizational "eggs" into one institutional basket. The adequacy of the statement that "in the beginning there were markets" is rejected not because it lacks explanatory value, but because it imposes a theoretically limited view of the world. The issue is which way does it make most sense to theorize about the world and the economy. Markets may be effective in organizing some types of economic behavior and not others. The same can be said of nonmarket organizations. Both markets and nonmarket organizational structures may fail. What is needed is a theory for correcting organizational failure of all varieties. If we could know when to correct non-market institutional failure by reorganizing transactions in the marketplace, this would be a great achievement. But it could also be the case that the failure of one type of nonmarket organization may require the development of another nonmarket structure. Nonmarket organizational failure may be corrected with either market or nonmarket solutions. What we need is a theory of how and why organizational failures are corrected – spontaneously and/or consciously by design.

WHY DOES SCIENCE EXIST? THE COMPLEMENTS VIEW

Although it could be extended to science as suggested above, science has been an anomaly for the substitutes conception of markets and firms. Hitherto, the processes and institutional arrangements by which science allocates resources have not been the subject of the substitutes theory of economic organization. This is an extraordinary deficiency. A substitutes perspective would lead us to the view that firms substitute for markets when complexity leads to high transactions costs and further that the peculiar institutional arrangements of science would substitute for firms when additional complexity leads to even higher transactions costs which cannot be internalized within either firms or markets. While I regard these statements as being informative in a significant way, they do not go far enough. The absence of an economic theory of science is one of the major flaws of mainstream economics.

A complements view of science is a less restrictive version of institutional pluralism accepting much of what the NIE substitutes theory would lead us to say about science. Science in fact is a transactions cost-minimizing, contractual coalition which forms the governance structure of an extremely complex and sophisticated arena of economic activity. What is different in the complements position is the explicitly broader assumptions of indeterminism and epistemic scarcity. In the complements view, the organizations of science help us produce knowledge, information, and specialized instruments that would never have been produced in the context of a commercial marketplace. Markets produce abstract indicators of what's happening in commercial economic processes. Because ordinary transactions are quantifiable in a monetized economy, numerical price indicators of economic activity can emerge quite readily. In comparison, science as an organizational process is engaged in the production of abstract theories about the fundamental properties of our world rather than prices. While these properties are often quantifiable, they cannot be mass produced in standard units and commodified. The properties of our world are not for sale. The properties of our world and the scientific theories of those properties are public goods. It is the production of fundamentally new abstractions which greatly enhances a reduction of epistemic scarcity. Markets and science both produce abstractions, but they are different types of abstractions. Both are needed and the abstractions of the marketplace cannot serve as a substitute for those of science. The economic role of science is to produce these theoretical abstractions and any specialized instrumentation otherwise unattainable through the marketplace or the firms.[24]

The fact that most scientific research cannot be organized adequately through the commercial marketplace is widely recognized with the emergence of a competing set of conceptions. What I have in mind is the conception of science as a marketplace of ideas.[25] If science could be organized as a commercial market activity or if the efficiencies of hierarchy were provided to science through firms, then there would be no need for a marketplace of ideas. The mere existence of the concept of a marketplace of ideas shows that we are beyond the realm of the commercial marketplace and firms. Of course there is some truth to the marketplace of ideas. Rival scientific theories and results do compete against one another so that those which stand the critical appraisal of the scientific community dominate the marketplace of scientific ideas. Michael Jensen expresses what I believe is a widely held viewpoint among professionals:

> In the end, competition in research is as important to innovation and progress as competition in product markets. Scholars will make their own judgements of what are currently useful results and where the productive and exciting research approaches and opportunities are. I have little doubt that with the passage of time, the "fit" (that is, the productive and useful results and approaches) will "survive".
>
> (Jensen 1983: 336)

The marketplace of ideas produces one category of scientific abstractions about our world and society while the commercial marketplace produces another category of abstractions about production, consumption, and borrowing and lending. The commercial marketplace is real while the marketplace of ideas is metaphorical.

If science exists to produce theoretical abstractions and specialized instruments that cannot be produced through any other organizational structures (the complements position), then how does science get the job done? Like any other human activity, science must solve its economic problems. At the most basic level, individual scientists and their support staff must earn a living and have adequate resources for research. At a more comprehensive level, the processes, organizations, and institutions of science must create an environment with attributes that engender the creation of knowledge and information about our

176

world. Neither the firm nor the market may work in isolation or in tandem, so other structures must exist that resolve the economic problems of science.

Using the complements theory of economic organization, both market and nonmarket organizational structures may be essential for science with the nonmarket structures of science being different than those found in any other set of arrangements in society. Previously in economics, the complementarity of market and nonmarket structures has been designated a dual economy.[26] In particular, it has been applied to labor in the form of primary and secondary jobs. Primary jobs are those attained only through access to career ladders existing within hierarchically structured organizations such as corporations, unions, government bureaucracies, and universities. Secondary jobs typically are those found through competitively functioning labor markets. They tend to be jobs with low skills, constant turnover, and dim prospects for improvement unless the job is the first step on one of the career ladders of the primary labor sector. The secondary part of the labor sector is characterized by competitive markets, while the primary part is dominated by structured organizations. If these notions are applied to science, a dual economy results. Primary science would be characterized by its unique nonmarket organizational structures and secondary science by its reliance on markets. The nonmarket institutions of primary science interface with real markets. The dual economy consists of nonmarket, noncommercial institutions, organizations, and processes which form the primary sector of scientific activity, and commercial markets which provide readily obtainable resources and relatively unskilled labor forming a secondary sector of science. The dual economy of the complements theory of science is portrayed in Figure 9.3.

Consider secondary science. Secondary science are those specialized firms and markets which serve the more conventional economic demands of science. Commercial markets and firms can be quite differentiated and specialized. They can be tailored to low levels of production as long as that process is profitable. Markets can be a source of computers, skilled and unskilled labor, the publication, production, and distribution of journals and texts, and the reproduction of supplies, materials, and machines essential for the conduct of scientific inquiry. For the scientist, it makes sense to rely on the commercial market to provide labor, resources, equipment, and technology if it is already available. Specialized commercial market products and processes should help the scientist economize on time and effort, allowing the scientist to focus greater attention on the basic research constituting primary science. Furthermore, the commercial economy establishes the relative wage structure that may be part of the decision to become a scientist or which science to choose. Secondary science is also that part of science which has gone commercial. In recent years, advances and discoveries in basic science have led to applications that are quite profitable in the conventional economic sense. For example, advances in human genetics have resulted in the creation of a biotech industry that has handsomely rewarded scientists and their business associates. New products are continually being

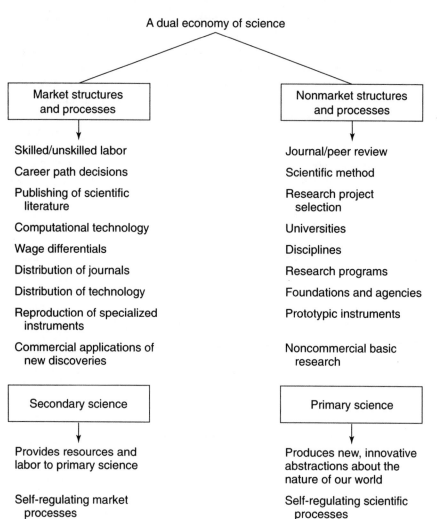

Figure 9.3 A dual economy of science from the complements theory of economic organization

created for the commercial marketplace. Once the basic research has occurred and fundamental discoveries have been made, the commercialization of new knowledge is no longer part of primary science. The commercialization of novel scientific discoveries by definition is part of secondary science.

Two well-known characterizations of primary science are those of Thomas Kuhn and Michael Polanyi. Kuhn (1970) has called attention to a broad conceptualization of primary science, normal science, which is dominated by a paradigm. The paradigm constitutes a scientific vision, a way of seeing the world. Kuhn conceives of normal science as a way of characterizing the main activities of science. Normal science includes not only the most advanced current science on the frontiers of new innovation, but also educational and organizational structures essential for the long-run survival of science. Normal science among many things includes the textbooks, the journals, the puzzles in the subject matter, the collegiate and graduate curricula that enable novices to enter science, the academic departments and research facilities, and the promotion and tenure rules that emphasize the necessity of innovative research. Furthermore, the vast majority of scientific education and a large portion of scientific research occur in the context of the modern university. The non-market institutions and organizations of Kuhnian normal science that constitute primary science are research programs, disciplines, journals, peer review, texts, universities, professional associations, foundations, and government agencies providing financial support.

A conception of primary science similar in many but not all respects to Kuhn's is Michael Polanyi's republic of science. Polanyi's conception of primary science as a rule-governed republic is similar to Kuhn's notions of normal science. A republic of science is a spontaneously ordering society of scientific explorers guided by rules and by tacit knowledge (Polanyi 1962a, 1962b). Much of what they know is more than they can tell and takes the form of tacit knowledge (Polanyi 1966). Scientists are also guided by shared theoretical constructs, by authority, and by mutually observed puzzle-solving. Theories and their applications are learned through professional apprenticeships in graduate school and in research projects. The authority of the scientific community encourages conformity to existing standards of scientific inquiry.[27] Puzzle solving plays a role analogous to markets in the economy. Polanyi has drawn important parallels between the market and science in a way that Kuhn has not done. For Polanyi, the market and science are two different instances of self-corrective social processes. Like Hayek, he calls such self-corrective processes spontaneous orders. For Polanyi, the self-correctiveness of primary science is located in scientific processes such as discovery, testing, puzzle-solving, and authority and not in economic processes. It is the shared investigation and observation of scientific puzzles done by individuals in a context in which each can learn from the efforts of others that allows science to be self-corrective. Polanyi's contribution is like Kuhn's in that it emphasizes the dominant nature of ordinary science as primary science. It is unlike Kuhn's view in that mutually observed puzzle-solving in Polanyi's republic of science is the key to the progress of primary science. In Kuhn's work, puzzle-solving seems more related to the training of new scientists in graduate instruction than to the self-correctiveness of science. Thus for Polanyi, those organizations and institutions of primary science which ensure communication within the community of investigators are essential for the progressiveness and self-correctability of science.

In summary, primary science is basic science facilitated by a unique array of noncommercial, nonmarket institutions and organizations governing the exploration of new domains of phenomena. Primary science is a process of peer reviewed judgements regarding the validity of abstractions created by individual members of the scientific community. Individuals produce abstractions called conclusions, empirical results, corollaries, theorems, laws, etc. and they construct the prototypic instruments and equipment to test those theories. These abstractions are produced using some variation of the team production process usually called the scientific method. The produced abstract results are reported as papers published in scientific journals. Most journals of any significance have peer reviewed publications weeding out papers of lesser merit. Papers publishing new findings can then be judged, imitated, replicated, and/or extended by other scientists. Beyond the arrangements affecting scientists at the individual level, primary science can be further characterized as groups of scientists pursuing similar topics and/or using similar research methods. They may form a small scientific community that inaugurates a professional association, publishes a journal, and authors textbooks. Several of such groups may form a scientific community or research program. The fact that multiple research groups occur within a discipline, research program, or paradigm permits a broader level of communication among scientists that may be essential for the creative expansion of science.[28] Science grows in the context of these unique organizational arrangements and processes called primary science. Primary science is based on a complements theory of institutions. The institutional structure of science is a dual economy which is just as essential for efficiency and growth as any other set of institutions in society.

A DUAL ECONOMY IN THE PHILOSOPHY OF SCIENCE LITERATURE

Since most of what happens in science could not be accomplished in the commercial sphere of the economy, science is a complement to the other fundamental organizational structures of the economy. Science utilizes commercial markets and firms in a secondary way to obtain specialized goods, services, and resources vital to science which science cannot efficiently produce internally. The complements theory of economic organization culminates in a dual economy of science. There is another application of the dual economy of science. Studies, theories, and philosophies of science can be appraised with regard to their implicit position regarding the economic organization of science. Various approaches can be reviewed for the level of institutional detail that is germane to an understanding of science. The question raised is whether science is viewed as an individualized process or one in which the scientist must function in a complex, organizational and social process similar to that found in the dual economy of science. This leads to a dual economy in the literature. The literary dual economy is more metaphorical than literal. In this literature, the primacy of the nonmarket character of science is readily apparent. Some views of science exclusively focus on the individual scientist while others emphasize the scientist in the context of a community of shared processes and institutions. One group of thinkers characterizes science as a highly individualized activity in which scientists interact in a competitive marketplace of ideas. There is minimal recognition, if any, of the institutional and organizational aspects of science. Another group of thinkers pays special attention to the nonmarket, organizational and institutional aspects of science and talks little of a marketplace of ideas.

The literary dual economy is not an actual dual economy as found in Figure 9.3. Neither those who emphasize an individualized marketplace of ideas in science nor those who emphasize other nonmarket organizational structures of science tell us what role real commercial markets and firms have in science. The significance of the marketplace of ideas is that it is tantamount to an admission of the irrelevance of the commercial marketplace to science. The marketplace of ideas is a metaphor which simultaneously denies the relevance of commercial markets and thereby implicitly asserts the noncommercial market character of the organizational structures of central importance to science. The metaphor "marketplace of ideas" is an institutionally nonspecific way to generically assert the noncommercial, self-regulative character of science.

The literary dual economy is portrayed in Figures 9.4 and 9.5. It is by no means comprehensive. The purpose is to highlight the two different approaches to science in recent philosophy of science. The dual economy of the literature is one category of thinkers who emphasize the individualized, but non-commercial market character of science with a marketplace of ideas and another category who emphasize the nonmarket, organizationally rich nature of science. To represent the individualized marketplace of ideas in science, I have chosen Milton Friedman, Friedrich Hayek, Karl Popper, William Bartley, and Donald McCloskey. To represent the organizationally robust conception of the complex institutional structures of science, I have chosen Thomas Kuhn, Michael Polanyi, Imre Lakatos, Nicholas Rescher, and David Hull. The contributions of Hayek and Polanyi were presented in the previous chapter. Hayek fits more with the first group and Polanyi more with the second. Only the briefest of sketches of the theories of these individuals can be presented. All methodologies, theories, and philosophies of science can be read for their economic content. These sketches direct our thinking to implicit notions concerning the economic organization of science in the ideas of these thinkers.[29]

Without going into exhaustive detail, there have been important discussions of the nature of science which emphasize the primacy of the individual researcher. In economics, Friedman's (1953) famous essay on method is exclusively oriented toward advice for the individual researcher. A good researcher is someone who has created testable theories, where a test consists of the predictive adequacy of the theory or hypothesis being tested. Friedman defends the economic theory of perfect competition in this way. Perfect competition is justifiable by the support it has received from repeated confirmations. Friedman's view has been labeled as instrumentalism (Boland 1979).[30] Competitive economic theories are useful instruments for generating predictions regarding economic phenomena. They

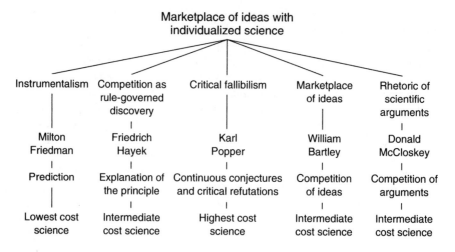

Figure 9.4 The dual economy of the literature: an individualized marketplace of ideas

are to be judged by their relative success in terms of prediction. Friedman does not explicitly use the metaphor marketplace of ideas. But Friedman clearly implies that scientific ideas compete with one another and that this rivalry should be judged by the relative predictive accuracy of rival theories. Friedman (1981) also believes that government intervention in science in the form of funding agencies has had an adverse impact on science. These concerns lead one to assert that Friedman's views are most compatible with a highly individualized marketplace of ideas as a conception of science.

Like Friedman, Popper has focused almost exclusively on the role of the individual in science. One of Popper's (1959) best-known ideas is falsification as found in the *Logic of Scientific Discovery*.[31] Initially, falsification was stated as a criterion for individual scientists to use in appraising a theory.[32] An individual scientist should aim to produce a falsifiable theory. Other scientists as individuals could criticize and appraise the work of another scientist on the basis of whether a contribution was falsified. Of course Popper has conceived of science as a community of individual scientists each interacting professionally on an individualistic basis. At one point, he compares the methodological rules of science to the rules of chess. In a similar comment, he asserts that the *Logic of Scientific Discovery* is an "inquiry in to the rules of the game of science" (Popper 1959: 53). Such comments suggest an awareness that science needs an institutional structure. Popper's most significant contribution has been to characterize the growth of knowledge as an evolutionary problem-focused selection process dominated by trial and error. Knowledge grows through conjectures and refutations as new problems replace old ones. Criticism is central to the conjectural creation of new theories and their refutation. In all of this, the emphasis seems to be more on the individual than the community.

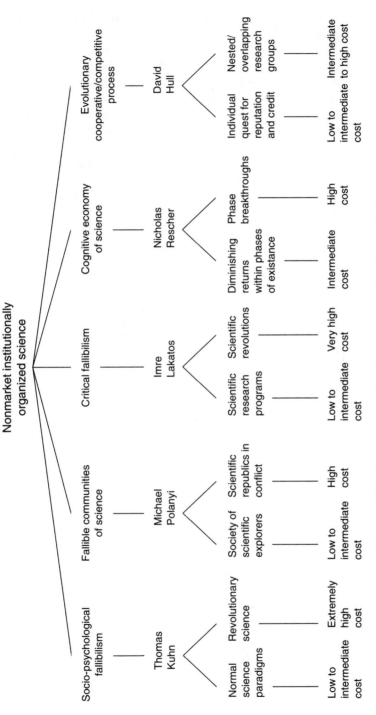

Figure 9.5 The dual economy of the literature: institutionally organized science

Hence I believe Popper's views can be better characterized as being consistent with the marketplace of ideas.

Most recently, Popper's approach to understanding science has been defended by his former student and colleague, the late William Bartley III. As elaborated in the previous chapter on market failure in the marketplace of ideas, Bartley (1990) maintains that Popper's contributions to science have been ignored by the community of professional philosophers who are located mostly in universities. Bartley recognizes that there is market failure in the marketplace of ideas. He directs attention to the institutional and organizational structures of science which he believes prevent free market competition in the marketplace of ideas in science. To remedy this neglect of Popper, Bartley advocates a strong dose of competition in the marketplace of ideas. Bartley believes that the growth of science and philosophy of science needs to be fostered outside of the domain of universities. He believes that universities stifle individual initiative and innovation.

Bartley clearly sees the organizational structures of science as a substitute for the marketplace of ideas. He seems totally unaware of the implications of a complements theory of economic organization. There may be organizational failure in science which Bartley may certainly perceive. However, the more fundamental problem is that science might not exist if it had to emerge in the context of real commercial markets or a literal marketplace of ideas. Aspects of market failure in the domain of science should be expected as part of the cost of having science as a separate, autonomous human enterprise. Bartley's criticisms of science seem naive in this regard.

Another conception of science which appears to be quite individualistic is D. N. McCloskey's (1985) *Rhetoric of Economics*. McCloskey maintains that a rhetoric of science is needed to understand how economists persuade others of the validity and fertility of their research. A rhetoric of science is needed because existing methodologies of economic science have failed. These methodologies have intellectual roots traceable to positivism. McCloskey labels them as modernism. Modernism requires that scientific achievements must be self-evident. However, the methodologies of the most successful researchers in economics have been modernist in name only. McCloskey reviews the research of Paul Samuelson, Robert Solow, Gary Becker, Robert Fogel, and others. If rhetoric were insignificant, then these seminal contributions would require little or no persuasion for their acceptance. McCloskey finds an inconsistency between the rich argumentation of their most important scientific contributions and their minimalist, modernist pronouncements.

McCloskey, in contrast to the isolated-man-in-nature vision of economic man that can be found in much of economics most notably in Robbins (1935), conceives of the scientist as a social individual. The centrality of language and rhetoric in McCloskey's conception of science emphasize the social nature of science. However, the organizational structures of science have no important place in McCloskey's view of science. Preeminent individual scientists persuade

184

others of the validity of their own views. The process is social, but there is no focus on the organizational structures conducive to persuasive communication in science.[33]

While the views of Friedman, Popper, Bartley, McCloskey, and Hayek emphasize the role of the individual and mostly ignore the organizational structures of science, other contributions emphasize the nonmarket institutional structures of science. Many of the institutional features of the dual economy of science that are highlighted in Figure 9.3 can be found in the contributions of Lakatos, Kuhn, Rescher, Hull, and Polanyi. They have focused on organizational structures such as disciplines, journals, texts, exemplars, etc. and are part of what Kuhn called normal science. His contributions regarding the nature of science are so well known, I will not repeat them in detail here. Nor will I present again a summary of Polanyi's view of science because this was accomplished in the previous chapter. Kuhn's emphasis on the unique institutional aspects of normal science makes it clear to see that Popper, by way of contrast, primarily theorizes in terms of individual revolutionary scientists epitomized by Albert Einstein.

Another of Popper's former students and colleagues, the late Imre Lakatos (1978a, 1978b) took much of what Kuhn had to say about the organizational structure of normal science and incorporated it within his notion of a research program. A research program rather than a normal science paradigm became the main locus of the institutional structures of normal science. Kuhn's idea of a paradigm introduced the prospect of a thoroughgoing relativism in science. Lakatos wanted a conception of science which made scientific progress rational and objective rather than irrational and subjective.

In several contributions that have received scant attention from economists, philosopher Nicholas Rescher (1976, 1978a, 1978b, 1989) has pioneered an economic approach to science. As mentioned in Chapter 4, Rescher's economic approach to science was inspired by Charles Sanders Peirce's (1879) project for an economics of research. Following the title of Rescher's book, *Cognitive Economy* (1989), I shall call Rescher's research project the cognitive economy of science. Like Kuhn and Lakatos, Rescher recognizes that science can no longer be done by individuals in isolation. In particular, Rescher focuses on the large scale and enormous costs of many of the most important projects in modern science. Rescher maintains that an implicit cost-benefit calculus pervades most scientific decisions and their magnitude requires team cooperation for the tasks of science to be accomplished.

The last conception of science I shall review is David Hull's (1988) recent *Science as a Process*. As his point of departure, Hull considers the comments by Popper, Kuhn, and Steven Toulmin characterizing science as an evolutionary process. Hull's goal is to create a comprehensive evolutionary approach to science. Such a task requires an intimate knowledge of the theory and evidence surrounding evolution as a scientific thesis. Likewise, an appraisal of Hull's theory would require the reader to have substantial knowledge of evolution.

Hull solves the problem partly by taking the development of the theory of evolution from Charles Darwin to the present as the case study for his evolutionary theory of science. For Hull, evolution is a process of selection which applies equally well to biological, social, and conceptual change. The development of the theory of evolution in biology, if itself evolutionary, ought to embody the very principles of social and conceptual change in Hull's evolutionary theory of science.

Hull's evolutionary theory of science is both individual and organizational. Individual scientists are broadly concerned with self-interest. They are motivated by curiosity about the world, by the desire for credit for their contributions, and by the desire to have their contributions checked and accepted by their peers (Hull 1988: 304). Organizationally science is structured into groups called "demes." Small demes are formed to carry out research projects. Larger demes exist as research programs and invisible colleges (Hull 1988: 508). Cooperation occurs within small and large demes, while competition takes place between demes. Characterized as a whole, science is a mixed, cooperative–competitive affair. The balance between competition and cooperation together with the unique organizational features of science as a social institution result in science being self-corrective (Hull 1988: 366). Science is exceptional in this regard when compared to other social processes (Hull 1988: 304).

TRANSACTIONS COSTS AND THE ECONOMIC ORGANIZATION OF SCIENCE

The dual economy of science in the literature on the history and philosophy of science has important economic content if interpreted collectively. Science is a specialized economic endeavor which must attract, support and retain scientists, support staff, financial capital, and other essential resources.[34] Otherwise science would fail because it would not be economically viable. Science at its pinnacle, particularly revolutionary science, is enormously expensive and risky. Organizational structures must be created which reduce the transactions costs for individual scientists below the level of costs faced by revolutionary scientists. We cannot all be revolutionary scientists.

The various views of science can be categorized by the implicit cost of doing science. Those views of science which exhort us to all be revolutionary scientists like Einstein place extraordinary demands of risk and cost on individuals. I believe that Karl Popper's falsificationist methodology, later broadened to bold conjectures and refutations, places the highest economic demands on individuals of any view of science. In contrast, Milton Friedman's instrumentalist approach to science prescribes an economically viable program for individual scientists. Friedman's ideas for doing science lower the entry barriers to science to a level which the average, doctorally trained scientist can attain and afford. I believe it is the implicit economic viability of Friedman's methodology that has contributed to the widespread acceptance of his essay in economics.

The other views of science implicitly embrace economic transactions costs between the extremes of Popper and Friedman. As stated previously, revolutionary science is the highest cost science because of greater explicit financial outlays, heightened uncertainty, and the inevitable obsolescence of the conception of science losing its dominance. While McCloskey, Bartley, and Hayek pay little attention to revolutions, others do. Kuhn and Polanyi's similar notions of scientific revolutions, Lakatos' conception of research program replacement, Rescher's (1978b) idea of phase breakthroughs, and Hull's vision of occasional but abrupt conceptual change in science, all imply periods of very high cost science. Kuhn, Lakatos, Polanyi, Rescher and Hull, also implicitly recognize that the enterprise of science consists of more than intermittent periods of revolutionary change or the path-breaking accomplishments of a few famous revolutionary figures. Indeed the very idea of sudden, revolutionary changes in science may be overstated and misguided. To their credit Kuhn, Polanyi, Lakatos, Rescher, and Hull have created various conceptions of ordinary scientific activity which make science economically viable for the nonrevolutionary scientist. Kuhn's normal science, Polanyi's republic of science, Lakatos' research programs, Rescher's research within phases of existence, and Hull's demic structure of science all have the effect of reducing the inherent transactions costs of science. Science would be mortally handicapped without the contributions of the average scientist. While some might disparage the mundane and pedestrian ordinary scientist, the organizational structures which provide support for such individuals are vital to scientific progress and to an economic understanding of science. From this point of view, the economic differences among these thinkers may be less than their philosophical differences. Science, among other things, is an economic enterprise and an economic approach to organizations enhances our understanding of both science and philosophy of science.

CONCLUSIONS

Economics is often portrayed as an equilibrium theoretical enterprise without any consideration of any institutions other than the commercial market. This impression is mistake. A substitutes theory of institutions pervades contemporary mainstream economics. This substitutes theory assumes that the market is the preeminent institution of society and that all other institutions substitute for market failure in one way or another. Except for an extension presented above, the substitutes perspective has not been applied to science. There is much to be learned by assuming, at least provisionally, that science is a substitute for both the failure of the market and the firm.

Because of the limitations of the substitutes approach, science has been characterized with a more expansive complements theory of institutions as a dual economy of primary and secondary science. Primary science is basic scientific research that is conducted within a unique array of organizational structures which exist to solve the peculiar economic problems faced by scientists. Primary

187

science is far removed from the influence of commercial markets and firms. Secondary science is the market-related, commercial side of science. A vast array of resources and skilled services can be provided to science from the economy, and particularly profitable applications may drive the creation of a new industry. Secondary science is predominantly commercial, while primary science is non-commercial.

In the complements theory, many varieties of institutions are needed both to create order in our evolving world and to create knowledge of that order through the production of appropriate abstractions. Science is a unique order-creating, order-informing, and order-destroying activity in our economy and society. Science produces theoretical abstractions and specialized instruments which would not otherwise come into existence. The complements theory also offers an explanation of why markets exist. In the substitutes theory, markets appear to be presupposed rather than explained. In the complements theory, markets exist like other organizations and institutions to help humanity cope with the disorder and chaos of an uncertain, indeterminate world. Markets, firms, and science are all needed both to create order in our evolving world and to create knowledge of that order through the production of appropriate abstractions. Markets, firms, and science are all order-creating, order-informing, and order-destroying activities in our economy and society. A complements theory of science has desirable epistemological implications as well. If science were pre-dominantly an economic activity, then science would lose a great deal of its objectivity. The search for fundamental knowledge would then be contingent on economic resources and incentives governed by markets or market-oriented conceptions of nonmarket processes. The dual economy of science is an economic way of expressing the nondominant role of economic factors in science. An economic theory can explain much about science but is necessarily incomplete.

From an economic perspective, the organizational structures of science exist to solve the peculiar economic problems faced by scientists. The economic metaphor of science as a marketplace of ideas provides no explanation of how scientists solve their economic problems. Commercial markets and traditional firms are not adequate to solve these problems. The peculiar economic problems of science can be characterized like those of the business sector as the transactions costs of doing science. Such transactions costs are due to the idiosyncracies and complexities of science, and to the fact that much of science exhibits the characteristics of public goods. Scientific theories are public goods and they are not divisible, saleable, and mass reproducible like private goods. The dual economy structure of science lowers the transactions costs of science to a functional level.

The complements theory also suggests that a metaphorical dual economy may exist in the philosophical literature about science. Some approaches wholly ignore the organizational features of science. Usually this is accomplished with a metaphorical application of the competitive, self-corrective forces of commercial market activity to science as a competitive marketplace of ideas. A metaphorical marketplace of ideas implicitly denies the literal relevance of commercial markets to science. Thus, it is an institutionally nonspecific way to assert the self-corrective and individualistic nature of science. Friedman, Popper, Hayek, Bartley, and McCloskey present the most individualistic conceptions of science of those surveyed. Other views of science, in differing ways, emphasize the essential role of the organizational structures and institutional processes of science. Kuhn, Polanyi, Lakatos, Rescher, and Hull emphasize not only the role of the individual scientist, but the social structures in which the scientist is educated and functions. Bartley's view of science is unusual in that he recognizes the organizational structures of science, but he believes they are responsible for the failure of a competitive marketplace of ideas. Philosophies, theories, and methodologies of science can also be categorized by the level of transactions cost they portray for scientists. Some methodologies impose the extremely high costs of revolutionary science, while others embrace intermediate or low cost conceptions of scientific activity. No doubt all conceptions of science can be appraised for the economic demands implicitly placed on the practitioners of science.

It should also be recognized that the economic functions of the organization of science, although vital to the ongoing nature of science as an enterprise, may have adverse economic implications. The economic security provided for scientists by the organizations of science may free the most creative to produce the best research results of science. But the economic security provided to many may decrease the critical attitude of some. Market and institutional failure in science may diminish the critical attitude as much as enhance it. An economic theory of science must acknowledge this possibility. The economic organization of science may facilitate the growth of science in some ways but retard it in others. Economics is not neutral in this regard. Economics matters if we want to understand science more fully.

10

TOWARDS AN EVOLUTIONARY CONCEPTION OF RATIONALITY IN SCIENCE AND ECONOMICS

> Economists who are zealous in insisting that economic actors maximize turn around and become satisficers when the evaluation of their own theories is concerned. They believe that businessmen maximize, but they know that economic theorists satisfice.
>
> (Simon 1979: 495)

TOWARDS AN EVOLUTIONARY, PROCESSIVE CONCEPTION OF RATIONALITY

One of the key aspects of an economics of science has been a conception of economic rationality. Chapters 2 through 4 were concerned with different aspects of the rational choices typically made by individual scientists. In those chapters, a mechanical optimizing conception of rationality was applied to the choices available to the scientist. However, in Chapters 6 through 9, the complexities of science as an evolutionary social process and the pervasiveness of market failure in the marketplace of ideas essentially suggested a more complicated view of rationality. Rational choice in science is much richer than the traditional optimizing approach to rationality in conventional neoclassical economic analysis. The broader, more complex activities of science require an evolutionary perspective that could imply the need for a processive, evolutionary conception of economic rationality. An evolutionary conception of rationality, whether in science or in economics, could show that logical, mechanical notions of rationality are special cases of something more general.[1]

The path for creating an evolutionary conception of rationality is not as straightforward as it may seem. In creating an evolutionary conception of rationality, I will first explore a conception of rationality in science. Philosophy of science and other studies of science can be interpreted as considering criteria for the rational conduct of science in the context of an evolutionary social process so that genuine knowledge is the outcome. Previously, I have started with economic ideas and applied them to science. In this chapter, I will start with rational conduct in science and argue for an evolutionary conception of the rationality of science. Then from the structure of an evolutionary conception of scientific rationality, I will create an evolutionary conception of economic rationality.[2] Finally, I will reconsider the nature of rationality in an economics of science. In an economics of science, is there one or are there two different aspects of rational conduct? In considering the rationality of science, the philosophical problem of induction is encountered. Induction embodies important aspects of the rational logic of scientific inquiry. But induction has led to questions regarding the rational foundation of knowledge. The problem of induction thus raises concern for the nature of rational behavior in science. An evolutionary conception of scientific rationality is offered to supersede induction. An evolutionary conception of rationality may not so much solve, but rather resolve, the problem of induction. It transforms the problem of rationality and so offers a suggestion that circumvents the problem of induction. Once an evolutionary conception of rationality is established for science, by analogy a similar one is created for ordinary economic decisions.

One reason for proceeding in this way previously was presented in Chapter 1. High levels of order and pattern exist even in an evolutionary world. Machines are models of high levels of order. Usually the order of man-made machines degrades or decays as they simply wear out. Mechanical phenomena in the natural world apparently endure much longer. In so far as human beings have domains of activity which are tightly patterned, mechanism is an appropriate but limited hypothesis. This same logic suggests a limited domain for the validity of rationality interpreted mechanistically as optimization. In an indeterministic evolving social world, mechanism is a description, but not an explanation of these high levels of order and pattern. Where human action is even more complex and less predictable, mechanism is no longer appropriate. What is needed besides the mechanical view of rationality is a conception of rationality for situations of evolutionary epistemic uncertainty. An evolutionary view postulates that all order is created. As order and pattern are created, knowledge is made possible. Whatever creates order, creates the possibility of knowing. To be rational in the context of epistemic scarcity and uncertainty not only means discovering knowledge of previously created order and pattern, but also engaging in processes creating order and pattern.

Another reason for reconsidering the issue of rationality is the precedent set by Peirce. Although his views on evolution have received little attention in the economics profession, Peirce was one of the foremost evolutionary thinkers of his time. Peirce's optimizing model of research project selection was created in the context of his evolutionary metaphysics and view of the world. Peirce thus establishes the precedent of an analytical economic theory within the broader context of an evolutionary conception of human behavior and action. In the broadest sense, this is how I would describe the contribution of an economics of science.

SCIENTIFIC RATIONALITY AND THE PROBLEM OF INDUCTION

In the methodologies of every scientific discipline one encounters the problem of rationally justifying knowledge claims. Most scientists consider the rationality of science to be based in empiricism. Empiricism traditionally has grounded knowledge in evidence based directly or indirectly on sense experience. Empiricists have maintained the necessity of an evidential justification of knowledge, even though modern technology has made observation quite complex and inseparable from theoretical, conceptual contamination. But there is a problem with the justification of knowledge claims within empiricism. Concern with the adequacy of the justification of empirical knowledge has become known as the problem of induction. A problem of induction occurs because our observational capacities are finite but scientific theories make claims that exceed those capacities. Thus we can never know when enough evidence is available to justify the claim that a specific scientific hypothesis constitutes empirically justified knowledge. In his well-known work, *Language, Truth, and Logic,* the logical empiricist A. J. Ayer puts the problem of induction this way:

> Having admitted that we are empiricists, we must now deal with the objection that is commonly brought against all forms of empiricism; the objection, namely, that it is impossible on empiricist principles to account for our knowledge of necessary truths. For as Hume conclusively showed, no general proposition whose validity is subject to the test of actual experience can ever be logically certain. No matter how often it is verified in practice, there still remains the possibility that it will be confuted on some future occasion. The fact that a law has been substantiated in $n-1$ cases affords no logical guarantee that it will be substantiated in the nth case also, no matter how large we take n to be. And this means that no general proposition referring to a matter of fact can ever be shown to be necessarily and universally true. It can at best be a probable hypothesis.
>
> (Ayer 1946: 72)

However, beyond the specific knowledge claims of the various scientific disciplines, the problem of induction occurs in a more fundamental sense. Empiricism is an abstract belief regarding the role of evidence in ascertaining human knowledge. A consistent rational empiricist would want some type of evidence that empiricism itself could be justified empirically. Ayer's statement of the problem of induction led him to suggest a way around the problem of induction. He wanted to resolve the problem of induction both at the level of specific scientific theories and at the doctrinal level of justifying the very idea of empiricism. Ayer's strategy was to suggest that a formal mathematical proof could not resolve the problem of induction and that empirical standards should simply be accepted as the most rational ones for doing science. This defense is sometimes known as a "limits of rationality" defense of empiricism.

The classic statement of the limits of rationality argument again can be found in another of Ayer's books, *The Problem of Knowledge*. Ayer presents the argument in a way that clearly raises a problem of self-reference. Self-reference raises either a concern with an infinite regress or circularity and this, in turn, raises the issues of irrationality and inconsistency. The problem of self-reference will be considered in much more detail in the next chapter. Here attention is confined to considering the issue in terms of a conception of rationality. Concerning the logical defense of empiricism and scientific method, Ayer writes:

> So, if circular proofs are not to count, there can be no proof. And the same applies to any other assumption which might be used to guarantee the reliability of inductive reasoning. A proof which is formally correct will not do the work, and a proof which does the work will not be formally correct.
>
> This does not mean that the use of the scientific method is irrational. It could be irrational only if there were a standard of rationality which it failed to meet; whereas in fact it goes to set the standard: arguments are judged to be rational or irrational by reference to it.
>
> (Ayer 1956: 75)

In the preceding statement, there is a clear self-referential dimension to Ayer's reasoning. Empiricism is its own standard. Empiricism is the rational standard for an empiricist. In a passage that closely follows the preceding one, the self-referential nature of Ayer's argument becomes even more explicit:

> Thus, here again the sceptic makes his point. There is no flaw in his logic: his demand for justification is such that it is necessarily true that it cannot be met. But here again it is a bloodless victory. When it is understood that there logically could be no court of superior jurisdiction, it hardly seems troubling that inductive reasoning should be left, as it were, to act as a judge in its own cause. The sceptic's merit is that he forces us to see that this must be so.
>
> (Ayer 1956: 75)

There is no doubt that the "bloodless victory" imagined by Ayer has not occurred. There is an inherent arbitrariness in making empiricism its own inductive judge. Such arbitrariness would be unacceptable to an empiricist at any other level of argument. Ayer's limits of rationality defense of empiricism does not give an adequate, rational justification of empiricism.

AN EVOLUTIONARY CONCEPTION OF RATIONALITY IN SCIENCE

Ayer's struggle with the foundations of empiricism exemplifies the sort of fundamental rethinking of the nature of science that has been underway for several decades. The paradigmatic version of empiricism was the logical positivism of the 1920s and 1930s. Logical postivists wanted to eliminate metaphysics from philosophy. They advocated a correspondence theory of truth. Theories were conceived as being analytic statements independent of events in the real world. Theories were given meaning by relating every theoretical term to an observational counterpart. This is the correspondence theory of truth. Any abstract entities which could not be represented were rejected as meaningless. Positivism was preceded by British empiricism represented by David Hume and John Stuart Mill and many others. Mill's views were still well known in the early decades of this century. Mill maintained that a scientific law was an inductive generalization that was valid because it was constructed out of the facts of our general experience. The idea of an inductive generalization does not reflect the correspondence theory of truth which came later. Mill's view of theories as inductive generalizations was quite well known to economists and was the view of economic theories that Lionel Robbins (1935) adopted in his influential *An Essay on the Nature and Significance of Economic Science*.

Ayer's rethinking of empiricism reflects an awareness of the problems with logical positivism. By the time Ayer wrote his two books, philosophers and scientists realized that verification at best could serve as a provisional scientific method, but not as a philosophical justification for empiricism. This awareness caused other variations of empiricism to appear. Popper (1959) attempted a substitution of falsification for verification in his work, *The Logic of Scientific Discovery*. Carnap and others argued for probabilistic confirmation of hypotheses. Conventionalists such as Duhem, Fisher, and Keynes saw the validity of scientific theories as a matter of norms accepted by the scientific community. Instrumentalists apparently chose to ignore the problem of induction and de-emphasized the significance of theories for science. For most instrumentalists, the truth or falsity of theories is irrelevant if they facilitate progress. Progress is usually defined as enhanced predictive power.

Since all of the preceding theories seem to share some common ways of conceiving of the role of theories in the search for knowledge, they can be grouped together as divergent instances of a single metatheory of science. Empiricism as a metatheory means that all varieties of empiricism exhibit a common logical and epistemological structure. Popper, Weimer, Bartley and others have noted the existence of this metatheory. Weimer (1979) has called this a justificationist metatheory of knowledge. All variations of empiricism require that knowledge be justified in some way even if the presumption of empirical justification cannot be justified. This use of justificationism seems quite close to another categorization scheme found in McCloskey's (1985) *The Rhetoric of Economics* called modernism. All of the justificationist varieties of empiricism are modernist. Modernism is the belief that knowledge can have secure foundations and that science is the best example of knowledge with a secure foundation.

By way of contrast, a new metatheory seems to be emerging in recent philosophy of science and in other disciplines concerned with the nature of human knowledge. The search for a secure foundation to knowledge appears to have been abandoned. A nonjustificational metatheory has emerged as a critical approach to epistemology. It is clearly post-modernist. It is critical because no uniquely authoritative criterion is offered as the rational criterion or justification of knowledge as is found in all justificationist epistemologies. Although criteria of empirical status can still be used in science, we now know that even logic and mathematics incorporate unprovable and hence arbitrary assumptions. In other words, a logical model of truth, certainty, and rationality is itself unprovable and uncertain. Furthermore, nonjustificationist philosophers of science like Kuhn and Lakatos have added additional dimensions to our understanding of scientific activity. No longer is the analysis of science confined to hypothetical statements of fact. Lakatos has extended analysis of science to research programs and Kuhn to paradigms and world views. Since Kuhn and Lakatos, others such as Laudan, Merton, Hull, Rescher, and Toulmin have continued this trend. The progressiveness of a research program or paradigm cannot be reduced to something so narrow as a single, monolithic authoritative criterion of theory appraisal like verification, falsification, or prediction.

My evolutionary conception of rationality proceeds from Walter Weimer's theory of science as a nonjustificational, rhetorical process.[3] Weimer's view of science is contained in his *Notes on the Methodology of Scientific Research* (1979). Weimer's title does not do justice to his work. Weimer's *Methodology* is nothing less than a synthesis of most philosophy of science up to the point in time when it was authored, and it has anticipated subsequent developments in studies of science, particularly the recent emphasis on scientific discourse as a rhetorical transaction. Weimer's work presents a key insight that is vital to the creation of my evolutionary conception of scientific rationality.

It is possible to create a structured account of an evolutionary conception of rationality.[4] Logic will form part of any conception of rationality. An evolutionary conception of rationality is multidimensional, requiring an important element of judgement and the balancing of multiple concerns. An evolutionary conception of rationality is processive in nature. Rationality as an evolutionary process moves beyond the notion that rational inference is an instantaneous logical inference in response to known or recently discovered facts. The depiction of an evolutionary process conception of rationality begins with a reconsideration of this concern in philosophy of science. Then the analysis shifts to creating an economic analogue of an evolutionary process conception of rationality.

Weimer's synthesis of recent philosophical contributions depends on a conceptual distinction. Weimer maintains that science proceeds on several levels of abstraction. The problem of induction that so concerned Ayer illustrates this well. Positivists like Ayer generally confine the appraisal of scientific theories to one level of analysis. Scientific theories are tested with evidence that is unambiguously considered relevant to the theory. The appraisal of scientific theories is thus at one level of analysis. Weimer calls this the "within theory" level of analysis. Popper and Kuhn also shifted the level of analysis and Weimer has clearly called attention to this fact.

Weimer's synthesis of the philosophical contributions of Popper, Lakatos, and Kuhn is schematically portrayed in Table 10.1. The views of Popper, Kuhn, and Lakatos are so well known that I will not take the time to review their philosophies in great detail. In traditional philosophy of science, the analysis of scientific theories is at one level of analysis. Scientific theories are tested against what is supposed to be an unproblematic empirical background. Weimer labels this as a justificationist conception of science. Logical positivists and their successors of several varieties maintained that scientific knowledge was valid only if it was empirically justified in some way. This is the sort of philosophy of science Ayer had in mind when he discussed the problem of induction. More recently Frederick Suppe (1974) has called this the received view.

It is the received view that Popper and Kuhn both opposed with the alternative conceptions of science they introduced. Popperians acknowledge that theoretical pluralism exists and that theories and research programs clash with one another. They also seem to suggest that all real science is revolutionary science. Justificationism based on or stemming from a conception of proof is abandoned. No finite amount of evidence can ever justify that a theory is valid and will never be replaced. Evidence is vital to scientific progress, but it is not uniquely decisive in the rise and fall of particular theories and research programs.

Table 10.1 Weimer's synthesis of Popper, Kuhn, and Lakatos

Level of analysis	Nature of science	
	Normal science	*Revolutionary science*
Within theory	(1) Testing of consequences (hypotheses) of particular theories within one research program.	(2) Anomaly collection
Between theories	(3) Evaluation of particular theories that constitute a research program.	(4) Rejection of all theories within the research program(s).
Beyond or behind theories	(5) Points of view: absolutely presupposed, never articulated or acknowledged. Commitment to (a) a metatheory, (b) a psychology of "seeing."	(6) Paradigm clashes – of incommensurate points of view.

Source: Weimer (1979: 65).

Thus if the justificationist position of the received view can be depicted as being confined to panel (1) of Table 10.1, then the Popperian view can be shown as being concerned with panels (2) and (4). Popperians see science as a clash between higher-level explanatory theories and lower-level theories of observation. All facts are theory laden. When a scientific test fails, it may be a failure of the observational theory as much as a failure of the explanatory theory being tested. Weimer portrays Kuhn's position as being more encompassing than either the received view or that of the Popperian critical fallibilists. Kuhn extends his conception of science to include clashes of views that go beyond the clash of theories within a research program, and is concerned with both traditional science and revolutionary science. Kuhn's view of science encompasses all six panels of Table 10.1.

Using Weimer's distinction of abstract levels of analysis, an evolutionary conception of scientific rationality can be created. The scientific process is one which is concerned with rationally eliminating errors in the way we think about the real world. The views of recent philosophers of science can be seen as attempts to ascertain the nature of scientific rationality if it is not entirely located decisively in evidence. The logical positivists who preceded Popper located the rationality of science in verification. As is well known by most economists, Popper has replaced verification with falsification. However, the impact of falsification is to make science pluralistic. Pluralism means that several unrefuted and competing theories with a degree of evidential support could exist simultaneously. Such theoretical pluralism requires a reconceptualization of the concept of scientific rationality. Because evidence is crucial but never exclusively decisive in scientific decision-making, I shall call this a nonjustificational evolutionary conception of scientific rationality. What is most significant for an evolutionary view of rationality are the levels of analysis from Weimer's synthesis of science as found in Table 10.1. Also, the major types of arguments that scientists use in their research provide an additional domain for developing a nonjustificational conception of rationality. The arguments of interest are threefold – empirical, analytical, and real.[5] The empirical argument is included because no view of scientific decision-making could be adequate without it. The analytical argument is included because theoretical work has become increasingly significant in science and economics in this century. The real argument is included because I believe that science is concerned with genuine problems in the real world.

Taking both the levels of abstraction and the types of arguments relevant to scientific inquiry, aspects of a nonjustificational conception of scientific rationality are found in Table 10.2.[6] Table 10.2 suggests that various types and levels of rational scientific activity exist for the practitioners of science. The various types and levels of argument suggest that a nonjustificational conception of rationality is a critical conception of rationality. No notion or assumption, no matter how surely it seems to be true and fundamental, is sheltered from criticism. The potential for error is pervasive for the scientist, even his/her

Table 10.2 Nonjustificational modes of criticism delineating aspects of a multidimensional, nonjustificational conception of scientific rationality

	Types of arguments		
Level of analysis	*Empirical*	*Analytical*	*Real*
Within theories	Are there falsifying observations?	Is the explanatory theory internally consistent?	Is there a real-world problem that this theory addresses and does not abstract from?
Between theories	Is the observational theory relevant to its explanatory theory?	Is the explanatory theory consistent with other similar explanatory theories?	Is this a problem that will generate alternative theoretical positions or research programs?
Beyond theories	Is the problem an empirical one?	Is the theory consistent with its conceptual framework?	Is the problem a genuine real-world problem in this conceptual framework?

Source: Wible (1984b).

most fundamental and rarely articulated concepts. Pragmatically, individual researchers accept aspects of their basic point of view in order to test and explore one theoretical approach or one domain of phenomena. However, as a matter of principle, all concepts which constitute a view of science are tentative and conjectural. This includes central assumptions like rationality. A rational scientist is one who is primarily committed to an open mind. A research commitment to a particular point of view is only pragmatic and of secondary intellectual importance.

AN EVOLUTIONARY CONCEPTION OF ECONOMIC RATIONALITY

It was Alfred Marshall ([1920] 1964: 1) who defined economics as "a study of mankind in the ordinary business of life" and John Dewey (1903: 9) who stated that "there is no difference of kind between the methods of science and those of the plain man." Furthermore, ever since Frederick W. Taylor (1947) announced his "scientific principles of management," the ordinary business of economic life has become increasingly affected by the scientific point of view. To the extent that the business community is trained by social scientists and emulates a scientific mode of inference in business decision-making, the problems of scientific inference may carry into actual economic affairs. In other words, the so-called methodological problems of economic science transcend the science and affect the economic activity being observed by the economist. If this argument has merit, that those in the marketplace have been taught implicitly to be scientific in their business activities, then it should be possible to formulate a non-justificational, evolutionary conception of economic rationality. A processive, evolutionary conception of economic rationality would be much more dynamic than the positivistic/maximizing conception of rationality.

Suppose that even just a *few* transactors are as sophisticated in their decision-making as practicing scientists.[7] This means that such businessmen and women conceive of several types of arguments relevant to business activity and at several different levels of analysis. As with scientific decision-making, three different levels of analysis and three types of arguments are presented. The three levels of analysis slightly reinterpreted are simple hypotheses, theoretical systems and conceptual frameworks, and the three types of arguments are informational, analytical and problematical; they correspond in design to those found in Table 10.2. Table 10.3 schematically presents a processive, evolutionary nonjustificational conception of economic rationality.

Table 10.3 A nonjustificational conception of economic rationality with maximization as a special case

Level of analysis	Types of arguments		
	Informational	*Analytical*	*Problematical*
Simple hypothesis	Is information available which implies a rejection of this project?	Are profits and present value being maximized for this project?	Is this project a solution to a genuine real-world problem, economic or otherwise?
Theoretical systems	Are the informational concepts relevant to the analytical concepts which are used to analyze the project?	Is there more than one mode of analysis in economics or otherwise which is relevant to this project?	Is the problem behind this project likely to generate alternative theoretical positions in and outside of economics?
Conceptual frameworks	Is information in principle available, given the role of uncertainty in my conceptual framework?	Are there limits to maximization and other modes of analysis, given my conceptual framework?	Is this problem a genuine problem in the analysis and in my conceptual framework?

Source: Wible (1984b).

There are several significant features of a nonjustificational, evolutionary conception of economic rationality. First, it is *multidimensional*. As such, its suggests the types of decision processes necessary to function in the context of genuine uncertainty. Second, the *problem orientation* of business takes a central place. This sharply contrasts with the traditional optimizing notion of rationality in which the businessman's only constraint is his limited ability to process huge amounts of data that could provide an instantaneous assessment of his economic circumstances. Third, business people are inherently skeptical about taking scientific theories too seriously – economic theories in particular. Such *skepticism* about economic theories corresponds rather nicely with the theoretical pluralism and skepticism found in recent works in studies of science.

Lastly, the most significant feature of a nonjustificational conception of economic rationality is that it explicitly portrays some of the major differences between the two major mainstream strands of microeconomics.[8] They are the Marshallian and the Walrasian views on economic rationality. While it might be unfair to simply equate the Marshallian view of economic activity with a nonjustificational conception of economic rationality, it does appear more compatible with Marshallian than Walrasian microeconomics. Two theorists who have commented on the nature of rationality as it relates to conceptions of economic activity are Robert Clower and Axel Leijonhufvud. Paralleling the analysis above, Clower has remarked:

> In Marshallian analysis, economic agents are conceived to be not so much rational as reasonable. Individuals fumble and grope rather than optimize. They are presumed to know little and care less about efficiency except as competition forces them to attend to it. . . . The contrast between the Marshallian conception of economic activity and that underlying the Neo-Walrasian literature could hardly be more stark. Neo-Walrasian analysis has no use for the bumbling oafs that populate a Marshallian world.
>
> (Clower 1975: 8–9)

Similarly Leijonhufvud has said:

> I tend like Clower, to the belief that the neo-Walrasian hard core is limiting . . . my suspicions focus (so far) on the Maximizing Behavior postulate in the particularly rigid form that it has come to take in neo-Walrasian economics, i.e., as a "necessary condition for the intelligibility of behavior."
>
> (Leijonhufvud 1976: 107)

TOWARDS AN ECONOMIC CONCEPTION OF SCIENTIFIC RATIONALITY

The nonjustificational conceptions of scientific and economic rationality in Tables 10.2 and 10.3 are meant to be suggestive rather than exhaustive. In an evolutionary sense, being rational is making good decisions subject to scarce resources in the context of hierarchically nested levels of conceptualization and a multitude of categories of arguments. There may be additional levels of analysis and other categories of argument which could expand the rows and columns of these tables. In principle, there may be no limit to the levels or to the types of arguments. The three-by-three tables of nonjustificational rationality take us part way in an attempt to infuse science with economic concepts. The two conceptions of nonjustificational rationality show what the cognitive structures of science and ordinary transactor activity may have in common. However, in spite of these cognitive similarities, the scientific conception of nonjustificational rationality ignores economic constraints.

The dichotomy between conceptions of rationality in science and economics (which has just been presented) presupposes a view that I have criticized since the opening pages of this economics of science. Science is studied as though economic issues are totally irrelevant to the conclusions which scientists reach. Throughout this economics of science, I have argued that science cannot proceed independently of economic concerns. Scarcity affects scientific endeavors just like any other human enterprise. The separate and distinct conceptions of scientific and economic rationality need to be integrated in some way for an economics of science to succeed.

In this economics of science, I would like to maintain that both conceptions of rationality are simultaneously operative in science. Economic limitations constrain the scientific process. Rather than adding new rows or columns to the tables of scientific and transactor nonjustificational rationality, I propose a somewhat different strategy. If the projects in the transactor version are interpreted as the research projects of the scientist rather than the investment projects of an enterprise in the commercial economy, then the economic side of nonjustificational rationality can be directly applied to science and the scientist. A conception of scientific rationality in an economics of science would encompass all of the levels of thought and types of argument shown in Tables 10.2 and 10.3. In the context of a cost-benefit approach to the legitimate activities of the scientist as developed in Chapter 5 and applied in Chapters 6 and 7, some of the wording of Table 10.3 may require alteration. For example, the content of the cell in the first row and second column, which now reads as: "Are profits and present value being maximized?" would need to be restated. In cost-benefit terms, the new paraphrase would be: "Is the net present value of this scientific research project being maximized?"

These tables can be seen as two sides of an intellectual Rubik's cube. One face of the cube would be philosophical, another economic, and the third could represent unexplicated aspects of rational scientific inquiry from other points of view. This multidimensional, multileveled, many-sided conception of scientific rationality is processive and incomplete. The unfinished third face of an intellectual Rubik's cube could represent the incompleteness of a nonjustificational conception of rationality. It is philosophical, scientific, and economic, but nevertheless incomplete.

CONCLUSIONS

In economics optimizing mechanical notions of rationality are often contrasted with evolutionary processive conceptions of rational action. Usually these two views of rationality are portrayed as contrary ideas. Previously I have argued that machines should be taken as special cases of evolutionary processes. With regard to rationality this means that mechanical notions of rationality should be conceived as special cases of an evolutionary theory of rationality. An evolutionary conception of scientific rationality was fashioned from the literature in philosophy of science. Often this literature has focused on the problem of induction. The problem of induction shows us that empirical evidence is a necessary but not a sufficient condition for rational scientific decisions. Consequently, this view of rationality has been termed nonjustificational scientific rationality. Once an evolutionary view of rationality in science was created, an economic version was reformulated for the decisions faced by ordinary transactors. Transactors in ordinary affairs must also create and appraise information relative to their most important business and financial decisions. A conception of economic rationality structured analogously to the nonjustificational conception of scientific rationality provided a richer evolutionary conception of economic rationality. This view of economic rationality has been called nonjustificational economic rationality. The last step was to suggest that a conception of rationality for an economics of science would integrate both the scientific and economic conceptions of nonjustificational rationality. Scientists function not only in the context of the philosophical, psychological, sociological, rhetorical, and theoretical complexities which constitute the scientist's discipline, but they also function in an economic context constrained by scarcity. The economic questions of science are intimately intertwined with all of the other important intellectual issues faced by the scientist. The rationality of science has a significant economic dimension.

11

INTERNAL CRITICISM
AND THE PROBLEM OF
SELF-REFERENCE

Although Gödel's "incompleteness" theorem applies, strictly speaking,
only to mathematics, it has much broader epistemological significance.
The Aristotelian ideal is shattered. Perfect deduction of truth from first
principles is not possible. Any formal model must be incomplete. The
theorist will, sooner or later, come upon a proposition that must be
accepted or rejected, not on the basis of logic, but through intuition, or
casual empiricism, or simple assumption.

(Fusfeld 1980: 7)

AN ECONOMICS OF SCIENCE AND SELF-REFERENCE

While an economics of science with an evolutionary interpretation of rational
action and behavior provides a coherent theoretical framework for understanding
much of science, it also raises a problem of self-reference. The problem of self-
reference is an important aspect of the problem of induction that was discussed
in the previous chapter. The problem of self-reference for an economics of
science can be formulated as follows. An economics of science must be applied
to and not exclude economics. If an economics of science were inapplicable to
economics, then an inconsistency would arise. An example would be the position
that the laws of economics are universal, but they exclude economists (and
economic methodologists). Such a position would be blatantly self-contradictory.
From a knowledge of recent intellectual history, a self-referential paradox or
inconsistency is the most significant non-ideological critique of a position that
I can imagine. Such an inconsistency could lead to the invalidation and perhaps
to a rejection of economics as a science. Self-referential inconsistency is an
example of internal criticism. It is the single, strongest internal criticism that
can be imagined. In philosophy, the problem of self-referentiality raises the
arbitrary nature of our most fundamental intellectual positions. The element
of arbitrariness of science that comes out of an economics of science is no
different than the uncertainty, if not agnosticism, attained in recent philosophy
of science.

Since an economics of science is already self-referential, a closer look at the problem in science, philosophy, and mathematics may be in order. William Bartley has formulated a philosophy of criticism as a way of dealing with the issues raised by the problem of self-reference. Following a presentation of Bartley's position, three different instances of self-reference are presented. They take the form of recursive regresses. A recursive version of the problem of induction is created. Then the problem of proof in mathematics is similarly reformulated. And finally the concept of falsification is restated as an infinite regress. In the last section, economic aspects of these instances of reflexivity are presented. In the next chapter the issue of a self-referential economics of science will be considered further.

WILLIAM BARTLEY ON SELF-REFERENCE AND THE *TU QUOQUE* DILEMMA

One response to the relativism of a self-referential theory has been articulated by the late William Bartley.[1] Bartley was a former student, colleague, and editor of some of Popper's writings. He was also an associate of Gerard Radnitzky. Until he wrote *Unfathomed Knowledge, Unmeasured Wealth*, Bartley's best known work was his *The Retreat to Commitment* (1984). The work contains his philosophy of critical rationalism and his response to the problem of self-reference. Critical rationalism is an intellectual position which attempts to balance commitment to new, unsupported ideas with the ideal that all beliefs should be rationally justified arguments. The idea of rational support raises the problem of self-reference. Although Bartley nowhere refers to Rescher's work on the underdetermination problem, the defense of the best intellectual positions of Western thought faces a similar problem. No individual can defend each intellectual argument he/she adopts. The human life span is simply not long enough for one person to check out completely every notion, conception, or argument which is central to an outlook on life. Thus no one can say either of the following statements: "I have examined every position I hold," or, "there is nothing I consider intellectually important which is unexamined or unjustified or unproven."

The problem is worse with an evolutionary conception of knowledge. In the context of an evolving growth of knowledge process, the implications of a new discipline or research program may be unclear for many years. Why does a scientist commit to a new research program in its infancy when it does not have the legitimacy of a more mature rival? If logical justification were the sole basis for knowledge, no mature scientist ever would reject an existing view of science in favor of a novel, infant research program. Or why does the young scientist in the infancy of a career commit to one research program rather than another? The young scientist must accept some starting point. If we demand that all commitments be completely rationally justifiable at every point in time, then such commitments cannot be rational. Obviously, every scientist understands that science is a community endeavor. One must trust the integrity of what other scientists have accomplished. Otherwise science would be continually in a process of reinvention, rediscovery, and rejustification.

Bartley continues this line of reasoning explaining the problem for the conception of rationality. Typically, being rational means that only justifiable positions should be maintained by the reasonable intellect, even if we allow for argumentative defenses fashioned by individuals other than ourselves. Yet this demand, the demand for rational justification, is also a position which must be rationally justified.[2] This is a problem of self-reference. Should the rational way of life itself be rationally justifiable? If we answer yes, this is an impossible demand because it would require us to know more than can be fathomed and have more resources than we do. If we answer no, then the defense of rational thought itself is recognized as being irrational. This opens the door to all sorts of irrational thoughts, behaviors, arguments, and points of view. Communication breaks down.

Bartley called this the *tu quoque* or boomerang argument. If the defense of a rational way of life is ultimately irrational, then anyone can make irrational arguments in support of any position no matter how absurd. The *tu quoque* argument entails a tremendous opportunity cost. The very essence of criticism loses its force. If all intellectual positions are equally irrational, then there is no basis for criticism of one point of view from another. Intellectual life becomes almost exclusively arbitrary. Self-reference leads to arbitrariness perhaps relativism.

THE PROBLEM OF INDUCTION IN SCIENCE AGAIN

The *tu quoque* problem existed long before Bartley dealt with the issue in his *The Retreat to Commitment*. The *tu quoque* problem, or defending rationality with an irrational argument, is raised by the problem of self-reference. An explicit awareness of the problem of self-reference has existed for nearly a century in mathematics, perhaps longer in philosophy. Other than its intrinsic interest as an important intellectual concern, self-reference is of significance as a way of conceiving internal criticism. The problem of self-reference provides a model of one type of internal criticism. As Bartley noted in *The Retreat to Commitment*, the real problem is the breakdown of communication among dissimilar, incommensurable points of view. An internal argument is an argument that might be heard even if its substance is rejected subsequently. In this economics of science, the shift from a substitutes to a complements theory of economic organizations is an attempt to broach a criticism more acceptable to those in the mainstream.

External criticisms abound in economics and they are easily dismissed. Most criticism of mainstream economics has been from an alien external point of view. Criticism of mainstream market economics can be categorized mostly as cross paradigmatic gibes that fall on deaf ears. Mainstream proponents often reciprocate criticizing paradigms to the ideological right or left. Such critiques of other paradigms similarly fall on deaf ears.[3] An effective critique of main-stream economics must take into account the tendency of most economists to ignore criticism from alternative ideological points of view.

Internal criticism is much more difficult to sustain. There are few if any genuine internal critiques of conceptions of economic science. In philosophy of science, Imre Lakatos has noted that the incentives and rewards of scientific research programs direct research away from anomalies and criticism toward an almost exclusive search for supporting evidence. In economics, Melvin Reder (1982: 22) has noted that only "paradigm preserving" research is tolerated at Chicago.[4] Thus it is not surprising that there are few good examples of internal dissent. Those internal critiques that have been published deal with thoughtful reflection rather than a systematic awareness of the nature of internal criticism. D. N. McCloskey's (1985) criticism of positive economics; Michael Howard's (1983) comparison of Marxist, neoclassical and Keynesian theories; Arjo Klamer's (1984) *Conversations with Economists* regarding the new classical macroeconomics; and Homa Katouzian's (1980) *Ideology and Method in Economics* are good examples.

Models of internal, self-referential criticism can be found in science and mathematics. In recent decades, internal criticism has been a significant issue for science and mathematics. Both disciplines have been criticized as being logically inconsistent or logically incomplete. Internal criticism has taken the form of a debate over the problem of self-reference, also called the limits of rationality, or perhaps most simply the liar's paradox. In mathematics a modern discussion of the self-reference problem began with a letter from Bertrand Russell (1902) to Gottlieb Frege around the turn of the century. Russell (1902) discovered a statement in Frege's mathematical logic that could be either true or false.[5] Since this involved a contradiction, it meant that Frege's logical system was inconsistent. Frege (1902) responded conceding the substance of Russell's discovery. In his *Principles of Mathematics*, Russell (1903) simply called his discovery "The Contradiction." Later, in his subsequent attempt to resolve this inconsistency, Russell (1907) related the contradiction to the ancient liar's paradox found in the Bible and other ancient literature:

> The oldest contradiction of the kind in question is the epimenides. Epimenides the Cretan said that all Cretans were liars, and all other state-ments made by Cretans were certainly lies. Was this a lie? The simplest form of this contradiction is afforded by the man who says "I am lying;" If he is lying, he is speaking the truth, and vice versa.
>
> (Russell 1907: 222)

Since then the contradiction has been known as "Russell's paradox" or more simply the "liar's paradox." There are many other versions of the paradox which are presented in Russell (1907), Martin (1970), and Nagel and Newman (1958). In order to reference the paradox efficiently, it shall be designated as the self-referential statement *LP* which is spoken by a liar:

LP. This statement is false.

Statement *LP* is obviously self-contradictory. The truth of *LP* implies that *LP* is false. This violates the law of the excluded middle, that a statement cannot be both true and false.

While the liar's paradox might seem to be a philosophical curiosity, avoidance of the liar's paradox has become one of the more significant intellectual issues of the century.[6] The liar's paradox, which was considered a problem with language, has reappeared in philosophy of science within empiricism and within mathematics. Thus it is possible to show that Russell's liar's paradox can be reformulated as an "inductive liar's" and as a "mathematical liar's" paradox.

Consider the problem of induction as presented in the previous chapter in the context of the discussion of the nature of rationality. The logical aspects of the problem of induction can be illustrated with a few succinctly stated propositions. An analytically consistent empiricist would require that all statements be empirically ascertainable. Ascertainable is meant to be a generic term which could be specified as any of the criteria of empirical reference that philosophers and scientists have considered: inductive generalization, verification, confirmation, falsification, testability, rejection of the null hypothesis, prediction, etc. The logic of the problem of induction and the problem of self-reference can be captured in the following statements. Let proposition *E-1* be a general statement about empirical ascertainment:

E-1. Any scientific statement must be empirically ascertainable.

Consistently interpreted, empiricism requires that *E-1* must also be empirically ascertainable. Formulate this requirement as *E-2*:

E-2. Statement *E-1* must be empirically ascertainable.

Again *E-2* implies that *E-2* must be empirically ascertainable: Formulate this as *E-3*:

E-3. Statement *E-2* must be empirically ascertainable.

If this procedure is repeated many times the process heads toward an infinite regress. If we enter the regress at stage *N*, we have:

E-N. Statement *E-(N − 1)* must be empirically ascertainable.

If we let *N* approach infinity, then an infinite regress occurs. A consistent form of empiricism is infinitely regressive and cannot be logically complete.

An infinite regress can be avoided if it is arbitrarily decided to end the regress with a nonempirical assumption like *E-X*, where *X* denotes the arbitrariness of the assumption ending the infinite regress:

E-X. Assume that empirical criteria are empirically valid and do not apply the demand for empirical ascertainment to *E-X*.[7]

In a rather well-known argument as quoted in the previous chapter, A. J. Ayer has formulated a "limits of rationality" position, that a statement like *E-X* does not have to be defended empirically. The core of the argument is that empiricism sets the standard for rationality and that an argument for empirical validation should not be extended to the very idea of empiricism.

While many might find Ayer's defense of empiricism rational, statement *E-X* fits the structure of the "liar's paradox." Reformulate *E-X* as an inductive liar's paradox:[8]

E-LP. The assumption that empiricism is empirically valid is false.

We now ask whether *E-LP* is true or false. If *E-LP* is true and supportable on empirical grounds, then criteria of empirical ascertainment are untrue and *E-LP* asserts an empirically based denial of the validity of empiricism. This is contradictory. If *E-LP* is false, then empiricism, although true, is without empirical justification. An infinite regress would appear as demonstrated previously. Thus if *E-LP* is either true or false, then empiricism breaks down. This would mean that true statements of fact exist which cannot be supported empirically. Such a state of affairs would suggest that empiricism is seriously incomplete.

SELF-REFERENCE IN MATHEMATICS AND GÖDEL'S THEOREMS

Next consider the problem of proof in mathematics. The arbitrariness of the *tu quoque*, the "liar's paradox," or the "limits of rationality" problem is not confined to the problem of induction.[9] As discussed above, the "liar's paradox" or the Russell contradiction actually originated in mathematical logic. Both Russell and Ernst Zermelo discovered that self-contradictory propositions could be formulated in mathematical logic. Such propositions suggest that there is some surprising aspect of mathematical proof not foreseen by the founders of mathematical logic. The aim of the founders was to obtain a mathematical system in which every statement was a tautological restatement of the axioms and definitions which constitute the system. The essence of proof in mathematics is tautology. If a statement or mathematical proposition could be found which was not a tautology and which was also "true", then this conception of proof would be called in question.

The task of demonstrating the insufficiency of tautological proof procedures as a conception of truth in mathematics was taken up by Kurt Gödel. In a famous paper in the 1930s, Gödel essentially "falsified" the adequacy of proof by providing a counter example.[10] His counter example was clearly motivated by the Russell contradiction or the liar's paradox. Gödel's counter example took the form of a statement that was ostensibly true yet unprovable and which is denoted as *M-KG'*:

M-KG'. This statement is not provable in mathematical system *A'*.

The essence of Gödel's contribution was in providing a demonstration rather than a proof for the truth of statement *M-KG'*. In place of a proof, Gödel offered a mapping relationship between two mathematical systems – arithmetic and metamathematics denoted as *A* and *A'* respectively. Gödel's original statement *M-KG'* was mapped into arithmetic using a technique now known as Gödel-numbering. For every term in *M-KG'*, Gödel provided a common whole-number raised to some whole number power like 11^8. Since each term in *M-KG'* was assigned a unique exponential number, the product of all of the numbers representing all the terms of *M-KG'* would also be a unique Gödel-number. In essence what Gödel created was a one-to-one mapping between statements in metamathematics and arithmetic through the process of factoring. Any number in arithmetic (*A*) that could be factored into a Gödel-number could represent a formula in metamathematics (*A'*). Conversely, every correctly specified proposition in metamathematics could have a unique Gödel-number.

In a schematic representation, Gödel's demonstration can be characterized in Figure 11.1. Let the left-hand side refer to arithmetic, the right-hand side to metamathematics and the arrows to the mapping between the two systems. It's at this point that Gödel's demonstration gets interesting. Three things have been established about *M-KG'*: (1) that *M-KG'* is correctly stated in *A'* (a well-formed formula); (2) that *M-KG* (Gödel-number) is correctly stated (factorable) in *A*, arithmetic; and (3) by virtue of the Gödel-numbering and mapping, that *M-KG'* can be considered as true statement.[11] Now reconsider *M-KG'*. Statement *M-KG'* asserts its unprovability in *A'*. If *M-KG'* is true, then we have found a formula in *A'* that is unprovable. Thus *A'* is *incomplete* because a true statement has been found in *A'* that is unprovable.[12] On the other hand if *M-KG'* is false, this means that *M-KG'* is provable. But if *M-KG'* is provable we have a contradiction. *M-KG'* cannot be both provable and unprovable in *A'*. If *M-KG'* is false (*M-KG'* is provable), mathematical system *A'* is *inconsistent*. Otherwise it is incomplete.

Gödel's demonstration regarding the incompleteness of arithmetic (*A*) and mathematical logic (*A'*) holds only if the analysis is confined to *A* and *A'*. In

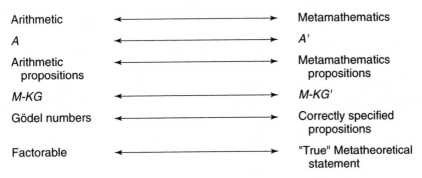

Figure 11.1 A schematic representation of Gödel's incompleteness demonstration

order to facilitate the generalization of the argument, redefine A and A' as A_1 and A_2 respectively. After Gödel, another mathematician demonstrated the consistency of A' now denoted as A_2, but this entailed an appeal to a more comprehensive system than either A_1 or A_2, call it A_3.[13] This succession of mathematical systems is similar to the beginning stages of the regressive conceptions of empiricism with the problem of induction. Taking account of the successive appeals to a higher-order mathematics in order to demonstrate the consistency of a lower level suggests the formulation of a mathematical regress.

Let us consider a sequence of mathematical systems that begins with simple arithmetic and expands to include more complex number and algebraic systems.[14] Arithmetic is denoted as A_1 and each successively more complex system as A_2, A_3, A_4 etc. until the nth system is reached and denoted simply as A_n. The very fact that there are many rather than just one mathematical system and that each successive one may contain its predecessor complicates the situation just a bit. The nesting of the mathematical systems can be represented as follows:

$$A_1 \subset A_2 \subset A_3 \subset \ldots \subset A_n \tag{1}$$

where A_2 contains A_1, A_3 contains A_2, and A_n contains A_{n-1}. Despite this complication, the situation is not all that different for mathematics than it is for science and the problem of induction. Mathematicians generally maintain that nonaxiomatic statements formulated within a mathematical system must be provable within the system. But we know from Gödel's work that this is impossible. The concern for proof involves an appeal to successively more encompassing mathematical systems. Even in this context the paradox reemerges. Let the concern for proof in mathematics be formulated in the following way beginning with arithmetic:

> *M-1.* In arithmetic (A_1), proof is the only procedure for establishing the validity of all nonaxiomatic propositions.

Now the logically consistent mathematician realizes that *M-1* is a meta-arithmetic statement about the role of proof in arithmetic (or A_1) which is not part of A_1 and that *M-1* also needs justification in a broader mathematical system A_2. Formulate this consideration as *M-2*:

> *M-2.* In mathematical system A_2, proof is the only procedure for establishing the validity of *M-1*.

Notice that we have moved to a higher-order system A_2 which contains *M-1*. While this resolves the issue of justifying proof in arithmetic (A_1), the issue of the general validity of proof is shifted from *M-1* to *M-2*. Can *M-2* be proven? Again following Gödel and others, proof of *M-2* seemingly requires an even more encompassing system A_3. Formulate this concern as *M-3*:

> *M-3.* In mathematical system A_3, proof is the only procedure for establishing the validity of *M-2*.

In analogous fashion, a similar demand could be directed to *M-3* and subsequent successors of *M-3*. This process could continue through many stages. At the *n*th stage we have:

> *M-N.* In mathematical system A_n, proof is the only procedure for establishing the validity of *M-(N − 1)*.

If we let *N* approach infinity, then this process like induction becomes infinitely regressive.

As with induction, the mathematical regress could be stopped with an arbitrary assumption that asserts the validity of proof procedures in mathematics:

> *M-X.* Assume that proof is a justification for mathematical validity but do not apply the demand for proof to *M-X* itself.

The self-contradictory nature of *M-X* suggests a mathematical version of the liar's paradox. Let's reformulate *M-X* as Russell-type paradox in the following statement:

> *M-LP.* The assumption that true mathematical propositions be provable in some mathematical system is false.

We now ask whether *M-LP* is true or false. In mathematics, truth is a matter of proof. If *M-LP* is true, then *M-LP* must be applied to itself and proven. However, if we prove *M-LP*, a contradiction results. A proof would have been given asserting the unprovability of *M-LP*. This is logically inconsistent.[15] If *M-LP* is false, then the notion of proof becomes quite problematic. If *M-LP* is false, the validity of truth being solely based on proof is reasserted and the problem of infinite regress reappears again. This implies that *M-LP* may not be provable and thus must be rejected. This means that proof as a criterion for the truth of a mathematical statement may be inadequate. A similar issue can be raised for science. Are there true statements of fact for which there is no empirical support?

FALSIFICATION AND THE PROBLEM OF SELF-REFERENCE

In the mid-1930s, Karl Popper was aware of the problem of induction and tried to provide a resolution to this issue so that scientific progress could continue. Like Gödel in mathematics, Popper (1959) almost single handedly convinced the scientific and philosophical communities that the scientific analogue of proof in mathematics, empirical verification, was logically invalid. Usually the argument against falsification is advanced by comparing the limits of human inquiry with the almost infinite number of observations that could be made by the scientific community. Verification it is argued would be acceptable if investigators could be sure that they had observed all possible outcomes relevant to the theory being tested. Of course, no finite human being can make this claim. A contrary instance might never be encountered. Thus the logic of scientific inference as verification will not work. Only if falsifying evidence is obtained can a theory be decisively rejected. Popper called this theory of scientific inference, falsification.

But the problem of induction is more fundamental than the shift from verification to falsification. Falsification is not an adequate response to the problem of induction when it is reformulated as an inductive liar's paradox. I would like to spare the reader yet another propositional representation of an infinite regress, but falsification has been such a widely accepted aspect of positive economic methodology that it bears repetition. Indeed the problem of induction can be reformulated totally within the notion of falsification. The sequence of conceptions of empiricism presented previously can be reformulated for falsification. Let *F-1* be the requirement that scientific statements be falsifiable:

F-1. All scientifically meaningful statements must be falsifiable.

Now a consistent falsificationist would also require that *F-1* be falsifiable. Denote this requirement as *F-2*:

F-2. F-1 must be falsifiable.

Similarly *F-2* should be falsifiable, if it is to be empirically meaningful. This demand for falsification if maintained to the nth degree would be:

F-N. Statement $F-(N-1)$ must be falsifiable.

Again if we let N tend to infinity, an infinite regress appears. The regress can be stopped by arbitrarily assuming that falsification is unfalsifiable:

F-X. Assume that falsification is the best criterion of scientific inference and do not try to falsify falsification.

Statement *F-X* is a falsificationist form of the liar's paradox. This can be more clearly reformulated as:

F-LP. The assumption that all scientific statements must be falsifiable is false.

If *F-LP* is meant to be a scientifically meaningful statement, then *F-LP* must be falsifiable. But if *F-LP* is falsifiable, then falsification as a criterion of scientific inference is false. *F-LP* cannot be both falsifiable and unfalsifiable. *F-LP* involves a contradiction. Otherwise we are caught in an infinite regress and the difficulties of incompleteness. Falsification does not solve the problem of induction.

Ever since the early 1960s and perhaps earlier, philosophers of science have been aware of the pervasive nature of the liar's paradox in Western thought. Philosophers of science typically presume that science is both the most rational and the most self-critical of all intellectual endeavors in Western culture. If an adequate answer or strategy cannot be found for the liar's paradox in science, then Western thought might be fundamentally irrational. If the conclusion regarding the irrationality of modern science and culture is to be avoided, then a new epistemic strategy is needed which alleviates the dilemma of the infinite regress. One response by Popper has been to create a proposition which does not result in a liar's paradox. Rather than making assumptions like E-X, M-X, or F-X that arbitrarily and uncritically end further inquiry, Popper essentially makes this suggestion:[16]

> F-CRIT. Assume only that falsification is a provisional criterion of scientific inference and do make this assumption known to others so that they can criticize it.

This is Popper's famous thesis of a critical open mind. Popper makes a decisive shift from emphasizing the logic of falsification to an evolutionary process of critical conjectures and refutations. Scientific progress requires that infinite regresses be provisionally stopped. Yet no one should declare that any particular stopping point is final and above or beyond evidential considerations or further criticism. Furthermore, all first premises which serve to stem the infinite regress should be "placed on the table" where they can be examined and criticized by others.

After Popper articulated his thesis regarding falsification and a theory of an open mind, many philosophers of science took Popper at his word and began to criticize Popper's conception of falsification. Some of them even reconstructed historical evidence which "falsified" Popper's original notion of falsification. Other notions of falsification were developed by Lakatos and Kuhn. It should not be surprising that these "newer" conceptions of falsification fit the early stages of an infinite regress. Of course, because of the relatively brief amount of time that has passed and resource constraints, only a few points of this infinitely regressive chain have appeared. The first five stages of a falsificationist infinite regress and a Darwinian generalization are presented in Table 11.1.[17] There are no necessary reasons why more conceptions of falsification may not be found. The problem of induction is still with us even though critical open-mindedness makes the situation a bit more tolerable.

AN ECONOMIC RESPONSE TO THE PROBLEMS GENERATED BY SELF-REFERENCE

By now so many infinite regresses have been formulated that it should be apparent how fundamentally ubiquitous they are. The problem of self-reference, once it is recognized, can be seen in almost all conceptual frameworks be they economic, scientific, mathematical, philosophical or otherwise. Self-reference leads to the *tu quoque* problem – that rational arguments apparently cannot be rationally defended. If this is the case, then all positions, no matter how apparently rational or irrational they be are equally irrational. Perhaps a new strategy is needed rather than the traditional one of attempting to justify a theory on the basis of some higher-level premise or assumption.

Table 11.1 An infinite regress of conceptions of falsification in recent philosophy of science

	Concept of falsification	Rationality of scientific progress in the conception of falsification	Proponent
F-1	Naive-dogmatic falsification	Evidence disproves a theory	$Popper_0$ (A strawman criticized by Ayer)
F-2	Methodological falsification	Rejection of a "falsified" theory is not accepted until conventional decision rules have been followed	$Popper_1$ Author of *LSD*
F-3	Sophisticated falsification	A theory generating excess empirical content (new facts) falsifies its rival. This is a pluralistic model of assessment because the observations may be just as theoretical as the facts	$Popper_2$ (Lakatos)
F-4	Programmatic falsification	A progressive scientific research program (SRP) "falsifies" a stagnating or degenerating rival	Lakatos
F-5	Paradigmatic falsification	A scientific paradigm is "falsified" when one paradigm is rejected in favor of another	Kuhn
	. . .	. . .	. . .
F-N	Unfathomed aspects of falsification	Scientific endeavors at whatever level may be falsified by unimagined hypotheses, theories, research programs, paradigms, metatheories	

In contrast to Ayer who argues that rational arguments set their own standards, Bartley takes Popper's notion of criticism and offers a different strategy. Rather than insulating a point of view from criticism with a *tu quoque* defense, Bartley proposes a different strategy. For Bartley, being rational means to be as self-critical of one's most basic principles as possible and to invite criticism from rivals. Rather than saying, "I cannot criticize your position and you cannot criticize mine because they are equally irrational," invite criticism from a rival. Ask your rival, given a momentary and provisional acceptance of your position, if there are any internal inconsistencies in your position. Alternatively, ask your rival, given your rival's position, if there are any relevant criticisms from his/her perspective. Bartley's strategy is this: Rather than defending a position, create the best representation of that position, criticize it yourself, and have it criticized by others on both sympathetic and antagonistic grounds. In brief, argue with others as you would have them argue with you. Or as Bartley remarks:

For if we treat our opponents in discussion *not as they treat us, but as we would have them treat us,* it is we who profit. When our object is to learn rather than win a debate, we must take our opponents' arguments seriously and not reject them unless we can refute them. As far as our aim, learning about the world and ourselves, is concerned, it does not matter whether our opponent reciprocates, or whether he treats our own arguments as no more than emotive signals. We may learn from the criticisms of our opponents even when their own practice prevents them from learning from us [original emphasis].

(Bartley 1984: 163–4)

One could ask whether Bartley has treated his opponents this way. And even if he has not, certainly one could raise this question about an economics of science. In my view, this is obviously the point of view one must have in creating an economic theory of science. Create the most coherent economic theory that can be imagined and then submit it to criticism both from internal and external perspectives. An internal perspective would be concerned with the coherence of the ideas in economic terms. An external criticism would come from others who have analyzed science from noneconomic points of view and who might oppose an economic theory of science.

Bartley's strategy in connection with the problem of self-reference can be given an economic interpretation. In Bartley's analysis in *The Retreat to Commitment,* the problem of self-reference lead to the *tu quoque* argument. The *tu quoque* argument is rooted in the realization that irrational and rational positions are equally irrational because neither can be rationally justified. The *tu quoque* means that if all intellectual commitments are equally irrational, then no criticism is possible. An economic interpretation of the *tu quoque* argument could be as follows. The demand that an individual rationally justify every position he or she holds is an economic impossibility. A human life span simply is not long enough for one person to ascertain if all of his most fundamental commitments are justifiable. The costs of absolutely justifying every position or theory are too high surpassing the availability of human resources. Consequently, because of scarcity, the demand for rational justification for isolated individuals is unattainable. Therefore because all intellectual positions or points of view face scarcity and insufficient resources, no one will be able to rationally defend their most fundamental intellectual commitments.

In the context of scarcity and an explicit recognition that real costs are involved in doing both science and philosophy, self-referential criticisms make a lot of economic sense. In economics, self-referential arguments economize on arguments already developed and applied to other phenomena. An economic theory of science can make use of arguments developed in consumer, producer, and welfare economics and in public finance. Taking care to avoid the problems of scientism, historicism, and reductionism, these arguments must be suitably reinterpreted to apply to science and may leave important aspects of science unexplained. But there is another concern. Although self-referential arguments allow an economizing of arguments in one way, in another way they open up the problem of infinite resources again. Self-referential arguments lead to an infinite regress. An economic theory of economics may require an economic metatheory. And the metatheory may require an even higher-level economic explanation and so on, perhaps infinitely.

Again the economic sense of Bartley's critical rationalism appears. Finite resources prevent us from further pursuing self-referential infinite regresses found in connection with the *tu quoque* argument. Thus, infinite rational justification of points of view needs to be rejected. In its place is needed an economically attainable conception of rationality which also encompasses the problem of self-reference. The evolutionary conception of nonjustificational rationality from the previous chapter is such a position. Bartley's critical rationalism may be such a position. Resources need to be devoted to the process of criticism including self-criticism. The discovery of errors, inconsistencies, irrelevancies, and other flaws requires something less than an infinite quantity of resources. Real, economically viable criticisms come one at a time or even in clusters. The economic demands for detecting error and fashioning relevant criticisms of either the internal or external variety must be within the realm of economic plausibility.

CONCLUSIONS

In this chapter, self-referential arguments were created for empiricism, for falsification, and for mathematics. The logical structure of the problem of self-reference for these three domains of inquiry was quite similar. When a criticism or argument was reflexively applied to itself, a problem of inconsistency or infinite regress arose. The inconsistencies took the form of liar's paradoxes and the infinite regresses raised a concern with incompleteness. The most plausible way out of this dilemma was a philosophy of criticism. A philosophy of open-minded criticism was suggested by Bartley and Popper, but there can be no doubt that others have come to a similar position so that a critical philosophy of science is much more widely accepted than my focus on Popper and Bartley would suggest.

The logic of philosophical problems such as the problem of induction in science and the problem of proof in mathematics suggests a shift from a logic of justification to criticism. Criticism comes in two forms, internal and external. External criticisms typically proliferate and multiply. Yet they are rarely effective in persuading a rational scientist, mathematician, or philosopher to alter a deeply rooted position. Internal criticisms, while often more readily received, rarely take the form of self-referential criticism.

Self-referential arguments economize on known modes of theory and criticism. Thus reflexive arguments make use of existing cognitive resources. Reflexive arguments should not be pursued to an infinite regress for economic reasons. As long as resources are scarce, infinite regresses should not be pursued endlessly. This would be a waste of cognitive resources. The nonjustificational conception of rationality should be viewed as an attempt to characterize rational thought and argument where the logical problems of philosophical justification get bogged down in paradoxes and regresses and waste resources. Pluralism is needed to generate effective external criticisms, and reflexive, self-referential arguments are needed to sharpen internal criticism. The next question of course is the role of an economics of science in creating a reflexive, self-referential criticism of economic science.

12

AN ECONOMIC CRITIQUE OF THE ARCHITECTURE OF ECONOMIC THEORY AND METHOD

When a man is about to build a house, what a power of thinking he has to do before he can safely break ground! With what pains he has to excogitate the precise wants that are to be supplied! What a study to ascertain the most available and suitable materials, to determine the mode of construction to which those materials are best adapted, and to answer a hundred such questions! Now without riding the metaphor too far, I think we may safely say that the studies preliminary to the construction of a great theory should be at least as deliberate and thorough as those that are preliminary to the building of a dwelling house.

That systems ought to be constructed architectonically has been preached since Kant.

(Peirce [1891] 1955: 315–16)

THE ECONOMICS OF SCIENCE AND THE PROBLEM OF SELF-REFERENCE

Problems of self-reference abound in Western thought. Once it is understood how a question of self-reference is raised, the conundrum seemingly breaks out everywhere. A problem of self-reference arises when a theory or conceptual framework is reflexively applied to itself. This has already been done in mathematics, philosophy, philosophy of science, sociology, evolutionary biology, and in other frameworks of inquiry but not in economics. An economics of science is clearly an application of the theories and methods of economic science reflexively on to the discipline of economics. Thus an economics of science in some sense is metalevel economics, economics being applied to the discipline of economics. But the reflexive strategy need not stop with an economics of science. An economics of science is also a resource-using activity requiring another level of reflexively directed economic analysis. It is clear that it would be quite easy to imagine an infinite regress of nested economic theories with a higher level theory analyzing the economic aspects of economic inquiry at a lower level.

In this chapter, I would like to propose a conceptual structure for characterizing the nature of economic theory and method. A conceptual structure can be constructed interrelating economic theory and method using the knowledge of the problem of self-reference and the nature of Gödel's proof from the previous chapter. This structure will incorporate reflexive regresses like those formed previously. Following Peirce's (1891) analysis of science and philosophy, I want to call this the architecture of economic theory. I believe there is a Gödel-like architecture to the theory and methodology held by many economists. Once this architectonic structure has been created, it will be criticized from the vantage point of the economics of science presented in previous chapters. The economics of science that I have developed does not fit this architecture of economic theory and method. Thus there is an extremely important sense in which an economics of science leads to a surprising result. My economics of science contradicts the theoretical architecture of economic science. This is particularly true for what economists call "Walrasian economics." An analytical evolutionary economics of science portrays those growth of knowledge processes in science and the economy which are necessary for economic efficiency and growth including those processes peculiar to science. Growth of knowledge processes are essential for a world of evolving order and pattern which falls somewhat short of equilibrium. They are unnecessary in the context of the Walrasian vision of economic activity. Notions of equilibrium essentially presuppose the growth of human knowledge of all varieties removing them from the economic process. This is why economic theory has no growth of knowledge processes and why economic methodology has very little economic content.

REGRESSIVE CONCEPTIONS OF ECONOMIC COMPETITION

For the purposes which follow, I propose a broad all-encompassing conception of the theory of competition for the economy and for science. It is this all-encompassing conceptual structure which I call "the architecture of economic theory and method." My purpose is both to present and to criticize the architecture of economic theory and method. A preview of the architecture of economic theory goes something like this. In economics, simpler theories of competition are nested within more complex theories of competition. Logically this nesting could be infinite but resource constraints prevent an infinite number of theories of competition from materializing. Similarly, in science simpler methodologies of scientific competition are nested within more complex competitive methodologies of science. The infinitely nested theories of economic competition can then be mapped with the competitive methodologies of science providing a Gödel-like structure of interrelated and infinitely nested theories of economic and scientific competition. Again scarce resources prevent the infinite logic from being attained in actual studies of science.

An exploration of the architecture of economic theory begins with a representation of theories of competition which is in most respects similar to the infinite regresses presented previously.[1] The infinite regress in mathematics took the form of a simpler mathematical system being nested within a broader one. Each level of the regress from $M–1$ to $M–X$ requires a broader mathematical system containing the simpler system of the previous level. The interpretation of competition which follows will take the same form of an infinite nesting of theories within theories. Perhaps theories of competition follow a similar structure.

Let's begin with the typical textbook presentation of competition and its assumptions letting C_1 stand for a principles-level explication of competition. The assumptions of the theory of competition with an accompanying abbreviation are: B, a large number of buyers; F, a large number of firms as sellers; Q, the existence of a homogeneous product; NG, no government restrictions on entry or exit; I, the presumed existence of adequate information; and P, the price that individual transactors take as given in the marketplace. This set of core assumptions of the theory of competition will be designated as C_1:

C_1 (B, F, Q, NG, I, P)   assumptions of economic competition

Being nothing more than a mere list of assumptions, C_1 is hardly an adequate theory of competition. What usually supplements C_1 is an analysis of competition in single markets. This is competitive market analysis here designated as C_2. It is competitive market analysis which is used to create a minimally acceptable notion of efficiency, i.e., where price equals minimum average total cost.[2] In the context of a single market, this means that economic profits are driven to zero in the long run under the forces of competition among sellers. It also means that the price charged for the product by a firm just covers all costs, implying that there is no waste in production and no overcharging or exploitation of consumers. Thus the relation of C_2 to C_1 can be represented in the following way:

$$C_1 \subset C_2 \tag{1}$$

or using implicit function notation we have:

C_2 (C_1, SM)   competitive market equilibrium

This means that competitive market analysis takes the heuristic assumptions of textbook competition, C_1, and applies them in the context of a single competitive market (SM).

As is known to every economist, the implications of competitive market analysis can be extended to a multimarket (MM) context. Many firms operate in several markets and so do households. If none of the conditions of C_1 or C_2 are violated in any of several related markets, then a multiple market equilibrium is possible. The preceding levels of competition are nested within this level of competition. This is designated as C_3:

$$C_2 \subset C_3 \qquad\qquad\qquad (2)$$

or,

C_3 (C_2, MM) multimarket equilibrium

From a theory of multiple market competitive equilibrium, the next step is to assume that all markets in the economy are in a mutually adjusting general equilibrium. Clusters of related competitive markets are so interlinked and the forces of competition are so strong that the whole economy and all of its markets can be portrayed in simultaneous, universal competitive equilibrium. In economic theory, this is the most consistent and the grandest conception of competition. It is the best of all possible actual and imagined economic worlds. It is known as Pareto optimal general equilibrium. The preceding levels of competition also are nested within this level of competition. If we let UM stand for all markets being universally and simultaneously in competitive equilibrium we have:

C_4 (C_3, UM) Pareto optimal general equilibrium

Recently the concept of optimization has been extended to the use of information. The notion that rational transactors do not waste any information has been designated as rational expectations. Since market clearing (MC) is already implicit in C_4, the addition of rational expectations essentially characterizes a view of economic analysis known as the New Classical macroeconomics. It can be fashioned as C_5:

$$C_4 \subset C_5 \qquad\qquad\qquad (3)$$

or,

C_5 (C_4, RE, MC) New Classical macro equilibrium

where RE stands for the assumption of rational expectations and MC explicitly represents the notion that all markets continually clear like auction markets.

As with the infinite regresses in mathematics and philosophy of science, the redefinition of competition could continue for many stages. While it might seem surprising, there does exist an nth level interpretation of competition. The nth level corresponds to the stopping of the infinite regress with an arbitrary assumption. In the previous regresses, arbitrary stopping points have been designated with an X. Thus C_n is augmented with C_n-X where C_n-X asserts:

C_n-X.   Assume that competition, however broadly interpreted, will yield the most successful predictions about actual economic events, but do not apply the demand for competition to C_n-X.

If an argument like C_n-X is used to stop the conceptual and theoretical infinite regresses in economic theory, then a liar's paradox C-LP results:

C-LP.   All statements of competition in economic theory must be "competitive" with those of rival economic theories, except C-LP.

Like the other paradoxes we ask whether *C-LP* itself is competitive with rival statements about economic theory and methodology. As a matter of logic, if *C-LP* is competitive with its rivals then *C-LP* might be replaced (refuted) by a rival theory. Thus if *C-LP* is in fact competitive, its existence may or may not endure.[3] On the other hand if *C-LP* is not competitive theoretically or methodologically as C_n-*X* asserts, then we have a contradiction. A contradiction results if competition can be sustained only by abandoning competition at the highest level of abstraction.[4]

METHODOLOGICAL COMPETITION IN THE SCIENTIFIC MARKETPLACE OF IDEAS

Moving from the economic to the scientific domain, the Gödel-like architecture of economic theory and methodology suggests the structure of an infinite array of nested competitive methodologies of science. Let *S* represent any methodology of science that says scientists should compete with each other within a competitively structured marketplace of ideas. Successively broader versions of methodological competition could include narrower versions of competition. The *n*-stage levels of economic competition could be reformulated for competitive scientific methodologies.[5]

As with the infinite nesting of theories of competition in the commercial marketplace, an analysis of competition in the scientific marketplace of ideas could begin with simple assumptions of economic competition. These assumptions are: *B*, a sufficiently large number of buyers of the services of scientists through universities and research institutes in business and government; *R*, large numbers of competing research scientists; *T*, the products of scientific research; *NG*, no government restriction on entry or exit from a given line of research; *I*, sufficient information about science as a career; and *W*, the average wage earned by a scientist. The assumptions of scientific competition appropriately reinterpreted for science are collectively designated as S_1:

S_1 *(B, R, T, NG, I, W)*   assumptions of scientific competition

Of course, mere definitions do not constitute much of a theory. In the economy, the lowest level of competition is among individual competitors in a single market. In science, a group of researchers often form a research group and compete with one another within the group. Such competition is restricted to scientists who do similar research. To compete in an effective way, scientists must be participating in one of the small research groups that do the same research. David Hull (1988) has named these groups with the term "demes" to refer to the various small circles of individuals that are apparent in science. Thus S_2 could represent competition within a research deme. The relation of S_2 to S_1 could be represented in the following way:

$$S_1 \subset S_2 \qquad\qquad (4)$$

or using implicit function notation we have:

S_2 (S_1, SRD)   competition within a single research deme

Moving to the next level of competition, it is also recognized that these Hullian research demes compete with each other for funds and prestige in advancing a research agenda common to several demes. This is probably the sense of competition which active scientists experience most intensely on a daily basis. If none of the conditions of S_1 or S_2 are violated, a higher level of competition emerges within science. The competition of one research deme with another can be designated as S_3. This level of competition can be represented as:

$$S_2 \subset S_3 \tag{5}$$

or

S_3 (S_2, MRD)   competition among multiple research demes within a research program

This is analogous to multimarket competition in the economy.

From competition among research demes within a research program, the next step is to look for an even higher level of competition in science. Groups of interrelated research demes constituting a research program may compete with other groups of demes forming another research program. Thus research programs compete with each other, even those which share a similar vision of science. This is the level of competition suggested in the writings of the late Imre Lakatos.[6] Let this be designated as S_4:

S_4 (S_3, RP)   competition among multiple research programs

At an even higher level, research programs could be viewed as existing within a philosophical paradigm. This is the level of competition found in Thomas Kuhn's (1970) *The Structure of Scientific Revolutions*.[7] Clashes of competing paradigms may represent an exceptionally high level of competition in science. Competition as the level of paradigms in science could be represented as:

$$S_4 \subset S_5 \tag{6}$$

or

S_5 (S_4, PDM)   competition among scientific paradigms

As with the theory of competition of ordinary economic affairs, competition in the marketplace of methodological ideas has an nth-stage version. The nth level corresponds to the stopping of an infinite regress with an arbitrary assumption designated with an X. Thus S_n is augmented and represented as S_n-X which asserts:

S_n-X. Assume that scientific competition however broadly interpreted will yield the best understanding of science, but do not apply the demand for competition to S_n-X.

If an argument like S_n-X is used to stop a methodological infinite regress, then a liar's paradox would result:

> S-LP. All statements of competition about science must be competitive with those of rival methodologies and scientific paradigms except S-LP.

As with the other regresses, one can ask whether *S-LP* is internally consistent allowing competition with rival statements of scientific methodology. As a matter of logic, if *S-LP* is in fact competitive with other methodological statements regarding the scientific process, then *S-LP* might be replaced by a rival theory. However, if *S-LP* asserts its own superiority and withdraws itself from relative appraisal of other conceptions of science, then we have a contradiction. As with economic theories of competition, if a competitive vision of science can be sustained only by abandoning it at the highest level of abstraction, then we have a contradiction.

Besides the conception of science represented in $S_1, \ldots, S_n$ above, we have already encountered two other instances of multiple versions of methodological competition from previous chapters. They could represent alternative ways of interpreting S_1 to S_n. In the preceding chapter, the problem of induction which was first formulated as an infinitely recursive sequence of conceptions of empiricism, *E-1* to *E-N*, was reformulated entirely in terms of falsification. There are so many conceptions and interpretations of falsification that they appear to fit the logical structure of a reflexive infinite regress. Thus *F-1* to *F-N* could correspond to S_1 to S_n and provide us with another way of focusing on falsification as the locus of competition in science regardless of the interpretation of falsification. More detail of the various conceptions of falsification is found in Table 11.2.

The second instance of a sequence of competitive methodologies are the various interpretations of Friedman's essay and positive economic methodology. These were detailed in Chapter 7 and highlighted in Tables 7.1 and 7.2. As new conceptions of falsification and other methodologies of science have been developed, new interpretations of Friedman's essay and positive economic methodology have proliferated. If the methodologies of science form the logical structure of a recursive regress, it is reasonable to expect that these same methodologies when brought into economics in the guise of a new interpretation of Friedman's essay would also fit the logical structure of a self-referential infinite regress. Thus many interpretations of Friedman's essay and positive economic methodology can be viewed as simply translating philosophical notions of scientific competition from philosophy into economic methodology.

THE ARCHITECTURE OF ECONOMIC THEORY AND METHOD

In conception, what I regard as the architecture of mainstream economic theory is a two-fold recursive nesting of theories of competition and theories of competitive science which can be related through a mapping. I propose that economic theory be conceived as a sequence of recursively nested theories of competition denoted with Cs such that:

$$C_1 \subset C_2 \subset C_3 \subset \ldots \subset C_n \tag{7}$$

where equation (7) means that theory C_1 is contained in C_2 and so on. I further propose that scientific methodologies be designated with Ss and represented as a sequence of recursively nested methodologies so that we have:

$$S_1 \subset S_2 \subset S_3 \subset \ldots \subset S_n \tag{8}$$

Following Peirce on the architecture of theories and the precedent set by Gödel's theorems, I propose a mapping between the economic theories of competition, $C_1, \ldots, C_n$, and the competitively interpreted scientific methodologies of science, $S_1, \ldots, S_n$. This mapping is schematically portrayed in Figure 12.1. Figure 12.1 portrays the architecture of mainstream economic theory and method.

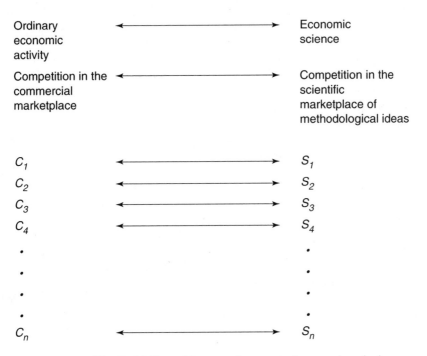

Figure 12.1 The Gödel-like architecture of economic theory and method

Besides Peirce's notion of the architecture of theories, an inspiration for this proposed architecture of economic theory is an awareness of the nature and importance of Gödel's demonstration of the incompleteness of mathematics. Figure 12.1 is closely modeled on Figure 11.1 which schematically portrays Gödel's contribution. Increasingly economic theory has been formalized with mathematics and logic. Like professional mathematicians, economic theorists have turned away from quantification as the frontier of the field to an exploration of qualitative results which result from the formalization of economic theory in the form of axioms, postulates, and set theory. Thus an emphasis on insights from Peirce and Gödel is consistent with the role of mathematics in contemporary economic theory. Another source of inspiration is an awareness that most economists instinctively apply economic theories outside the domain of ordinary commerce to nonmarket phenomena. Science is a nonmarket phenomenon. Indeed one possible interpretation of the concept of science as a marketplace of ideas is that some version of the theory of competition, C_i, is mapped into the domain of science and forms the basis of a corresponding theory of scientific competition, S_i, in the marketplace of ideas. Whether this whole strategy makes sense intellectually, historically, and empirically is precisely what is at issue. Regardless of the conclusion which may result, this strategy needs to be considered as a possibility even if it were ultimately rejected.

To my knowledge no one else has called attention to the competitive architecture of economic theory and method. The Gödel-like architecture of economic theory and method seemingly pervades almost all of mainstream economic analysis. One could think of it as the ultimate extension of the substitutes conception of economic science. Not only do nonmarket processes substitute for the market when market failure appears, but economic theorists also model nonmarket phenomena as imperfect, market-like competitive economic processes. Competition, equilibrium, and the primacy of markets are deeply embedded in the mindset of most economists. Economists instinctively presume the primacy of the market and competitive equilibrium theory as a way of understanding these processes.

The interrelated doubly recursive and infinitely regressive architecture of economic theory and method is quite remarkable. I believe it represents one of the most sophisticated, complex, and logically rigorous conceptual structures that mankind has yet created. Few disciplines except philosophy, physics, and mathematics appear to have reached such a high plane of theoretically unified abstraction. The architecture of economic science is the economist's equivalent of a grand unified theory. It is a two-fold vision of competition at many levels of interpretation pervading both ordinary commerce and science. In principle, the competitive architecture of economic theory could be expanded and applied to every imaginable economic process, every scientific process, and every other nonmarket process.

AN ECONOMICS OF SCIENCE CRITIQUE OF THE ARCHITECTURE OF ECONOMIC SCIENCE

The major difficulty with the architecture of economic theory is that it has not explained science in general nor the discipline of economic science in particular. The widespread existence of market failure in the marketplace of ideas and the problems resulting from economic concentration within science have led me to portray science in the context of the complements theory of institutions as a flawed, rule-governed, dual economy of primary and secondary science. Science is self-corrective over very long periods of time when the rule-governed processes of science manage to surmount the market failure problems due to economic concentration in science and the public good nature of scientific theories. What all of this means is that my economics of science cannot qualify as any of the competitive equilibrium theories of science which through a mapping, could be a nonmarket analogue of an equilibrium theory of competition. To put is more simply, my conception of an economics of science as an evolutionary social process is not any of the S_i which are mapped from a C_i in the Gödel-like architecture of economic theory. My economics of science clearly embraces a vision of science as an evolutionary social process which cannot be conceived in any manner as a sophisticated extension of any of the equilibrium theories of economic competition in the history of economic analysis.

It should be clear why I have spent so much time dealing with misconduct and market failure in science. The architecture of economic theory forms the intellectual core of mainstream economic science. In intellectual terms, the architecture of economic science is one of the most powerful and persuasive theoretical constructs that has ever been fashioned in the social sciences or perhaps any science. The success of the economic theories and economic methodologies which have flowed from this architecture have not been surpassed by any rivals. This is why I took such great care in showing that a marketplace of ideas is a denial rather than an extension of the relevance of conceptions of competition premised on commercial markets to science. Science may be self-corrective, but the stability of corrective processes in science results in spite of, not because of, stabilizing competitive commercial market forces.

Certainly an economics of science raises the problem of self-reference. And many disciplines have attempted self-referential applications of the main theoretical constructs of their discipline. An economics of science must therefore raise the reflexive question. However, my economics of science turns out to be more a critique than another extension of conventional economic analysis to nonmarket phenomena. This is especially true of the Walrasian vision of economic processes. In that view the economy is conceived as a grand, multi-market machine with individual households and firms as cogs in the machine. My economics of science is less critical of the Marshallian evolutionary view of economics. But even the Marshallian view fails to theorize about science and economic science. This is a gaping anomaly. Science needs to be considered as an economic process. Otherwise economics is woefully incomplete as an intellectual enterprise.

This evolutionary economics of science can also be compared briefly to the other evolutionary approaches to economics. An economics of science shares some important aspects with the evolutionary economics of the American Institutional school. American institutionalism can be traced to the philosophy of John Dewey and the economics of Thorstein Veblen. I believe these institutionalists have always held a complements approach to comparative institutions and organizations. Where I most differ is in the use of analytical microeconomics to represent some of the more rigidly patterned choices of the scientist. Institutionalists typically prefer a psychological theory of the individual based on behaviorism or a functionalist theory of instincts. In this regard, I have been more influenced by Peirce than by Dewey. In its broadest perspective, this analytical evolutionary economics of science was inspired by Peirce's vision of economic processes as found in his "Note on the Economy of Research." Peirce may have been the first to use analytical microeconomics explicitly in the context of an evolutionary vision of the world. This economics of science also shares important dimensions of the evolutionary economics of the Austrian school in so far as Friedrich Hayek is taken as a representative figure. The subjectivity of the cost-benefit logic of choice clearly has an Austrian tinge to it. And the conception of science as an extremely long-run, rule-governed process is clearly present in Hayek's writings on science (Butos 1987). Where Austrians may most differ is the analytical microeconomics of individual choice found in the discussion on misconduct in science.

From an evolutionary growth of knowledge view of science, it is the conception of equilibrium which most strongly deprives economics of an epistemic conception of economic processes. By epistemic I mean two things. In ordinary commerce, economic processes are viewed as information creating and destroying processes and similarly, in science, epistemic processes are seen as knowledge creating and destroying processes. The presumption of economic equilibrium presupposes such a high degree of social order that epistemic processes are no longer needed in economic theory and analysis. Thus we have a discipline where economic theory is devoid of commonsense growth of knowledge processes and we have economic methodology without much economic content.

What I have done is create an analytical evolutionary approach to the economics of science. Recognizing its limitations, I have used analytical microeconomics to theorize about the more rigidly patterned activities of individual choice in science realizing that such rigidity is constructed and created in an evolutionary world. As a social process, the determinacy of individual choice gives way to an adaptive evolutionary view of science as a social process. Revolutions are rare in science. Science is a long-run, adaptive process of change. Among economists, Karl Popper's philosophy of science is probably best known and most widely cited. Popper's views of science are clearly evolutionary in nature. Popper (1972a: 67) considers himself to be a post-Darwinian epistemologist. Popper maintains that knowledge grows through a trial and error selection process which he has called "conjectures and refutations."[8]

> All this may be expressed by saying that the growth of our knowledge is the result of a process closely resembling what Darwin called 'natural selection': that is, *the natural selection of hypotheses*: our knowledge consists, at every moment, of those hypotheses which have shown their (comparative) fitness by surviving so far in their struggle for existence; a competitive struggle which eliminates those hypotheses which are unfit.
>
> This interpretation may be applied to animal knowledge, pre-scientific knowledge, and to scientific knowledge . . . scientific criticism often makes our theories perish in our stead, eliminating our mistaken beliefs before such beliefs lead to our own elimination.
>
> This statement of the situation is meant to describe how knowledge really grows. It is not meant metaphorically, though of course it makes use of metaphors. The theory of knowledge which I wish to propose is a largely Darwinian theory of the growth of knowledge [original emphasis].
>
> (Popper 1972a: 261)

More recently and outside of economics, the most elaborate evolutionary view of science is David Hull's (1988) *Science as a Process*. Hull takes up the challenge posed by Popper, Kuhn, and others to create a richer evolutionary theory of science. Hull's evolutionary theory of science would be the next place to turn to more fully elaborate an evolutionary economics of science. Hull's case study is the theory of evolution. Hull shows that the theory of evolution has also developed in an evolutionary fashion. Thus *Science as a Process* shares the concern with the problem of self-reference which has been a central concern of this economics of science. Evolutionary interpretations of economics and economic methodology have been offered and, occasionally, in the history of economics. However, evolutionary interpretations of economics including my own need to be separated from the Gödel-like architecture of economic theory. An evolutionary theory of economic activity is really a different theory than a mechanistic, Walrasian equilibrium theory. Economists need to be clear about the conceptual foundations of economics in so far as this is possible.

CONCLUSIONS

An economics of science because of its reflexive nature must address the problem of self-reference. An awareness of many aspects of the problem of self-reference is a minimal requirement for an economics of science. In this chapter, a broadly encompassing conceptual structure which I have called the architecture of economic theory and method was created. This architecture consists of two nested, recursive regresses of theories of economic and scientific competition which are mapped to each other. The notion of an architecture of a theory or philosophy comes from Peirce and the idea of recursive mapping comes from

Gödel's theorems. The purpose was to characterize the logic of economic analysis as coherently and efficiently as possible thus facilitating a critique of the architecture of economic science. The major critique is that the economics of science which I have developed is not compatible with the conceptual architecture of economic science. The problem is the presumption of equilibrium. There are so many problems with market failure in science and there are the concomitant issues of inefficient concentrations of resources by dominant points of view. Thus it is impossible to think of science as a competitive economic process as economists typically use that term. More precisely, scientific competition cannot be described with economic theories of competitive equilibrium. Science is an evolutionary process fraught with flaws, imperfections, and other problems due to the public good nature of scientific theories. Science as a process is not an equilibrium process.

This economics of science is a critique of the very core of contemporary economic science. In light of the problem of self-reference, an intellectually honest criticism of the architecture of economic theory and method is possibly the best one could hope for from an economics of science. Intellectual honesty means not exempting oneself from the arguments, theories, criticisms, and intellectual standards applied to others. This economics of science attempts to be self-critical of the profession of economic science in the same way that economists criticize other professions and ordinary economic activity.

NOTES

1 WHY AN ECONOMICS OF SCIENCE?

1 There are several papers that place scientists, professors, or economists in a formal or informal optimizing framework. W. E. Becker (1975) has created a model of the university professor as a utility maximizer. Robert Tollison has argued that the activities of economists as scientists should be the subject of economic analysis: "Economists are not outside the economy. . . . The economist is a rational, maximizing individual, subject to the predictions of economic science (Tollison 1986: 911). In a review of research on the economics profession, David Colander (1989) has asserted that the economics profession should make an excellent case study for the application of economic theory. Several other pieces on the economics of science which are of worthy of note are Blank and Stigler (1957), Nelson (1959), and Machlup (1962).

2 An exception is Nelson and Winter (1982).

3 Michael Ghiselin has argued for an evolutionary synthesis of biology and economics. He explores the thesis "that biology and economics are subdivisions of a single branch of knowledge called 'general economy'" (Ghiselin 1987: 271).

4 Another is Nicholas Georgescu-Roegen (1971) whose book, *The Entropy Law and the Economic Process*, I have used repeatedly in my graduate seminar on methodology.

5 To the extent that scientific theories are correct and truthfully and/or usefully capture ordered aspects of the nature of our world, they become public goods in the economic sense. Public goods are goods that, once produced and provided for one, are provided for all.

6 An exception in the nineteenth century would be Thorstein Veblen.

7 Another important figure in the sociology of the economics profession has been A. W. Coats (1984).

8 Merton (1973) has written several interesting essays on the reward structure of science.

9 David Levy has written several pieces on the economics of science. Levy (1988) has analyzed the scientist's trade-off between fame and fortune using a utility function approach to scientific choice. In his other contributions, Levy and Susan Feigenbaum (1993) have used econometrics to explore many aspects of the replication of scientific research. Another contribution of Feigenbaum and Levy (1993) drew fifteen commentaries in the journal in which it appeared, *Social Epistemology*. In a more recent article, Levy and Feigenbaum (1996) create a rational choice model of fraud in science.

10 In mathematics self-criticism has taken the form of the liar's or Russell's (1907) paradox. This paradox eventually led to Gödel's famous incompleteness theorems

which are interpreted by Nagel and Newman (1958). The problem of self-reference is exhaustively presented and discussed in Douglas Hofstadter's (1979) *Gödel, Escher, Bach: An Eternal Golden Braid*. Self-reference is an important issue in music, art, mathematics, philosophy, artificial intelligence, and other disciplines. More on this subject can be found in Chapter 11.

11 Besides the reference in the text, others articles on the relationship of economics and the sociology of science are Hands (1994a, 1994b, 1996, 1997) and Diamond (1996).

12 Other recent papers of relevance are those of Mirowski (1994) and Mirowski and Sklivas (1991).

2 AN ECONOMIC THEORY OF REPLICATION FAILURE

1 This chapter is a significantly revised version of Wible (1991).

2 Another empirical study of replication has been done by Feigenbaum *et al.* (1986).

3 An example of replication failure which may not fit the theory is an honest mistake which results from legitimate research design. In economics there is the case of the disreplication of Martin Feldstein's research of the impact of social security on personal savings as discussed in Feigenbaum and Levy (1994).

Ten years after the *JMCB* project, Anderson and Dewald (1994) reviewed the responses of the economics profession to the problems of replication failure. They indicate that the importance of replication has not really changed much in the past decade.

4 The lack of routine direct replication may not be of concern if later research can expose undetected mistakes unless the subject matter involves human subjects. Those scientists in the medical and allied health fields would seem to have an obligation to a higher proportion of direct replications before new drugs and therapies are widely administered to human patients.

5 Suppose we have a positive economist whose professional goal is to create scientific investigations of ordinary transactor behavior that are important enough and of sufficient quality to gain publication in the very best economics journals. This is a worthy aim. In general, I assume the aims and motivations of science as typically espoused among positive economists are among the highest that can be imagined. Furthermore, I wish to assume that the economist being considered is one whose skills and publications are held in high esteem, that he or she is among the best and brightest of the profession. In all cases suppose that the research produced by this person would be of sufficient quality that a disinterested and professionally informed third party would approve of our economist's research, if this third party were able to *completely* review and preserve an economist's work as it was being done. But this is where methodological problems begin. It would be inordinately expensive to have a third party monitor the research endeavors of each economist. The individual economist must be responsible for preserving all important aspects of a scientific investigation. The methodological implications of the model would be stronger if the analysis were extended to the economist of average skill and motivation.

6 The investigation being attempted could be any of the three types of scientific replication studies discussed in the previous section. The project could aim to make a fundamentally innovative contribution of the sort associated with conceptual replication. The project could be a test of a new method to establish a known result more fully as in design replication. Or the project being undertaken could be a direct replication of someone else's work.

7 The nature of complex transactional settings is discussed by Williamson *et al.* (1975) and Nelson and Winter (1982). Tacit knowledge may play an important role in such processes.

8 If the two wage rates are weighted by the time spent in each type of activity, A_1 and A_2, then the actual wage, w is a weighted average of w_1 and w_2:

$$w = (\frac{t_1}{t_1 + t_2})\ w_1\ +\ (\frac{t_2}{t_1 + t_2})\ w_2$$

where $w_1 > w > w_2$ and t_1 and t_2 are the hours spent in activities A_1 and A_2 respectively.

9 The fixed coefficient production functions are: $t_i = b_i Z_i$ and $x_i = a_i Z_i$ where the x_i are the inputs and the t_i the amounts of time devoted to producing each Z_i.

10 If the time horizon of this maximization problem were taken to be a year, then Z_1 and Z_2 could be defined as the number of SRAs and GRAs produced each year, while Z_3 could be defined as the number of nonwork days per year.

11 Use of a joint income and time constraint permits avoidance of a Lagrangian with two constraints and implicitly assumes the wage could be adjusted upward in the current period.

12 Implicit contract theory is summarized by Azariadis and Stiglitz (1983) and Rosen (1985). They make no application of their work to economic science.

13 A corner solution also could be achieved with negatively sloped indifference curves. Corner solutions resulting from lexicographic and positively sloped indifference maps are more interesting given a topic like science.

14 The lexicographic approach to understanding the behavior of economists is explored by Earl (1983, 1988). Earl also explores psychological dimensions of academic careerism versus scientific integrity. Furthermore Earl relates nontraditional microeconomic ideas like bounded rationality, cognitive dissonance, and informational impactedness to the economics profession rather than to managers and firms.

15 Grantsmanship could also alter the relative cost of applied empirical research versus traditional "desk research." Successful grants would make empirical research less costly most likely stimulating more production of this type of inquiry. I am grateful to an anonymous reader for making this point.

16 Some might object to this implication on the grounds that the "brightest and best" of the economics profession would not be bound by a publication rate requirement. The tenure and promotion constraint, TT in Figure 2.3, could lie so far to the left for high achievers that it may not intersect the joint resource constraint or not alter the optimization solution if it does intersect. This is indeed possible, so that this application may apply more to the typical rather than the extraordinary economist. Nevertheless, in many cases, tenure and promotion requirements can have the adverse consequence of lowering the quality of scientific research in economics.

3 AN ECONOMIC THEORY OF FRAUD IN SCIENCE

1 Fraud in science has also been the subject of NOVA, the PBS program devoted to science. See NOVA (1988). Recent episodes of fraud in science are also the subject of Friedlander (1995) and Weinstein (1979). This chapter is based on Wible (1992a).

2 Burt's biographer Leslie Hearnshaw (1979: 228 ff.) is a particularly good source of information.

3 Hearnshaw's discussion can be found in the preface of his biography of Burt.

4 Other works commenting on the Burt affair are Lewontin et al. (1984) and Eysenck and Kamin (1981).

5 This account of the Darsee affair is a summary of the report of Broad and Wade (1982: 13–15).

6 The Darsee affair was carried beyond Darsee. Walter Stewart and Ned Feder (1987b) investigated 18 of Darsee's full-length research papers. These papers were published with forty-seven coauthors. They found an abundance of errors that referees or co-authors should have found. Darsee's former mentor Braunwald (1987) commented on the Stewart and Feder critique. The editor of *Nature* also commented at length on the Darsee affair and the work of Stewart and Feder ([Maddox] 1987b).

7 Darsee was later banned from receiving government research grants for a period of ten years (Budiansky, 1983b).

8 Details of the Breuning case are from Holden (1986) and Anderson (1988a). The case is also discussed in NOVA (1988: 4–5).

9 A great deal has been written about the Baltimore case. See [Maddox] (1987), Anderson (1988b), Palca and Anderson (1988), Culliton (1988a, 1988b), Foreman (1988), Boffey (1988), and Foreman and Howe (1996).

10 The story was reported by Hilts (1991). More recently Saransohn (1993) has written a full-length account of this episode in science.

11 Another major episode of fraud concerns the research of Robert Gallo and Daniel Zagury. They are attempting to create a vaccine against AIDS. Sloppy procedures have lead apparently to the unnecessary deaths of several patients. Research findings were published that no deaths occurred (Warsh 1991). Also Gallo may have taken the virus from the French rather than making an independent discovery (Saransohn 1993: 269).

12 Fraud in science has gained so much attention that the National Library of Medicine compiled a selected bibliography on the problem. The bibliography covers 1977–87 and contains 450 citations. See van de Kamp and Cummings (1987).

13 Baltimore apparently had no intention of deceiving his peers.

14 Anthologies containing articles of the economics of crime are Becker and Landes (1974), McPheters and Stronge (1976), and Heineke (1978).

15 Pertinent literature surveys of choice under uncertainty are those of Machina (1987), Shoemaker (1982), and Hirshleifer and Riley (1979).

16 The model largely follows Ehrlich's development of the topic. The variables have been designated differently to apply to the problem of fraud in science. See Ehrlich (1973: 521–9).

17 Because we are dealing with people who are already highly trained and have lab facilities available to them, these assumptions are not very restrictive.

4 PEIRCE'S ECONOMICS OF RESEARCH PROJECT SELECTION

1 One presentation of the ideas in pragmatism is Wiener (1949). For an overview of the relevance of Peirce and pragmatism to controversial issues in economics see Kevin Hoover (1994). This chapter is mostly based on Wible (1994a).

2 The classic statement of Peirce's (1878) pragmatism is his essay, "How to Make Our Ideas Clear."

3 Brent's (1993) biography documents that Peirce became an outcast in academia, government, and publishing.

4 A more complete edition of the correspondence with Newcomb is found in Eisele (1979b).

5 Cited in Baumol and Goldfeld (1968: 161–9).

6 My source is Eisele (1979b: 58).

7 Peirce (1871a) in Baumol and Goldfeld (1968: 187).

8 Eisele (1979c) discusses Peirce's interest in Ricardo.

9 See Eisele (1979c, 1979d) and Peirce (1871b, 1882).

10 Eisele (1979c: 253) and Fisch (1982: xxxv).

11 Wible (1984a) discusses this aspect of Dewey's philosophy.

12 See Mach (1893, 1898).

13 Presently there are four places where Peirce's Note has appeared. The Note was originally published in a report to the Coast Survey in 1879. This published report apparently was lost but then rediscovered in the 1960s. A reprinting of the Coast Survey version appeared in *Operations Research* in 1967 (Peirce [1879] 1967: 642–8). A brief discussion of the Coast Survey version can be found in Cushen (1967). The Note previously appeared in the *Collected Papers of Charles Sanders Peirce*, vol. 7 (Peirce [1879] 1967: 76–83) as edited by the department of philosophy at Harvard. The Harvard version is published from a handwritten manuscript in Widener library. Also, the Note has been reprinted as part of a much more comprehensive edition of Peirce's papers than the *Collected Papers*. These are the *Writings of Charles S. Peirce: A Chronological Edition*. The Note appears in vol. 4 (Peirce [1879] 1986: 72–8). Most recently, the Note has been republished as an appendix to Wible (1994b) in the *Journal of Economic Methodology*.

14 Brent's (1993) biography of Peirce documents that Peirce spent most of his professional life trying to measure differences in the earth's gravity at different geographic locations in Europe and North America. Peirce continually appealed for additional funding to support research at new locations and the construction of more accurate pendulums to reduce the inaccuracies introduced by the equipment. Peirce considered himself a first-rate gravimetric researcher and was well known in Europe for his skill.

15 This statement is taken from private correspondence with Professor Dorfman. His comments sent me searching for a better understanding of the term "probable error."

16 See Fisch (1982: xxi–xxiii).

17 An estimator is a measure of a true parameter of a population under investigation. The true parameter is unknown unless the entire population is known. As an example consider the mean. A mean can be calculated from a random sample of the population and compared to the mean of the population. The sample mean is an estimator of the true mean of the population. What we want to know at this point is how accurate the sample mean is as an estimator of the true mean.

18 I am indebted to Jeff Sohl for suggesting this interpretation of probable error. It seems consistent with Hacking's (1990) interpretation of probable error in Peirce's writings. Kmenta (1971: 186–91) has a thorough explanation of the meaning of a confidence interval.

19 Peirce used the term "probable error" in a manuscript in 1861. See Peirce ([1861] 1982: 70).

20 For example, Kmenta's (1971: 125–8) econometrics text provides a discussion of economic aspects of choosing the correct sample size.

21 A search through recent articles regarding mathematical economics in the nineteenth century reveals that Peirce's contributions are unknown in economics except for the Baumol and Goldfeld volume. For example, Stigler (1972) does not include Peirce in his survey of the adoption of marginal utility theory in the late nineteenth century. Similarly, Peirce's contributions are not among those listed by Howey (1972) in recounting the origins of marginalism.

22 Suppe (1974: 12) discusses the impact of *Principia Mathematica* on positivism.

23 See Eisele (1979e: 153).

24 There has been other research on economic aspects of science. Boland (1971) presents an economic analysis of conventionalism using welfare theory. I became aware of Boland's piece and Peirce's Note almost simultaneously while in graduate school in the 1970s. At that time, Boland's article lead me to attach a great deal of significance to Peirce's Note (Wible 1991, 1992a, 1992b).

25 Rescher's use of cost-benefit rhetoric and terminology stimulated a search of the cost-benefit literature. In searching that literature, a utility approach to research project evaluation was encountered in the work of F. M. Scherer (1965). What is so unusual about Scherer's model is that he chose a utility rather than a cost-benefit model for research project evaluation. Furthermore, it is astonishing to find that Scherer's model yields results that are nearly identical to those attained by Peirce almost a century earlier. Comparison of Peirce's and Scherer's models reveals the uncanny prescience of Peirce's model.

26 In *Cognitive Economy*, Rescher (1989) also focuses on large-scale science that has become enormously vast and expensive:

> This technological escalation has massive economic ramifications. The economics of scientific inquiry presents a picture of ongoing cost escalation that is strongly reminiscent of an arms race. The technical escalation inherent in scientific research parallels that familiar arms race situation of inescapable technological obsolescence, as the opposition escalates to the next phase of sophistication.
>
> (Rescher 1989: 137)

27 Rescher (1978a: 72 ff.) maintains that an economic approach helps to deal with several disputes regarding aspects of induction. Among them are Carnap's total evidence requirement, Hempel's paradox of the ravens, Goodman's grue paradox, and Popper's notion of falsification.

28 Recently another important evolutionary approach to science has appeared by David Hull (1988). His lengthy treatise, *Science as a Process*, has been reviewed and critiqued by Donoghue (1990), Oldroyd (1990), and Rosenberg (1992). Oldroyd (1990: 484) comments that Hull relies on invisible hand type arguments rather than those which depend on discredited altruistic norms to explain the behavior of scientists.

29 Wade Hands (1985: 85–6) also considers economic aspects of Popper's philosophy of science.

30 The use of economic models to study economic science raises some extraordinary issues. The most important issue concerns reflexivity or self-reference. The issues are summarized in later chapters and by Hands (1994b).

5 A COST-BENEFIT APPROACH TO RESEARCH PROJECT SELECTION, POPPER'S METHODOLOGY, AND SCIENTIFIC PROGRESS

1 Radnitzky (1987a: 291) constructs his rationality principle using both cost-benefit and utility concepts.

2 The very idea of creating a mathematical model of science, particularly from a growth of knowledge point of view, may be repugnant to some. Besides the economic models found in this paper, Jason Wittenberg (1992) discusses creating a computer model of Kuhn's *Structure of Scientific Revolutions* using a systems dynamics model.

3 The classic statement of cost-benefit analysis is E. J. Mishan's (1976) work *Cost Benefit Analysis*. Graham (1981) extends cost-benefit analysis to conditions of uncertainty and Kitcher (1990) analyzes the division of cognitive labor under conditions of uncertainty. Philosopher Elliott Sober (1992) has explored cost-benefit aspects of evolutionary biology using the prisoner's dilemma.

4 Gramlich (1981) and Campen (1986) provide a brief history of cost-benefit analysis. Campen also constructs a radical critique of cost-benefit analysis. A widely cited collection of essays was edited by Dorfman (1965).

5 There are several critical appraisals of the limitations of cost-benefit analysis such as Williams (1972), Wolf (1979), Gramlich (1981), and Campen (1986). Machlup (1965) suggests that there are five different types of cost-benefit analysis: (1) an intuition of the implicit worth of some project; (2) an explicit personal valuation of what is best for society; (3) an explicit collective evaluation by a segment of society of what is best for society; (4) a theoretical analysis of costs and benefits, and (5) an actual calculation of costs and benefits.

6 A discussion of the formal representation of the cost-benefit problem can be found in Rosen (1988: 230 ff.) and Gramlich (1981).

7 Perhaps the most widely used criterion has been the benefit cost ratio (B/C). Benefits and costs can be compared in each period and a composite B/C ratio for an entire project can be computed. Again this would require that both costs and benefits be discounted appropriately. However, the B/C ratio can be quite misleading. Projects with higher B/C ratios may actually have lower net present values. This is possible if the magnitude of the project with the higher B/C ratio is of a much smaller magnitude. It is also possible if the time path of the costs and benefits are remarkably dissimilar.

8 The difficulties associated with fully implementing cost-benefit analysis are also essential in understanding Bartley's interpretation of Popper and his treatment by philosophers and sociologists.

9 Fundamental insights come from two of Ronald Coase's (1937, 1960) well-known articles. Like Coase's explanation for the existence of the firm, I believe that science exists because it is a contractual coalition which is more efficient than the market given the complexity of the situation. Because of the remoteness of science from the marketplace, significant problems of social cost arise which are conceptualized in welfare economics and cost-benefit theory.

10 There is a distributional concern for publicly financed scientific projects. Those who receive benefits will not be the same group who pay for those projects with their tax dollars.

11 Research in developing complex technologies may be an exception. Research which is funded by the government and deals with the development of complex technology for military or industrial purposes may be no different than those envisioned in traditional cost-benefit analysis. Beyond the development of technology is basic science.

12 Gramlich (1981: 95 ff.) discusses problems associated with choosing a rate of discount for cost-benefit analysis.

13 While it may be quite impractical to rely totally on cost-benefit analysis to make most public sector investment decisions, cost-benefit analysis could play a significant role in rejecting certain options. If the benefit-cost ratio is less than one or the net present value of a project is negative, then it is clear that a project should be rejected. In practice, the benefits may be routinely overestimated and the costs understated by those preparing the cost-benefit analysis in a government agency. Thus if negative results are achieved even under the most liberal assumptions, then surely such projects need to be rejected. Thus cost-benefit analysis could function like the notion of falsification in methodology. Cost-benefit analysis could be used to reject wasteful projects in the planning stage but need to be supplemented with other criteria when a positive selection among future projects or termination of existing programs needs to be made.

14 There are self-corrective processes in the marketplace and in science. Cost-benefit analysis is an attempt to reformulate the self-corrective aspects of market processes so that they apply to science. The experimental method is a self-corrective process within science. The real issue is whether cost-benefit analysis will lead to additional improvement beyond the self-corrective experimental methods already in place in

science. Of course economic imperfections in science could undermine the self-corrective processes of science.

15 The subjective understanding of the quantitative results of cost-benefit analysis has a strong parallel with Keynes' understanding of probabilities. They both appear to be subjective.

16 Perhaps Rescher was really on the right track in applying Peirce's marginal utility model to the selection of research topics and to Popper's methodology.

17 Popper's original work on the natural and social sciences is *The Poverty of Historicism* (1961). His 1966 work, *The Open Society and its Enemies*, particularly the second volume, contains more of Popper's comparison of the sciences. Jarvie (1982), Hands (1985), and Caldwell (1991) provide various insights into Popper's views on the methodologies of the natural and the social sciences.

18 Radnitzky (1987a: 285) writes: "The expression '*economic approach*' is used here in the *wide* sense which corresponds to Karl Popper's 'situational logic,' or '*rational problem-solving approach*' (as I would prefer to call it). I consider Popper's 'situational logic,' which stands in the tradition of 'Austrian methodology,' as a forerunner of the economic approach to *all* human action" [original emphasis].

19 This is ultimately a question of the nature of objectivity in science which has led Popper to advocate the realist position. Hattiangadi (1985) provides an analysis of Popper's realism and compares it with Bertrand Russell's.

6 MARKET FAILURE IN THE MARKETPLACE OF IDEAS: THE CASES OF KARL POPPER AND THE ECONOMICS PROFESSION

1 An internal explanation of science concerns the intellectual context of science while external influences deal with socioeconomic and cultural factors relevant for specific periods in history. Lakatos (1978b: 102) and Kuhn (1977) discuss internal and external aspects of science. As mentioned in Chapter 1, Milton Friedman (1953: 42–3) did not consider economic factors relevant to explaining the progress of economic science.

2 Michael Polanyi (1962b: 54–6) explores similarities between science and economics. Bertrand de Jouvenel (1961) comments on Polanyi's ideas about science. Bartley (1990: 25–6) gives a brief history regarding the marketplace of ideas. Ronald Coase (1974) also draws on analogies between the market for goods and the marketplace of ideas.

3 For universities, Bartley (1990: 145) suggests abandoning tenure at all levels and giving students vouchers so that they can select and thus reward the best teachers.

4 Bartley (1990: 114) maintains that universities are feudal in character resembling fiefdoms, guilds, and mutual-protection rackets.

5 The author emphasizes that the data is presented to contend Bartley's conclusion that Popper has been neglected in the marketplace of ideas. Citation data can be biased and it may not be very clear if references to other authors with similar names are mixed into the reference list. This seemed to be the case for R. K. Merton and the financial specialist R. C. Merton. Some figures also had separate reference lists with only their last names. For example, citations to Marx were listed under Marx and Karl Marx. It appeared that there was no significant double counting. Also the selection of journals to be included in *SSCI* may or may not be representative of the relevant disciplines.

6 Being in academics for many years, it appears that other disciplines have dominant views about the economy. The economic views of other academic professions seem to be liberal-interventionist or radical left-wing in nature. The dominance of these

views could be the consequence of the same type of market imperfections that lead to the ascendancy of free market economics in the economics profession.

7 Bartley (1990: 91, 136 ff.) believes that Walrasian general equilibrium theory, macroeconomics, and econometrics have dominated the economics profession. Bartley seems to be unaware of the recent literature in the New Keynesian economics which is beginning to incorporate the role of ideas in a theory of implicit contracts.

8 Cf. Lucas and Sargent (1981b).

7 MARKET FAILURE IN THE MARKETPLACE OF IDEAS: THE CASE OF FRIEDMAN'S ESSAY

1 Friedman's comments regarding Marshall's view of competition include two illustrative examples, wheat farming and cigarette production:

> Wheat farming is frequently taken to exemplify perfect competition. Yet, while for some problems it is appropriate to treat cigarette producers as if they comprised a perfectly competitive industry, for some it is not appropriate to treat wheat producers as if they did. For example, it may not be if the problem is the differential in prices paid by local elevator operators for wheat.
>
> Marshall's apparatus turned out to be most useful for problems in which a group of firms is affected by common stimuli, and in which the firms can be treated *as if* they were perfect competitors. This is the source of the misconception that Marshall "assumed" perfect competition in some descriptive sense [original emphasis].
>
> (Friedman 1953: 37–8)

2 Cf. with Weimer (1979) and Baum (1974).

3 Boland's essay resulted in several lengthy replies like those of Caldwell (1980), Wible (1982), and Stanley (1985). Katouzian (1980) has also portrayed Friedman's essay as being instrumentalist.

4 For a lengthy discussion of conceptions of instrumentalism see Wible (1984a).

5 This line of interpreting Boland's essay as a noncompetitive episode was suggested to me by Wade Hands. In any event, responsibility for the argument is, of course, the author's.

6 With regard to Samuelson's critique, Boland confined himself to Samuelson's direct criticisms of Friedman's essay. The significance of Samuelson's comments on operational behaviorism were not discussed in Boland's (1979) article.

7 The noted late philosopher Ernest Nagel (1971) in assessing Friedman's essay perceives little that is truly innovative from a philosophical point of view.

8 There is another possible level of interpretation to the market failure view of the dominance of Friedman's essay in economics. For a time, perhaps several decades, it is conceivable that Friedman's essay left economics with a more flexible and error-correcting scientific methodology than any of the justificationist alternatives. Not only does Table 7.1 illustrate a pattern of dominance by Friedman's essay, it also shows a period of rapidly changing philosophies of science. Conceptions of science were being revised and reconceived faster than nonspecialists could follow. Practising scientists want to do science, not philosophy of science or methodology. The dominance of Friedman's essay effectively insulated economics for a time, from unprecedented chaotic innovation in thinking about science. Such insulation required market failure in the marketplace of ideas in economics. Table 7.1 portrays philosophy of science as approaching intellectual chaos. In the short run, intellectual chaos can waste the time and effort of many good scientists. In this

context, the arguments made by Boland for the intellectual superiority of Friedman's essay could also be consistent with an awareness of market failure in the marketplace of ideas in economics. Friedman's essay, despite its errors and flaws and in spite of market failure in the marketplace of ideas could have been the best methodology of science available to economists. Friedman's essay simply could have presented a less flawed and more stable vision of science than any of the rapidly changing proposed alternatives. So despite significant flaws in the essay and in the degree of competitiveness in economics, it is possible to maintain that Friedman's essay temporarily lead to more scientific progress in economics than rival visions of the nature of economic science.

8 SELF-CORRECTIVE SCIENCE IN THE CONTEXT OF MARKET FAILURE: THE MARKETPLACE OF IDEAS IS NOT REALLY A MARKET

1 There are other philosophers who have written about the self-correctiveness of science. Popper views science as a trial and error process which solves problems by conjectured theories and critically scrutinized refutations of those theories. To the extent science corrects its errors, it must solve new problems. But according to Popper (1972a: 17), such progress is not assured. Lakatos is known for his thesis that scientific research programs can be either progressive or degenerating.

2 While Blaug does not mention the problems of misconduct such as fraud and replication failure, Blaug is aware of the faults of science and that scientists make mistakes. Blaug takes a Popperian, falsificationist view of the economics profession. His conception of falsification has been modified for the significant changes introduced by Lakatos. Blaug believes a Lakatosian notion of falsification is the scientific standard by which mainstream, neoclassical economics should be judged. Scientific progress and self-correctability must take the path of falsifiable theories. In his work *The Methodology of Economics* (Blaug 1980), he appraises the scientific status of many contributions to economics and concludes that economists do not create falsifiable research. This critique is even extended to human capital theory which Blaug similarly claims is untestable. What Blaug is describing from his viewpoint is a significant degree of failure in the marketplace of economic ideas. Mainstream neoclassical economics has dominated economics even though it has failed to succeed as a science. Despite such an awareness of the failure of falsification in scientific practice in economics, Blaug continues to assert the self-correctability of science.

3 Milton's *Areopagitica* does not represent the first expression of the marketplace of ideas. Bartley (1990: 26) maintains that the market in books and manuscripts played an important role in stimulating the emergence of democracy in Athens in the fifth century BC.

4 Further discussion of the themes introduced by Coase can be found in Breton and Wintrobe (1992).

5 Criticism of Polanyi's conception of science can be found in de Jouvenel (1961).

6 Much of what Hayek has to say about economic competition and spontaneous orders is not accepted by mainstream economists. The mainstream conception of economic competition is quite different from the Hayekian self-ordering processes just described. Most economists view Hayek as a subjectivist who has rejected an objective basis for ordinary economic knowledge.

7 Besides the eclipsing of the scientism of Keynesian and New Classical macro-economics, in economic methodology inquiry has moved beyond a preoccupation with Friedman's essay and an emphasis on positive economic science. Among philosophers and methodologists, there is an awareness that economic science could

not be practiced according to the more naturalistic, hard science interpretation of Friedman's essay. Again, the half century or so of dominance by Friedman's essay as a possible instance of scientism and market failure in the marketplace of ideas needs to be contrasted with the apparent receding of the essay into the background of professional discourse.

8 This discussion of *Scientific Progress* is drawn from Wible (1994b).

9 The first part of *Scientific Progress* ends with a discussion of the growth rate of science. Rescher documents that science has been growing at an exponential rate for almost a century and perhaps two. He calls this Adams' law of exponential growth. In terms of manpower, literature, information, facilities, and expenditure, a great deal of descriptive evidence is presented supporting an exponential growth path for science. Then Rescher inquires whether an Adams' law view of scientific progress can be maintained in a world where there is little or zero growth in resources.

9 ON THE ECONOMIC ORGANIZATION OF SCIENCE, THE FIRM, AND THE MARKETPLACE

1 The perfect information interpretation of competition has been significantly modified in the past two decades with rational expectations. I would not want my characterization of the substitutes argumentative structure to be criticized because it presents a naive view of the role of information in economic theory. This chapter is in partly based on Wible (1995).

2 Williamson repeatedly makes this point in his research. See Williamson (1990: 62, 1991: 161).

3 Arrow (1969: 51) denies the universality of markets: "The bulk of meaningful future transactions cannot be carried out on any existing present market, so that assumption (M), the universality of markets, is not valid."

4 William Baumol (1982) has reinterpreted the theory of economic competition with a theory of contestable markets. Contestability expands the successful domain of invisible-hand processes in the market and reduces the scope of market failure.

5 A classical economist such as Adam Smith has viewed the market as a substitute for the failure of simple barter. As the division of labor encourages specialization, productive surpluses begin to create problems in trade. Smith remarked: "But when the division of labour first began to take place, this power of exchanging must frequently have been very much clogged and embarrassed in its operations" (Smith 1910: ch. iv, 20). One solution is for individuals to hold stocks of relatively marketable items that are in high demand by others. Trading arrangements such as these constitute a more complex form of barter. Another solution to the problem of trade is the emergence of money and markets.

6 Alchian and Demsetz (1972: 791) state the issue in the following way: "To this point the discussion has examined why firms, as we have defined them, exist? That is, why is there an owner-employer who is the common party to contracts with other owners of inputs in team activity?"

7 In 1987 Coase (1991a, 1991b, 1991c) gave three lectures on the 1937 essay which was one of the main works cited for his Nobel prize. Coase apparently conceived of the core of his ideas when he was twenty-one years old. The historical background to the essay can be found in the first lecture. The other two lectures deal with the impact and interpretation of the essay. Coase's lectures and other essays regarding Coase's contributions can be found in Williamson and Winter (1991).

8 If the firm borrows money, another problem appears of who monitors the monitor or who monitors the owner. The incentives of borrowers and lenders may differ so

that the promised behavior of the borrower may be different once the borrowed funds are committed.

9 The substitutes theory of various institutions may be adequate for most of the issues faced in an attempt to understand the nature of the firm. Science however is another matter. I have actually tried to reread the NIE literature from the opposing position, that the primacy of markets is not presupposed. But I believe the substitutes position is the better interpretation of the literature summarized in the text.

10 Earlier in the essay Coase (1937: 335) remarked that: "Our task is to attempt to discover why a firm emerges at all in a specialized economy."

11 Williamson's analysis of the role of the divisional structure of the corporation and the internalization of the capital market within the corporation clearly portray these corporate processes as substitutes for the market. Kay (1992: 324) provides commentary and criticism of Williamson's position.

12 In *Markets and Hierarchies*, Williamson (1975: 20) authored a similar genesis statement. However, he asserted that it was made "for expositional convenience."

13 Whether the transactions cost approach can be applied to science is an important question. Williamson (1992: 335) asserts that transactions cost theory is not an "all purpose theory of economic organization." He also remarks that "just because an issue has not yet been addressed in transactions cost economizing terms does not mean that the issue is beyond the reach of transactions cost economics reasoning" (Williamson 1992: 337). I believe that Williamson's transactions cost approach can add to our understanding of science and that science, because of its peculiarities, will illustrate important limitations of the transactions cost approach.

14 The noncapitalist nature of science raises an important question. How does science acquire its capital? In the private sector, capital is raised in financial markets and from financial institutions. For individual scientists and research teams, access to financial markets is prohibitively costly. Usually the investigation could not be organized within a corporate structure or other form of business organization. So how is it that scientists acquire the large sums of capital they need to finance their experiments? The obvious answer is grantsmanship. Like the ordinary firm which has good access to capital or the conglomerate firm which internalizes some of the functions of capital markets, science has created institutional structures providing access to large sums of support. Government agencies provide access for science to the capital markets through the credit rating and borrowing powers of the fiscal agent of any level of government. Usually the fiscal agent is a department of the treasury or revenue. To the extent that the sciences rely on government for access to capital, the federal treasury provides a substitute to capital markets. The creation of agencies like the NSF and NIH provide an institutional mechanism for acquiring and allocating capital for science through the public sector.

15 A similarly phrased question is often raised in the economics literature: Does market failure exist? Failure of markets appears to be a more significant issue than their existence.

16 Compare with Hodgson (1989) and Rutherford (1989).

17 One of the most approachable discussions of indeterminism is Popper (1972b). Other recent works encompassing evolutionary indeterminism are Robbins (1935: 131–2), Bohm (1957: 36), Georgescu-Roegen (1971), and Shackle (1972).

18 In the history of economics, an example of one economist who assumed an evolutionary complements position with regard to science and other economic institutions was Thorstein Veblen. Veblen's complements position can serve as an inspiration but not as a detailed guide to a modern, reconstructed complements approach to institutions and organizations that also embraces mainstream economics. Veblen did not present an abstract generalized scheme of evolution and he based his theory of

human behavior on an instinct psychology that was not incorporated subsequently into mainstream economics.

Veblen (1906) held that science played a formative role in culture and civilization. A matter of fact attitude rooted in science came to dominate the mindset of the common man through the dispersion of ideas accompanying technological advance and modern economic growth. Although he does not use the terminology, Veblen depicts something like a common-sense version of positivism:

> But whatever the common-sense of earlier generations may have held in this respect, modern common-sense holds that the scientist's answer is the only ultimately true one. In the last resort enlightened common-sense sticks by the opaque truth and refuses to go behind the returns given by the tangible facts.
>
> (Veblen [1906] 1961: 4)

For Veblen, modern science emerges when anthropomorphic conceptualization is replaced with an understanding of cause and effect based on natural law. Such laws best apply to machines and machine-like phenomena. Veblen believes that: "The machine process has displaced the workman as the archetype in whose image causation is conceived by the scientific investigators" (Veblen [1906] 1961: 16). Consequently a mechanistic attitude permeates science and culture and even economic science. Veblen (1898) asserts that economics is not an evolutionary science because it has become dominated with mechanistic conceptions of facts and behavior that are prevalent in culture more generally. Science and economic science, like other culture processes, exist to create theoretical concepts which become embedded in conduct and social processes. Unfortunately, economics in Veblen's (1898) view has not followed the other more highly developed sciences and has not become an evolutionary science. It has become dominated by the very mechanical concepts it helped to create. It is also interesting to note that one of Veblen's teachers was Charles Sanders Peirce.

19 Uncertainty is discussed by Williamson (1975: 4, 1985: 57, 79) and Coase (1937: 336–7). They relate uncertainty to the role of the firm but not to an understanding of the existence of markets.

20 Shackle (1972) provides a rich depiction of a monetary economy characterized by indeterminism and epistemic scarcity.

21 See Hayek (1948).

22 Arrow (1969: 48) notes that money is a transactions-cost reducing creation. For a discussion of the role of accounting in the economy see Jensen (1983).

23 If I had to choose one institution as being more important above all others it would be the household or the family. Hayek (1948: 23) states: "true individualism affirms the value of the family and all the common efforts of the small community and group."

24 The role of technology and instrumentation in science is considered in great detail by Rescher (1978b, 1989).

25 The relevant references are de Jouvenel (1961), Polanyi (1962a, 1962b), Stigler (1963), Coase (1974), Breton and Wintrobe (1992), and Bartley (1990).

26 Okun (1981) presented a dual economy model of the entire economy while Doeringer and Piore (1971) pioneered the dual markets hypothesis for labor markets.

27 According to Polanyi (1962a), the authority of science is subject to methodological rules and evolutionary change and is slowly self-correcting.

28 Much of the sociology of science can be found in Merton (1973). Other significant literature is Radnitzky's (1987a) economic approach to scientific discovery, Hull's (1988) conception of science in terms of visible and invisible hand explanations,

and Colander's (1989) analysis of the economics profession using an invisible hand argument.

29 For example, Merton (1973) would most likely be categorized as emphasizing the organizational complexity of science.

30 Klappholz and Agassi (1959: 65) have criticized Friedman's instrumentalism even though it was not specifically identified as such in their article. Comparing Friedman to Popper's critical approach, they assert: "Friedman's position . . . is an example of the acceptance of the methodological rules which are part and parcel of the critical approach, yet without the wholehearted adoption of the approach itself."

31 For a discussion of falsification see Hausman (1985) and Salanti (1987).

32 The idea of falsification has been broadened and reinterpreted in Lakatos (1978a) to the point that it is a rival theory rather than evidence which really leads to the rejection of a theory.

33 William Butos (1987) has noted this limitation of McCloskey's *Rhetoric* and has argued that taken as a whole, science is a Hayekian evolutionary, spontaneous order. In this conception of science, the traditions of scientific communities as embedded in rules of conduct guide individual actions of members of the community. Such rules prevent the sort of intellectual anarchy and chaos suggested by Paul Feyerabend. Methodological rules are given at a point in time, but change in a gradual evolutionary manner reflecting many particularized and specialized developments in science. These rules reflect the presence of an inquisitive human intelligence consciously exploring the world, but they are not the product of a single conscious mind.

34 How science gains access to financial capital in capitalism is discussed in note 14.

10 TOWARDS AN EVOLUTIONARY CONCEPTION OF RATIONALITY IN SCIENCE AND ECONOMICS

1 In this chapter, rationality is used in two senses: (1) as a hypothetical logic of transactor deliberation and (2) as a concern for the sequences of deliberation in real, complex situations. The latter sense is often denoted as "process rationality" or reasonability. I do not wish to cede the semantic turf to those who would argue that the definition of rationality should be narrowly confined to a logical conception. In economics, the rhetoric of rationality is central to the discipline.

2 Some economists have developed processive notions of rationality. See Shackle (1972), Godelier (1972), Georgescu-Roegen (1971), Simon (1976, 1978, 1979), and March (1978) on conceptions of rationality.

3 Weimer, a cognitive psychologist, is somewhat like H.A. Simon in being interested in cognitive processes. Rather than using computers to investigate the "bounded rationality" of complex decisions, Weimer focuses on the complexity of scientific decision-making presumed in various philosophies of science. While Weimer's work does not have the technological sophistication of Simon's, it does have the advantage of not imposing the inherent limitations of computer algorithms and artificial intelligence devices. Simon (1976: 144) even recognizes such limitations: "There are still many areas of decision – particularly those that are ill-structured – where human cognitive processes are more effective than the best available optimization techniques or artificial intelligence methods."

4 Some may believe that modeling economic man using science as a precedent smacks of scientism because it imposes the prejudices of a narrow naturalistic view on economic phenomena where they do not belong. However, an alternative point of view is to focus on complex decision-making maintaining that scientific decision-making is different in degree but not in kind from choices in other domains of

human activity. Science is merely a domain in which some aspects of decision-making complexity may be more apparent.

5 Bartley (1984) lists four types of arguments for eliminating error in science: the check of logic, the check of sense observation, the check of scientific theory, and the check of the problem. My approach expands on the points made by Bartley.

6 This part of the chapter is based on Wible (1984b).

7 It must be emphasized that only a small minority of transactors as individuals may exhibit the decision-making sophistication of nonjustificational economic rationality. Indeed, for many individuals such sophistication may be impossible. However, it is possible to specialize in the various argumentative dimensions summarized in Table 10.3. Collectively, it may take a corporation, bureaucratic institution, or academic profession to handle all aspects of rational argument. In an organizational sense, the rational decision then becomes a process of collective judgement involving committees, boards, seminars, etc. Thus nonjustificational economic rationality may be either an individual or social conception of rationality depending on the individuals and the specific organizational context.

8 The importance of nonjustificational notions of knowledge and rationality as they relate to macroeconomics is explored in Wible (1990). See also see Boland (1981).

11 INTERNAL CRITICISM AND THE PROBLEM OF SELF-REFERENCE

1 For a discussion of the problem of self-reference, see Nagel and Newman (1958) and Rucker (1982). For a discussion of the problem of self-reference in economics see Winrich (1984). Jarvie (1982) and Hull (1988) discuss the problem of a self-referential theory of science.

2 The classic work on this issue is Ayer (1956).

3 Arjo Klamer (1984), D. N. McCloskey (1985), and Melvin Reder (1982) acknowledge this problem.

4 Lakatos' terminology is "positive heuristic." A positive heuristic is a research orientation that extends an existing view of economic science and supports these extensions with appropriate empirical evidence.

5 Ernst Zermelo claims to have discovered the Russell paradox before Russell. Evidence exists that Zermelo sent handwritten notes describing the paradox to selected colleagues before Russell published his version in 1903. The issues are reprised by Rang and Thomas (1981).

6 Russell (1907) attempted to circumvent the paradox with his "Theory of Types." He claims that a statement like *LP* is meaningless.

7 Russell (1907) attempted to circumvent the liar's paradox by maintaining the independence of each statement *E-1* to *E-N*. A statement is true or false relative to its level of order. *E-3* is a third order proposition because it refers to *E-2* and *E-1*. Russell maintains that *E-3* can be true even if *E-2* and *E-1* are false. Similarly *E-X* and *E-LP* do not involve a contradiction for Russell because they are higher order propositions (*X*) making assertions about lower order (*X-1*) propositions. Russell (1907: 241) concludes: "This solves the liar."

8 To my knowledge, Russell did not extend his concern with paradox to scientific inference. His theory of types does not seem adequate to convince us that empiricism is empirically defensible.

9 J. Steven Winrich's (1984) article raises the issue of a mathematical liar.

10 An acceptable English translation is Gödel (1931). One of the best accounts of Gödel's work is the Nagel and Newman (1958) monograph, *Gödel's Proof.* A more recent account can be found in mathematician Rudy Rucker's (1982) monograph,

Infinity and Mind. Other pertinent works are those by Martin (1970), Wilder (1965), and Hofstadter (1985).

11 Cf. Nagel and Newman (1958: 86).

12 In mathematical logic, a system of calculus is complete if all theorems in the system can be derived from axioms. If a valid theorem were discovered that could not be generated from the axioms, then this system would be incomplete. See Nagel and Newman (1958: 55–6).

13 Nagel and Newman (1958: 97) tell us that Gerhard Gentzen has established the consistency of arithmetic by creating "new forms of metamathematical constructions." His arguments apparently involve an infinite regress.

14 My presentation of the proof involves a succession of more encompassing mathematical systems. Gödel dealt with just two, arithmetic and metamathematics. Each stage of my regress takes us to a higher order system. My view implies that the consistency of each mathematical system is dependent on the consistency of a higher order system which in turn depends on the consistency of even higher order systems. The result is an infinite hierarchy of mathematical systems with mathematics as a totality being incomplete. This is a much broader result than Gödel's theorem. I have included it because this seems to be an obvious implication of Gödel's theorem.

15 Mathematicians typically require that proofs be of finite length (Nagel and Newman 1958: 97, n. 30). Philip Davis and Rubin Hersh (1981: 375 ff.) describe the difficulties that computers cause for mathematicians. Should mathematicians accept proofs which are the product of computer algorithms? Computers would enable mathematicians to formulate much longer proofs than otherwise. Yet the issue of the provability of the algorithm arises. Will errors be found in the algorithm? Could it be proven that an algorithm would generate no erroneous results? These are some questions which make mathematicians reticent to rely on computers let alone infinite regresses.

16 This is my reconstruction of Popper's remarks on induction and his critical response to Thomas Kuhn claiming that normal scientists are uncritical. See Popper (1965: 54–5, 1970, 1972a: 22 ff.).

17 Of course the relevant literature is Kuhn (1970, 1977), Popper (1959, 1965, 1972a), Lakatos (1978a, 1978b), and Lakatos and Musgrave (1970). Philosophically minded economists should consult Caldwell (1982), Boland (1982), Katouzian (1980), and Blaug (1980) for appraisals of the relevance of this research to economics.

12 AN ECONOMIC CRITIQUE OF THE ARCHITECTURE OF ECONOMIC THEORY AND METHOD

1 In this section I will use an alternative device for representing an infinite regress with sequences of nested parentheses. These issues are discussed in Rucker (1982: 146 ff., 196 ff.).

2 This statement presumes more of a Walrasian than a Marshallian view of economic processes.

3 The attempt to justify the validity of perfect competition would also return the argument to an infinite regress.

4 Katouzian (1980: 70) suggests that such an inconsistency exists: "It is a paradox when a system of thought [positive economics] preaches a certain methodology which it does not observe; it is even a greater paradox when the same system of thought ruthlessly insists that alternative theories, both old and new, should observe the methodological criteria which the orthodoxy observes but refuses to practice!"

5 For the concerned reader, these methodological conceptions of competition provide

a basis for arguments discussed later in this essay. The realism of these conceptions is considered in the next part of this chapter.

6 My remarks should not be construed to imply that Lakatos conceived science as an equilibrium process. I call attention only to the level, but not to the nature of competition in Lakatos' conception of science.

7 As with Lakatos, these remarks should refer to the level but not the nature of competition in Kuhn's theory of science.

8 Note that Popper's view applies to all kinds of knowledge not just science. Popper (1972a: 66, 261) claims that scientific knowledge differs from other forms of knowledge because of the role of criticism and evidence in scientific investigation. However, Popper's work needs to be modified for economic constraints.

BIBLIOGRAPHY

Alchian, A. A. and Demsetz, H. (1972) "Production, Information Costs, and Economic Organization," *American Economic Review*, vol. 62, pp. 777–95.

Anderson, A. (1988a) "Criminal Charge in Scientific Fraud Case," *Nature*, April 21, p. 670.

—— (1988b) "U.S. Congressional Committee Takes on Role of Reviewer," *Nature*, April 21, p. 670.

—— (1988c) "First Scientific Fraud Conviction," *Nature*, September 29, p. 89.

Anderson, R. G. and Dewald, W. G. (1994) "Replication and Scientific Standards in Applied Economics a Decade After the *Journal of Money, Credit, and Banking Project*," *Review*, Federal Reserve Bank of St Louis, November/December, pp. 79–83.

Arrow, K. (1963) "Uncertainty and the Economics of Medical Care," *American Economic Review*, vol. 53, pp. 941–73.

—— (1969) "The Organization of Economic Activity: Issues Pertinent to the Choice of Market versus Nonmarket Allocation," in *The Analysis and Evaluation of Public Expenditures: The PPB System*, Washington: Joint Economic Committee.

Ashmore, M. (1989) *The Reflexive Thesis: Wrighting Sociology of Scientific Knowledge*, Chicago: University of Chicago Press.

Ayer, A. J. (1946) *Language, Truth, and Logic*, New York: Dover Publications.

—— (1956) *The Problem of Knowledge*, Baltimore: Penguin Books.

Azariadis, C. and Stiglitz, J. E. (1983) "Implicit Contracts and Fixed Price Equilibria," *Quarterly Journal of Economics*, vol. 98, pp. 1–22.

Backhouse, R. E. (ed.) (1994) *New Directions in Economic Methodology*, London: Routledge.

Bartley, W. W., III (1984) *The Retreat to Commitment*, 2nd edn, La Salle, Ill.: Open Court.

—— (1990) *Unfathomed Knowledge, Unmeasured Wealth: On Universities and the Wealth of Nations*, La Salle, Ill.: Open Court.

Baum, R. F. (1974) "Popper, Kuhn, Lakatos: A Crisis of Modern Intellect," *Intercollegiate Review*, vol. 9, pp. 99–110.

Baumol, W. J. (1982) "Contestable Markets: An Uprising in the Theory of Industry Structure," *American Economic Review*, vol. 72, pp. 1–15.

Baumol, W. J. and Goldfeld, S. M. (1968) *Precursors in Mathematical Economics: An Anthology*, London: London School of Economics and Political Science.

Bear, D. V. T. and Orr, D. (1967) "Logic and Expediency in Economic Theorizing," *Journal of Political Economy*, April, pp. 188–96.

Beckor, G. S. (1965) "A Theory of the Allocation of Time," *Economic Journal*, vol. 75, pp. 493–517.

—— (1968) "Crime and Punishment: An Economic Approach," *Journal of Political Economy*, vol. 76, pp. 169–217.

—— (1971) *Economic Theory*, New York: A. A. Knopf.

Becker, G. S. and Landes, W. M. (1974) *Essays in the Economics of Crime and Punishment*, New York: National Bureau of Economic Research.

Becker, W. E. Jr (1975) "The University Professor as a Utility Maximizer and Producer of Learning, Research, and Income," *Journal of Human Resources*, vol. 10, pp. 107–15.

Blank, D. M. and Stigler, G. J. (1957) *The Demand and Supply of Scientific Personnel*, New York: National Bureau of Economic Research.

Blaug, M. (1976) "Kuhn versus Lakatos *or* Paradigms versus Research Programmes in the History of Economics," in Latsis (1976), pp. 149–80.

—— (1980) *The Methodology of Economics*, Cambridge: Cambridge University Press.

Boffey, P. M. (1988) "Nobel Winner is Caught Up in a Dispute over Study," *New York Times*, April 12, pp. C1 and C10.

Bohm, D. (1957) *Causality and Chance in Modern Physics*, Philadelphia: University of Pennsylvania Press.

Boland, L. A. (1971) "Methodology as an Exercise in Economic Analysis," *Philosophy of Science*, vol. 38, pp. 105–17.

—— (1979) "A Critique of Friedman's Critics," *Journal of Economic Literature*, vol. 17, pp. 503–22.

—— (1981) "On the Futility of Criticizing the Neoclassical Maximization Hypothesis," *American Economic Review*, vol. 71, pp. 1031–6.

—— (1982) *The Foundations of Economic Method*, London: Allen and Unwin.

Braunwald, E. (1987) "On Analyzing Scientific Fraud," *Nature*, January 15, pp. 215–16.

Brent, J. (1993) *Charles Sanders Peirce: A Life*, Bloomington, Ind.: Indiana University Press.

Breton, A. and Wintrobe, R. (1992) "Freedom of Speech vs. Efficient Regulation," *Journal of Economic Behavior and Organization*, vol. 17, pp. 217–39.

Broad, W. and Wade, N. (1982) *Betrayers of the Truth*, New York: Simon and Schuster.

Budiansky, S. (1983a) "Research Fraud: False Data Confessed," *Nature*, January 13, p. 101.

—— (1983b) "Data Falsification: NIH Decrees Ten-year Ban on Research Grants," *Nature*, February 24, p. 645.

Butos, W. N. (1987) "Rhetoric and Rationality: A Review Essay of McCloskey's *The Rhetoric of Economics*," *Eastern Economic Journal*, July–September, pp. 295–304.

Caldwell, B. J. (1980) "A Critique of Friedman's Methodological Instrumentalism," *Southern Economic Journal*, October, pp. 366–74.

—— (1982) *Beyond Positivism: Economic Methodology in the Twentieth Century*, London: Allen and Unwin.

—— (1991) "Clarifying Popper," *Journal of Economic Literature*, vol. 29, March, pp. 1–33.

Campbell, K. E. and Jackson, T. T. (1979) "The Role and Need for Replication Research in Social Psychology," *Replications in Social Psychology*, vol. 1, pp. 3–15.

Campen, J. T. (1986) *Benefit, Cost, and Beyond: The Political Economy of Benefit-Cost Analysis*, Cambridge: Ballinger Publishing.

Clower, R. W. (1975) "Reflections on the Keynesian Perplex," *Zeitschrift für Nationalökonomie*, vol. 35, no. 1, pp. 1–24.

Coase, R. H. (1937) "The Nature of the Firm," *Economica*, NS, vol. 4, pp. 366–405.

—— (1960) "The Problem of Social Cost," *Journal of Law and Economics*, October, pp. 1–44.

—— (1974) "The Market for Goods and the Market for Ideas," *American Economic Review*, vol. 64, pp. 384–91.

—— (1991a) "The Nature of the Firm: Origin," in Williamson and Winter (1991) pp. 34–47.

—— (1991b) "The Nature of the Firm: Meaning," in Williamson and Winter (1991) pp. 48–60.

—— (1991c) "The Nature of the Firm: Influence," in Williamson and Winter (1991) pp. 61–74.

Coats, A. W. (1969) "Is There a 'Structure of Scientific Revolutions' in Economics?" *Kyklos*, vol. 22, pp. 289–94.

—— (1984) "The Sociology of Knowledge and the History of Economics," *Research in the History of Economic Thought and Methodology*, a research annual, vol. 2, pp. 211–34.

Colander, D. (1989) "Research on the Economics Profession," *Journal of Economic Perspectives*, vol. 3, no. 4, pp. 137–48.

Collins, H. M. (1985) *Changing Order: Replication and Induction in Scientific Practice*, London: Sage Publications.

Commons, J. R. (1934) *Institutional Economics*, New York: Macmillan.

Cournot, A. (1929) [1838] *Researches into the Mathematical Principles of the Theory of Wealth*, trans. N. T. Bacon, New York: Macmillan.

Culliton, B. J. (1986) "Harvard Researchers Retract Data in Immunology Paper," *Science*, November 28, p. 1069.

—— (1988a) "A Bitter Battle Over Error," *Science*, June 24, pp. 1720–3.

—— (1988b) "A Bitter Battle Over Error (II)," *Science*, July 1, pp. 18–21.

Cushen, W. E. (1967) "C.S. Peirce on Benefit-Cost Analysis of Scientific Activity," *Operations Research*, vol. 15, p. 641.

Dasgupta, P. and David, P. A. (1994) "Toward a New Economics of Science," *Research Policy*, vol. 23, pp. 487–521.

Davis, P. J. and Hersh, R. (1981) *The Mathematical Experience*, Boston: Houghton Mifflin.

Dewald, W. G., Thursby, J. G. and Anderson, R. G. (1986) "Replication in Empirical Economics," *American Economic Review*, vol. 76, pp. 587–603.

Dewey, J. (1903) *Studies in Logical Theory*, Chicago: University of Chicago Press.

Diamond, A. (1988) "Science as a Rational Enterprise," *Theory and Decision*, vol. 24, pp. 147–67.

—— (1994) "The Determinants of a Scientist's Choice of Research Projects," in T. Horowitz and A. I. Janis, (eds) *Scientific Failure*, London: Rowman and Littlefield, pp. 167–204.

—— (1995) "George Stigler's Contributions to the Economics of Science," University of Nebraska, May 28, paper presented to the History of Economics Society at Notre Dame on June 4.

—— (1996) "The Economics of Science?," *The International Journal of Knowledge Transfer and Utilization*, vol. 9, pp. 6–49.

Doeringer, P. B. and Piore, M. J. (1971) *Internal Labor Markets and Manpower Analysis*, Lexington, Mass: Heath.

Donoghue, M. J. (1990) "Sociology, Selection, and Success: A Critique of David Hull's Analysis of Science and Systematics," *Biology and Philosophy*, vol. 5, pp. 459–72.

Dorfman, R. (ed.) (1965) *Measuring the Benefits of Government Investments*, Washington, D.C.: Brookings.

Earl, P. E. (1983) "A Behavioral Theory of Economist's Behavior," in A. S. Eichner (ed.) *Why Economics is Not Yet a Science*, New York: Macmillan, pp. 90–125.

—— (1988) "On Being a Psychological Economist and Winning the Games Economists Play," in P. Earl (ed.) *Psychological Economics: Development, Tensions, Prospects*, Boston: Kluwer, pp. 227–42.

Ehrlich, I. (1973) "Participation in Illegitimate Activities: An Economic Analysis," *Journal of Political Economy*, vol. 81, no. 3, pp. 521–65.

Eisele, C. (1979a) *Studies in the Mathematical Philosophy of Charles S. Peirce*, R. M. Martin (ed.), New York: Mouton Publishers.
—— (1979b) "The Correspondence with Simon Newcomb," in Eisele (1979a) pp. 52–93.
—— (1979c) "The Mathematics of Economics," in Eisele (1979a) pp. 251–4.
—— (1979d) "Introductions to *The New Elements of Mathematics*," in Eisele (1979a) pp. 308–76.
—— (1979e) "The Problem of Map Projection," in Eisele (1979a) pp. 145–59.
Eysenck, H. J. and Kamin, L. (1981) *The Intelligence Controversy*, New York: Wiley and Sons.
Feigenbaum, S. and Levy, D. M. (1993) "The Market for (Ir)Reproducible Econometrics," *Social Epistemology*, vol. 7, pp. 215–32.
—— (1994) "The Self Enforcement Mechanism in Science?," paper presented to the American Economic Association, January 1993.
Feigenbaum, S., Levy, D. and Tullock, G. (1986) "Some Economics of Econometrics: An Empirical Exploration of Replication," paper presented to the American Economics Association meeting.
Fisch, M. (1982) "The Decisive Year and Its Early Consequences," introduction to E. C. Moore, *et al.* (eds) *Writings of Charles S. Peirce: A Chronological Edition*, vol. 2 1867–1871, Indianapolis: Indiana University Press.
Foreman, J. (1988) "Baltimore Speaks Out on Disputed Study," *Boston Globe*, May 23, pp. 31 and 32.
Foreman, J. and Howe, P. J. (1996) "Ex-MIT Scientist is Cleared of Fraud," *Boston Globe*, June 22, pp. 1 and 7.
Frege, G. (1902) [1967] "Letter to Russell (1902)," in J. van Heijenoort (ed.) *From Frege to Gödel: A Sourcebook in Mathematical Logic*, Cambridge: Harvard University Press, pp. 126–8.
Friedlander, M. W. (1995) *At the Fringes of Science*, Boulder: Westview Press.
Friedman, M. (1953) "The Methodology of Positive Economics," in M. Friedman *Essays in Positive Economics*, Chicago: University of Chicago Press.
—— (1981) "An Open Letter on Grants," *Newsweek*, May 18, p. 99.
Friedmann, T. (1992) "Ethical Duties of Scientists, their Institutions, and the Guild of Science," *Journal of NIH Research*, vol. 4, February, pp. 19–22.
Fusfeld, D. R. (1980) "The Conceptual Framework of Modern Economics," *Journal of Economic Issues*, vol. 14, pp. 1–52.
Georgescu-Roegen, N. (1971) *The Entropy Law and the Economic Process*, Cambridge: Harvard University Press.
Ghiselin, M. T. (1987) "The Economics of Scientific Discovery," in G. Radnitzky and P. Bernholz (eds) *Economic Imperialism: The Economic Approach Applied Outside the Field of Economics*, New York: Paragon House, pp. 271–82.
Gödel, K. (1931) [1970]. "On Formally Undecidable Propositions of *Principia Mathematica* and Related Systems I," English translation published in J. van Heijenoort (ed.), *Frege and Gödel: Two Fundamental Texts in Mathematical Logic*, Cambridge: Harvard University Press.
Godelier, M. (1972) *Rationality and Irrationality in Economics*, trans. B. Pearce, New York: Monthly Review Press.
Gosselin, P. (1988) "Scientists Grapple with Rising Fraud," *Boston Globe*, December 4, pp. 1 and 28.
Graham, D. A. (1981) "Cost-Benefit Analysis Under Uncertainty," *American Economic Review*, vol. 71, pp. 715–25.
Gramlich, E. M. (1981) *Benefit-Cost Analysis of Government Programs*, Englewood Cliffs N.J.: Prentice Hall.
Hacking, I. (1990) *The Taming of Chance*, Cambridge: Cambridge University Press.

Hands, D. W. (1985) "Karl Popper and Economic Methodology: A New Look," *Economics and Philosophy*, vol. 1, pp. 83–99.

—— (1994a) "The Sociology of Scientific Knowledge and Economics: Some Thoughts on the Possibilities," in R. Backhouse (ed.) *New Perspectives in Economic Methodology*, London: Routledge, pp. 75–106.

—— (1994b) "Blurred Boundaries: Recent Changes in the Relationship Between Economics and the Philosophy of Natural Science," *Studies in the History and Philosophy of Science.*, vol. 25, pp. 751–72.

—— (1996) "Economics and Laudan's Normative Naturalism: Bad News from Instrumental Rationality's Front Line," *Social Epistemology*, vol. 10, pp. 137–52.

—— (1997) "Caveat Emptor: Economics and Contemporary Philosophy of Science," unpublished research paper, University of Puget Sound.

Hattiangadi, J. N. (1985) "The Realism of Popper and Russell," *Philosophy of the Social Sciences*, vol. 15, pp. 461–86.

Hausman, Daniel M. 1985. "Is Falsificationism Unpractised or Unpractisable?," *Philosophy of the Social Sciences*, vol. 15, pp. 313–19.

Hayek, F. A. (1942) "Scientism and the Study of Society," *Economica*, NS, vol. 9, pp. 267–91.

—— (1946) "The Meaning of Competition," in F. A. Hayek (1948) *Individualism and Economic Order*, Chicago: University of Chicago Press, pp. 92–106.

—— (1948) "The Use of Knowledge in Society," in F. A. Hayek *Individualism and Economic Order*, Chicago: University of Chicago Press, pp. 77–91.

—— (1967) [1978] "The Confusion of Language in Political Thought," reprinted in *New Studies in Philosophy, Politics, Economics and the History of Ideas*, Chicago: University of Chicago Press, pp. 71–97.

—— (1968) [1978] "Competition as a Discovery Procedure," in *New Studies in Philosophy, Politics, Economics and the History of Ideas*, Chicago: University of Chicago Press, pp. 179–90.

Hearnshaw, L. S. (1979) *Cyril Burt: Psychologist*, Ithaca: Cornell University Press.

Heineke, J. M. (ed.) (1978) *Economic Models of Criminal Behavior*, Amsterdam: North Holland.

Helmholtz, Hermann von (1895) *Popular Lectures on Scientific Subjects*, 2nd series, London: Longmans, Green, and Co.

Hilts, P. J. (1991) "Science and the Stain of Scandal," *New York Times*, December 4, pp. B1 and B11.

Hirsch, A., and Marchi, N. de (1990) *Milton Friedman: Economics in Theory and Practice*, Ann Arbor: University of Michigan Press.

Hirshleifer, J. and Riley, J. G. (1979) "The Analytics of Uncertainty and Information: An Expositional Survey," *Journal of Economic Literature*, vol. 17, pp. 1375–421.

Hodgson, G. M. (1989) "Institutional Economic Theory: The Old versus the New," *Review of Political Economy*, November, pp. 249–69.

Hofstadter, D. R. (1979) *Gödel, Escher, Bach: An Eternal Golden Braid*, New York: Basic Books.

—— (1985) *Metamagical Themas*, New York: Basic Books.

Holden, C. (1986) "NIMH Fraud Charge Moves Slowly," *Science*, December 19, pp. 1488–9.

Hollis, M. and Nell, E. J. (1975) *Rational Economic Man: A Philosophical Critique of Neoclassical Economics*, London: Cambridge University Press.

Hoover, K. D. (1994) "Pragmatism, Pragmaticism, and Economic Theory," in R. Backhouse (ed.) *New Perspectives on Economic Methodology*, London: Routledge, pp. 286–315.

Howard, M. (1983) *Profits in Economic Theory*, New York: St Martin's Press.

Howey, R. S. (1972) "The Origins of Marginalism," *History of Political Economy*, vol. 2, Fall, pp. 281–302.

Hull, D. (1988) *Science as a Process: An Evolutionary Account of the Social and Conceptual Development in Science*, Chicago: University of Chicago Press.

Hutchison, T. W. (1964) *Positive Economics and Policy Objectives*, Cambridge: Harvard University Press.

Jarvie, I. C. (1982) "Popper on the Difference between the Natural and the Social Sciences," in P. Levinson (ed.) *In Pursuit of Truth*, Atlantic Highlands, N.J.: Humanities Press, pp. 83–107.

Jensen, M. C. (1983) "Organization Theory and Methodology," *The Accounting Review*, vol. 68, pp. 319–39.

Jensen, M. C. and Meckling, W. H. (1976) "Theory of the Firm: Managerial Behavior, Agency Costs, and Ownership Structure," *Journal of Financial Economics*, vol. 3, pp. 305–60.

Jevons, W. S. [1871] (1957) *The Theory of Political Economy*, 5th edn, London: Macmillan.

Johnson, W. E. (1913) [1968] "The Pure Theory of Utility Curves," in Baumol and Goldfeld (1968), pp. 97–124.

Jouvenel, B. de (1961) "The Republic of Science," in *The Logic of Personal Knowledge*, essays presented to M. Polanyi on his seventieth birthday, Glencoe, Ill.: Free Press, pp. 131–41.

Kamin, L. J. (1974) *The Science and Politics of I.Q.*, New York: John Wiley and Sons.

Katouzian, M. A. H. (1980) *Ideology and Method in Economics*, New York: New York University Press.

Kay, N. M. (1992) "Markets, False Hierarchies, and the Evolution of the Modern Corporation," *Journal of Economic Behavior and Organization*, vol. 17, pp. 315–33.

Keynes, J. N. (1917) [1963] *The Scope and Method of Political Economy*, 4th edn, New York: A. M. Kelley.

Kitcher, P. (1990) "The Division of Cognitive Labor," *Journal of Philosophy*, vol. 87, pp. 5–20.

—— (1993) *The Advancement of Science: Science without Legend, Objectivity without Illusions*, New York: Oxford University Press.

Klamer, A. (1984) *Conversations with Economists*, Totowa, N.J: Rowman and Allanheld.

Klamer, A. and Colander, D. (1990) *The Making of an Economist*, Boulder: Westview Press.

Klappholz, K. and Agassi, J. (1959) "Methodological Prescriptions in Economics," *Economica*, vol. 26, pp. 60–74.

Kmenta, J. (1971) *Elements of Econometrics*, New York: Macmillan.

Koshland, D. (1988a) "Balance in Science," *Science*, January 15, p. 241.

—— (1988b) "Science, Journalism, and Whistle Blowing," *Science*, April 29, p. 585.

—— (1988c) "The Price of Progress," *Science*, August 5, p. 637.

Kuhn, T. S. (1970) *The Structure of Scientific Revolutions*, 2nd edn, Chicago: University of Chicago Press.

—— (1977) *The Essential Tension*, Chicago: University of Chicago Press.

Lakatos, I. (1978a) "Falsification and the Methodology of Scientific Research Programmes," in *Philosophical Papers*, vol. 1, Cambridge: Cambridge University Press, pp. 8–101.

—— (1978b) "History of Science and its Rational Reconstructions," in *Philosophical Papers*, vol. 1, Cambridge: Cambridge University Press, pp. 102–38.

Lakatos, I. and A. Musgrave (eds) (1970) *Criticism and the Growth of Knowledge*, Cambridge: Cambridge University Press.

Latsis, S. J. (ed.) (1976) *Method and Appraisal in Economics*, Cambridge: Cambridge University Press.

Leijonhufvud, A. (1976) "Schools, 'Revolutions,' and Research Programmes in Economic Theory," in S. J. Latsis (ed.) *Method and Appraisal in Economics*, Cambridge: Cambridge University Press.

Levy, D. (1988) "The Market for Fame and Fortune," *History of Political Economy*, vol. 20, pp. 615–25.

Levy, D. and Feigenbaum, S. (1993) "Testing the Replication Hypothesis When the Data Set is Subject to Gross Error," *Economic Letters*, vol. 34, pp. 49–53.

—— (1996) "The Technological Obsolescence of Scientific Fraud," *Rationality and Society*, vol. 8, pp. 261–76.

Lewontin, R. C., Rose, S. and Kamin, L. J. (1984) *Not in Our Genes*, New York: Pantheon Books.

Lucas, R. E. and Sargent, T. J. (1981a) *Rational Expectations and Econometric Practice*, Minneapolis: University of Minnesota Press.

—— (1981b) "After Keynesian Macroeconomics," in Lucas and Sargent (1981a), pp. 295–320.

McCloskey, D. N. (1985) *The Rhetoric of Economics*, Madison: University of Wisconsin Press.

Mach, E. (1893) "The Economy of Science," in E. Mach, *The Science of Mechanics*, 6th American edition (1960). La Salle, Ill.: Open Court, pp. 577–95.

—— (1898) "The Economical Nature of Inquiry in Physics," in T. J. McCormack (trans.) *Popular Scientific Lectures* of Mach, 3rd edn, revised, Chicago: Open Court, pp. 188–213.

Machina, M. (1987) "Choice Under Uncertainty: Problems Solved and Unsolved," *Journal of Economic Perspectives*, vol. 1, pp. 121–54.

Machlup, F. (1962) *The Production and Distribution of Knowledge in the United States*, Princeton: Princeton University Press.

—— (1965) "Comment," in R. Dorfman (ed.) *Measuring the Benefits of Government Investments*, Washington D.C.: Brookings, pp. 149–57.

McPheters, L. R. and Stronge, W. B. (eds) (1976) *The Economics of Crime and Law Enforcement*, Springfield, Ill: C. C. Thomas Publisher.

Mäki, U. (1995) "Diagnosing McCloskey," *Journal of Economic Literature*, vol. 33, pp. 1300–18.

March, J. G. (1978) "Bounded Rationality, Ambiguity, and the Engineering of Choice," *Bell Journal of Economics*, Autumn, pp. 587–610.

Marshall, A. (1920) [1964] *Principles of Economics*, 8th edn, London: Macmillan.

Martin, R. L. (ed.) (1970) *The Paradox of the Liar*, New Haven: Yale University Press.

Mason, W. E. (1980–81) "Some Negative Thoughts on Friedman's Positive Economics," *Journal of Post Keynesian Economics*, Winter, pp. 235–55.

Mayer, T. (1993) *Truth versus Precision in Economics*, Brookfield, Vt: Edward Elgar.

[Maddox, J.] (1987) "Fraud, Libel, and the Literature," *Nature*, unsigned editorial, January 15.

Merton, R. K. (1973) *The Sociology of Science: Theoretical and Empirical Investigations*, ed. N. W. Storer, Chicago: University of Chicago Press.

Milanese, C., Richardson, N. E. and Reinherz, E. L. (1986a) "Identification of T Helper Cell-derived Lymphokine that Activates Resting T Lymphocytes," *Science*, March 7, pp. 1118–22.

—— (1986b) "Retraction of Data," *Science*, November, p. 1056.

Milton, J. (1644) [1952] *Areopagitica*, in R. M. Hutchins (ed.) *Great Books of the Western World*, vol. 32, Chicago: Encyclopedia Britannica Inc., pp. 381–412.

Mirowski, P. (1994) "A Visible Hand in the Marketplace of Ideas: Precision Measurement as Arbitrage," *Science in Context*, vol. 3, pp. 563–89.

—— (1995) "Philip Kitcher's *Advancement of Science*: A Review Article," *Review of Political Economy*, vol. 7, pp. 227–41.

Mirowski, P. and Sklivas, S. (1991) "Why Econometricians, Don't Replicate (Although They Do Reproduce)," *Review of Political Economy*, vol. 3, pp. 146–63.

Mishan, E. J. (1976) *Cost Benefit Analysis*, 2nd edn, New York: Praeger.

Mulkay, M. and Gilbert, N. (1991) "Replication and Mere Replication," in M. Mulkay, *Sociology of Science: A Sociological Pilgrimage*, Bloomington: Indiana University Press, pp. 154–223.

Muma, J. R. (1993) "The Need for Replication," *Journal of Speech and Hearing Research*, vol. 36, pp. 927–30.

Nagel, E. [1963] (1971) "Assumptions in Economic Theory," in W. Breit and H. M. Hochman (eds), *Readings in Microeconomics*, 2nd edn, New York: Holt, Rinehart, and Winston, pp. 48–54.

Nagel, E. and Newman, J. R. (1958) *Gödel's Proof*, New York: New York University Press.

Nelson, R. R. (1959) "The Simple Economics of Basic Scientific Research," *Journal of Political Economy*, vol. 67, pp. 297–306.

Nelson, R. R. and Winter, S. G. (1982) *An Evolutionary Theory of Economic Change*, Cambridge: Harvard University Press.

Newcomb, S. (1886) *Principles of Political Economy*, reprinted 1966, New York: A. M. Kelley.

NOVA (1988) "Do Scientists Cheat?," WGBH transcripts, Boston: Public Broadcasting System, October 25.

Okun, A. M. (1981) *Prices and Quantities: A Macroeconomic Analysis*, Washington D.C.: Brookings.

Oldroyd, D. (1990) "David Hull's Evolutionary Model for the Progress and Process of Science," *Biology and Philosophy*, vol. 5, pp. 473–87.

Palca, J. and Anderson, A. (1988) "NIH Speeds to Preserve Charges of Scientific Error," *Nature*, June 20, p. 788.

Peirce, C. S., (1861) [1982] "[A Treatise on Metaphysics]," in M. Fisch *et al.* (eds) *Writings of Charles S. Peirce: A Chronological Edition*, vol. 1, 1857–1866, pp. 57–84.

—— (1871a) [1982] "Letter to Simon Newcomb," in Baumol and Goldfeld (1968), pp. 186–7.

—— (1871b) [1982] "[Charles Babbage]," *Nation*, vol. 13, November, in *Writings of Charles S. Peirce: A Chronological Edition*, vol. 2, 1867–1871, E. C. Moore *et al.* (eds), Indianapolis: Indiana University Press, pp. 457–9.

—— (1878) [1955] "How to Make Our Ideas Clear," in J. Buchler (ed.), *Philosophical Writings of Peirce*, New York: Dover Publications, pp. 23–41.

—— (1879) "Note on the Theory of the Economy of Research," *United States Coast Survey* for the fiscal year ending June 1876, US Government Printing Office 1879, reprinted in *Operations Research*, vol. 15, (1967) [1879], pp. 642–8. Also reprinted in A. W. Burks, (ed.) (1958) *The Collected Papers of Charles Sanders Peirce*, vol. 7, Cambridge: Harvard University Press, pp. 76–83; and in C. J. W. Kloesel (ed.) (1986) *The Writings of Charles S. Peirce: A Chronological Edition*, vol. 4, 1879–1884, Indianapolis: Indiana University Press, pp. 72–8.

—— (1880) [1955] "What is a Leading Principle?," in J. Buchler (ed.), *Philosophical Writings of Peirce*, New York: Dover Publications, pp. 129–34.

—— (1882) [1986] "Introductory Lecture on the Study of Logic," in C. J. W. Kloesel (ed.) *Writings of Charles S. Peirce*, vol. 4, 1879–1884, Indianapolis: Indiana University Press, pp. 378–81.

—— (1891) [1955] "The Architecture of Theories," in J. Buchler (ed.), *Philosophical Writings of Peirce*, New York: Dover Publications, pp. 315–23.

—— (1893) [1960] "The Logic of Quantity," in C. Hartshorne and P. Weiss (eds), *Collected Papers of Charles Sanders Peirce*, vol. 4, Cambridge: Harvard University Press, pp. 59–131.

—— (1896) [1960] "The Economy of Research," in C. Hartshorne and P. Weiss (eds), "Lessons from the History of Science," *Collected Papers of Charles Sanders Peirce*, vol. 1, Cambridge: Harvard University Press, pp. 48–9.

—— (1897) [1960] "Multitude and Number," in C. Hartshorne and P. Weiss (eds), *Collected Papers of Charles Sanders Peirce*, vol. 4, Cambridge: Harvard University Press, pp. 145–88.

—— (1901) [1985]. "On the Logic of Drawing History from Ancient Documents especially from Testimonies," in C. Eisele (ed.), *Historical Perspectives on Peirce's Logic of Science*, Berlin: Mouton Publishers, pp. 705–800.

—— (1902a) [1985]. "Carnegie Institution. Application for a Grant," in C. Eisele (ed.), *Historical Perspectives on Peirce's Logic of Science*, Berlin: Mouton Publishers, pp. 1022–41.

—— (1902b) [1985]. "On the Economics of Research," Memoir no. 28 of Peirce (1902a), pp. 1036–9.

Pheby, J. (1988) *Methodology and Economics: A Critical Introduction*, Arkmonk, N.Y.: M. E. Sharpe.

Polanyi, M. (1962a) *Personal Knowledge: Towards a Post-Critical Philosophy*, Chicago: University of Chicago Press.

—— (1962b) "The Republic of Science: Its Political and Economic Theory," *Minerva*, vol. 1, pp. 54–73.

—— (1966) *The Tacit Dimension*, Garden City, N.Y.: Anchor Books.

Popper, K. R. (1959) *The Logic of Scientific Discovery*, New York: Harper and Row.

—— (1961) *The Poverty of Historicism*, New York: Harper and Row.

—— (1965) *Conjectures and Refutations: The Growth of Scientific Knowledge*, New York: Harper and Row.

—— (1966) *The Open Society and its Enemies*, vol 2, Princeton: Princeton University Press.

—— (1970) "Normal Science and Its Dangers," in I. Lakatos and A. Musgrave (eds), *Criticism and the Growth of Knowledge*, Cambridge: Cambridge University Press, pp. 51–8.

—— (1972a) *Objective Knowledge: An Evolutionary Approach*, Oxford: Oxford University Press.

—— (1972b) "Of Clouds and Clocks: An Approach to the Problem of Rationality and the Freedom of Man," in Popper (1972a), pp. 206–55.

—— (1976) *Unended Quest: An Intellectual Biography*, Oxford: Clarendon Press.

Prelli, L. J. (1989) *A Rhetoric of Science: Inventing Scientific Discourse*, Columbia, S.C.: University of South Carolina Press.

Priestley, J. (1767) *The History and Present State of Electricity*, London: J. Dodsley.

Radnitzky, G. (1987a) "Cost-Benefit Thinking in the Methodology of Research: The 'Economic Approach' Applied to Key Problems of the Philosophy of Science," in G. Radnitzky and P. Bernholz (eds), *Economic Imperialism: The Economic Approach Applied Outside the Field of Economics*, New York: Paragon House Publishers, pp. 283–331.

—— (1987b) "The 'Economic' Approach to the Philosophy of Science," *British Journal for the Philosophy of Science*, vol. 38, pp. 159–79.

Rang, B. and Thomas, W. (1981) "Zermelo's Discovery of the 'Russell Paradox'," *Historia Mathematica*, vol. 8, no. 1, pp. 15–22.

Reder, M. W. (1982) "Chicago Economics: Permanence and Change," *Journal of Economic Literature*, vol. 20, no. 1, pp. 1–38.

Redman, D. A. (1991) *Economics and the Philosophy of Science*, New York: Oxford University Press.

Rescher, N. (1976) "Peirce and the Economy of Research," *Philosophy of Science*, vol. 43, pp. 71–98.

—— (1977) *Methodological Pragmatism*, New York: New York University Press.

—— (1978a) *Peirce's Philosophy of Science*, University of Notre Dame Press: Notre Dame.

—— (1978b) *Scientific Progress: A Philosophical Essay on the Economics of the Natural Sciences*, Oxford: Basil Blackwell.

—— (1989) *Cognitive Economy: The Economic Dimension of the Theory of Knowledge*, Pittsburgh: University of Pittsburgh Press.

—— (1996) *Priceless Knowledge: Natural Science in Economic Perspective*, Lanham, Md: Rowman and Littlefield.

Robbins, L. (1935) *An Essay on the Nature and Significance of Economic Science*, London: St Martin's Press.

Rosen, H. S. (1988) *Public Finance*, 2nd edn, Homewood, Ill: Richard D. Irwin.

Rosen, S. (1985) "Implicit Contracts: A Survey," *Journal of Economic Literature*, vol. 23, pp. 1144–75.

Rosenberg, A. (1992) "Selection and Science: Critical Notice of David Hull's *Science as a Process*," *Biology and Philosophy*, vol. 7, pp. 217–28.

Rosenthal, R. (1979) "Replications and their Relative Utilities," *Replications in Social Psychology*, vol. 1, pp. 15–23.

Rotwein, E. (1959) "On 'The Methodology of Positive Economics'," *Quarterly Journal of Economics*, vol. 73, November, pp. 554–75.

Rucker, R. (1982) *Infinity and Mind: The Science and Philosophy of the Infinite*, Boston: Birkhauser.

Russell, B. (1902) [1967] "Letter to Frege (1902)," in J. van Heijenoort (ed.) *From Frege to Gödel: A Sourcebook in Mathematical Logic, 1879–1931*, Cambridge: Harvard University Press, pp. 124–5.

—— (1903) *The Principles of Mathematics*, Cambridge: Cambridge University Press.

—— (1907) "Mathematical Logic as Based on the Theory of Types," *American Journal of Mathematics*, vol. 24, pp. 222–63.

Rutherford, M. (1989) "What is Wrong with the New Institutional Economics (and What is Still Wrong with the Old)?," *Review of Political Economy*, November, pp. 299–318.

Salanti, A. (1987) "Falsificationism and Fallibilism as Epistemic Foundations of Economics: A Critical View," *Kyklos*, vol. 40, pp. 368–92.

Samuels, W. J. (1992) *Essays on the Methodology and Discourse of Economics*, Washington Square, N.Y.: New York University Press.

Samuelson, P. A. (1947) *Foundations of Economic Analysis*, Cambridge: Harvard University Press.

Saransohn, J. (1993) *Science on Trial: The Whistle-blower, the Accused, and the Nobel Laureate*, New York: St Martins.

Scherer, F. M. (1965) "Government Research and Development Programs," in R. Dorfman (ed.) *Measuring the Benefits of Government Investments*, Washington D.C.: Brookings, pp. 12–70.

Sent, E.-M. (1997) "The Need for a New Economics of Science," unpublished paper, University of Notre Dame.

Shackle, G. L. S. (1967) *The Years of High Theory*, Cambridge: Cambridge University Press.

—— (1972) *Epistemics and Economics: A Critique of Economic Doctrines*, Cambridge: Cambridge University Press.

Shoemaker, P. J. H. (1982) "The Expected Utility Model: Its Variants, Purposes, Evidence, and Limitations," *Journal of Economic Literature*, vol. 20, pp. 529–63.

Simon, H. A. (1976) "From Substantive to Procedural Rationality," in S. J. Latsis (ed.) *Method and Appraisal in Economics*, Cambridge: Cambridge University Press, pp. 129–48.

—— (1978) "Rationality as Process and as Product of Thought," *American Economic Review*, vol. 68, pp. 1–16.

—— (1979) "Rational Decision-Making in Business Organizations," *American Economic Review*, vol. 69, pp. 493–513.

Smith, A. [1776] (1910) *The Wealth of Nations*, London: J. M. Dent and Sons.

Smith, N. C., Jr (1970) "Replication Studies: A Neglected Aspect of Psychological Research," *American Psychologist*, vol. 25, pp. 970–4.

Sober, E. (1992) "The Evolution of Altruism: Correlation, Cost, and Benefit," *Biology and Philosophy*, vol. 72, pp. 177–87.

Stanley, T. D. (1985) "Positive Economics and Its Instrumental Defence," *Economica*, vol. 52, pp. 305–19.

Stephan, P. (1996) "The Economics of Science," *Journal of Economic Literature*, vol. 34, pp. 1199–235.

Stewart, W. and Feder, N. (1987a) "Why Research Fraud Thrives," *Boston Globe*, November 30, pp. A1 and A24.

—— (1987b) "The Integrity of the Scientific Literature," *Nature*, January 15, pp. 207–14.

—— (1988) "Battle Over Error," *Science*, October 14, p. 67.

Stigler, G. J. (1963) "The Intellectual and the Marketplace," Occasional Paper no. 11 of IEA.

—— (1972) "The Adoption of the Marginal Utility Theory," *History of Political Economy*, vol. 4, Fall, pp. 571–86.

—— (1982a) *The Economist as Preacher and Other Essays*, Chicago: University of Chicago Press.

—— (1982b) "Does Economics Have a Useful Past?," in Stigler (1982a), pp. 107–18.

—— (1984) *The Intellectual and the Marketplace*, Cambridge: Harvard University Press.

—— (1986) "The Process and Progress of Economics," Nobel Memorial Lecture December 8, 1982, in K. R. Leube and T. G. Moore (eds) *The Essence of Stigler*, Chicago: University of Chicago Press, pp. 134–49.

Suppe, F. (1974) *The Structure of Scientific Theories*, Urbana, Ill: University of Illinois Press.

Tarascio, V. J. and Caldwell, B. (1979) "Theory Choice in Economics: Philosophy and Practice," *Journal of Economic Issues*, December, pp. 983–1006.

Taylor, F. W. [1911] (1947) *Scientific Management*, New York: Harper.

Teich, A. H. and Frankel, M. S. (1992) "Good Science and Responsible Scientists: Meeting the Challenge of Fraud and Misconduct in Science," American Association for the Advancement of Science: Washington D.C., March, 35 pp.

Tollison, R. D. (1986) "Economists as the Subject of Economic Inquiry," *Southern Economic Journal*, vol. 52, pp. 909–22.

van de Kamp, J. and Cummings, M. M. (1987) *Misconduct and Fraud in the Life Sciences: Literature Search*, Bethesda, Mass.: National Library of Medicine, National Institutes of Health.

Veblen, T. (1898) [1961] "Why Economics is Not an Evolutionary Science?," in T. Veblen, *The Place of Science in Modern Civilization*, New York: Russell and Russell, pp. 56–81.

—— (1906) [1961] "The Place of Science in Modern Civilization," in T. Veblen, *The Place of Science in Modern Civilization*, New York: Russell and Russell, pp. 1–31.

Warsh, D. (1991) "The End of the Fraud Game?," *Boston Globe*, June 23, pp. 29 and 33.

Weaver, D., Reis, M. H., Albanese, C., Costantini, F., Baltimore, D. and Imanishi-Kari, T. (1986) "Altered Repertoire of Endogenous Immunoglobulin Gene Expression in

Transgenic Mice Containing a Rearranged Mu Heavy Chain Gene," *Cell*, vol. 45, April 25, pp. 247–59.

Weimer, W. B. (1979) *Notes on the Methodology of Scientific Research*, New York: Lawrence Erlbaum.

Weinstein, D. (1979) "Fraud in Science," *Social Science Quarterly*, vol. 59, pp. 639–52.

Wible, J. R. (1982) "Friedman's Positive Economics and Philosophy of Science," *Southern Economic Journal*, vol. 49, no. 2, pp. 350–60.

—— (1984a) "The Instrumentalisms of Dewey and Friedman," *Journal of Economic Issues*, vol. 18, no. 4, pp. 1049–70.

—— (1984b) "Towards a Process Conception of Rationality in Economics and Science," *Review of Social Economy*, vol. 42, October, pp. 89–104.

—— (1990) "Implicit Contracts, Rational Expectations, and Theories of Knowledge," *Review of the History of Economic Thought and Methodology*, vol. 7, pp. 141–70.

—— (1991) "Maximization, Replication, and the Economic Rationality of Positive Economic Science," *Review of Political Economy*, vol. 3, pp. 164–86.

—— (1992a) "Fraud in Science: An Economic Approach," *Philosophy of the Social Sciences*," vol. 22, pp. 5–27.

—— (1992b) "Cost-Benefit Analysis, Utility Theory, and Economic Aspects of Peirce's and Popper's Conceptions of Science," manuscript, University of New Hampshire, 80 pp.

—— (1994a) "Charles Sanders Peirce's Economy of Research," *Journal of Economic Methodology*, vol. 1, pp. 135–60.

—— (1994b) "Rescher's Economic Philosophy of Science," *Journal of Economic Methodology*, vol. 1, pp. 314–29.

—— (1995) "The Economic Organization of Science, the Firm, and the Marketplace," *Philosophy of the Social Sciences*, vol. 25, March, pp. 35–68.

Wiener, P. P. (1949) *Evolution and the Founders of Pragmatism*, New York: Harper and Row.

—— (1958) "Introduction," in *Values in a Universe of Chance: Selected Writings of Charles S. Peirce* 1839–1914, Garden City, N.Y.: Doubleday Anchor.

Wilber, C. K. and J. D. Wisman, (1975) "The Chicago School: Positivism or Ideal Type?," *Journal of Economic Issues*, December, pp. 665–79.

Wilder, R. L. (1965) *Introduction to the Foundations of Mathematics*, New York: J. Wiley.

Williams, A. (1972) "Cost-benefit Analysis: Bastard Science? and/or Insidious Poison in the Body Politick?," *Journal of Public Economics*, vol. 1, pp. 199–225.

Williamson, O. (1975) *Markets and Hierarchies: Analysis and Antitrust Implications*, New York: Free Press.

—— (1985) *The Economic Institutions of Capitalism*, New York: Free Press.

—— (1990) "A Comparison of Alternative Approaches to Economic Organization," *Journal of Institutional and Theoretical Economics*, vol. 146, pp. 61–71.

—— (1991) "Economic Institutions: Spontaneous and Intentional Governance," *Journal of Law, Economics, and Organization*, vol. 7, pp. 159–87.

—— (1992) "Markets, Hierarchies, and the Modern Corporation: An Unfolding Perspective," *Journal of Economic Behavior and Organization*, vol. 17, pp. 335–52.

Williamson, O. E., Wachter, M. L. and Harris, J. E. (1975) "Understanding the Employment Relation: The Analysis of Idiosyncratic Exchange," *Bell Journal of Economics*, vol. 6, pp. 250–79.

Williamson, O. E. and Winter, S. G. (eds) (1991) *The Nature of the Firm: Origins, Evolution, and Development*, Oxford: Oxford University Press.

Winrich, J. S. (1984) "Self Reference and the Incomplete Structure of Neoclassical Economics," *Journal of Economic Issues*, vol. 17, pp. 987–1005.

Wittenberg, J. (1992) "On the Very Idea of a System Dynamics Model of Kuhnian Science," *System Dynamics Review*, vol. 8, pp. 21–33.

Wolf, C. (1979) "A Theory of Nonmarket Failure: Framework of Implementation Analysis," *Journal of Law and Economics*, vol. 22, April, pp. 107–39.

Woolgar, S. (1988) *Knowledge and Reflexivity: New Frontiers in the Sociology of Knowledge*, London: Sage.

INDEX

abduction 65
Alchian, A. 165–7, 169, 170, 171
allocation of time and science 24–5,
    32–7, 41, 51–2, 99–100, 134, 232
    n5
analytical evolutionary economics xv
Andersen, R. 24–5, 28, 31, 33, 35, 232
    n3
Anderson, A. 47
architecture of theory and method
    218–19, 225–7, 229–30
argumentative golden rule 22, 214–15
Arrow, K. 165, 168, 171, 241 n3
Ashmore, M. 13
Austrian economics 21, 111, 169, 228
Ayer, A. 13, 121, 192–5, 208, 214

Babbage, C. 64
Backhouse, R. 122
Baltimore, D. 23, 47, 49, 234 n13
Bartley, W. 3, 18, 21, 96–110, 113, 119,
    122, 128, 133, 181–2, 184–5, 187,
    189, 194, 204–5, 214–16
Baumol, W. 63–4, 73, 75–6
Bear, D. 121
Becker, G. S. 32, 35, 52, 108, 184
Becker, W. E. 231 n1
Bernoulli, D. 50
Blank, D. 231 n1
Blaug, M. 11, 115–16, 121, 124, 135-7,
    240 n2
Boland, L. 12, 121-6, 129–31, 181, 235
    n24, 239 n3, 239 n6, 245 n8
Boring, E. G. 12, 121
Braunwald, E. 46–7
Brent, J. 81
Breuning, S. 47–8
Bridgeman, P. 121

Broad, W. 45, 47, 50
Budiansky, S. 47–8
Burt, C. 44–7
Butos, W. 153, 228, 244 n33

Caldwell, B. 116, 121–2, 239 n3
Campbell, K. 26–7
Carnap, R. 121, 194
censorship 138
citations 106–10, 238 n5
Clower, R. 200
Coase, R. 108, 126, 139–40, 165–72,
    237 n9, 241 n7
Coats, A. W. 122, 231 n7
Colander, D. xvi, 23, 231 n1
Collins, H. M. 26
Commons, J. R. 167
competition in science 93, 96, 102, 113,
    126, 131, 140, 147–8, 150, 176,
    219–20, 222–4, 230
complements theory: of economic
    organization 168, 172–5, 187–8, 205,
    227–8, 242 n18; of markets 172–5; of
    science 175–80
complexity 10, 25, 56, 92, 151–2, 170,
    175, 188, 190–1, 244 n3
confirmation 121
conventionalism 121, 194
Cort, J. 47–8
cost-benefit analysis 3, 19, 76, 79,
    83–94, 96, 102, 104, 110–11, 127,
    158, 201, 236 n3, 237 n14
cost escalation in science 151–2
Cournot, A. 63
Culliton, B. 47–9

Dalton 50
Dana-Farber Cancer Institute 48

Darsee, J. 46–8
Dasgupta, P. 13
David, P. 13
Demsetz, H. 165–7, 169, 170–1
Descartes, R. 8
DeWald, W. 24–5, 28, 31, 33, 35, 232 n3
Dewey, J. 63–4, 107–8, 122–3, 128, 130–1, 172, 198, 228
Diamond, A. 12, 122, 232 n11
Dingell, J. 44
Dorfman, R. 71
dual economy of science 177–80, 185–6, 227
dual economy of the scientific literature 180–6, 188–9
Duhem, P. 121, 194

Earl, P. 38, 233 n14
ecology of knowledge 99, 103–4, 113
econometrics 25–6, 71–3, 99, 149, 231 n9
economic critique of universities 100–1, 103, 128
economic epistemology 99
economic methodology xii–xv, 1, 11, 13, 15, 20, 37–40, 129, 131, 184, 192, 199, 203, 219, 222–26, 239 n8, 240 n7
economic rationality xiv, 1, 14, 18–20, 36–41, 52–7, 61, 63, 84, 92, 94, 104, 118, 141, 170, 190, 198–203, 244 n1, 245 n7
economy of research 62, 65, 67–70, 75–7, 81, 83, 143, 235 n14
Ehrlich, I. 52, 57
Einstein, A. 186
empiricism 120–1, 192–4, 197, 207–8, 210, 212
epistemic microfoundation 15
epistemic scarcity 91, 99, 145, 173–6, 219, 243 n20; see also scarcity
error 100, 115, 138, 149, 197, 216, 229, 245 n5
evolution 8, 82, 185–6, 195, 203, 213, 228–9
evolutionary economics xv, 9, 62, 99, 161, 190–204, 215–17, 219, 227–8, 230, 242 n18
evolutionary rationality 19, 62, 148, 185, 190–1, 195, 197, 199–202, 203–5, 213, 215–16
externalities 88–9, 160–1

fallibilism 122, 183
falsification 2, 52, 57, 62, 78–80, 83, 117, 121, 182, 186, 198, 207–8, 211–14, 224, 237 n13, 240 n2
falsified data 46–50
Feder, N. 47, 49, 50
Feldstein social security disreplication 232 n3
Feyerabend, P. 108–9
firm as an anomaly 162–3
Fisher, I. 64
Fisher, R. A. 121, 194
Fogel, R. 184
Foucault, M. 107
Foreman, J. 47, 49
Frankel, M. 51
fraud in science 43–56, 61–2, 116, 134, 140, 143, 157, 170, 234 n11
Frege, G. 206
Freud, S. 107–9
Friedman, B. 25, 35
Friedman, M. 10–11, 107–9, 116–19, 126, 129–30, 181–2, 185–7, 239 n1; "Methodology of Positive Economics" 10–11, 106, 116–33, 150, 158, 181, 224, 239 n8, 240 n7, 244 n30; positive economics 4, 11, 127
Friedmann, T. 43
Fusfeld, D. 203

Gallo, R. 234 n11
general equilibrium theory 9, 99, 149, 221, 227
Ghiselin, M. 231 n3
Gilbert, N. 26,27
Gödel, K. 13, 19, 203, 208–11, 219, 222, 225–6, 229–30, 231 n10, 246 n14
Goldfeld, S. 63–4, 73, 75–6
Gosselin, P. 47, 50
government failure 6, 90, 140, 149, 161–2, 175
grantsmanship 15, 126, 143, 233 n15, 233 n16
Great Depression 111-12
growth of knowledge 96, 99, 122, 145, 147, 219

Hacking, I. 71–2
Hands, D. W. xvii, 15, 83, 92, 122, 232 n11, 237 n5
Harvard Medical School 46, 48
Hayek, F. A. 19, 98, 102, 119, 126,

134–5, 141, 144–50, 152–4, 157, 167, 179, 181–2, 185, 187, 189, 228, 240 n6, 243 n23
Hearnshaw, L. 44–7
Helmholz, H. 139
Hempel, C. 81, 121, 236 n27
Hirsch, A. 122, 130–1
Holden, C. 47–8
Hollis, M. 121
Hoover, K. 234 n1
Howard, M. 206
Howe, P. 47, 49
Hull, D. xvii, 13, 122, 158, 181, 183, 185–7, 189, 195, 222–3, 229
Hume, D. 194
Hutchison, T. W. 117

Imanishi-Kari, T. 47, 49
incompleteness xv, 6, 14, 77, 168, 170, 188, 201, 203, 206–9, 216, 226, 228, 246 n12
indeterminism 9, 78, 173–5, 191, 243 n20
induction 61, 117–18, 191–2, 194, 202–3, 205, 207, 210–12
inference: hypothetical 64, 74, 198–9; statistical 71–3, 77
infinite regress 78, 193, 204, 207, 210–13, 216–17, 219–26, 229
Institutionalists 7, 9, 21, 81–2, 111, 129, 169, 172, 228
institutions of science 159
instrumentalism 64, 121, 123–6, 129–30, 186, 194, 244 n30
internal criticism xv, 15, 19–22, 203, 205–6, 215–16, 224, 230
invisible hand and science 133, 137, 141–2, 144, 153, 236 n28, 241 n4, 243 n28

Jackson, T. 26–7
James, W. 63, 66, 130
Jensen, M. 176
Jevons, W.S. 75
Johnson, W.E. 75
Journal of Money, Credit, and Banking replication project 24, 31
justificationist metatheory 120–1, 194, 196–7

Kamin, L. 45, 47
Kant, I. 108
Katouzian, H. 206

Keynes, J. M. 108, 111, 121, 194
Keynes, J. N. 11, 117, 122
Keynesians 7, 21, 111–12, 149–50
Kitcher, P. 16–17, 236 n3
Klamer, A. xvi, 122, 206
Kmenta, J. 72–3
Koshland, D. 43, 50, 51, 55
Kuhn, T.S. 12, 17, 28, 77, 100–1, 108–9, 119–20, 122, 133, 151, 178–9, 181, 183, 185, 187, 189, 195–7, 213–14, 223, 229

Lakatos, I. 13, 91, 108–9, 119–20, 122, 124, 181, 183, 185, 187, 189, 195–6, 206, 213–14, 223
Laudan, L. 195
Leijonhufvud, A. 200
levels of abstraction 151, 195–7, 199, 201, 210, 213, 220–1, 223
levels of order 9, 151, 191
levels of observation 152, 197, 199
Levy, D. 12, 122, 231 n9, 232 n3
lexicograpic preferences 37–8
liar's paradox 206–8, 211-12, 221–22, 224
London School of Economics 124

McCloskey, D. N. 120–1, 131, 181–2, 184–5, 187, 189, 194, 206
Mach, E. 64
macroeconomics xiv, 6–7, 155, 161, 239 n7
Maddox, J. 49
Malthus, T. 64
de Marchi, N. 122, 130–1
market failure 1–2, 5, 96–7, 102–3, 105, 110, 112–13, 116, 125, 128, 132, 134, 144, 150, 156, 158, 161–4, 173, 190, 227, 239 n8, 240 n2, 242 n42
marketplace of ideas 1, 97, 99, 100, 102, 105, 110, 113, 125, 132, 134, 138–43, 158, 172, 176, 181, 189–90, 222, 227, 240 n2
markets as an anomaly 165
Marshallian economics 81, 119, 200, 227
Martin, R. 206
Marx, K. 98, 107, 108, 109
Marxian economics 21, 111, 169
Mason, W. E. 122
Massachusetts Insititute of Technology 49

Mayer, T. 122, 133
measurement and precision 67
mechanism 8, 62, 81–2, 190–1, 202, 227, 243 n18
Mendel, G. 50
Merton, R.K. 12, 107, 195
methodological competition 126, 131, 222–4
methodological rules 144, 148–9, 182, 227–8
methodological unity of the sciences 93–5
microeconomics xv, 6, 9, 10, 18, 61–2, 68, 81, 134, 228, 237 n7
Milanese, C. 47–9
Mill, J. S. 11, 64, 122, 194
Millikan 50
Milton, J. 137–8
Mirowski, P. 16, 17, 31, 122, 232 n12
misconduct in science 1–3, 15, 20, 23–4, 43–50, 61, 83, 95, 96, 116, 134, 144, 156, 158, 227–8
Monetarists 7, 21, 111–12
Mulkay, M. 26, 27
Muma, J. 27, 28

Nagel, E. 121, 206
National Institutes of Health 46, 48
Nell, E. 121
neoclassical economics 21, 62, 145, 150, 159
New Classical economics 7, 111-12, 149, 150, 221
New Institutionalists 7, 165, 167, 168, 170, 172, 175
New Keynesians 7
Newcomb, S. 63, 64, 71, 74–5
Newman, J. 206
Newton, I. 8, 50
nonjustificationist metatheory 120, 122, 195, 197–202, 245 n7
normal science 3, 15, 23, 15, 61–2, 179, 185
Notre Dame economics of science conference xiii, 13

operational behaviorism 136
opportunity cost and science 2, 15, 78, 80, 91, 99–100, 205
optimizing theories of science 14, 32–41, 52–9, 61–2, 67–71, 79, 80–1, 83, 96, 118, 143, 172, 190–1, 200

organizations of science 159, 177
Orr, D. 121
O'Toole, M. 49

Peirce, B. 64
Peirce, C. S. 3, 9, 12, 18, 61–82, 83, 86, 87, 90, 91, 94, 95, 102, 122, 130, 135, 136, 137, 185, 191, 218–19, 226, 228, 235 n14, 235 n24, 243 n18
Pheby, J. 115, 122
pluralism 2, 17–18, 92, 105, 144, 197, 218
Polanyi, M. 18, 122, 133, 134, 141–4, 150, 152–4, 157, 178–9, 181, 183, 185, 187, 189
Popper, K. 3, 9, 10, 32, 67, 78–81, 83–4, 86, 92, 94–5, 97–8, 101–10, 113, 115, 119, 121–2, 181–2, 185–7, 194, 197, 204, 211–12, 214, 216, 228–9, 240 n1, 240 n2
positivism 77, 118, 121, 124, 184, 194, 196–7, 243 n18
Post Keynesians 111
pragmatism 9, 63, 129
Priestley, J. 135, 137
Prelli, L. 122
primary science 177–80, 187, 227
probable error 71–3
proof in mathematics 208–11
present value 86–90; of facts 91–2; of research programs 88, 91, 104, 110–11, 127; of research projects 91–2; of theories 91
Ptolemy 50
promotion and tenure requirements 40, 233 n16
public goods and science 87–8, 154, 160, 176, 227, 230, 231 n5
pure theorist 41
puzzle of science 153
puzzle-solving 25, 142, 149–50, 153, 179

Radnitzky, G. 3, 12, 18, 83–6, 88, 90–5, 102, 122, 204
rational expectations xiv, 221, 241 n1
rationality, see economic rationality, evolutionary rationality, scientific rationality
realism of assumptions 119, 197
Reder, M. 206
Redman, B. 122

reflexivity xiv, 13, 14, 110, 193, 203–18, 224, 227
Reinherz, E. 48
replication 27–31, 33–4, 36, 42, 51
replication failure 24, 31–42, 43, 51, 61, 84, 115, 134, 170, 232 n3
Rescher, N. 1, 3, 12, 18, 19, 61, 62, 76–81, 83, 84, 86, 90, 94, 95, 102, 122, 134, 135, 150–4, 157, 181, 183, 185, 187, 189, 195, 204, 236 n26, 236 n27
rhetoric of economics 184–5, 194
rhetoric of science 17, 151, 182, 195, 202
Ricardo, D. 64
Richardson, N. 47–9
Robbins, L. 1, 23, 184, 194
Rorty, R. 108, 122
Rosenthal, R. 26
Rotwein, E. 121, 125
Russell, B. 13, 74, 121, 206–8, 245 n6, n7, n8

Samuels, W. 122
Samuelson, P. 8, 130, 131, 184
satisficing 190
scarcity 10, 19, 79–80, 87, 93–4, 99, 113, 145, 148, 151, 163, 165, 173, 200–2, 215, 217, 219; see also epistemic scarcity
science: as an anomaly 6, 53, 157–9, 164, 170, 175, 227; failure 2, 43, 55, 57, 106, 184, 186, 189, 240 n2; as partially endogenous 2, 10, 134, 154–6, 170, 172, 231 n1; and property rights 171
scientific progress 2, 22, 77, 79, 83, 137, 150–3, 185, 195–6, 211, 213
scientific rationality 57, 84, 92, 94, 104, 170, 191–8, 200–2, 204, 207, 214, 245 n7
scientific revolutions 3, 23, 185–7, 189, 196, 228
scientism 148–9, 157
secondary science 177–80, 187, 227
self-corrective science 2, 4, 135–7, 141, 144, 147–8 , 150, 155–6, 158, 227, 240 n1, 240 n2
self-reference 13, 18, 22, 125, 193, 203, 205–17, 218, 227, 229, 245 n1
selection: of facts 83–6, 90–2, 94, 117, 195; of research projects 18, 61–71, 80–1, 86–8, 90–2, 94, 104, 109, 111;

of research programs 91–2, 127, 185, 204; of theories 83–6, 90–2, 94
Sent, E. 13
Shackle, G. 74, 243 n20
Simon, H. A. 99, 167, 190, 244 n3
Sklivas, S. 26, 31
Smith, A. 99, 141, 241 n5
Smith, N. C. 26
sociology: of science 10, 15, 98, 100, 135; of scientific knowledge 15, 98,100–1
Sohl, J. 235 n17
Solow, R. 184
Stephan, P. 13
spontaneous order 98, 102, 143, 145, 147, 167, 175, 240 n6
Sprague, R. 48
Stewart, W. 47, 49, 50
Stigler, G. 12, 108, 126, 135, 139–40, 141, 231 n1, 235 n21
substitutes argumentative structure 5–8, 102, 159–64
substitutes theory: of economic organization 163, 169, 205, 241 n5, 242 n9; of the firm 162–3, 165–9, 242 n9; of science 170–2, 187
Suppe, F. 196

Tarascio, V. 121
tautology 208
Taylor, F. W. 198
team production and science 166–8, 171, 180, 185
theory of economic competition 98, 113, 118–19, 126, 145–6, 161, 181–2, 220–2, 225–7, 230
Teich, A. 51
Thursby, J. 24–5, 28, 31, 33, 35, 232 n3
Times, The (London) 45
Tollison, R. 231 n1
Toulmin, S. 122, 185, 195
transactions cost of science 158, 165–7, 170–1, 182–3, 186–7, 242, n13
truth 19, 77, 115, 129, 136, 138, 144, 150, 164, 194, 195, 203, 208, 211, 231 n 5

uncertainty 52–6, 134, 173–4, 191, 200, 203, 243 n19
underdetermination in science 79, 86, 204
unfathomed knowledge 98, 112, 205

United States Coast Survey 63, 66, 74, 75

Veblen, T. 129, 172, 228, 231 n6, 242 n18

Wade, N. 45, 47, 50
Walrasian economics 81, 111–12, 119, 200, 219, 227, 229, 239 n7
Weimer, W. 119, 122, 194–7, 244 n3
Whitehead, A. N. 74
Wible, J. R. 20, 121, 122, 130, 198, 199, 232 n1, 233 n1, 234 n1, 235 n1, 235 n24, 237 n3, 237 n4, 241 n1, 241 n8, 245 n6, 245 n8
Wiener, P. 63
Wilbur, C. 121
Williamson, O. 158, 165, 167, 169, 170, 242 n13
Wisman, J. 121
Wittgenstein, L. 108, 121
Woolgar, S. 13

Zermelo, E. 208, 245 n5